D1403464

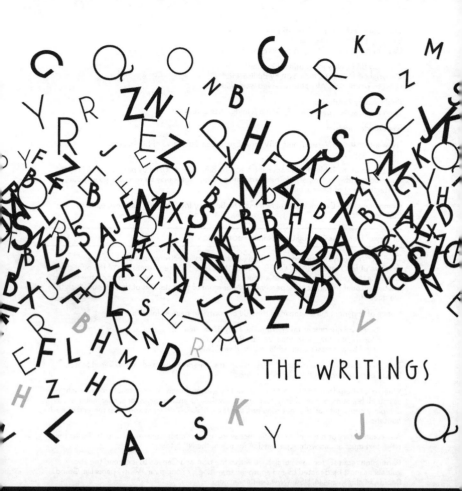

THE WRITINGS

THE
BOOKS OF THE BIBLE
THE
NEW INTERNATIONAL VERSION

FIND WISDOM IN STORIES, POETRY, AND SONGS

ZONDERVAN®

THE DRAMA OF THE BIBLE IN SIX ACTS

The Bible is a collection of letters, poems, stories, visions, prophetic oracles, wisdom and other kinds of writing. The first step to good Bible reading and understanding is to engage these collected works as the different kinds of writing that they are, and to read them as whole books. We encourage you to read big, to not merely take in little fragments of the Bible. The introductions at the start of each book will help you to do this.

But it is also important not to view the Bible as a gathering of unrelated writings. Overall, the Bible is a narrative. These books come together to tell God's true story and his plan to set the world right again. This story of the Bible falls naturally into six key major acts, which are briefly summarized below.

> "I had always felt life first as a story: and if there is a story, there is a story-teller."
>
> G. K. Chesterton

But even more precisely, we can say the story of the Bible is a drama. The key to a drama is that it has to be acted out, performed, lived. It can't remain as only words on a page. A drama is an activated story. The Bible was written so we could enter into its story. It is meant to be lived.

All of us, without exception, live our lives as a drama. We are on stage every single day. What will we say? What will we do? According to which story will we live? If we are not answering these questions with the biblical script, we will follow another. We can't avoid living by someone's stage instructions, even if merely our own.

This is why another key to engaging the Bible well is to recognize that its story has not ended. God's saving action continues. We are all invited to take up our own roles in this ongoing story of redemption and new creation. So, welcome to the drama of the Bible. Welcome to the story of how God intends to renew your life, and the life of the world. God himself is calling you to engage with his word.

ACT 1: GOD'S INTENTION

The drama begins (in the first pages of the book of Genesis) with God already on the stage creating a world. He makes a man and a woman, Adam and Eve, and places them in the Garden of Eden to work it and take care of it. The earth is created to be their home. God's intention is for humanity to be in close, trusting relationship with him and in harmony with the rest of creation that surrounds them.

In a startling passage, the Bible tells us that human beings are God's image-bearers, created to share in the task of bringing God's wise and beneficial rule to the rest of the world. Male and female together, we are significant, decision-making, world-shaping beings. This is our vocation, our purpose as defined in the biblical story.

An equally remarkable part of Act 1 is the description of God as coming into the garden to be with the first human beings. Not only is the earth the God-intended place for humanity, God himself comes to make the beautiful new creation his home as well.

God then gives his own assessment of the whole creation: *God saw all that he had made, and it was very good.* Act 1 reveals God's original desire for the world. It shows us that life itself is a gift from the Creator. It tells us what we were made for and provides the setting for all the action that follows.

ACT 2: EXILE

 Tension and conflict are introduced to the story when Adam and Eve decide to go their own way and seek their own wisdom. They listen to the deceptive voice of God's enemy, Satan, and doubt God's trustworthiness. They decide to live apart from the word that God himself has given them. They decide to be a law to themselves.

The disobedience of Adam and Eve—the introduction of sin into our world—is presented in the Bible as having devastating consequences. Humans were created for healthy, life-giving relationship: with God, with each other, and with the rest of creation. But now humanity must live with the fracturing of all these relations and with the resulting shame, brokenness, pain, loneliness—and death.

Heaven and earth—God's realm and our realm—were intended to be united. God's desire from the beginning was clearly to live with us in the world he made. But now God is hidden. Now it is possible to be in our world and not know him, not experience his presence, not follow his ways, not live in gratitude.

As a result of this rebellion, the first exile in the story takes place. The humans are driven away from God's presence. Their offspring throughout history will seek to find their way back to the source of life. They will devise any number of philosophies and religions, trying to make sense of a fallen, yet haunting world. But death now stalks them, and they will find that they cannot escape it. Having attempted to live apart from God and his good word, humans will find they have neither God nor life.

New questions arise in the drama: Can the curse on creation be overcome and the relationship between God and humanity restored? Can heaven and earth be reunited? Or did God's enemy effectively end the plan and subvert the story?

ACT 3: CALLING ISRAEL TO A MISSION

 We see the direction of God's redemptive plan when he calls Abraham, promising to make him into a great nation. God narrows his focus and concentrates on one group of people. But the ultimate goal remains the same: to bless all the peoples on earth and remove the curse from creation.

When Abraham's descendants are enslaved in Egypt, a central pattern in the story is set: God hears their cries for help and comes to set them free. God makes a covenant with this new nation of Israel at Mt. Sinai. Israel is called by God to be a light to the nations, showing the world what it means to follow God's ways for living. If they will do this, he will bless them in their new land and will come to live with them.

However, God also warns them that if they are not faithful to the covenant, he will send them away, just as he did with Adam and Eve. In spite of God's repeated warnings through his prophets, Israel seems determined to break the covenant. So God abandons the holy temple—the sign of his presence with his people—and it is smashed by pagan invaders. Israel's capital city Jerusalem is sacked and burned.

Abraham's descendants, chosen to reverse the failure of Adam, have now apparently also failed. The problem this poses in the biblical story is profound. Israel, sent as the divine answer to Adam's fall, cannot escape Adam's sin. God, however, remains committed to his people and his plan, so he sows the seed of a different outcome. He promises to send a new king, a descendant of Israel's great King David, who will lead the nation back to its destiny. The very prophets who warned Israel of the dire consequences of its wrongdoing also pledge that the good news of God's victory will be heard in Israel once again.

Act 3 ends tragically, with God apparently absent and the pagan nations ruling over Israel. But the hope of a promise remains. There is one true God. He has chosen Israel. He will return to his people to live with them again. He will bring justice, peace and healing to Israel, and then to the world. He will do this in a final and climactic way. God will send his anointed one—the Messiah. He has given his word on this.

ACT 4: THE SURPRISING VICTORY OF JESUS

 "He is the god made manifest . . . the universal savior of human life." These words, referring to Caesar Augustus (found in a Roman inscription from 4 BC in Ephesus), proclaim the gospel of the Roman Empire. This version of the good news announces that Caesar is the lord who brings peace and prosperity to the world.

Into this empire a son of David is born, and he announces the gospel of God's kingdom. Jesus of Nazareth brings the good news of the coming of God's reign. He begins to show what God's new creation looks like. He announces the end of Israel's exile and the forgiveness of sins. He heals the sick and raises the dead. He overcomes the dark spiritual powers. He welcomes sinners and those considered unclean. Jesus renews the nation, rebuilding the twelve tribes of Israel around himself in a symbolic way.

But the established religious leaders are threatened by Jesus and his kingdom, so they have him brought before the Roman governor. During the very week that the Jews were remembering and celebrating Passover—God's ancient rescue of his people from slavery in Egypt—the Romans nail Jesus to a cross and kill him as a false king.

But the Bible claims that this defeat is actually God's greatest victory. How? Jesus willingly gives up his life as a sacrifice on behalf of the nation, on behalf of the world. Jesus takes onto himself the full force of evil and empties it of its power. In this surprising way, Jesus fights and wins Israel's ultimate battle. The real enemy was never Rome, but the spiritual powers that lie behind Rome and every other kingdom whose weapon is death. Through his blood Jesus pays the price and reconciles everything in heaven and on earth to God.

God then publicly declares this victory by reversing Jesus' death sentence and raising him back to life. The resurrection of Israel's king shows that the great enemies of God's creation—sin and death—really have been defeated. The resurrection is the great sign that the new creation has begun.

Jesus is the fulfillment of Israel's story and a new start for the entire human race. Death came through the first man, Adam. The resurrection of the dead comes through the new man, Jesus. God's original intention is being reclaimed.

ACT 5: THE RENEWED PEOPLE OF GOD

 If the key victory has already been secured, why is there an Act 5? The answer is that God wants the victory of Jesus to spread to all the nations of the world. The risen Jesus says to his disciples, *"Peace be with you! As the Father has sent me, I am sending you."* So this new act in the drama tells the story of how the earliest followers of Jesus began to spread the good news of God's reign.

According to the New Testament, all those who belong to Israel's Messiah are children of Abraham, heirs of both the ancient promises and the ancient mission. The task of bringing blessing to the peoples of the world has been given again to Abraham's family. Their mission is to live out the liberating message of the good news of God's kingdom.

God is gathering people from all around the world and forming them into assemblies of Jesus-followers—his church. Together they are God's new temple, the place where his Spirit lives. They are the community of those who have pledged their allegiance to Jesus as the true Lord of the world. They have crossed from death into new life, through the power of God's Spirit. They demonstrate God's love across the usual boundaries of race, class, tribe and nation.

Forgiveness of sins and reconciliation with God can now be announced to all. Following in the steps of Jesus, his followers proclaim this gospel in both word and deed. The power of this new, God-given life breaking into the world is meant to be shown by the real-world actions of the Christian community. But the message also has a warning. When the Messiah returns, he will come as the rightful judge of the world.

The Bible is the story of the central struggle weaving its way through the history of the world. And now the story arrives at our own time, enveloping us in its drama.

So the challenge of a decision confronts us. What will we do? How will we fit into this story? What role will we play? God is inviting us to be a part of his mission of re-creation—of bringing restoration, justice and forgiveness. We are to join in the task of making things new, to be a living sign of what is to come when the drama is complete.

ACT 6: GOD COMES HOME

 God's future has come into our world through the work of Jesus the Messiah. But for now, the present evil age also continues. Brokenness, wrongdoing, sickness and even death remain. We live in the time of the overlap of the ages, the time of in-between. The final Act is coming, but it has not yet arrived.

We live in the time of invitation, when the call of the gospel goes out to every creature. Of course, many still live as though God doesn't exist. They do not acknowledge the rule of the Messiah. But the day is coming when Jesus will return to earth and the reign of God will become an uncontested reality throughout the world.

God's presence will be fully and openly with us once again, as it was at the beginning of the drama. God's plan of redemption will reach its goal. The creation will experience its own Exodus, finding freedom from its bondage to decay. Pain and tears, regret and shame, suffering and death will be no more.

When the day of resurrection arrives God's people will find that their hope has been realized. The dynamic force of an indestructible life will course through their bodies. Empowered by the Spirit, and unhindered by sin and death, we will pursue our original vocation as a renewed humanity. We will be culture makers, under God but over the world. Having been remade in the image of Christ, we will share in bringing his wise, caring rule to the earth.

At the center of it all will be God himself. He will return and make his home with us, this time in a new heavens and a new earth. We, along with the rest of creation, will worship him perfectly and fulfill our true calling. God will be all in all, and the whole world will be full of his glory.

WHAT NOW?

The preceding overview of the drama of the Bible is meant to give you a framework so you can begin to read the books that make up the story. The summary we've provided is merely an invitation for you to engage the sacred books themselves.

Many people today follow the practice of reading only small, fragmentary snippets of the Bible—verses—and often in isolation from the books of which they are a part. This does not lead

Go deep and read big.

to good Bible understanding. We encourage you instead to take in whole books, the way their authors wrote them. This is really the only way to gain deep insight to the Scriptures.

The more you immerse yourself in the script of this drama, the better you will be able to find your own place in the story. The following page, called *Living the Script*, will help you with practical next steps for taking up your role in the Bible's drama of renewal.

LIVING
THE SCRIPT

From the beginning God made it clear that he intends for us to be significant players in his drama. No doubt, it is first and foremost God's story. But we can't passively sit back and just watch what happens. At every stage he invites humans to participate with him.

Here are three key steps to finding your place in the drama:

1. IMMERSE YOURSELF IN THE BIBLE

If we are unfamiliar with the text of the drama itself, there's no chance of living our parts well. Only when we read both deeply and widely in the Bible, marinating in it and letting it soak into our lives, will we be prepared to effectively take up our roles. The more we read the Bible, the better readers we will become. Rather than skimming the surface, we will become skilled at interpreting and practicing what we read.

2. COMMIT TO FOLLOW JESUS

We've all taken part in the brokenness and wrongdoing that came into the story in Act 2. The victory of Jesus in Act 4 now offers us the opportunity to have our lives turned around. Our sins can be forgiven. We can become part of God's story of new creation.

Turn away from your wrongdoing. God has acted through the death and resurrection of the Messiah to deal decisively with evil—in your life and in the life of the world. His death was a sacrifice, and his resurrection a new beginning. Acknowledge that Jesus is the rightful ruler of the world, and commit to follow him and join with God's people.

3. LIVE YOUR PART

Followers of Jesus are gospel players in local communities living out the biblical drama together. But we do not have an exact script for our lines and actions in the drama today. Our history has not yet been written. And we can't just repeat lines from earlier acts in the drama. So what do we do?

We read the Bible to understand what God has already done, especially through Jesus the Messiah, and to know how we carry this story forward. The Bible helps us answer the key question about everything we say and do: Is this an appropriate and fitting way to live out the story of Jesus today? This is how we put the Scriptures into action. Life's choices can be messy, but God has given us his word and promised us his Spirit to guide us on the way. You are God's artwork, created to do good works. May your life be a gift of beauty back to him.

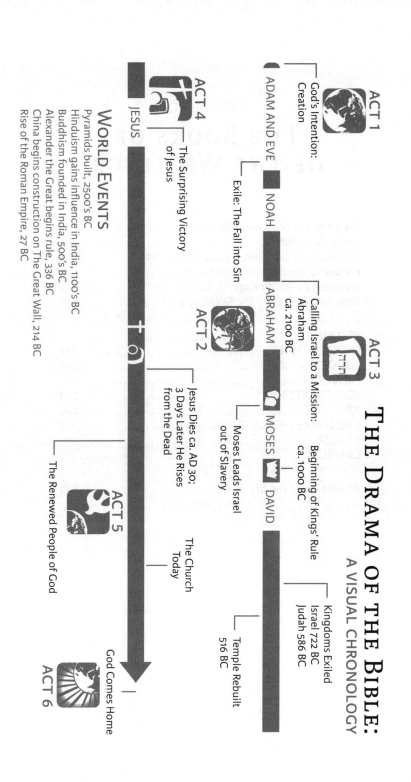

THE DRAMA OF THE BIBLE:
A VISUAL CHRONOLOGY

ACT 1

God's Intention:
Creation

ADAM AND EVE

Exile: The Fall into Sin

NOAH

ACT 3

Calling Israel to a Mission:
Abraham
ca. 2100 BC

ABRAHAM

Beginning of Kings' Rule
ca. 1000 BC

MOSES

Moses Leads Israel
out of Slavery

DAVID

ACT 2

ACT 4

JESUS

The Surprising Victory
of Jesus

Jesus Dies ca. AD 30;
3 Days Later He Rises
from the Dead

Kingdoms Exiled
Israel 722 BC
Judah 586 BC

Temple Rebuilt
516 BC

The Church
Today

ACT 5

The Renewed People of God

God Comes Home

ACT 6

WORLD EVENTS

Pyramids built, 2500's BC
Hinduism gains influence in India, 1100's BC
Buddhism founded in India, 500's BC
Alexander the Great begins rule, 336 BC
China begins construction on The Great Wall, 214 BC
Rise of the Roman Empire, 27 BC

A GUIDE TO

The Books of
of the Writings

PREFACE TO

THE BOOKS
OF THE BIBLE

The Bible isn't a single book. It's a collection of many books that were written, preserved and gathered together so that they could be shared with new generations of readers. Reading, of course, is not an end in itself. Especially in the case of the Bible, reading is a means of entering into the story. Overall, the Bible is an invitation to the reader first to view the world in a new way, and then to become an agent of the world's renewal. Reading is a step in this journey. *The Books of the Bible* is intended to help readers have a more meaningful encounter with the sacred writings and to read with more understanding, so they can take their places more readily within this story of new creation.

Just as the Bible is not a single book, the Bible is more than bare words. Those who wrote its books chose to put them in particular forms, using the literary conventions appropriate to those forms. Many different kinds of writing are found in the Bible: poetry, narrative, wisdom collections, letters, law codes, apocalyptic visions and more. All of these forms must be read as the literature they really are, or else misunderstanding and distortion of meaning are bound to follow. In order to engage the text on its own terms, good readers will honor the agreement between themselves and the biblical writers implied by the choices of particular forms. Good readers will respect the conventions of these forms. In other words, they'll read poetry as poetry, songs as songs, stories as stories, and so forth.

Unfortunately, for some time now the Bible has been printed in a format that hides its literary forms under a mask of numbers. These break the text into bits and sections that the authors never intended. And so *The Books of the Bible* seeks instead to present the books in their distinctive literary forms and structures. It draws on the key insight that visual presentation can be a crucial aid to right reading, good understanding and a better engagement with the Bible.

Specifically, this edition of the Bible differs from the most common current format in several significant ways:

: chapter and verse numbers have been removed from the text;
: the books are presented instead according to the internal divisions that we believe their authors have indicated;
: a single-column setting is used to present the text more clearly and naturally, and to avoid disrupting the intended line breaks in poetry;
: footnotes, section headings and any other additional materials have been removed from the pages of the sacred text;

: individual books that later tradition divided into two or more parts are put back together again; and

: the books have been placed in an order that we hope will help readers understand them better.

Why have we made these changes? First of all, the chapters and verses in the Bible weren't put there by the original authors. The present system of chapter divisions was devised in the thirteenth century, and our present verse divisions weren't added until the sixteenth. Chapters and verses have imposed a foreign structure on the Bible and made it more difficult to read with understanding. Chapter divisions typically don't correspond with the actual divisions of thought. They require readers to make sense of only part of a longer discussion as if it were complete in itself, or else to try to combine two separate discussions into one coherent whole. Moreover, because the Bible's chapters are all roughly the same length, they can at best only indicate sections of a certain size. This hides the existence of both larger and smaller units of thought within biblical books.

When verses are treated as intentional units (as their numbering suggests they should be), they encourage the Bible to be read as a giant reference book, perhaps as a collection of rules or as a series of propositions. Also, when "Bible verses" are treated as independent and free-standing statements, they can be taken selectively out of context and arranged in such a way as to suggest that the Bible supports beliefs and positions that it really doesn't.

It is true that chapter and verse numbers allow ease of reference. But finding passages at this speed may be a dubious benefit since this can encourage ignoring the text *around* the sought out citation. In order to encourage greater understanding and more responsible use of the Bible, we've removed chapter and verse numberings from the text entirely. (A chapter-and-verse range is included at the bottom of each page.)

Because the biblical books were handwritten, read out loud and then hand-copied long before standardized printing, their authors and compilers needed a way to indicate divisions within the text itself. They often did this by repeating a phrase or expression each time they made a transition from one section to another. We can confirm that particular phrases are significant in this way by observing how their placement reinforces a structure that can already be recognized implicitly from other characteristics of a book, such as changes in topic, movement in place or time, or shifts from one kind of writing to another. Through line spacing, we've marked off sections of varying sizes. The smallest are indicated by one blank line, the next largest by two lines, and so on, up to four-line breaks in the largest books. We've also indicated key divisions with a large initial capital letter of new sections. Our goal is to encourage meaningful units to be read in their entirety and so with greater appreciation and understanding.

Footnotes, section headings and other supplemental materials have been removed from the page in order to give readers a more direct and immediate experience of the word of God. At the beginning of each biblical book we've included an invitation to that particular writing with background information on why it was written and how we understand it to be put together. Beyond this, we encourage readers to study the Bible in community. We believe that if they do, they and their teachers, leaders and peers will provide one another with much more information and many more insights than could ever be included in notes added by publishers.

The books of the Bible were written or recorded individually. When they were gathered together, they were placed into a variety of orders. Unfortunately, the order in which today's readers typically encounter these books is yet another factor that hinders their understanding. Paul's letters, for example, have been put in order of length. They are badly out of historical order, and this makes it difficult to read them with an appreciation for where they fit in the course of his life or how they express the development of his thought. The traditional order of the biblical books can also encourage misunderstandings of what kind of writing a particular work is. For example, the book of James has strong affinities with other biblical books in the wisdom tradition. But it's typically placed within a group of letters, suggesting that it, too, should be read as a letter. To help readers overcome such difficulties, we've sought to order the books so that their literary types, their circumstances of composition and the theological traditions they reflect will be evident. Our introductions to each of the different parts of the Bible will explain how we have ordered the books in these sections, and why.

Just as the work of Bible translation is never finished, the work of formatting the Bible on the principles described here will never be completed. Advances in the literary interpretation of the biblical books will undoubtedly enable the work we've begun here to be extended and improved in the years ahead. Yet the need to help readers overcome the many obstacles inherent in the Bible's current format is urgent, so we humbly offer the results of our work to those seeking an improved visual presentation of its sacred books.

We gratefully acknowledge the assistance of many lay people, clergy, scholars and people engaged in active Scripture outreach who've reviewed our work. They've shared their considerable knowledge and expertise with us and continue to provide valuable insights and guidance. However, final responsibility for all of the decisions in this format rests with us. We trust that readers will gain a deeper appreciation for, and a greater understanding of, these sacred texts. Our hope and prayer is that their engagement with *The Books of the Bible* will enable them to take up their own roles in God's great drama of redemption.

The Bible Design Group
Biblica
Colorado Springs, Colorado
March 2011

INVITATION TO THE
WRITINGS

The Writings are the third major division of the First Testament. They represent a much looser grouping than those in the first and second divisions. They've been drawn together from a wider range of traditions, genres (types of literature), and time periods. They're presented here grouped by genre, so that each work can be read meaningfully alongside other examples of the same kind of literature.

: Three of the books in the Writings are collections of song lyrics. These songs were composed over the course of many centuries. Psalms contains nearly 150 worship songs that were written for individual or community use over a period of some 700 years, from the time of Moses up to the time when the Jerusalem temple was rebuilt. Lamentations is a small collection of five songs that all mourn the destruction of Jerusalem. Song of Songs contains half a dozen wedding songs that could have been used for years in marriage celebrations before being gathered together.

: The Writings also contain several books from the "wisdom" tradition. This was a school of thought that flourished in Israel and in other countries of the ancient Near East. In Israel this tradition claimed that wisdom ultimately came from the Lord. Even when human ability and skill were involved, these were really means of discerning the order God himself had placed in the creation. Wisdom came from finding the right way to live in God's world. So for Israel's writers, the acknowledgment of God was the first step of the truly wise. The wisdom teachers loved to formulate and collect "proverbs"—pithy sayings that expressed vital truths about life in a compact and striking way. King Solomon was one of the most outstanding of these teachers. Two collections of his sayings, one likely recorded in his lifetime and the other a couple of centuries later, constitute the bulk of the book of Proverbs. Solomon may also be the author of Ecclesiastes, a book that weaves short reflections together with autobiographical musings to provide a perspective on life that complements the one in Proverbs. Wisdom teachers also cast their reflections in the form of dialogues between people who take turns making poetic speeches. The book of Job provides an example of this type of wisdom literature.

: The two historical books among the Writings were created, like the Psalms, within the worship experience of the community. Chronicles–Ezra–Nehemiah is a sprawling history that runs all the way from the beginning of the human race to the Judeans' return from exile. Its central concern, however, is with how God chose Jerusalem as the place where he'd be worshiped. It describes how a temple was built there, how it was destroyed, and how it was rebuilt as a place where people of all nations could come to seek the true God. The book of Esther is much shorter and more narrowly focused. It explains why a new worship festival, Purim, was added to the ones Moses commanded the people to observe. But in the process, this book offers profound insights into the workings of God's invisible hand in history and into the calling that each individual has to be part of God's work.

: The remaining book in the Writings, Daniel, is a combination of two different kinds of literature. It's half history and half apocalypse. It first tells six stories of how God preserved and protected Daniel and his friends in exile because they remained exclusively devoted to him. The second half of the book describes how, on four occasions, Daniel spoke with angels after praying or seeing a vision. These angels explained God's purposes for his people in the years to come.

In terms of the overall movement of the Bible, the Writings add depth, texture and color to the drama. While for the most part they are not in narrative form themselves, they reveal that the story is rooted in all the complexities of real life. This group of books thus completes the First Testament by drawing a diverse collection of books into its pages. They review the history of the covenant people and they display the theological and literary riches they possessed since, as one of the psalmists wrote, God *has revealed his word to Jacob, his laws and decrees to Israel.*

Israel's ancient songs of
PRAISE, LAMENT AND WONDER,
wise words to craft
A GOOD LIFE
and ponder
LIFE'S DEEPEST CHALLENGES,
stories of Israel's
TEMPLE AND WORSHIP,
the birth of a
FESTIVAL,
and visions of
**GOD'S COMING RULE
OVER THE WORLD,**

THE
WRITINGS

THE WORLD OF ABRAHAM, ISAAC AND JACOB

MEDITERRANEAN SEA

EGYPT

RED SEA

CANAAN
• Shechem
• Bethel
• Hebron
• Beersheba

ARABIAN DESERT

• Haran

Euphrates River

Tigris River

• Babylon

CHALDEA

• Ur

THE KINGDOM OF ISRAEL
and Surrounding Nations

Damascus •

MEDITERRANEAN SEA

• Samaria

Shechem •

Shiloh
•

Bethel •

Jerusalem •

• Jericho

Bethlehem •

Jordan River

AMMON

PHILISTIA

MOAB

• Gaza

Hebron •

Beersheba •

EDOM

David Thomason 2010

INVITATION TO
PSALMS

The book of Psalms is a collection of poems that were originally set to music. In other words, the psalms are song lyrics. Many of them contain musical notations. Their introductions sometimes include musical instructions and the names of their tunes. Like the songs we know today, they were originally written in response to specific occasions in the lives of the songwriters. (Some of their introductions indicate what these occasions were.) But they were then used in worship at various times by the whole community of believers. After the people of Israel returned from exile in Babylon and rebuilt the temple in Jerusalem, many of the songs that had been written and sung over the centuries were collected and used in worship in this second temple. That collection forms the basis of the book of Psalms as we know it today.

This book contains the words to 147 different songs. (They've traditionally been numbered from 1 to 150, but two of them have been split in half, 9–10 and 42–43, while another has been included twice and numbered both 14 and 53.) Because each of the songs is an independent composition, they're all meaningful when read individually. The different psalms describe the broad range of experiences the people of Israel had in their covenant journey with God. They provide a way for us to enter into the story, by reading or singing them, as we live the script of the biblical drama today.

At the same time, the book as a whole has been deliberately structured. This adds a further level of meaning. The collection is divided into five parts by four variations on the formula, *Praise be to the* LORD . . . *Amen and Amen!* This creates five "books" within the collection. This seems intended to remind the reader of the five "books" that the law of Moses was divided into. The implication is that even though these poems were originally sung in worship, they can also be read and studied for instruction in God's ways. The psalm that comes first in the collection (#1) emphasizes the value of reading them this way. It appears to have been placed there deliberately to make this point. This theme is also stressed at the beginning of book three (in #73) and near the end of the whole collection (in #145).

These five "books," in their general outlines, also tell a three-part story. They trace Israel's history in its successive stages: monarchy, exile and return:

: The first two books consist mostly of psalms by David, whom God established as king over Israel and as the head of its royal line. Taken together, these two books begin and end with psalms about God establishing the king on the throne (#2 and #72).

: But the third book then begins with the question of why the wicked prosper (#73) and with a lament over the destruction of Jerusalem (#74). This book ends with a similar complaint that God has abandoned David's line (#89). In other words, book three recalls the situation of exile.

: The fourth book then opens with a reminder that God is the true dwelling place of the people of Israel (#90). The psalms in this section state repeatedly that *the LORD reigns* (#93, 97, 99)—in other words, Israel's true king is still on the throne. This fourth book nevertheless ends with a plea for God to bring the exiled people home (#106).

: The fifth book begins with a declaration that God has indeed brought the exiles back (#107). It includes many "songs of ascents" (#120–134), psalms that were sung by travelers going up to the temple in Jerusalem. This suggests a context in which the people have returned to the land. Therefore, appropriately, this fifth book (and the whole collection) ends with a call to praise God (at the end of #145), followed by five songs of praise (#146–150).

In other words, the very form in which Israel's worship songs have been collected illustrates one foundational reason for its worship: God has been faithful to the nation, judging it by means of exile but then bringing it back home again. And so two principles largely account for the structure and meaning of the book of Psalms when it's read as a whole collection: the call to meditate on these psalms in the same way as on the law of Moses, and the call to remember God's continuing faithfulness in history and then respond with our own continuing praise.

Psalms

BOOK I

Psalms 1 – 41

Psalm 1

Blessed is the one
who does not walk in step with the wicked

or stand in the way that sinners take
or sit in the company of mockers,

but whose delight is in the law of the Lord,
and who meditates on his law day and night.

That person is like a tree planted by streams of water,
which yields its fruit in season

and whose leaf does not wither—
whatever they do prospers.

Not so the wicked!
They are like chaff
that the wind blows away.

Therefore the wicked will not stand in the judgment,
nor sinners in the assembly of the righteous.

For the Lord watches over the way of the righteous,
but the way of the wicked leads to destruction.

Psalm 2

Why do the nations conspire
and the peoples plot in vain?

The kings of the earth rise up
and the rulers band together
against the Lord and against his anointed, saying,

"Let us break their chains
and throw off their shackles."

The One enthroned in heaven laughs;
the Lord scoffs at them.

He rebukes them in his anger
and terrifies them in his wrath, saying,

"I have installed my king
on Zion, my holy mountain."

I will proclaim the LORD's decree:

He said to me, "You are my son;
today I have become your father.

Ask me,
and I will make the nations your inheritance,
the ends of the earth your possession.

You will break them with a rod of iron;
you will dash them to pieces like pottery."

Therefore, you kings, be wise;
be warned, you rulers of the earth.

Serve the LORD with fear
and celebrate his rule with trembling.

Kiss his son, or he will be angry
and your way will lead to your destruction,

for his wrath can flare up in a moment.
Blessed are all who take refuge in him.

Psalm 3

A psalm of David. When he fled from his son Absalom.

LORD, how many are my foes!
How many rise up against me!

Many are saying of me,
"God will not deliver him."

But you, LORD, are a shield around me,
my glory, the One who lifts my head high.

I call out to the LORD,
and he answers me from his holy mountain.

I lie down and sleep;
I wake again, because the LORD sustains me.

I will not fear though tens of thousands
assail me on every side.

Arise, LORD!
Deliver me, my God!
Strike all my enemies on the jaw;
break the teeth of the wicked.

From the LORD comes deliverance.
May your blessing be on your people.

Psalm 4

*For the director of music. With stringed instruments.
A psalm of David.*

Answer me when I call to you,
my righteous God.
Give me relief from my distress;
have mercy on me and hear my prayer.

How long will you people turn my glory into shame?
How long will you love delusions and seek false gods?
Know that the LORD has set apart his faithful servant for
himself;
the LORD hears when I call to him.

Tremble and do not sin;
when you are on your beds,
search your hearts and be silent.
Offer the sacrifices of the righteous
and trust in the LORD.

Many, LORD, are asking, "Who will bring us prosperity?"
Let the light of your face shine on us.
Fill my heart with joy
when their grain and new wine abound.

In peace I will lie down and sleep,
for you alone, LORD,
make me dwell in safety.

Psalm 5

For the director of music. For pipes. A psalm of David.

Listen to my words, Lord,
consider my lament.

Hear my cry for help,
my King and my God,
for to you I pray.

In the morning, Lord, you hear my voice;
in the morning I lay my requests before you
and wait expectantly.

For you are not a God who is pleased with wickedness;
with you, evil people are not welcome.

The arrogant cannot stand
in your presence.

You hate all who do wrong;
you destroy those who tell lies.

The bloodthirsty and deceitful
you, Lord, detest.

But I, by your great love,
can come into your house;

in reverence I bow down
toward your holy temple.

Lead me, Lord, in your righteousness
because of my enemies —
make your way straight before me.

Not a word from their mouth can be trusted;
their heart is filled with malice.

Their throat is an open grave;
with their tongues they tell lies.

Declare them guilty, O God!
Let their intrigues be their downfall.

Banish them for their many sins,
for they have rebelled against you.

But let all who take refuge in you be glad;
let them ever sing for joy.

Spread your protection over them,
that those who love your name may rejoice in you.

Surely, Lord, you bless the righteous;
you surround them with your favor as with a shield.

Psalm 6

*For the director of music. With stringed instruments.
According to* sheminith. *A psalm of David.*

Lord, do not rebuke me in your anger
or discipline me in your wrath.

Have mercy on me, Lord, for I am faint;
heal me, Lord, for my bones are in agony.

My soul is in deep anguish.
How long, Lord, how long?

Turn, Lord, and deliver me;
save me because of your unfailing love.

Among the dead no one proclaims your name.
Who praises you from the grave?

I am worn out from my groaning.

All night long I flood my bed with weeping
and drench my couch with tears.

My eyes grow weak with sorrow;
they fail because of all my foes.

Away from me, all you who do evil,
for the Lord has heard my weeping.

The Lord has heard my cry for mercy;
the Lord accepts my prayer.

All my enemies will be overwhelmed with shame and
anguish;
they will turn back and suddenly be put to shame.

Psalm 7

A shiggaion *of David, which he sang to the Lord concerning Cush,
a Benjamite.*

Lord my God, I take refuge in you;
save and deliver me from all who pursue me,

or they will tear me apart like a lion
and rip me to pieces with no one to rescue me.

Lord my God, if I have done this
and there is guilt on my hands —

if I have repaid my ally with evil
or without cause have robbed my foe —

then let my enemy pursue and overtake me;
let him trample my life to the ground
and make me sleep in the dust.

Arise, Lord, in your anger;
rise up against the rage of my enemies.
Awake, my God; decree justice.

Let the assembled peoples gather around you,
while you sit enthroned over them on high.
Let the Lord judge the peoples.

Vindicate me, Lord, according to my righteousness,
according to my integrity, O Most High.

Bring to an end the violence of the wicked
and make the righteous secure —

you, the righteous God
who probes minds and hearts.

My shield is God Most High,
who saves the upright in heart.

God is a righteous judge,
a God who displays his wrath every day.

If he does not relent,
he will sharpen his sword;
he will bend and string his bow.

He has prepared his deadly weapons;
he makes ready his flaming arrows.

Whoever is pregnant with evil
conceives trouble and gives birth to disillusionment.

Whoever digs a hole and scoops it out
falls into the pit they have made.

The trouble they cause recoils on them;
their violence comes down on their own heads.

I will give thanks to the Lord because of his
    righteousness;
I will sing the praises of the name of the Lord Most High.

Psalm 8

For the director of music. According to gittith. *A psalm of David.*

LORD, our Lord,
how majestic is your name in all the earth!

You have set your glory
in the heavens.

Through the praise of children and infants
you have established a stronghold against your enemies,
to silence the foe and the avenger.

When I consider your heavens,
the work of your fingers,

the moon and the stars,
which you have set in place,

what is mankind that you are mindful of them,
human beings that you care for them?

You have made them a little lower than the angels
and crowned them with glory and honor.

You made them rulers over the works of your hands;
you put everything under their feet:

all flocks and herds,
and the animals of the wild,

the birds in the sky,
and the fish in the sea,
all that swim the paths of the seas.

LORD, our Lord,
how majestic is your name in all the earth!

Psalm 9–10

For the director of music. To the tune of "The Death of the Son."
A psalm of David.

I will give thanks to you, LORD, with all my heart;
I will tell of all your wonderful deeds.

I will be glad and rejoice in you;
I will sing the praises of your name, O Most High.

My enemies turn back;
they stumble and perish before you.

For you have upheld my right and my cause,
sitting enthroned as the righteous judge.

You have rebuked the nations and destroyed the wicked;
you have blotted out their name for ever and ever.

Endless ruin has overtaken my enemies,
you have uprooted their cities;
even the memory of them has perished.

The Lord reigns forever;
he has established his throne for judgment.

He rules the world in righteousness
and judges the peoples with equity.

The Lord is a refuge for the oppressed,
a stronghold in times of trouble.

Those who know your name trust in you,
for you, Lord, have never forsaken those who seek you.

Sing the praises of the Lord, enthroned in Zion;
proclaim among the nations what he has done.

For he who avenges blood remembers;
he does not ignore the cries of the afflicted.

Lord, see how my enemies persecute me!
Have mercy and lift me up from the gates of death,

that I may declare your praises
in the gates of Daughter Zion,
and there rejoice in your salvation.

The nations have fallen into the pit they have dug;
their feet are caught in the net they have hidden.

The Lord is known by his acts of justice;
the wicked are ensnared by the work of their hands.

The wicked go down to the realm of the dead,
all the nations that forget God.

But God will never forget the needy;
the hope of the afflicted will never perish.

Arise, Lord, do not let mortals triumph;
let the nations be judged in your presence.

Strike them with terror, Lord;
let the nations know they are only mortal.

Why, LORD, do you stand far off?
Why do you hide yourself in times of trouble?

In his arrogance the wicked man hunts down the weak,
who are caught in the schemes he devises.

He boasts about the cravings of his heart;
he blesses the greedy and reviles the LORD.

In his pride the wicked man does not seek him;
in all his thoughts there is no room for God.

His ways are always prosperous;
your laws are rejected by him;
he sneers at all his enemies.

He says to himself, "Nothing will ever shake me."
He swears, "No one will ever do me harm."

His mouth is full of lies and threats;
trouble and evil are under his tongue.

He lies in wait near the villages;
from ambush he murders the innocent.

His eyes watch in secret for his victims;
like a lion in cover he lies in wait.

He lies in wait to catch the helpless;
he catches the helpless and drags them off in his net.

His victims are crushed, they collapse;
they fall under his strength.

He says to himself, "God will never notice;
he covers his face and never sees."

Arise, LORD! Lift up your hand, O God.
Do not forget the helpless.

Why does the wicked man revile God?
Why does he say to himself,
"He won't call me to account"?

But you, God, see the trouble of the afflicted;
you consider their grief and take it in hand.

The victims commit themselves to you;
you are the helper of the fatherless.

Break the arm of the wicked man;
call the evildoer to account for his wickedness
that would not otherwise be found out.

The LORD is King for ever and ever;
the nations will perish from his land.

You, LORD, hear the desire of the afflicted;
you encourage them, and you listen to their cry,

defending the fatherless and the oppressed,
so that mere earthly mortals
will never again strike terror.

Psalm 11

For the director of music. Of David.

In the LORD I take refuge.
How then can you say to me:
"Flee like a bird to your mountain.

For look, the wicked bend their bows;
they set their arrows against the strings

to shoot from the shadows
at the upright in heart.

When the foundations are being destroyed,
what can the righteous do?"

The LORD is in his holy temple;
the LORD is on his heavenly throne.

He observes everyone on earth;
his eyes examine them.

The LORD examines the righteous,
but the wicked, those who love violence,
he hates with a passion.

On the wicked he will rain
fiery coals and burning sulfur;
a scorching wind will be their lot.

For the LORD is righteous,
he loves justice;
the upright will see his face.

Psalm 12

For the director of music. According to sheminith.
A psalm of David.

Help, LORD, for no one is faithful anymore;
those who are loyal have vanished from the human race.

Everyone lies to their neighbor;
they flatter with their lips
but harbor deception in their hearts.

May the Lord silence all flattering lips
and every boastful tongue —

those who say,
"By our tongues we will prevail;
our own lips will defend us — who is lord over us?"

"Because the poor are plundered and
the needy groan,
I will now arise," says the Lord.
"I will protect them from those who
malign them."

And the words of the Lord are flawless,
like silver purified in a crucible,
like gold refined seven times.

You, Lord, will keep the needy safe
and will protect us forever from the wicked,

who freely strut about
when what is vile is honored by the human race.

Psalm 13

For the director of music. A psalm of David.

How long, Lord? Will you forget me forever?
How long will you hide your face from me?

How long must I wrestle with my thoughts
and day after day have sorrow in my heart?
How long will my enemy triumph over me?

Look on me and answer, Lord my God.
Give light to my eyes, or I will sleep in death,

and my enemy will say, "I have overcome him,"
and my foes will rejoice when I fall.

But I trust in your unfailing love;
my heart rejoices in your salvation.

I will sing the Lord's praise,
for he has been good to me.

Psalm 14

For the director of music. Of David.

The fool says in his heart,
"There is no God."
They are corrupt, their deeds are vile;
there is no one who does good.

The Lord looks down from heaven
on all mankind
to see if there are any who understand,
any who seek God.

All have turned away, all have become corrupt;
there is no one who does good,
not even one.

Do all these evildoers know nothing?

They devour my people as though eating bread;
they never call on the Lord.
But there they are, overwhelmed with dread,
for God is present in the company of the righteous.
You evildoers frustrate the plans of the poor,
but the Lord is their refuge.

Oh, that salvation for Israel would come out of Zion!
When the Lord restores his people,
let Jacob rejoice and Israel be glad!

Psalm 15

A psalm of David.

Lord, who may dwell in your sacred tent?
Who may live on your holy mountain?

The one whose walk is blameless,
who does what is righteous,
who speaks the truth from their heart;
whose tongue utters no slander,
who does no wrong to a neighbor,
and casts no slur on others;
who despises a vile person
but honors those who fear the Lord;

who keeps an oath even when it hurts,
and does not change their mind;

who lends money to the poor without interest;
who does not accept a bribe against the innocent.

Whoever does these things
will never be shaken.

Psalm 16

A miktam *of David.*

Keep me safe, my God,
for in you I take refuge.

I say to the Lord, "You are my Lord;
apart from you I have no good thing."
I say of the holy people who are in the land,
"They are the noble ones in whom is all my delight."
Those who run after other gods will suffer more
        and more.
I will not pour out libations of blood to such gods
or take up their names on my lips.

Lord, you alone are my portion and my cup;
you make my lot secure.
The boundary lines have fallen for me in
        pleasant places;
surely I have a delightful inheritance.
I will praise the Lord, who counsels me;
even at night my heart instructs me.
I keep my eyes always on the Lord.
With him at my right hand, I will not be shaken.

Therefore my heart is glad and my tongue
        rejoices;
my body also will rest secure,

because you will not abandon me to the realm
        of the dead,
nor will you let your faithful one see decay.

You make known to me the path of life;
you will fill me with joy in your presence,
with eternal pleasures at your right hand.

Psalm 17

A prayer of David.

Hear me, Lᴏʀᴅ, my plea is just;
listen to my cry.

Hear my prayer —
it does not rise from deceitful lips.

Let my vindication come from you;
may your eyes see what is right.

Though you probe my heart,
though you examine me at night and test me,

you will find that I have planned no evil;
my mouth has not transgressed.

Though people tried to bribe me,
I have kept myself from the ways of the violent
through what your lips have commanded.

My steps have held to your paths;
my feet have not stumbled.

I call on you, my God, for you will answer me;
turn your ear to me and hear my prayer.

Show me the wonders of your great love,
you who save by your right hand
those who take refuge in you from their foes.

Keep me as the apple of your eye;
hide me in the shadow of your wings

from the wicked who are out to destroy me,
from my mortal enemies who surround me.

They close up their callous hearts,
and their mouths speak with arrogance.

They have tracked me down, they now surround me,
with eyes alert, to throw me to the ground.

They are like a lion hungry for prey,
like a fierce lion crouching in cover.

Rise up, Lᴏʀᴅ, confront them, bring them down;
with your sword rescue me from the wicked.

By your hand save me from such people, Lᴏʀᴅ,
from those of this world whose reward is in this life.

May what you have stored up for the wicked fill their
    bellies;
may their children gorge themselves on it,
and may there be leftovers for their little ones.

As for me, I will be vindicated and will see your face;
when I awake, I will be satisfied with seeing your
    likeness.

Psalm 18

*For the director of music. Of David the servant of the Lord. He sang
to the Lord the words of this song when the Lord delivered him from
the hand of all his enemies and from the hand of Saul. He said:*

I love you, Lord, my strength.

The Lord is my rock, my fortress and my deliverer;
my God is my rock, in whom I take refuge,
my shield and the horn of my salvation, my stronghold.

I called to the Lord, who is worthy of praise,
and I have been saved from my enemies.
The cords of death entangled me;
the torrents of destruction overwhelmed me.
The cords of the grave coiled around me;
the snares of death confronted me.

In my distress I called to the Lord;
I cried to my God for help.
From his temple he heard my voice;
my cry came before him, into his ears.
The earth trembled and quaked,
and the foundations of the mountains shook;
they trembled because he was angry.
Smoke rose from his nostrils;
consuming fire came from his mouth,
burning coals blazed out of it.
He parted the heavens and came down;
dark clouds were under his feet.
He mounted the cherubim and flew;
he soared on the wings of the wind.

He made darkness his covering, his canopy
   around him —
the dark rain clouds of the sky.

Out of the brightness of his presence clouds advanced,
with hailstones and bolts of lightning.

The Lord thundered from heaven;
the voice of the Most High resounded.

He shot his arrows and scattered the enemy,
with great bolts of lightning he routed them.

The valleys of the sea were exposed
and the foundations of the earth laid bare

at your rebuke, Lord,
at the blast of breath from your nostrils.

He reached down from on high and took hold of me;
he drew me out of deep waters.

He rescued me from my powerful enemy,
from my foes, who were too strong for me.

They confronted me in the day of my disaster,
but the Lord was my support.

He brought me out into a spacious place;
he rescued me because he delighted in me.

The Lord has dealt with me according to my
   righteousness;
according to the cleanness of my hands he has rewarded
   me.

For I have kept the ways of the Lord;
I am not guilty of turning from my God.

All his laws are before me;
I have not turned away from his decrees.

I have been blameless before him
and have kept myself from sin.

The Lord has rewarded me according to my
   righteousness,
according to the cleanness of my hands in his sight.

To the faithful you show yourself faithful,
to the blameless you show yourself blameless,

to the pure you show yourself pure,
but to the devious you show yourself shrewd.

You save the humble
but bring low those whose eyes are haughty.

You, Lord, keep my lamp burning;
my God turns my darkness into light.

With your help I can advance against a troop;
with my God I can scale a wall.

As for God, his way is perfect:
The Lord's word is flawless;
he shields all who take refuge in him.

For who is God besides the Lord?
And who is the Rock except our God?

It is God who arms me with strength
and keeps my way secure.

He makes my feet like the feet of a deer;
he causes me to stand on the heights.

He trains my hands for battle;
my arms can bend a bow of bronze.

You make your saving help my shield,
and your right hand sustains me;
your help has made me great.

You provide a broad path for my feet,
so that my ankles do not give way.

I pursued my enemies and overtook them;
I did not turn back till they were destroyed.

I crushed them so that they could not rise;
they fell beneath my feet.

You armed me with strength for battle;
you humbled my adversaries before me.

You made my enemies turn their backs in flight,
and I destroyed my foes.

They cried for help, but there was no one to save them —
to the Lord, but he did not answer.

I beat them as fine as windblown dust;
I trampled them like mud in the streets.

You have delivered me from the attacks of the people;
you have made me the head of nations.

People I did not know now serve me,
foreigners cower before me;
as soon as they hear of me, they obey me.

They all lose heart;
they come trembling from their strongholds.

The Lord lives! Praise be to my Rock!
Exalted be God my Savior!

He is the God who avenges me,
who subdues nations under me,
who saves me from my enemies.

You exalted me above my foes;
from a violent man you rescued me.

Therefore I will praise you, Lord, among the nations;
I will sing the praises of your name.

He gives his king great victories;
he shows unfailing love to his anointed,
to David and to his descendants forever.

Psalm 19

For the director of music. A psalm of David.

The heavens declare the glory of God;
the skies proclaim the work of his hands.

Day after day they pour forth speech;
night after night they reveal knowledge.

They have no speech, they use no words;
no sound is heard from them.

Yet their voice goes out into all the earth,
their words to the ends of the world.

In the heavens God has pitched a tent for the sun.
It is like a bridegroom coming out of his chamber,
like a champion rejoicing to run his course.

It rises at one end of the heavens
and makes its circuit to the other;
nothing is deprived of its warmth.

The law of the Lord is perfect,
refreshing the soul.

The statutes of the Lord are trustworthy,
making wise the simple.

The precepts of the Lord are right,
giving joy to the heart.

The commands of the Lord are radiant,
giving light to the eyes.

The fear of the Lord is pure,
enduring forever.

The decrees of the Lord are firm,
and all of them are righteous.

They are more precious than gold,
than much pure gold;

they are sweeter than honey,
than honey from the honeycomb.

By them your servant is warned;
in keeping them there is great reward.

But who can discern their own errors?
Forgive my hidden faults.

Keep your servant also from willful sins;
may they not rule over me.

Then I will be blameless,
innocent of great transgression.

May these words of my mouth and this meditation of my
heart
be pleasing in your sight,
Lord, my Rock and my Redeemer.

Psalm 20

For the director of music. A psalm of David.

May the Lord answer you when you are in distress;
may the name of the God of Jacob protect you.

May he send you help from the sanctuary
and grant you support from Zion.

May he remember all your sacrifices
and accept your burnt offerings.

May he give you the desire of your heart
and make all your plans succeed.

May we shout for joy over your victory
and lift up our banners in the name of our God.

May the Lord grant all your requests.

Now this I know:
The Lord gives victory to his anointed.

He answers him from his heavenly sanctuary
with the victorious power of his right hand.

Some trust in chariots and some in horses,
but we trust in the name of the Lord our God.

They are brought to their knees and fall,
but we rise up and stand firm.

Lord, give victory to the king!
Answer us when we call!

Psalm 21

For the director of music. A psalm of David.

The king rejoices in your strength, Lord.
How great is his joy in the victories you give!

You have granted him his heart's desire
and have not withheld the request of his lips.

You came to greet him with rich blessings
and placed a crown of pure gold on his head.

He asked you for life, and you gave it to him —
length of days, for ever and ever.

Through the victories you gave, his glory is great;
you have bestowed on him splendor and majesty.

Surely you have granted him unending blessings
and made him glad with the joy of your presence.

For the king trusts in the Lord;
through the unfailing love of the Most High
he will not be shaken.

Your hand will lay hold on all your enemies;
your right hand will seize your foes.

When you appear for battle,
you will burn them up as in a blazing furnace.

The Lord will swallow them up in his wrath,
and his fire will consume them.

You will destroy their descendants from the earth,
their posterity from mankind.

Though they plot evil against you
and devise wicked schemes, they cannot succeed.

You will make them turn their backs
when you aim at them with drawn bow.

Be exalted in your strength, Lord;
we will sing and praise your might.

For the director of music. To the tune of "The Doe of the Morning."
A psalm of David.

My God, my God, why have you forsaken me?
Why are you so far from saving me,
so far from my cries of anguish?

My God, I cry out by day, but you do not answer,
by night, but I find no rest.

Yet you are enthroned as the Holy One;
you are the one Israel praises.

In you our ancestors put their trust;
they trusted and you delivered them.

To you they cried out and were saved;
in you they trusted and were not put to shame.

But I am a worm and not a man,
scorned by everyone, despised by the people.

All who see me mock me;
they hurl insults, shaking their heads.

"He trusts in the Lord," they say,
"let the Lord rescue him.

Let him deliver him,
since he delights in him."

Yet you brought me out of the womb;
you made me trust in you, even at my mother's breast.

From birth I was cast on you;
from my mother's womb you have been my God.

Do not be far from me,
for trouble is near
and there is no one to help.

Many bulls surround me;
strong bulls of Bashan encircle me.

Roaring lions that tear their prey
open their mouths wide against me.

I am poured out like water,
and all my bones are out of joint.

My heart has turned to wax;
it has melted within me.

My mouth is dried up like a potsherd,
and my tongue sticks to the roof of my mouth;
you lay me in the dust of death.

Dogs surround me,
a pack of villains encircles me;
they pierce my hands and my feet.

All my bones are on display;
people stare and gloat over me.

They divide my clothes among them
and cast lots for my garment.

But you, Lord, do not be far from me.
You are my strength; come quickly to help me.

Deliver me from the sword,
my precious life from the power of the dogs.

Rescue me from the mouth of the lions;
save me from the horns of the wild oxen.

I will declare your name to my people;
in the assembly I will praise you.

You who fear the Lord, praise him!
All you descendants of Jacob, honor him!
Revere him, all you descendants of Israel!

For he has not despised or scorned
the suffering of the afflicted one;

he has not hidden his face from him
but has listened to his cry for help.

From you comes the theme of my praise in the great
assembly;
before those who fear you I will fulfill my vows.

The poor will eat and be satisfied;
those who seek the Lord will praise him —
may your hearts live forever!

All the ends of the earth
will remember and turn to the Lord,

and all the families of the nations
will bow down before him,

for dominion belongs to the Lord
and he rules over the nations.

All the rich of the earth will feast and
worship;
all who go down to the dust will kneel
before him—
those who cannot keep themselves alive.

Posterity will serve him;
future generations will be told about the Lord.

They will proclaim his righteousness,
declaring to a people yet unborn:
He has done it!

Psalm 23

A psalm of David.

The Lord is my shepherd, I lack nothing.
He makes me lie down in green pastures,

he leads me beside quiet waters,
he refreshes my soul.

He guides me along the right paths
for his name's sake.

Even though I walk
through the darkest valley,

I will fear no evil,
for you are with me;

your rod and your staff,
they comfort me.

You prepare a table before me
in the presence of my enemies.

You anoint my head with oil;
my cup overflows.

Surely your goodness and love will
follow me
all the days of my life,

and I will dwell in the house of the Lord
forever.

Of David. A psalm.

The earth is the Lord's, and everything in it,
the world, and all who live in it;
for he founded it on the seas
and established it on the waters.

Who may ascend the mountain of the Lord?
Who may stand in his holy place?
The one who has clean hands and a pure heart,
who does not trust in an idol
or swear by a false god.

They will receive blessing from the Lord
and vindication from God their Savior.
Such is the generation of those who seek him,
who seek your face, God of Jacob.

Lift up your heads, you gates;
be lifted up, you ancient doors,
that the King of glory may come in.
Who is this King of glory?
The Lord strong and mighty,
the Lord mighty in battle.
Lift up your heads, you gates;
lift them up, you ancient doors,
that the King of glory may come in.
Who is he, this King of glory?
The Lord Almighty—
he is the King of glory.

Psalm 25

Of David.

In you, Lord my God,
I put my trust.

I trust in you;
do not let me be put to shame,
nor let my enemies triumph over me.
No one who hopes in you
will ever be put to shame,

but shame will come on those
who are treacherous without cause.

Show me your ways, LORD,
teach me your paths.

Guide me in your truth and teach me,
for you are God my Savior,
and my hope is in you all day long.

Remember, LORD, your great mercy and love,
for they are from of old.

Do not remember the sins of my youth
and my rebellious ways;

according to your love remember me,
for you, LORD, are good.

Good and upright is the LORD;
therefore he instructs sinners in his ways.

He guides the humble in what is right
and teaches them his way.

All the ways of the LORD are loving and faithful
toward those who keep the demands of his covenant.

For the sake of your name, LORD,
forgive my iniquity, though it is great.

Who, then, are those who fear the LORD?
He will instruct them in the ways they should choose.

They will spend their days in prosperity,
and their descendants will inherit the land.

The LORD confides in those who fear him;
he makes his covenant known to them.

My eyes are ever on the LORD,
for only he will release my feet from the snare.

Turn to me and be gracious to me,
for I am lonely and afflicted.

Relieve the troubles of my heart
and free me from my anguish.

Look on my affliction and my distress
and take away all my sins.

See how numerous are my enemies
and how fiercely they hate me!

Guard my life and rescue me;
    do not let me be put to shame,
    for I take refuge in you.
May integrity and uprightness protect me,
    because my hope, LORD, is in you.

Deliver Israel, O God,
    from all their troubles!

Psalm 26

Of David.

Vindicate me, LORD,
    for I have led a blameless life;
I have trusted in the LORD
    and have not faltered.
Test me, LORD, and try me,
    examine my heart and my mind;
for I have always been mindful of your unfailing love
    and have lived in reliance on your faithfulness.

I do not sit with the deceitful,
    nor do I associate with hypocrites.
I abhor the assembly of evildoers
    and refuse to sit with the wicked.
I wash my hands in innocence,
    and go about your altar, LORD,
proclaiming aloud your praise
    and telling of all your wonderful deeds.

LORD, I love the house where you live,
    the place where your glory dwells.
Do not take away my soul along with sinners,
    my life with those who are bloodthirsty,
in whose hands are wicked schemes,
    whose right hands are full of bribes.
I lead a blameless life;
    deliver me and be merciful to me.

My feet stand on level ground;
    in the great congregation I will praise the LORD.

Psalm 27

Of David.

The LORD is my light and my salvation—
whom shall I fear?
The LORD is the stronghold of my life—
of whom shall I be afraid?

When the wicked advance against me
to devour me,
it is my enemies and my foes
who will stumble and fall.
Though an army besiege me,
my heart will not fear;
though war break out against me,
even then I will be confident.

One thing I ask from the LORD,
this only do I seek:
that I may dwell in the house of the LORD
all the days of my life,
to gaze on the beauty of the LORD
and to seek him in his temple.
For in the day of trouble
he will keep me safe in his dwelling;
he will hide me in the shelter of his sacred tent
and set me high upon a rock.

Then my head will be exalted
above the enemies who surround me;
at his sacred tent I will sacrifice with shouts of joy;
I will sing and make music to the LORD.

Hear my voice when I call, LORD;
be merciful to me and answer me.
My heart says of you, "Seek his face!"
Your face, LORD, I will seek.
Do not hide your face from me,
do not turn your servant away in anger;
you have been my helper.
Do not reject me or forsake me,
God my Savior.

Though my father and mother forsake me,
the Lord will receive me.

Teach me your way, Lord;
lead me in a straight path
because of my oppressors.

Do not turn me over to the desire of my foes,
for false witnesses rise up against me,
spouting malicious accusations.

I remain confident of this:
I will see the goodness of the Lord
in the land of the living.

Wait for the Lord;
be strong and take heart
and wait for the Lord.

Psalm 28

Of David.

To you, Lord, I call;
you are my Rock,
do not turn a deaf ear to me.

For if you remain silent,
I will be like those who go down to the pit.

Hear my cry for mercy
as I call to you for help,
as I lift up my hands
toward your Most Holy Place.

Do not drag me away with the wicked,
with those who do evil,
who speak cordially with their neighbors
but harbor malice in their hearts.

Repay them for their deeds
and for their evil work;
repay them for what their hands have done
and bring back on them what they deserve.

Because they have no regard for the deeds of the Lord
and what his hands have done,
he will tear them down
and never build them up again.

Praise be to the Lord,
for he has heard my cry for mercy.

The Lord is my strength and my shield;
my heart trusts in him, and he helps me.

My heart leaps for joy,
and with my song I praise him.

The Lord is the strength of his people,
a fortress of salvation for his anointed one.

Save your people and bless your inheritance;
be their shepherd and carry them forever.

Psalm 29

A psalm of David.

Ascribe to the Lord, you heavenly beings,
ascribe to the Lord glory and strength.

Ascribe to the Lord the glory due his name;
worship the Lord in the splendor of his holiness.

The voice of the Lord is over the waters;
the God of glory thunders,
the Lord thunders over the mighty waters.

The voice of the Lord is powerful;
the voice of the Lord is majestic.

The voice of the Lord breaks the cedars;
the Lord breaks in pieces the cedars of Lebanon.

He makes Lebanon leap like a calf,
Sirion like a young wild ox.

The voice of the Lord strikes
with flashes of lightning.

The voice of the Lord shakes the desert;
the Lord shakes the Desert of Kadesh.

The voice of the Lord twists the oaks
and strips the forests bare.

And in his temple all cry, "Glory!"

The Lord sits enthroned over the flood;
the Lord is enthroned as King forever.

The Lord gives strength to his people;
the Lord blesses his people with peace.

Psalm 30

A psalm. A song. For the dedication of the temple. Of David.

I will exalt you, Lord,
for you lifted me out of the depths
and did not let my enemies gloat over me.
Lord my God, I called to you for help,
and you healed me.
You, Lord, brought me up from the realm
of the dead;
you spared me from going down to the pit.

Sing the praises of the Lord, you his faithful
people;
praise his holy name.
For his anger lasts only a moment,
but his favor lasts a lifetime;
weeping may stay for the night,
but rejoicing comes in the morning.

When I felt secure, I said,
"I will never be shaken."
Lord, when you favored me,
you made my royal mountain stand firm;
but when you hid your face,
I was dismayed.

To you, Lord, I called;
to the Lord I cried for mercy:
"What is gained if I am silenced,
if I go down to the pit?
Will the dust praise you?
Will it proclaim your faithfulness?
Hear, Lord, and be merciful to me;
Lord, be my help."

You turned my wailing into dancing;
you removed my sackcloth and clothed
me with joy,
that my heart may sing your praises and
not be silent.
Lord my God, I will praise you forever.

Psalm 31

For the director of music. A psalm of David.

In you, Lord, I have taken refuge;
let me never be put to shame;
deliver me in your righteousness.

Turn your ear to me,
come quickly to my rescue;

be my rock of refuge,
a strong fortress to save me.

Since you are my rock and my fortress,
for the sake of your name lead and guide me.

Keep me free from the trap that is set for me,
for you are my refuge.

Into your hands I commit my spirit;
deliver me, Lord, my faithful God.

I hate those who cling to worthless idols;
as for me, I trust in the Lord.

I will be glad and rejoice in your love,
for you saw my affliction
and knew the anguish of my soul.

You have not given me into the hands
of the enemy
but have set my feet in a spacious place.

Be merciful to me, Lord, for I am in distress;
my eyes grow weak with sorrow,
my soul and body with grief.

My life is consumed by anguish
and my years by groaning;

my strength fails because of my affliction,
and my bones grow weak.

Because of all my enemies,
I am the utter contempt of my neighbors

and an object of dread to my closest friends —
those who see me on the street flee from me.

I am forgotten as though I were dead;
I have become like broken pottery.

For I hear many whispering,
"Terror on every side!"

They conspire against me
and plot to take my life.

But I trust in you, Lord;
I say, "You are my God."

My times are in your hands;
deliver me from the hands of my enemies,
from those who pursue me.

Let your face shine on your servant;
save me in your unfailing love.

Let me not be put to shame, Lord,
for I have cried out to you;

but let the wicked be put to shame
and be silent in the realm of the dead.

Let their lying lips be silenced,
for with pride and contempt
they speak arrogantly against the righteous.

How abundant are the good things
that you have stored up for those who fear you,

that you bestow in the sight of all,
on those who take refuge in you.

In the shelter of your presence you hide them
from all human intrigues;

you keep them safe in your dwelling
from accusing tongues.

Praise be to the Lord,
for he showed me the wonders of his love
when I was in a city under siege.

In my alarm I said,
"I am cut off from your sight!"

Yet you heard my cry for mercy
when I called to you for help.

Love the Lord, all his faithful people!
The Lord preserves those who are
    true to him,
but the proud he pays back in full.

Be strong and take heart,
all you who hope in the Lord.

Of David. A maskil.

Blessed is the one
whose transgressions are forgiven,
whose sins are covered.

Blessed is the one
whose sin the Lord does not count against them
and in whose spirit is no deceit.

When I kept silent,
my bones wasted away
through my groaning all day long.

For day and night
your hand was heavy on me;
my strength was sapped
as in the heat of summer.

Then I acknowledged my sin to you
and did not cover up my iniquity.

I said, "I will confess
my transgressions to the Lord."
And you forgave
the guilt of my sin.

Therefore let all the faithful pray to you
while you may be found;
surely the rising of the mighty waters
will not reach them.

You are my hiding place;
you will protect me from trouble
and surround me with songs of deliverance.

I will instruct you and teach you in the way you should go;
I will counsel you with my loving eye on you.

Do not be like the horse or the mule,
which have no understanding

but must be controlled by bit and bridle
or they will not come to you.

Many are the woes of the wicked,
but the Lord's unfailing love
surrounds the one who trusts in him.

Rejoice in the LORD and be glad, you righteous;
sing, all you who are upright in heart!

Psalm 33

Sing joyfully to the LORD, you righteous;
it is fitting for the upright to praise him.

Praise the LORD with the harp;
make music to him on the ten-stringed lyre.

Sing to him a new song;
play skillfully, and shout for joy.

For the word of the LORD is right and true;
he is faithful in all he does.

The LORD loves righteousness and justice;
the earth is full of his unfailing love.

By the word of the LORD the heavens were made,
their starry host by the breath of his mouth.

He gathers the waters of the sea into jars;
he puts the deep into storehouses.

Let all the earth fear the LORD;
let all the people of the world revere him.

For he spoke, and it came to be;
he commanded, and it stood firm.

The LORD foils the plans of the nations;
he thwarts the purposes of the peoples.

But the plans of the LORD stand firm forever,
the purposes of his heart through all generations.

Blessed is the nation whose God is the LORD,
the people he chose for his inheritance.

From heaven the LORD looks down
and sees all mankind;

from his dwelling place he watches
all who live on earth —

he who forms the hearts of all,
who considers everything they do.

No king is saved by the size of his army;
no warrior escapes by his great strength.

A horse is a vain hope for deliverance;
despite all its great strength it cannot save.

But the eyes of the Lord are on those who fear him,
on those whose hope is in his unfailing love,

to deliver them from death
and keep them alive in famine.

We wait in hope for the Lord;
he is our help and our shield.

In him our hearts rejoice,
for we trust in his holy name.

May your unfailing love be with us, Lord,
even as we put our hope in you.

Psalm 34

Of David. When he pretended to be insane before Abimelek,
who drove him away, and he left.

I will extol the Lord at all times;
his praise will always be on my lips.

I will glory in the Lord;
let the afflicted hear and rejoice.

Glorify the Lord with me;
let us exalt his name together.

I sought the Lord, and he answered me;
he delivered me from all my fears.

Those who look to him are radiant;
their faces are never covered with shame.

This poor man called, and the Lord heard him;
he saved him out of all his troubles.

The angel of the Lord encamps around those who fear
    him,
and he delivers them.

Taste and see that the Lord is good;
blessed is the one who takes refuge in him.

Fear the Lord, you his holy people,
for those who fear him lack nothing.

The lions may grow weak and hungry,
but those who seek the Lord lack no good thing.

Come, my children, listen to me;
I will teach you the fear of the LORD.

Whoever of you loves life
and desires to see many good days,

keep your tongue from evil
and your lips from telling lies.

Turn from evil and do good;
seek peace and pursue it.

The eyes of the LORD are on the righteous,
and his ears are attentive to their cry;

but the face of the LORD is against those who do evil,
to blot out their name from the earth.

The righteous cry out, and the LORD hears them;
he delivers them from all their troubles.

The LORD is close to the brokenhearted
and saves those who are crushed in spirit.

The righteous person may have many troubles,
but the LORD delivers him from them all;

he protects all his bones,
not one of them will be broken.

Evil will slay the wicked;
the foes of the righteous will be condemned.

The LORD will rescue his servants;
no one who takes refuge in him will be condemned.

Psalm 35

Of David.

Contend, LORD, with those who contend with me;
fight against those who fight against me.

Take up shield and armor;
arise and come to my aid.

Brandish spear and javelin
against those who pursue me.

Say to me,
"I am your salvation."

May those who seek my life
be disgraced and put to shame;

may those who plot my ruin
be turned back in dismay.

May they be like chaff before the wind,
with the angel of the LORD driving them away;

may their path be dark and slippery,
with the angel of the LORD pursuing them.

Since they hid their net for me without cause
and without cause dug a pit for me,

may ruin overtake them by surprise —
may the net they hid entangle them,
may they fall into the pit, to their ruin.

Then my soul will rejoice in the LORD
and delight in his salvation.

My whole being will exclaim,
"Who is like you, LORD?

You rescue the poor from those too strong for them,
the poor and needy from those who rob them."

Ruthless witnesses come forward;
they question me on things I know nothing about.

They repay me evil for good
and leave me like one bereaved.

Yet when they were ill, I put on sackcloth
and humbled myself with fasting.

When my prayers returned to me unanswered,
I went about mourning
as though for my friend or brother.

I bowed my head in grief
as though weeping for my mother.

But when I stumbled, they gathered in glee;
assailants gathered against me without my knowledge.
They slandered me without ceasing.

Like the ungodly they maliciously mocked;
they gnashed their teeth at me.

How long, Lord, will you look on?
Rescue me from their ravages,
my precious life from these lions.

I will give you thanks in the great assembly;
among the throngs I will praise you.

Do not let those gloat over me
who are my enemies without cause;

do not let those who hate me without reason
maliciously wink the eye.

They do not speak peaceably,
but devise false accusations
against those who live quietly in the land.

They sneer at me and say, "Aha! Aha!
With our own eyes we have seen it."

Lord, you have seen this; do not be silent.
Do not be far from me, Lord.

Awake, and rise to my defense!
Contend for me, my God and Lord.

Vindicate me in your righteousness, Lord my God;
do not let them gloat over me.

Do not let them think, "Aha, just what we wanted!"
or say, "We have swallowed him up."

May all who gloat over my distress
be put to shame and confusion;

may all who exalt themselves over me
be clothed with shame and disgrace.

May those who delight in my vindication
shout for joy and gladness;

may they always say, "The Lord be exalted,
who delights in the well-being of his servant."

My tongue will proclaim your righteousness,
your praises all day long.

Psalm 36

For the director of music. Of David the servant of the Lord.

I have a message from God in my heart
concerning the sinfulness of the wicked:

There is no fear of God
before their eyes.

In their own eyes they flatter themselves
too much to detect or hate their sin.

The words of their mouths are wicked and deceitful;
they fail to act wisely or do good.

Even on their beds they plot evil;
they commit themselves to a sinful course
and do not reject what is wrong.

Your love, Lord, reaches to the heavens,
your faithfulness to the skies.

Your righteousness is like the highest mountains,
your justice like the great deep.
You, Lord, preserve both people and animals.

How priceless is your unfailing love, O God!
People take refuge in the shadow of your wings.

They feast on the abundance of your house;
you give them drink from your river of delights.

For with you is the fountain of life;
in your light we see light.

Continue your love to those who know you,
your righteousness to the upright in heart.

May the foot of the proud not come against me,
nor the hand of the wicked drive me away.

See how the evildoers lie fallen—
thrown down, not able to rise!

Psalm 37

Of David.

Do not fret because of those who are evil
or be envious of those who do wrong;

for like the grass they will soon wither,
like green plants they will soon die away.

Trust in the Lord and do good;
dwell in the land and enjoy safe pasture.

Take delight in the Lord,
and he will give you the desires of your heart.

Commit your way to the Lord;
trust in him and he will do this:

He will make your righteous reward shine like the dawn,
your vindication like the noonday sun.

Be still before the Lord
and wait patiently for him;

do not fret when people succeed in their ways,
when they carry out their wicked schemes.

Refrain from anger and turn from wrath;
do not fret — it leads only to evil.

For those who are evil will be destroyed,
but those who hope in the Lord will inherit the land.

A little while, and the wicked will be no more;
though you look for them, they will not be found.

But the meek will inherit the land
and enjoy peace and prosperity.

The wicked plot against the righteous
and gnash their teeth at them;

but the Lord laughs at the wicked,
for he knows their day is coming.

The wicked draw the sword
and bend the bow

to bring down the poor and needy,
to slay those whose ways are upright.

But their swords will pierce their own hearts,
and their bows will be broken.

Better the little that the righteous have
than the wealth of many wicked;

for the power of the wicked will be broken,
but the Lord upholds the righteous.

The blameless spend their days under the Lord's care,
and their inheritance will endure forever.

In times of disaster they will not wither;
in days of famine they will enjoy plenty.

But the wicked will perish:
Though the Lord's enemies are like the flowers of the
field,
they will be consumed, they will go up in smoke.

The wicked borrow and do not repay,
but the righteous give generously;

those the Lord blesses will inherit the land,
but those he curses will be destroyed.

The Lord makes firm the steps
of the one who delights in him;
though he may stumble, he will not fall,
for the Lord upholds him with his hand.

I was young and now I am old,
yet I have never seen the righteous forsaken
or their children begging bread.
They are always generous and lend freely;
their children will be a blessing.

Turn from evil and do good;
then you will dwell in the land forever.
For the Lord loves the just
and will not forsake his faithful ones.

Wrongdoers will be completely destroyed;
the offspring of the wicked will perish.
The righteous will inherit the land
and dwell in it forever.

The mouths of the righteous utter wisdom,
and their tongues speak what is just.
The law of their God is in their hearts;
their feet do not slip.

The wicked lie in wait for the righteous,
intent on putting them to death;
but the Lord will not leave them in the power of the
        wicked
or let them be condemned when brought to trial.

Hope in the Lord
and keep his way.
He will exalt you to inherit the land;
when the wicked are destroyed, you will see it.

I have seen a wicked and ruthless man
flourishing like a luxuriant native tree,
but he soon passed away and was no more;
though I looked for him, he could not be found.

Consider the blameless, observe the upright;
a future awaits those who seek peace.

But all sinners will be destroyed;
there will be no future for the wicked.

The salvation of the righteous comes from the Lord;
he is their stronghold in time of trouble.

The Lord helps them and delivers them;
he delivers them from the wicked and saves them,
because they take refuge in him.

Psalm 38

A psalm of David. A petition.

Lord, do not rebuke me in your anger
or discipline me in your wrath.

Your arrows have pierced me,
and your hand has come down on me.

Because of your wrath there is no health in my body;
there is no soundness in my bones because of my sin.

My guilt has overwhelmed me
like a burden too heavy to bear.

My wounds fester and are loathsome
because of my sinful folly.

I am bowed down and brought very low;
all day long I go about mourning.

My back is filled with searing pain;
there is no health in my body.

I am feeble and utterly crushed;
I groan in anguish of heart.

All my longings lie open before you, Lord;
my sighing is not hidden from you.

My heart pounds, my strength fails me;
even the light has gone from my eyes.

My friends and companions avoid me because of my
    wounds;
my neighbors stay far away.

Those who want to kill me set their traps,
those who would harm me talk of my ruin;
all day long they scheme and lie.

I am like the deaf, who cannot hear,
like the mute, who cannot speak;
I have become like one who does not hear,
whose mouth can offer no reply.

Lord, I wait for you;
you will answer, Lord my God.
For I said, "Do not let them gloat
or exalt themselves over me when my feet slip."

For I am about to fall,
and my pain is ever with me.
I confess my iniquity;
I am troubled by my sin.
Many have become my enemies without cause;
those who hate me without reason are numerous.
Those who repay my good with evil
lodge accusations against me,
though I seek only to do what is good.

Lord, do not forsake me;
do not be far from me, my God.
Come quickly to help me,
my Lord and my Savior.

Psalm 39

For the director of music. For Jeduthun. A psalm of David.

I said, "I will watch my ways
and keep my tongue from sin;
I will put a muzzle on my mouth
while in the presence of the wicked."
So I remained utterly silent,
not even saying anything good.
But my anguish increased;
my heart grew hot within me.
While I meditated, the fire burned;
then I spoke with my tongue:

"Show me, Lord, my life's end
and the number of my days;
let me know how fleeting my life is.

You have made my days a mere handbreadth;
the span of my years is as nothing before you.

Everyone is but a breath,
even those who seem secure.

"Surely everyone goes around like a mere phantom;
in vain they rush about, heaping up wealth
without knowing whose it will finally be.

"But now, Lord, what do I look for?
My hope is in you.

Save me from all my transgressions;
do not make me the scorn of fools.

I was silent; I would not open my mouth,
for you are the one who has done this.

Remove your scourge from me;
I am overcome by the blow of your hand.

When you rebuke and discipline anyone for their sin,
you consume their wealth like a moth—
surely everyone is but a breath.

"Hear my prayer, Lord,
listen to my cry for help;
do not be deaf to my weeping.

I dwell with you as a foreigner,
a stranger, as all my ancestors were.

Look away from me, that I may enjoy life again
before I depart and am no more."

Psalm 40

For the director of music. Of David. A psalm.

I waited patiently for the Lord;
he turned to me and heard my cry.

He lifted me out of the slimy pit,
out of the mud and mire;

he set my feet on a rock
and gave me a firm place to stand.

He put a new song in my mouth,
a hymn of praise to our God.

Many will see and fear the Lord
and put their trust in him.

Blessed is the one
who trusts in the Lord,
who does not look to the proud,
to those who turn aside to false gods.

Many, Lord my God,
are the wonders you have done,
the things you planned for us.

None can compare with you;
were I to speak and tell of your deeds,
they would be too many to declare.

Sacrifice and offering you did not desire—
but my ears you have opened—
burnt offerings and sin offerings you did not require.

Then I said, "Here I am, I have come—
it is written about me in the scroll.

I desire to do your will, my God;
your law is within my heart."

I proclaim your saving acts in the great assembly;
I do not seal my lips, Lord,
as you know.

I do not hide your righteousness in my heart;
I speak of your faithfulness and your saving help.

I do not conceal your love and your faithfulness
from the great assembly.

Do not withhold your mercy from me, Lord;
may your love and faithfulness always protect me.

For troubles without number surround me;
my sins have overtaken me, and I cannot see.

They are more than the hairs of my head,
and my heart fails within me.

Be pleased to save me, Lord;
come quickly, Lord, to help me.

May all who want to take my life
be put to shame and confusion;
may all who desire my ruin
be turned back in disgrace.

May those who say to me, "Aha! Aha!"
be appalled at their own shame.

But may all who seek you
rejoice and be glad in you;

may those who long for your saving help always say,
"The LORD is great!"

But as for me, I am poor and needy;
may the Lord think of me.

You are my help and my deliverer;
you are my God, do not delay.

Psalm 41

For the director of music. A psalm of David.

Blessed are those who have regard for the weak;
the LORD delivers them in times of trouble.

The LORD protects and preserves them—
they are counted among the blessed in the land—
he does not give them over to the desire of their foes.

The LORD sustains them on their sickbed
and restores them from their bed of illness.

I said, "Have mercy on me, LORD;
heal me, for I have sinned against you."

My enemies say of me in malice,
"When will he die and his name perish?"

When one of them comes to see me,
he speaks falsely, while his heart gathers slander;
then he goes out and spreads it around.

All my enemies whisper together against me;
they imagine the worst for me, saying,

"A vile disease has afflicted him;
he will never get up from the place where he lies."

Even my close friend,
someone I trusted,

one who shared my bread,
has turned against me.

But may you have mercy on me, LORD;
raise me up, that I may repay them.

I know that you are pleased with me,
for my enemy does not triumph over me.

Because of my integrity you uphold me
and set me in your presence forever.

Praise be to the Lord, the God of Israel,
from everlasting to everlasting.
                    Amen and Amen.

BOOK II

Psalms 42 – 72

Psalm 42–43

For the director of music. A maskil *of the Sons of Korah.*

As the deer pants for streams of water,
so my soul pants for you, my God.

My soul thirsts for God, for the living God.
When can I go and meet with God?

My tears have been my food
day and night,

while people say to me all day long,
"Where is your God?"

These things I remember
as I pour out my soul:

how I used to go to the house of God
under the protection of the Mighty One

with shouts of joy and praise
among the festive throng.

Why, my soul, are you downcast?
Why so disturbed within me?

Put your hope in God,
for I will yet praise him,
my Savior and my God.

My soul is downcast within me;
therefore I will remember you

from the land of the Jordan,
the heights of Hermon — from Mount Mizar.

Deep calls to deep
in the roar of your waterfalls;

all your waves and breakers
have swept over me.

By day the LORD directs his love,
at night his song is with me —
a prayer to the God of my life.

I say to God my Rock,
"Why have you forgotten me?

Why must I go about mourning,
oppressed by the enemy?"

My bones suffer mortal agony
as my foes taunt me,

saying to me all day long,
"Where is your God?"

Why, my soul, are you downcast?
Why so disturbed within me?

Put your hope in God,
for I will yet praise him,
my Savior and my God.

Vindicate me, my God,
and plead my cause
against an unfaithful nation.

Rescue me from those who are
deceitful and wicked.

You are God my stronghold.
Why have you rejected me?

Why must I go about mourning,
oppressed by the enemy?

Send me your light and your faithful care,
let them lead me;

let them bring me to your holy mountain,
to the place where you dwell.

Then I will go to the altar of God,
to God, my joy and my delight.

I will praise you with the lyre,
O God, my God.

Why, my soul, are you downcast?
Why so disturbed within me?

Put your hope in God,
for I will yet praise him,
my Savior and my God.

Psalm 44

For the director of music. Of the Sons of Korah. A maskil.

We have heard it with our ears, O God;
our ancestors have told us

what you did in their days,
in days long ago.

With your hand you drove out the nations
and planted our ancestors;

you crushed the peoples
and made our ancestors flourish.

It was not by their sword that they won the land,
nor did their arm bring them victory;

it was your right hand, your arm,
and the light of your face, for you loved them.

You are my King and my God,
who decrees victories for Jacob.

Through you we push back our enemies;
through your name we trample our foes.

I put no trust in my bow,
my sword does not bring me victory;

but you give us victory over our enemies,
you put our adversaries to shame.

In God we make our boast all day long,
and we will praise your name forever.

But now you have rejected and humbled us;
you no longer go out with our armies.

You made us retreat before the enemy,
and our adversaries have plundered us.

You gave us up to be devoured like sheep
and have scattered us among the nations.

You sold your people for a pittance,
gaining nothing from their sale.

You have made us a reproach to our neighbors,
the scorn and derision of those around us.

You have made us a byword among the nations;
the peoples shake their heads at us.

I live in disgrace all day long,
and my face is covered with shame

at the taunts of those who reproach and revile me,
because of the enemy, who is bent on revenge.

All this came upon us,
though we had not forgotten you;
we had not been false to your covenant.

Our hearts had not turned back;
our feet had not strayed from your path.

But you crushed us and made us a haunt for jackals;
you covered us over with deep darkness.

If we had forgotten the name of our God
or spread out our hands to a foreign god,

would not God have discovered it,
since he knows the secrets of the heart?

Yet for your sake we face death all day long;
we are considered as sheep to be slaughtered.

Awake, Lord! Why do you sleep?
Rouse yourself! Do not reject us forever.

Why do you hide your face
and forget our misery and oppression?

We are brought down to the dust;
our bodies cling to the ground.

Rise up and help us;
rescue us because of your unfailing love.

Psalm 45

*For the director of music. To the tune of "Lilies." Of the Sons
of Korah. A maskil. A wedding song.*

My heart is stirred by a noble theme
as I recite my verses for the king;
my tongue is the pen of a skillful writer.

You are the most excellent of men
and your lips have been anointed with grace,
since God has blessed you forever.

Gird your sword on your side, you mighty one;
clothe yourself with splendor and majesty.

In your majesty ride forth victoriously
in the cause of truth, humility and justice;
let your right hand achieve awesome deeds.

Let your sharp arrows pierce the hearts of the king's
    enemies;
let the nations fall beneath your feet.

Your throne, O God, will last for ever and ever;
a scepter of justice will be the scepter of your kingdom.

You love righteousness and hate wickedness;
therefore God, your God, has set you above your
    companions
by anointing you with the oil of joy.

All your robes are fragrant with myrrh and aloes and
    cassia;
from palaces adorned with ivory
the music of the strings makes you glad.

Daughters of kings are among your honored women;
at your right hand is the royal bride in gold of Ophir.

Listen, daughter, and pay careful attention:
Forget your people and your father's house.

Let the king be enthralled by your beauty;
honor him, for he is your lord.

The city of Tyre will come with a gift,
people of wealth will seek your favor.

All glorious is the princess within her chamber;
her gown is interwoven with gold.

In embroidered garments she is led to the king;
her virgin companions follow her —
those brought to be with her.

Led in with joy and gladness,
they enter the palace of the king.

Your sons will take the place of your fathers;
you will make them princes throughout the land.

I will perpetuate your memory through all generations;
therefore the nations will praise you for ever and ever.

Psalm 46

For the director of music. Of the Sons of Korah. According to
alamoth. A song.

God is our refuge and strength,
an ever-present help in trouble.

Therefore we will not fear, though the earth give way
and the mountains fall into the heart of the sea,

though its waters roar and foam
and the mountains quake with their surging.

There is a river whose streams make glad the city of God,
the holy place where the Most High dwells.

God is within her, she will not fall;
God will help her at break of day.

Nations are in uproar, kingdoms fall;
he lifts his voice, the earth melts.

The Lord Almighty is with us;
the God of Jacob is our fortress.

Come and see what the Lord has done,
the desolations he has brought on the earth.

He makes wars cease
to the ends of the earth.

He breaks the bow and shatters the spear;
he burns the shields with fire.

He says, "Be still, and know that I am God;
I will be exalted among the nations,
I will be exalted in the earth."

The Lord Almighty is with us;
the God of Jacob is our fortress.

Psalm 47

For the director of music. Of the Sons of Korah. A psalm.

Clap your hands, all you nations;
shout to God with cries of joy.

For the LORD Most High is awesome,
the great King over all the earth.

He subdued nations under us,
peoples under our feet.

He chose our inheritance for us,
the pride of Jacob, whom he loved.

God has ascended amid shouts of joy,
the LORD amid the sounding of trumpets.

Sing praises to God, sing praises;
sing praises to our King, sing praises.

For God is the King of all the earth;
sing to him a psalm of praise.

God reigns over the nations;
God is seated on his holy throne.

The nobles of the nations assemble
as the people of the God of Abraham,

for the kings of the earth belong to God;
he is greatly exalted.

Psalm 48

A song. A psalm of the Sons of Korah.

Great is the LORD, and most worthy of praise,
in the city of our God, his holy mountain.

Beautiful in its loftiness,
the joy of the whole earth,

like the heights of Zaphon is Mount Zion,
the city of the Great King.

God is in her citadels;
he has shown himself to be her fortress.

When the kings joined forces,
when they advanced together,

they saw her and were astounded;
they fled in terror.

Trembling seized them there,
pain like that of a woman in labor.

You destroyed them like ships of Tarshish
shattered by an east wind.

As we have heard,
so we have seen

in the city of the Lord Almighty,
in the city of our God:

God makes her secure
forever.

Within your temple, O God,
we meditate on your unfailing love.

Like your name, O God,
your praise reaches to the ends of the earth;
your right hand is filled with righteousness.

Mount Zion rejoices,
the villages of Judah are glad
because of your judgments.

Walk about Zion, go around her,
count her towers,

consider well her ramparts,
view her citadels,

that you may tell of them
to the next generation.

For this God is our God for ever and ever;
he will be our guide even to the end.

Psalm 49

For the director of music. Of the Sons of Korah. A psalm.

Hear this, all you peoples;
listen, all who live in this world,

both low and high,
rich and poor alike:

My mouth will speak words of wisdom;
the meditation of my heart will give you understanding.

I will turn my ear to a proverb;
with the harp I will expound my riddle:

Why should I fear when evil days come,
when wicked deceivers surround me —

those who trust in their wealth
and boast of their great riches?

No one can redeem the life of another
or give to God a ransom for them —

the ransom for a life is costly,
no payment is ever enough —

so that they should live on forever
and not see decay.

For all can see that the wise die,
that the foolish and the senseless also perish,
leaving their wealth to others.

Their tombs will remain their houses forever,
their dwellings for endless generations,
though they had named lands after themselves.

People, despite their wealth, do not endure;
they are like the beasts that perish.

This is the fate of those who trust in
themselves,
and of their followers, who approve their
sayings.

They are like sheep and are destined to die;
death will be their shepherd
(but the upright will prevail over them
in the morning).

Their forms will decay in the grave,
far from their princely mansions.

But God will redeem me from the realm
of the dead;
he will surely take me to himself.

Do not be overawed when others grow rich,
when the splendor of their houses increases;

for they will take nothing with them when they die,
their splendor will not descend with them.

Though while they live they count themselves
blessed —
and people praise you when you prosper —

they will join those who have gone before them,
who will never again see the light of life.

People who have wealth but lack
understanding
are like the beasts that perish.

Psalm 50

A psalm of Asaph.

The Mighty One, God, the Lord,
speaks and summons the earth
from the rising of the sun to where it sets.

From Zion, perfect in beauty,
God shines forth.

Our God comes
and will not be silent;

a fire devours before him,
and around him a tempest rages.

He summons the heavens above,
and the earth, that he may judge his people:

"Gather to me this consecrated people,
who made a covenant with me by sacrifice."

And the heavens proclaim his righteousness,
for he is a God of justice.

"Listen, my people, and I will speak;
I will testify against you, Israel:
I am God, your God.

I bring no charges against you concerning your
    sacrifices
or concerning your burnt offerings, which are
    ever before me.

I have no need of a bull from your stall
or of goats from your pens,

for every animal of the forest is mine,
and the cattle on a thousand hills.

I know every bird in the mountains,
and the insects in the fields are mine.

If I were hungry I would not tell you,
for the world is mine, and all that is in it.

Do I eat the flesh of bulls
or drink the blood of goats?

"Sacrifice thank offerings to God,
fulfill your vows to the Most High,

and call on me in the day of trouble;
I will deliver you, and you will honor me."

But to the wicked person, God says:

> "What right have you to recite my laws
> or take my covenant on your lips?
>
> You hate my instruction
> and cast my words behind you.
>
> When you see a thief, you join with him;
> you throw in your lot with adulterers.
>
> You use your mouth for evil
> and harness your tongue to deceit.
>
> You sit and testify against your brother
> and slander your own mother's son.
>
> When you did these things and I kept silent,
> you thought I was exactly like you.
> But I now arraign you
> and set my accusations before you.
>
> "Consider this, you who forget God,
> or I will tear you to pieces, with no one
>   to rescue you:
> Those who sacrifice thank offerings
>   honor me,
> and to the blameless I will show my
>   salvation."

Psalm 51

For the director of music. A psalm of David. When the prophet Nathan came to him after David had committed adultery with Bathsheba.

> Have mercy on me, O God,
> according to your unfailing love;
> according to your great compassion
> blot out my transgressions.
> Wash away all my iniquity
> and cleanse me from my sin.
>
> For I know my transgressions,
> and my sin is always before me.
> Against you, you only, have I sinned
> and done what is evil in your sight;

so you are right in your verdict
and justified when you judge.

Surely I was sinful at birth,
sinful from the time my mother conceived me.

Yet you desired faithfulness even in the womb;
you taught me wisdom in that secret place.

Cleanse me with hyssop, and I will be clean;
wash me, and I will be whiter than snow.

Let me hear joy and gladness;
let the bones you have crushed rejoice.

Hide your face from my sins
and blot out all my iniquity.

Create in me a pure heart, O God,
and renew a steadfast spirit within me.

Do not cast me from your presence
or take your Holy Spirit from me.

Restore to me the joy of your salvation
and grant me a willing spirit, to sustain me.

Then I will teach transgressors your ways,
so that sinners will turn back to you.

Deliver me from the guilt of bloodshed, O God,
you who are God my Savior,
and my tongue will sing of your righteousness.

Open my lips, Lord,
and my mouth will declare your praise.

You do not delight in sacrifice, or I would
    bring it;
you do not take pleasure in burnt offerings.

My sacrifice, O God, is a broken spirit;
a broken and contrite heart
you, God, will not despise.

May it please you to prosper Zion,
to build up the walls of Jerusalem.

Then you will delight in the sacrifices
    of the righteous,
in burnt offerings offered whole;
then bulls will be offered on
    your altar.

Psalm 52

For the director of music. A maskil of David. When Doeg the Edomite had gone to Saul and told him: "David has gone to the house of Ahimelek."

Why do you boast of evil, you mighty hero?
Why do you boast all day long,
you who are a disgrace in the eyes of God?

You who practice deceit,
your tongue plots destruction;
it is like a sharpened razor.

You love evil rather than good,
falsehood rather than speaking the truth.

You love every harmful word,
you deceitful tongue!

Surely God will bring you down to everlasting ruin:
He will snatch you up and pluck you from your tent;
he will uproot you from the land of the living.

The righteous will see and fear;
they will laugh at you, saying,

"Here now is the man
who did not make God his stronghold

but trusted in his great wealth
and grew strong by destroying others!"

But I am like an olive tree
flourishing in the house of God;

I trust in God's unfailing love
for ever and ever.

For what you have done I will always praise you
in the presence of your faithful people.

And I will hope in your name,
for your name is good.

Psalm 53

For the director of music. According to mahalath. *A maskil of David.*

The fool says in his heart,
"There is no God."

They are corrupt, and their ways are vile;
there is no one who does good.

God looks down from heaven
on all mankind

to see if there are any who understand,
any who seek God.

Everyone has turned away, all have become
        corrupt;
there is no one who does good,
not even one.

Do all these evildoers know nothing?

They devour my people as though eating bread;
they never call on God.

But there they are, overwhelmed with dread,
where there was nothing to dread.

God scattered the bones of those who attacked you;
you put them to shame, for God despised them.

Oh, that salvation for Israel would come out of Zion!
When God restores his people,
let Jacob rejoice and Israel be glad!

Psalm 54

*For the director of music. With stringed instruments.
A* maskil *of David. When the Ziphites had gone to Saul
and said, "Is not David hiding among us?"*

Save me, O God, by your name;
vindicate me by your might.

Hear my prayer, O God;
listen to the words of my mouth.

Arrogant foes are attacking me;
ruthless people are trying to kill me —
people without regard for God.

Surely God is my help;
the Lord is the one who sustains me.

Let evil recoil on those who slander me;
in your faithfulness destroy them.

I will sacrifice a freewill offering to you;
I will praise your name, LORD, for it is good.

You have delivered me from all my troubles,
and my eyes have looked in triumph on my foes.

For the director of music. With stringed instruments.
A maskil *of David.*

Listen to my prayer, O God,
do not ignore my plea;
hear me and answer me.

My thoughts trouble me and I am distraught
because of what my enemy is saying,
because of the threats of the wicked;

for they bring down suffering on me
and assail me in their anger.

My heart is in anguish within me;
the terrors of death have fallen on me.

Fear and trembling have beset me;
horror has overwhelmed me.

I said, "Oh, that I had the wings of a dove!
I would fly away and be at rest.

I would flee far away
and stay in the desert;

I would hurry to my place of shelter,
far from the tempest and storm."

Lord, confuse the wicked, confound their words,
for I see violence and strife in the city.

Day and night they prowl about on its walls;
malice and abuse are within it.

Destructive forces are at work in the city;
threats and lies never leave its streets.

If an enemy were insulting me,
I could endure it;

if a foe were rising against me,
I could hide.

But it is you, a man like myself,
my companion, my close friend,

with whom I once enjoyed sweet
    fellowship
at the house of God,

as we walked about
among the worshipers.

Let death take my enemies by surprise;
let them go down alive to the realm
    of the dead,
for evil finds lodging among them.

As for me, I call to God,
and the LORD saves me.

Evening, morning and noon
I cry out in distress,
and he hears my voice.

He rescues me unharmed
from the battle waged against me,
even though many oppose me.

God, who is enthroned from of old,
who does not change—

he will hear them and humble them,
because they have no fear of God.

My companion attacks his friends;
he violates his covenant.

His talk is smooth as butter,
yet war is in his heart;

his words are more soothing than oil,
yet they are drawn swords.

Cast your cares on the LORD
and he will sustain you;

he will never let
the righteous be shaken.

But you, God, will bring down
    the wicked
into the pit of decay;

the bloodthirsty and deceitful
will not live out half their days.

But as for me, I trust in you.

For the director of music. To the tune of "A Dove on Distant Oaks."
Of David. A miktam. *When the Philistines had seized him in Gath.*

Be merciful to me, my God,
for my enemies are in hot pursuit;
all day long they press their attack.

My adversaries pursue me all day long;
in their pride many are attacking me.

When I am afraid, I put my trust in you.
In God, whose word I praise —

in God I trust and am not afraid.
What can mere mortals do to me?

All day long they twist my words;
all their schemes are for my ruin.

They conspire, they lurk,
they watch my steps,
hoping to take my life.

Because of their wickedness do not let
them escape;
in your anger, God, bring the nations down.

Record my misery;
list my tears on your scroll —
are they not in your record?

Then my enemies will turn back
when I call for help.
By this I will know that God is for me.

In God, whose word I praise,
in the Lord, whose word I praise —

in God I trust and am not afraid.
What can man do to me?

I am under vows to you, my God;
I will present my thank offerings to you.

For you have delivered me from death
and my feet from stumbling,

that I may walk before God
in the light of life.

Psalm 57

For the director of music. To the tune of "Do Not Destroy."
Of David. A miktam. *When he had fled from Saul into the cave.*

Have mercy on me, my God, have mercy on me,
for in you I take refuge.
I will take refuge in the shadow of your wings
until the disaster has passed.

I cry out to God Most High,
to God, who vindicates me.
He sends from heaven and saves me,
rebuking those who hotly pursue me —
God sends forth his love and his faithfulness.

I am in the midst of lions;
I am forced to dwell among ravenous beasts —
men whose teeth are spears and arrows,
whose tongues are sharp swords.

Be exalted, O God, above the heavens;
let your glory be over all the earth.

They spread a net for my feet —
I was bowed down in distress.
They dug a pit in my path —
but they have fallen into it themselves.

My heart, O God, is steadfast,
my heart is steadfast;
I will sing and make music.
Awake, my soul!
Awake, harp and lyre!
I will awaken the dawn.

I will praise you, Lord, among the nations;
I will sing of you among the peoples.
For great is your love, reaching to the
heavens;
your faithfulness reaches to the skies.

Be exalted, O God, above the heavens;
let your glory be over all the earth.

Psalm 58

For the director of music. To the tune of "Do Not Destroy."
Of David. A miktam.

Do you rulers indeed speak justly?
Do you judge people with equity?
No, in your heart you devise injustice,
and your hands mete out violence on the earth.

Even from birth the wicked go astray;
from the womb they are wayward, spreading lies.
Their venom is like the venom of a snake,
like that of a cobra that has stopped its ears,
that will not heed the tune of the charmer,
however skillful the enchanter may be.

Break the teeth in their mouths, O God;
Lord, tear out the fangs of those lions!
Let them vanish like water that flows away;
when they draw the bow, let their arrows fall short.
May they be like a slug that melts away as it
    moves along,
like a stillborn child that never sees the sun.

Before your pots can feel the heat of the thorns—
whether they be green or dry—the wicked will
    be swept away.

The righteous will be glad when they are avenged,
when they dip their feet in the blood of the wicked.
Then people will say,
"Surely the righteous still are rewarded;
surely there is a God who judges the earth."

Psalm 59

For the director of music. To the tune of "Do Not Destroy."
Of David. A miktam. When Saul had sent men to watch
David's house in order to kill him.

Deliver me from my enemies, O God;
be my fortress against those who are attacking me.
Deliver me from evildoers
and save me from those who are after my blood.

See how they lie in wait for me!
Fierce men conspire against me
for no offense or sin of mine, LORD.

I have done no wrong, yet they are ready
    to attack me.
Arise to help me; look on my plight!

You, LORD God Almighty,
you who are the God of Israel,

rouse yourself to punish all the nations;
show no mercy to wicked traitors.

They return at evening,
snarling like dogs,
and prowl about the city.

See what they spew from their mouths—
the words from their lips are sharp as swords,
and they think, "Who can hear us?"

But you laugh at them, LORD;
you scoff at all those nations.

You are my strength, I watch for you;
you, God, are my fortress,
my God on whom I can rely.

God will go before me
and will let me gloat over those who slander me.

But do not kill them, Lord our shield,
or my people will forget.

In your might uproot them
and bring them down.

For the sins of their mouths,
for the words of their lips,
let them be caught in their pride.

For the curses and lies they utter,
consume them in your wrath,
consume them till they are no more.

Then it will be known to the ends of the earth
that God rules over Jacob.

They return at evening,
snarling like dogs,
and prowl about the city.

They wander about for food
and howl if not satisfied.

But I will sing of your strength,
in the morning I will sing of your love;

for you are my fortress,
my refuge in times of trouble.

You are my strength, I sing praise to you;
you, God, are my fortress,
my God on whom I can rely.

For the director of music. To the tune of "The Lily of the Covenant."
A miktam *of David. For teaching. When he fought Aram Naharaim*
and Aram Zobah, and when Joab returned and struck down twelve
thousand Edomites in the Valley of Salt.

You have rejected us, God, and burst upon us;
you have been angry—now restore us!

You have shaken the land and torn it open;
mend its fractures, for it is quaking.

You have shown your people desperate times;
you have given us wine that makes us stagger.

But for those who fear you, you have raised a banner
to be unfurled against the bow.

Save us and help us with your right hand,
that those you love may be delivered.

God has spoken from his sanctuary:
"In triumph I will parcel out Shechem
and measure off the Valley of Sukkoth.

Gilead is mine, and Manasseh is mine;
Ephraim is my helmet,
Judah is my scepter.

Moab is my washbasin,
on Edom I toss my sandal;
over Philistia I shout in triumph."

Who will bring me to the fortified city?
Who will lead me to Edom?

Is it not you, God, you who have now rejected us
and no longer go out with our armies?

Give us aid against the enemy,
for human help is worthless.

With God we will gain the victory,
and he will trample down our enemies.

Psalm 61

For the director of music. With stringed instruments. Of David.

Hear my cry, O God;
listen to my prayer.

From the ends of the earth I call to you,
I call as my heart grows faint;
lead me to the rock that is higher than I.
For you have been my refuge,
a strong tower against the foe.

I long to dwell in your tent forever
and take refuge in the shelter of your wings.
For you, God, have heard my vows;
you have given me the heritage of those who
fear your name.

Increase the days of the king's life,
his years for many generations.
May he be enthroned in God's presence forever;
appoint your love and faithfulness to protect him.

Then I will ever sing in praise of your name
and fulfill my vows day after day.

Psalm 62

For the director of music. For Jeduthun. A psalm of David.

Truly my soul finds rest in God;
my salvation comes from him.
Truly he is my rock and my salvation;
he is my fortress, I will never be shaken.

How long will you assault me?
Would all of you throw me down —
this leaning wall, this tottering fence?

Surely they intend to topple me
from my lofty place;
they take delight in lies.

With their mouths they bless,
but in their hearts they curse.

Yes, my soul, find rest in God;
my hope comes from him.

Truly he is my rock and my salvation;
he is my fortress, I will not be shaken.

My salvation and my honor depend on God;
he is my mighty rock, my refuge.

Trust in him at all times, you people;
pour out your hearts to him,
for God is our refuge.

Surely the lowborn are but a breath,
the highborn are but a lie.

If weighed on a balance, they are nothing;
together they are only a breath.

Do not trust in extortion
or put vain hope in stolen goods;

though your riches increase,
do not set your heart on them.

One thing God has spoken,
two things I have heard:

"Power belongs to you, God,
and with you, Lord, is unfailing love";

and, "You reward everyone
according to what they have done."

Psalm 63

A psalm of David. When he was in the Desert of Judah.

You, God, are my God,
earnestly I seek you;

I thirst for you,
my whole being longs for you,

in a dry and parched land
where there is no water.

I have seen you in the sanctuary
and beheld your power and your glory.

Because your love is better than life,
my lips will glorify you.

I will praise you as long as I live,
and in your name I will lift up my hands.

I will be fully satisfied as with the richest
      of foods;
with singing lips my mouth will praise you.

On my bed I remember you;
I think of you through the watches
      of the night.

Because you are my help,
I sing in the shadow of your wings.

I cling to you;
your right hand upholds me.

Those who want to kill me will be destroyed;
they will go down to the depths of the earth.

They will be given over to the sword
and become food for jackals.

But the king will rejoice in God;
all who swear by God will glory in him,
while the mouths of liars will be silenced.

Psalm 64

For the director of music. A psalm of David.

Hear me, my God, as I voice my complaint;
protect my life from the threat of the enemy.

Hide me from the conspiracy of the wicked,
from the plots of evildoers.

They sharpen their tongues like swords
and aim cruel words like deadly arrows.

They shoot from ambush at the innocent;
they shoot suddenly, without fear.

They encourage each other in evil plans,
they talk about hiding their snares;
they say, "Who will see it?"

They plot injustice and say,
"We have devised a perfect plan!"
Surely the human mind and heart are cunning.

But God will shoot them with his arrows;
they will suddenly be struck down.

He will turn their own tongues against them
and bring them to ruin;
all who see them will shake their heads in scorn.

All people will fear;
they will proclaim the works of God
and ponder what he has done.

The righteous will rejoice in the LORD
and take refuge in him;
all the upright in heart will glory in him!

Psalm 65

For the director of music. A psalm of David. A song.

Praise awaits you, our God, in Zion;
to you our vows will be fulfilled.

You who answer prayer,
to you all people will come.

When we were overwhelmed by sins,
you forgave our transgressions.

Blessed are those you choose
and bring near to live in your courts!
We are filled with the good things
of your house,
of your holy temple.

You answer us with awesome and
righteous deeds,
God our Savior,

the hope of all the ends of the earth
and of the farthest seas,

who formed the mountains by your power,
having armed yourself with strength,

who stilled the roaring of the seas,
the roaring of their waves,
and the turmoil of the nations.

The whole earth is filled with awe
    at your wonders;
where morning dawns, where evening fades,
you call forth songs of joy.

You care for the land and water it;
    you enrich it abundantly.
The streams of God are filled with water
    to provide the people with grain,
    for so you have ordained it.
You drench its furrows and level its ridges;
    you soften it with showers and bless its crops.
You crown the year with your bounty,
    and your carts overflow with abundance.
The grasslands of the wilderness overflow;
    the hills are clothed with gladness.
The meadows are covered with flocks
    and the valleys are mantled with grain;
    they shout for joy and sing.

Psalm 66

For the director of music. A song. A psalm.

Shout for joy to God, all the earth!
Sing the glory of his name;
    make his praise glorious.
Say to God, "How awesome are
    your deeds!
So great is your power
    that your enemies cringe before you.
All the earth bows down to you;
    they sing praise to you,
    they sing the praises of your name."

Come and see what God has done,
    his awesome deeds for mankind!
He turned the sea into dry land,
    they passed through the waters on foot—
    come, let us rejoice in him.
He rules forever by his power,
    his eyes watch the nations—
    let not the rebellious rise up against him.

Praise our God, all peoples,
let the sound of his praise be heard;

he has preserved our lives
and kept our feet from slipping.

For you, God, tested us;
you refined us like silver.

You brought us into prison
and laid burdens on our backs.

You let people ride over our heads;
we went through fire and water,
but you brought us to a place of abundance.

I will come to your temple with burnt offerings
and fulfill my vows to you —

vows my lips promised and my
mouth spoke
when I was in trouble.

I will sacrifice fat animals to you
and an offering of rams;
I will offer bulls and goats.

Come and hear, all you who fear God;
let me tell you what he has done for me.

I cried out to him with my mouth;
his praise was on my tongue.

If I had cherished sin in my heart,
the Lord would not have listened;

but God has surely listened
and has heard my prayer.

Praise be to God,
who has not rejected my prayer
or withheld his love from me!

Psalm 67

For the director of music. With stringed instruments.
A psalm. A song.

May God be gracious to us and bless us
and make his face shine on us —

so that your ways may be known on earth,
your salvation among all nations.

May the peoples praise you, God;
may all the peoples praise you.

May the nations be glad and sing for joy,
for you rule the peoples with equity
and guide the nations of the earth.

May the peoples praise you, God;
may all the peoples praise you.

The land yields its harvest;
God, our God, blesses us.

May God bless us still,
so that all the ends of the earth will fear him.

Psalm 68

For the director of music. Of David. A psalm. A song.

May God arise, may his enemies be scattered;
may his foes flee before him.

May you blow them away like smoke—
as wax melts before the fire,
may the wicked perish before God.

But may the righteous be glad
and rejoice before God;
may they be happy and joyful.

Sing to God, sing in praise of his name,
extol him who rides on the clouds;
rejoice before him—his name is the Lord.

A father to the fatherless, a defender
      of widows,
is God in his holy dwelling.

God sets the lonely in families,
he leads out the prisoners with singing;
but the rebellious live in a sun-scorched land.

When you, God, went out before your people,
when you marched through the wilderness,

the earth shook, the heavens poured down rain,
before God, the One of Sinai,
before God, the God of Israel.

You gave abundant showers, O God;
you refreshed your weary inheritance.

Your people settled in it,
and from your bounty, God, you provided for the poor.

The Lord announces the word,
and the women who proclaim it are a mighty throng:
"Kings and armies flee in haste;
the women at home divide the plunder.

Even while you sleep among the sheep pens,
the wings of my dove are sheathed with silver,
its feathers with shining gold."

When the Almighty scattered the kings in the land,
it was like snow fallen on Mount Zalmon.

Mount Bashan, majestic mountain,
Mount Bashan, rugged mountain,

why gaze in envy, you rugged mountain,
at the mountain where God chooses to reign,
where the Lord himself will dwell forever?

The chariots of God are tens of thousands
and thousands of thousands;
the Lord has come from Sinai into his sanctuary.

When you ascended on high,
you took many captives;
you received gifts from people,

even from the rebellious—
that you, Lord God, might dwell there.

Praise be to the Lord, to God our Savior,
who daily bears our burdens.

Our God is a God who saves;
from the Sovereign Lord comes escape from death.

Surely God will crush the heads of his enemies,
the hairy crowns of those who go on in their sins.

The Lord says, "I will bring them from Bashan;
I will bring them from the depths of the sea,

that your feet may wade in the blood of your foes,
while the tongues of your dogs have their share."

Your procession, God, has come into view,
the procession of my God and King into the sanctuary.

In front are the singers, after them the musicians;
with them are the young women playing the timbrels.

Praise God in the great congregation;
praise the Lord in the assembly of Israel.

There is the little tribe of Benjamin, leading them,
there the great throng of Judah's princes,
and there the princes of Zebulun and of Naphtali.

Summon your power, God;
show us your strength, our God, as you have done
before.

Because of your temple at Jerusalem
kings will bring you gifts.

Rebuke the beast among the reeds,
the herd of bulls among the calves of the nations.

Humbled, may the beast bring bars of silver.
Scatter the nations who delight in war.

Envoys will come from Egypt;
Cush will submit herself to God.

Sing to God, you kingdoms of the earth,
sing praise to the Lord,

to him who rides across the highest heavens, the ancient
heavens,
who thunders with mighty voice.

Proclaim the power of God,
whose majesty is over Israel,
whose power is in the heavens.

You, God, are awesome in your sanctuary;
the God of Israel gives power and strength to his people.

Praise be to God!

Psalm 69

For the director of music. To the tune of "Lilies." Of David.

Save me, O God,
for the waters have come up to my neck.

I sink in the miry depths,
where there is no foothold.

I have come into the deep waters;
the floods engulf me.

I am worn out calling for help;
my throat is parched.

My eyes fail,
looking for my God.

Those who hate me without reason
outnumber the hairs of my head;

many are my enemies without cause,
those who seek to destroy me.

I am forced to restore
what I did not steal.

You, God, know my folly;
my guilt is not hidden from you.

Lord, the LORD Almighty,
may those who hope in you
not be disgraced because of me;

God of Israel,
may those who seek you
not be put to shame because of me.

For I endure scorn for your sake,
and shame covers my face.

I am a foreigner to my own family,
a stranger to my own mother's children;

for zeal for your house consumes me,
and the insults of those who insult you fall on me.

When I weep and fast,
I must endure scorn;

when I put on sackcloth,
people make sport of me.

Those who sit at the gate mock me,
and I am the song of the drunkards.

But I pray to you, LORD,
in the time of your favor;

in your great love, O God,
answer me with your sure salvation.

Rescue me from the mire,
do not let me sink;

deliver me from those who hate me,
from the deep waters.

Do not let the floodwaters engulf me
or the depths swallow me up
or the pit close its mouth over me.

Answer me, LORD, out of the goodness of your love;
in your great mercy turn to me.

Do not hide your face from your servant;
answer me quickly, for I am in trouble.

Come near and rescue me;
deliver me because of my foes.

You know how I am scorned, disgraced and shamed;
all my enemies are before you.

Scorn has broken my heart
and has left me helpless;

I looked for sympathy, but there was none,
for comforters, but I found none.

They put gall in my food
and gave me vinegar for my thirst.

May the table set before them become a snare;
may it become retribution and a trap.

May their eyes be darkened so they cannot see,
and their backs be bent forever.

Pour out your wrath on them;
let your fierce anger overtake them.

May their place be deserted;
let there be no one to dwell in their tents.

For they persecute those you wound
and talk about the pain of those you hurt.

Charge them with crime upon crime;
do not let them share in your salvation.

May they be blotted out of the book of life
and not be listed with the righteous.

But as for me, afflicted and in pain —
may your salvation, God, protect me.

I will praise God's name in song
and glorify him with thanksgiving.

This will please the LORD more than an ox,
more than a bull with its horns and hooves.

The poor will see and be glad —
you who seek God, may your hearts live!

The LORD hears the needy
and does not despise his captive people.

Let heaven and earth praise him,
the seas and all that move in them,

for God will save Zion
and rebuild the cities of Judah.

Then people will settle there and possess it;
the children of his servants will inherit it,
and those who love his name will dwell there.

Psalm 70

For the director of music. Of David. A petition.

Hasten, O God, to save me;
come quickly, Lord, to help me.

May those who want to take my life
be put to shame and confusion;
may all who desire my ruin
be turned back in disgrace.

May those who say to me, "Aha! Aha!"
turn back because of their shame.

But may all who seek you
rejoice and be glad in you;
may those who long for your saving help
always say,
"The Lord is great!"

But as for me, I am poor and needy;
come quickly to me, O God.

You are my help and my deliverer;
Lord, do not delay.

Psalm 71

In you, Lord, I have taken refuge;
let me never be put to shame.

In your righteousness, rescue me and
deliver me;
turn your ear to me and save me.

Be my rock of refuge,
to which I can always go;
give the command to save me,
for you are my rock and my fortress.

Deliver me, my God, from the hand of the wicked,
from the grasp of those who are evil and cruel.

For you have been my hope, Sovereign LORD,
my confidence since my youth.

From birth I have relied on you;
you brought me forth from my mother's womb.
I will ever praise you.

I have become a sign to many;
you are my strong refuge.

My mouth is filled with your praise,
declaring your splendor all day long.

Do not cast me away when I am old;
do not forsake me when my strength is gone.

For my enemies speak against me;
those who wait to kill me conspire together.

They say, "God has forsaken him;
pursue him and seize him,
for no one will rescue him."

Do not be far from me, my God;
come quickly, God, to help me.

May my accusers perish in shame;
may those who want to harm me
be covered with scorn and disgrace.

As for me, I will always have hope;
I will praise you more and more.

My mouth will tell of your righteous deeds,
of your saving acts all day long—
though I know not how to relate them all.

I will come and proclaim your mighty acts,
Sovereign LORD;
I will proclaim your righteous deeds,
yours alone.

Since my youth, God, you have taught me,
and to this day I declare your marvelous deeds.

Even when I am old and gray,
do not forsake me, my God,

till I declare your power to the next generation,
your mighty acts to all who are to come.

Your righteousness, God, reaches
    to the heavens,
you who have done great things.
Who is like you, God?

Though you have made me see troubles,
many and bitter,
you will restore my life again;

from the depths of the earth
you will again bring me up.

You will increase my honor
and comfort me once more.

I will praise you with the harp
for your faithfulness, my God;

I will sing praise to you with the lyre,
Holy One of Israel.

My lips will shout for joy
when I sing praise to you—
I whom you have delivered.

My tongue will tell of your righteous acts
all day long,

for those who wanted to harm me
have been put to shame and confusion.

Psalm 72

Of Solomon.

Endow the king with your justice, O God,
the royal son with your righteousness.

May he judge your people in righteousness,
your afflicted ones with justice.

May the mountains bring prosperity to the people,
the hills the fruit of righteousness.

May he defend the afflicted among the people
and save the children of the needy;
may he crush the oppressor.

May he endure as long as the sun,
as long as the moon, through all generations.

May he be like rain falling on a mown field,
like showers watering the earth.

In his days may the righteous flourish
and prosperity abound till the moon
     is no more.

May he rule from sea to sea
and from the River to the ends of the earth.

May the desert tribes bow before him
and his enemies lick the dust.

May the kings of Tarshish and of distant
     shores
bring tribute to him.

May the kings of Sheba and Seba
present him gifts.

May all kings bow down to him
and all nations serve him.

For he will deliver the needy who cry out,
the afflicted who have no one to help.

He will take pity on the weak and the needy
and save the needy from death.

He will rescue them from oppression
     and violence,
for precious is their blood in his sight.

Long may he live!
May gold from Sheba be given him.

May people ever pray for him
and bless him all day long.

May grain abound throughout the land;
on the tops of the hills may it sway.

May the crops flourish like Lebanon
and thrive like the grass of the field.

May his name endure forever;
may it continue as long as the sun.

Then all nations will be blessed
     through him,
and they will call him blessed.

Praise be to the LORD God, the God of Israel,
who alone does marvelous deeds.

Praise be to his glorious name forever;
may the whole earth be filled with his glory.

Amen and Amen.

This concludes the prayers of David son of Jesse.

BOOK III

Psalms 73 – 89

Psalm 73

A psalm of Asaph.

Surely God is good to Israel,
to those who are pure in heart.

But as for me, my feet had almost slipped;
I had nearly lost my foothold.
For I envied the arrogant
when I saw the prosperity of the wicked.

They have no struggles;
their bodies are healthy and strong.
They are free from common human burdens;
they are not plagued by human ills.
Therefore pride is their necklace;
they clothe themselves with violence.
From their callous hearts comes iniquity;
their evil imaginations have no limits.
They scoff, and speak with malice;
with arrogance they threaten oppression.
Their mouths lay claim to heaven,
and their tongues take possession of the earth.
Therefore their people turn to them
and drink up waters in abundance.
They say, "How would God know?
Does the Most High know anything?"

This is what the wicked are like —
always free of care, they go on amassing wealth.

Surely in vain I have kept my heart pure
and have washed my hands in innocence.

All day long I have been afflicted,
and every morning brings new punishments.

If I had spoken out like that,
I would have betrayed your children.

When I tried to understand all this,
it troubled me deeply

till I entered the sanctuary of God;
then I understood their final destiny.

Surely you place them on slippery
      ground;
you cast them down to ruin.

How suddenly are they destroyed,
completely swept away by terrors!

They are like a dream when one awakes;
when you arise, Lord,
you will despise them as fantasies.

When my heart was grieved
and my spirit embittered,

I was senseless and ignorant;
I was a brute beast before you.

Yet I am always with you;
you hold me by my right hand.

You guide me with your counsel,
and afterward you will take me
      into glory.

Whom have I in heaven but you?
And earth has nothing I desire
      besides you.

My flesh and my heart may fail,
but God is the strength of my heart
and my portion forever.

Those who are far from you will perish;
you destroy all who are unfaithful to you.

But as for me, it is good to be near God.
I have made the Sovereign Lord my refuge;
I will tell of all your deeds.

Psalm 74

A maskil of Asaph.

O God, why have you rejected us forever?
Why does your anger smolder against the sheep of your
      pasture?

Remember the nation you purchased long ago,
the people of your inheritance, whom you redeemed—
Mount Zion, where you dwelt.

Turn your steps toward these everlasting ruins,
all this destruction the enemy has brought on the
      sanctuary.

Your foes roared in the place where you met with us;
they set up their standards as signs.

They behaved like men wielding axes
to cut through a thicket of trees.

They smashed all the carved paneling
with their axes and hatchets.

They burned your sanctuary to the ground;
they defiled the dwelling place of your Name.

They said in their hearts, "We will crush them
      completely!"
They burned every place where God was worshiped in
      the land.

We are given no signs from God;
no prophets are left,
and none of us knows how long this will be.

How long will the enemy mock you, God?
Will the foe revile your name forever?

Why do you hold back your hand, your right hand?
Take it from the folds of your garment and
      destroy them!

But God is my King from long ago;
he brings salvation on the earth.

It was you who split open the sea by your power;
you broke the heads of the monster in the waters.

It was you who crushed the heads of Leviathan
and gave it as food to the creatures of the desert.

It was you who opened up springs and streams;
you dried up the ever-flowing rivers.

The day is yours, and yours also the night;
you established the sun and moon.

It was you who set all the boundaries of the earth;
you made both summer and winter.

Remember how the enemy has mocked you, Lord,
how foolish people have reviled your name.

Do not hand over the life of your dove to wild beasts;
do not forget the lives of your afflicted people forever.

Have regard for your covenant,
because haunts of violence fill the dark places
          of the land.

Do not let the oppressed retreat in disgrace;
may the poor and needy praise your name.

Rise up, O God, and defend your cause;
remember how fools mock you all day long.

Do not ignore the clamor of your adversaries,
the uproar of your enemies, which rises continually.

Psalm 75

For the director of music. To the tune of "Do Not Destroy."
A psalm of Asaph. A song.

We praise you, God,
we praise you, for your Name is near;
people tell of your wonderful deeds.

You say, "I choose the appointed time;
it is I who judge with equity.

When the earth and all its people quake,
it is I who hold its pillars firm.

To the arrogant I say, 'Boast no more,'
and to the wicked, 'Do not lift up your horns.

Do not lift your horns against heaven;
do not speak so defiantly.'"

No one from the east or the west
or from the desert can exalt themselves.

It is God who judges:
He brings one down, he exalts another.

In the hand of the Lord is a cup
full of foaming wine mixed with spices;

he pours it out, and all the wicked of the earth
drink it down to its very dregs.

As for me, I will declare this forever;
I will sing praise to the God of Jacob,

who says, "I will cut off the horns of all the wicked,
but the horns of the righteous will be lifted up."

Psalm 76

For the director of music. With stringed instruments.
A psalm of Asaph. A song.

God is renowned in Judah;
in Israel his name is great.

His tent is in Salem,
his dwelling place in Zion.

There he broke the flashing arrows,
the shields and the swords, the weapons of war.

You are radiant with light,
more majestic than mountains rich with game.

The valiant lie plundered,
they sleep their last sleep;

not one of the warriors
can lift his hands.

At your rebuke, God of Jacob,
both horse and chariot lie still.

It is you alone who are to be feared.
Who can stand before you when you are angry?

From heaven you pronounced judgment,
and the land feared and was quiet —

when you, God, rose up to judge,
to save all the afflicted of the land.

Surely your wrath against mankind brings you praise,
and the survivors of your wrath are restrained.

Make vows to the Lord your God and fulfill them;
let all the neighboring lands
bring gifts to the One to be feared.

Psalm 77

For the director of music. For Jeduthun. Of Asaph. A psalm.

I cried out to God for help;
I cried out to God to hear me.

When I was in distress, I sought the Lord;
at night I stretched out untiring hands,
and I would not be comforted.

I remembered you, God, and I groaned;
I meditated, and my spirit grew faint.

You kept my eyes from closing;
I was too troubled to speak.

I thought about the former days,
the years of long ago;

I remembered my songs in the night.
My heart meditated and my spirit asked:

"Will the Lord reject forever?
Will he never show his favor again?

Has his unfailing love vanished forever?
Has his promise failed for all time?

Has God forgotten to be merciful?
Has he in anger withheld his compassion?"

Then I thought, "To this I will appeal:
the years when the Most High stretched out his right
    hand.

I will remember the deeds of the LORD;
yes, I will remember your miracles of long ago.

I will consider all your works
and meditate on all your mighty deeds."

Your ways, God, are holy.
What god is as great as our God?

You are the God who performs miracles;
you display your power among the peoples.

With your mighty arm you redeemed your people,
the descendants of Jacob and Joseph.

The waters saw you, God,
the waters saw you and writhed;
the very depths were convulsed.

The clouds poured down water,
the heavens resounded with thunder;
your arrows flashed back and forth.

Your thunder was heard in the whirlwind,
your lightning lit up the world;
the earth trembled and quaked.

Your path led through the sea,
your way through the mighty waters,
though your footprints were not seen.

You led your people like a flock
by the hand of Moses and Aaron.

Psalm 78

A maskil of Asaph.

My people, hear my teaching;
listen to the words of my mouth.

I will open my mouth with a parable;
I will utter hidden things, things from of old—

things we have heard and known,
things our ancestors have told us.

We will not hide them from their descendants;
we will tell the next generation

the praiseworthy deeds of the Lord,
his power, and the wonders he has done.

He decreed statutes for Jacob
and established the law in Israel,

which he commanded our ancestors
to teach their children,

so the next generation would know them,
even the children yet to be born,
and they in turn would tell their children.

Then they would put their trust in God
and would not forget his deeds
but would keep his commands.

They would not be like their ancestors—
a stubborn and rebellious generation,

whose hearts were not loyal to God,
whose spirits were not faithful to him.

The men of Ephraim, though armed with bows,
turned back on the day of battle;

they did not keep God's covenant
and refused to live by his law.

They forgot what he had done,
the wonders he had shown them.

He did miracles in the sight of their ancestors
in the land of Egypt, in the region of Zoan.

He divided the sea and led them through;
he made the water stand up like a wall.

He guided them with the cloud by day
and with light from the fire all night.

He split the rocks in the wilderness
and gave them water as abundant as the seas;

he brought streams out of a rocky crag
and made water flow down like rivers.

But they continued to sin against him,
rebelling in the wilderness against the Most High.

They willfully put God to the test
by demanding the food they craved.

They spoke against God;
they said, "Can God really
spread a table in the wilderness?

True, he struck the rock,
and water gushed out,
streams flowed abundantly,

but can he also give us bread?
Can he supply meat for his people?"

When the LORD heard them, he was furious;
his fire broke out against Jacob,
and his wrath rose against Israel,

for they did not believe in God
or trust in his deliverance.

Yet he gave a command to the skies above
and opened the doors of the heavens;

he rained down manna for the people to eat,
he gave them the grain of heaven.

Human beings ate the bread of angels;
he sent them all the food they could eat.

He let loose the east wind from the heavens
and by his power made the south wind blow.

He rained meat down on them like dust,
birds like sand on the seashore.

He made them come down inside their camp,
all around their tents.

They ate till they were gorged —
he had given them what they craved.

But before they turned from what they craved,
even while the food was still in their mouths,

God's anger rose against them;
he put to death the sturdiest among them,
cutting down the young men of Israel.

In spite of all this, they kept on sinning;
in spite of his wonders, they did not believe.

So he ended their days in futility
and their years in terror.

Whenever God slew them, they would seek him;
they eagerly turned to him again.

They remembered that God was their Rock,
that God Most High was their Redeemer.

But then they would flatter him with their mouths,
lying to him with their tongues;

their hearts were not loyal to him,
they were not faithful to his covenant.

Yet he was merciful;
he forgave their iniquities
and did not destroy them.

Time after time he restrained his anger
and did not stir up his full wrath.

He remembered that they were but flesh,
a passing breeze that does not return.

How often they rebelled against him
in the wilderness
and grieved him in the wasteland!

Again and again they put God to the test;
they vexed the Holy One of Israel.

They did not remember his power—
the day he redeemed them from the oppressor,

the day he displayed his signs in Egypt,
his wonders in the region of Zoan.

He turned their river into blood;
they could not drink from their streams.

He sent swarms of flies that devoured them,
and frogs that devastated them.

He gave their crops to the grasshopper,
their produce to the locust.

He destroyed their vines with hail
and their sycamore-figs with sleet.

He gave over their cattle to the hail,
their livestock to bolts of lightning.

He unleashed against them his hot anger,
his wrath, indignation and hostility—
a band of destroying angels.

He prepared a path for his anger;
he did not spare them from death
but gave them over to the plague.

He struck down all the firstborn of Egypt,
the firstfruits of manhood in the tents of Ham.

But he brought his people out like a flock;
he led them like sheep through the wilderness.

He guided them safely, so they were unafraid;
but the sea engulfed their enemies.

And so he brought them to the border of his holy land,
to the hill country his right hand had taken.

He drove out nations before them
and allotted their lands to them as an inheritance;
he settled the tribes of Israel in their homes.

But they put God to the test
and rebelled against the Most High;
they did not keep his statutes.

Like their ancestors they were disloyal and faithless,
as unreliable as a faulty bow.

They angered him with their high places;
they aroused his jealousy with their idols.

When God heard them, he was furious;
he rejected Israel completely.

He abandoned the tabernacle of Shiloh,
the tent he had set up among humans.

He sent the ark of his might into captivity,
his splendor into the hands of the enemy.

He gave his people over to the sword;
he was furious with his inheritance.

Fire consumed their young men,
and their young women had no wedding songs;

their priests were put to the sword,
and their widows could not weep.

Then the Lord awoke as from sleep,
as a warrior wakes from the stupor of wine.

He beat back his enemies;
he put them to everlasting shame.

Then he rejected the tents of Joseph,
he did not choose the tribe of Ephraim;

but he chose the tribe of Judah,
Mount Zion, which he loved.

He built his sanctuary like the heights,
like the earth that he established forever.

He chose David his servant
and took him from the sheep pens;

from tending the sheep he brought him
to be the shepherd of his people Jacob,
of Israel his inheritance.

And David shepherded them with integrity of heart;
with skillful hands he led them.

Psalm 79

A psalm of Asaph.

O God, the nations have invaded your inheritance;
they have defiled your holy temple,
they have reduced Jerusalem to rubble.

They have left the dead bodies of your servants
as food for the birds of the sky,
the flesh of your own people for the animals of the wild.

They have poured out blood like water
all around Jerusalem,
and there is no one to bury the dead.

We are objects of contempt to our neighbors,
of scorn and derision to those around us.

How long, Lord? Will you be angry forever?
How long will your jealousy burn like fire?

Pour out your wrath on the nations
that do not acknowledge you,

on the kingdoms
that do not call on your name;

for they have devoured Jacob
and devastated his homeland.

Do not hold against us the sins of past generations;
may your mercy come quickly to meet us,
for we are in desperate need.

Help us, God our Savior,
for the glory of your name;

deliver us and forgive our sins
for your name's sake.

Why should the nations say,
"Where is their God?"

Before our eyes, make known among the nations
that you avenge the outpoured blood of your servants.

May the groans of the prisoners come before you;
with your strong arm preserve those condemned to die.

Pay back into the laps of our neighbors seven times
the contempt they have hurled at you, Lord.

Then we your people, the sheep of your pasture,
will praise you forever;

from generation to generation
we will proclaim your praise.

Psalm 80

*For the director of music. To the tune of "The Lilies
of the Covenant." Of Asaph. A psalm.*

Hear us, Shepherd of Israel,
you who lead Joseph like a flock.

You who sit enthroned between the cherubim,
shine forth before Ephraim, Benjamin and Manasseh.

Awaken your might;
come and save us.

Restore us, O God;
make your face shine on us,
that we may be saved.

How long, LORD God Almighty,
will your anger smolder
against the prayers of your people?

You have fed them with the bread of tears;
you have made them drink tears by the bowlful.

You have made us an object of derision to our
    neighbors,
and our enemies mock us.

Restore us, God Almighty;
make your face shine on us,
that we may be saved.

You transplanted a vine from Egypt;
you drove out the nations and planted it.

You cleared the ground for it,
and it took root and filled the land.

The mountains were covered with its shade,
the mighty cedars with its branches.

Its branches reached as far as the Sea,
its shoots as far as the River.

Why have you broken down its walls
so that all who pass by pick its grapes?

Boars from the forest ravage it,
and insects from the fields feed on it.

Return to us, God Almighty!
Look down from heaven and see!

Watch over this vine,
the root your right hand has planted,
the son you have raised up for yourself.

Your vine is cut down, it is burned with fire;
at your rebuke your people perish.

Let your hand rest on the man at your right hand,
the son of man you have raised up for yourself.

Then we will not turn away from you;
revive us, and we will call on your name.

Restore us, LORD God Almighty;
make your face shine on us,
that we may be saved.

Psalm 81

For the director of music. According to gittith. *Of Asaph.*

Sing for joy to God our strength;
shout aloud to the God of Jacob!

Begin the music, strike the timbrel,
play the melodious harp and lyre.

Sound the ram's horn at the New Moon,
and when the moon is full, on the day
        of our festival;

this is a decree for Israel,
an ordinance of the God of Jacob.

When God went out against Egypt,
he established it as a statute for Joseph.

I heard an unknown voice say:

"I removed the burden from their shoulders;
their hands were set free from the basket.

In your distress you called and I rescued you,
I answered you out of a thundercloud;
I tested you at the waters of Meribah.

Hear me, my people, and I will warn you —
if you would only listen to me, Israel!

You shall have no foreign god among you;
you shall not worship any god other than me.

I am the LORD your God,
who brought you up out of Egypt.

Open wide your mouth and I will fill it.

"But my people would not listen to me;
Israel would not submit to me.

So I gave them over to their stubborn hearts
to follow their own devices.

"If my people would only listen to me,
if Israel would only follow my ways,

how quickly I would subdue their enemies
and turn my hand against their foes!

Those who hate the Lord would cringe before him,
and their punishment would last forever.

But you would be fed with the finest of wheat;
with honey from the rock I would satisfy you."

Psalm 82

A psalm of Asaph.

God presides in the great assembly;
he renders judgment among the "gods":

"How long will you defend the unjust
and show partiality to the wicked?

Defend the weak and the fatherless;
uphold the cause of the poor and the oppressed.

Rescue the weak and the needy;
deliver them from the hand of the wicked.

"The 'gods' know nothing, they understand nothing.
They walk about in darkness;
all the foundations of the earth are shaken.

"I said, 'You are "gods";
you are all sons of the Most High.'

But you will die like mere mortals;
you will fall like every other ruler."

Rise up, O God, judge the earth,
for all the nations are your inheritance.

Psalm 83

A song. A psalm of Asaph.

O God, do not remain silent;
do not turn a deaf ear,
do not stand aloof, O God.

See how your enemies growl,
how your foes rear their heads.

With cunning they conspire against your people;
they plot against those you cherish.

"Come," they say, "let us destroy them as a nation,
so that Israel's name is remembered no more."

With one mind they plot together;
they form an alliance against you—

the tents of Edom and the Ishmaelites,
of Moab and the Hagrites,

Byblos, Ammon and Amalek,
Philistia, with the people of Tyre.

Even Assyria has joined them
to reinforce Lot's descendants.

Do to them as you did to Midian,
as you did to Sisera and Jabin at the river Kishon,

who perished at Endor
and became like dung on the ground.

Make their nobles like Oreb and Zeeb,
all their princes like Zebah and Zalmunna,

who said, "Let us take possession
of the pasturelands of God."

Make them like tumbleweed, my God,
like chaff before the wind.

As fire consumes the forest
or a flame sets the mountains ablaze,

so pursue them with your tempest
and terrify them with your storm.

Cover their faces with shame, Lord,
so that they will seek your name.

May they ever be ashamed and dismayed;
may they perish in disgrace.

Let them know that you, whose name is the Lord—
that you alone are the Most High over all the earth.

Psalm 84

For the director of music. According to gittith.
Of the Sons of Korah. A psalm.

How lovely is your dwelling place,
Lord Almighty!

My soul yearns, even faints,
for the courts of the Lord;
my heart and my flesh cry out
for the living God.

Even the sparrow has found a home,
and the swallow a nest for herself,
where she may have her young—
a place near your altar,
Lord Almighty, my King and my God.

Blessed are those who dwell in your house;
they are ever praising you.

Blessed are those whose strength is in you,
whose hearts are set on pilgrimage.

As they pass through the Valley of Baka,
they make it a place of springs;
the autumn rains also cover it with pools.

They go from strength to strength,
till each appears before God in Zion.

Hear my prayer, Lord God Almighty;
listen to me, God of Jacob.

Look on our shield, O God;
look with favor on your anointed one.

Better is one day in your courts
than a thousand elsewhere;
I would rather be a doorkeeper in the house of my God
than dwell in the tents of the wicked.

For the Lord God is a sun and shield;
the Lord bestows favor and honor;
no good thing does he withhold
from those whose walk is blameless.

Lord Almighty,
blessed is the one who trusts in you.

Psalm 85

For the director of music. Of the Sons of Korah. A psalm.

You, Lord, showed favor to your land;
you restored the fortunes of Jacob.

You forgave the iniquity of your people
and covered all their sins.

You set aside all your wrath
and turned from your fierce anger.

Restore us again, God our Savior,
and put away your displeasure toward us.

Will you be angry with us forever?
Will you prolong your anger through all
     generations?

Will you not revive us again,
that your people may rejoice in you?

Show us your unfailing love, LORD,
and grant us your salvation.

I will listen to what God the LORD says;
he promises peace to his people, his faithful
     servants —
but let them not turn to folly.

Surely his salvation is near those who fear him,
that his glory may dwell in our land.

Love and faithfulness meet together;
righteousness and peace kiss each other.

Faithfulness springs forth from the earth,
and righteousness looks down from heaven.

The LORD will indeed give what is good,
and our land will yield its harvest.

Righteousness goes before him
and prepares the way for his steps.

Psalm 86

A prayer of David.

Hear me, LORD, and answer me,
for I am poor and needy.

Guard my life, for I am faithful to you;
save your servant who trusts in you.

You are my God; have mercy on me, Lord,
for I call to you all day long.

Bring joy to your servant, Lord,
for I put my trust in you.

You, Lord, are forgiving and good,
abounding in love to all who call to you.

Hear my prayer, Lord;
listen to my cry for mercy.

When I am in distress, I call to you,
because you answer me.

Among the gods there is none
    like you, Lord;
no deeds can compare with yours.

All the nations you have made
will come and worship before you, Lord;
they will bring glory to your name.

For you are great and do marvelous deeds;
you alone are God.

Teach me your way, Lord,
that I may rely on your faithfulness;

give me an undivided heart,
that I may fear your name.

I will praise you, Lord my God, with
    all my heart;
I will glorify your name forever.

For great is your love toward me;
you have delivered me from the depths,
from the realm of the dead.

Arrogant foes are attacking me, O God;
ruthless people are trying to kill me—
they have no regard for you.

But you, Lord, are a compassionate and
    gracious God,
slow to anger, abounding in love and
    faithfulness.

Turn to me and have mercy on me;
show your strength in behalf of your servant;

save me, because I serve you
just as my mother did.

Give me a sign of your goodness,
that my enemies may see it and be put
    to shame,
for you, Lord, have helped me and
    comforted me.

Of the Sons of Korah. A psalm. A song.

He has founded his city on the holy mountain.
The LORD loves the gates of Zion
more than all the other dwellings of Jacob.

Glorious things are said of you,
city of God:

"I will record Rahab and Babylon
among those who acknowledge me —
Philistia too, and Tyre, along with Cush —
and will say, 'This one was born in Zion.'"

Indeed, of Zion it will be said,
"This one and that one were born in her,
and the Most High himself will establish her."
The LORD will write in the register of the peoples:
"This one was born in Zion."

As they make music they will sing,
"All my fountains are in you."

*A song. A psalm of the Sons of Korah. For the director of music.
According to* mahalath leannoth. *A maskil of Heman the Ezrahite.*

LORD, you are the God who saves me;
day and night I cry out to you.
May my prayer come before you;
turn your ear to my cry.

I am overwhelmed with troubles
and my life draws near to death.
I am counted among those who go down to the pit;
I am like one without strength.
I am set apart with the dead,
like the slain who lie in the grave,
whom you remember no more,
who are cut off from your care.

You have put me in the lowest pit,
in the darkest depths.

Your wrath lies heavily on me;
you have overwhelmed me with all your waves.

You have taken from me my closest friends
and have made me repulsive to them.

I am confined and cannot escape;
my eyes are dim with grief.

I call to you, Lord, every day;
I spread out my hands to you.

Do you show your wonders to the dead?
Do their spirits rise up and praise you?

Is your love declared in the grave,
your faithfulness in Destruction?

Are your wonders known in the place of darkness,
or your righteous deeds in the land of oblivion?

But I cry to you for help, Lord;
in the morning my prayer comes before you.

Why, Lord, do you reject me
and hide your face from me?

From my youth I have suffered and been close to death;
I have borne your terrors and am in despair.

Your wrath has swept over me;
your terrors have destroyed me.

All day long they surround me like a flood;
they have completely engulfed me.

You have taken from me friend and neighbor —
darkness is my closest friend.

Psalm 89

A maskil of Ethan the Ezrahite.

I will sing of the Lord's great love forever;
with my mouth I will make your faithfulness known
through all generations.

I will declare that your love stands firm forever,
that you have established your faithfulness
    in heaven itself.

You said, "I have made a covenant with my
        chosen one,
I have sworn to David my servant,

'I will establish your line forever
and make your throne firm through all generations.'"

The heavens praise your wonders, L ORD,
your faithfulness too, in the assembly of the holy ones.

For who in the skies above can compare with the L ORD?
Who is like the L ORD among the heavenly beings?

In the council of the holy ones God is greatly feared;
he is more awesome than all who surround him.

Who is like you, L ORD God Almighty?
You, L ORD, are mighty, and your faithfulness
        surrounds you.

You rule over the surging sea;
when its waves mount up, you still them.

You crushed Rahab like one of the slain;
with your strong arm you scattered your enemies.

The heavens are yours, and yours also the earth;
you founded the world and all that is in it.

You created the north and the south;
Tabor and Hermon sing for joy at your name.

Your arm is endowed with power;
your hand is strong, your right hand exalted.

Righteousness and justice are the foundation of your
        throne;
love and faithfulness go before you.

Blessed are those who have learned to acclaim you,
who walk in the light of your presence, L ORD.

They rejoice in your name all day long;
they celebrate your righteousness.

For you are their glory and strength,
and by your favor you exalt our horn.

Indeed, our shield belongs to the L ORD,
our king to the Holy One of Israel.

Once you spoke in a vision,
to your faithful people you said:
"I have bestowed strength on a warrior;
I have raised up a young man from among the people.

I have found David my servant;
with my sacred oil I have anointed him.

My hand will sustain him;
surely my arm will strengthen him.

The enemy will not get the better of him;
the wicked will not oppress him.

I will crush his foes before him
and strike down his adversaries.

My faithful love will be with him,
and through my name his horn will be exalted.

I will set his hand over the sea,
his right hand over the rivers.

He will call out to me, 'You are my Father,
my God, the Rock my Savior.'

And I will appoint him to be my firstborn,
the most exalted of the kings of the earth.

I will maintain my love to him forever,
and my covenant with him will never fail.

I will establish his line forever,
his throne as long as the heavens endure.

"If his sons forsake my law
and do not follow my statutes,

if they violate my decrees
and fail to keep my commands,

I will punish their sin with the rod,
their iniquity with flogging;

but I will not take my love from him,
nor will I ever betray my faithfulness.

I will not violate my covenant
or alter what my lips have uttered.

Once for all, I have sworn by my holiness—
and I will not lie to David—

that his line will continue forever
and his throne endure before me like the sun;

it will be established forever like the moon,
the faithful witness in the sky."

But you have rejected, you have spurned,
you have been very angry with your anointed one.

You have renounced the covenant with your servant
and have defiled his crown in the dust.

You have broken through all his walls
and reduced his strongholds to ruins.

All who pass by have plundered him;
he has become the scorn of his neighbors.

You have exalted the right hand of his foes;
you have made all his enemies rejoice.

Indeed, you have turned back the edge of his sword
and have not supported him in battle.

You have put an end to his splendor
and cast his throne to the ground.

You have cut short the days of his youth;
you have covered him with a mantle of shame.

How long, LORD? Will you hide yourself forever?
How long will your wrath burn like fire?

Remember how fleeting is my life.
For what futility you have created all humanity!

Who can live and not see death,
or who can escape the power of the grave?

Lord, where is your former great love,
which in your faithfulness you swore to David?

Remember, Lord, how your servant has been mocked,
how I bear in my heart the taunts of all the nations,

the taunts with which your enemies, LORD, have mocked,
with which they have mocked every step of your
anointed one.

Praise be to the LORD forever!

Amen and Amen.

BOOK IV
Psalms 90–106

Psalm 90

A prayer of Moses the man of God.

Lord, you have been our dwelling place
throughout all generations.

Before the mountains were born
or you brought forth the whole world,
from everlasting to everlasting you are God.

You turn people back to dust,
saying, "Return to dust, you mortals."

A thousand years in your sight
are like a day that has just gone by,
or like a watch in the night.

Yet you sweep people away in the sleep
    of death —
they are like the new grass of the morning:

In the morning it springs up new,
but by evening it is dry and withered.

We are consumed by your anger
and terrified by your indignation.

You have set our iniquities before you,
our secret sins in the light of your presence.

All our days pass away under your wrath;
we finish our years with a moan.

Our days may come to seventy years,
or eighty, if our strength endures;

yet the best of them are but trouble and sorrow,
for they quickly pass, and we fly away.

If only we knew the power of your anger!
Your wrath is as great as the fear that is
    your due.

Teach us to number our days,
that we may gain a heart of wisdom.

Relent, Lord! How long will it be?
Have compassion on your servants.

Satisfy us in the morning with your
    unfailing love,
that we may sing for joy and be glad all our days.

Make us glad for as many days as you have
    afflicted us,
for as many years as we have seen trouble.

May your deeds be shown to your servants,
your splendor to their children.

May the favor of the Lord our God rest on us;
establish the work of our hands for us —
yes, establish the work of our hands.

Psalm 91

Whoever dwells in the shelter of the Most High
will rest in the shadow of the Almighty.
I will say of the Lord, "He is my refuge and my fortress,
my God, in whom I trust."

Surely he will save you
from the fowler's snare
and from the deadly pestilence.
He will cover you with his feathers,
and under his wings you will find refuge;
his faithfulness will be your shield and rampart.
You will not fear the terror of night,
nor the arrow that flies by day,
nor the pestilence that stalks in the darkness,
nor the plague that destroys at midday.
A thousand may fall at your side,
ten thousand at your right hand,
but it will not come near you.
You will only observe with your eyes
and see the punishment of the wicked.

If you say, "The Lord is my refuge,"
and you make the Most High your dwelling,
no harm will overtake you,
no disaster will come near your tent.
For he will command his angels concerning you
to guard you in all your ways;
they will lift you up in their hands,
so that you will not strike your foot against a stone.
You will tread on the lion and the cobra;
you will trample the great lion and the serpent.

"Because he loves me," says the Lord, "I will
    rescue him;
I will protect him, for he acknowledges my name.
He will call on me, and I will answer him;
I will be with him in trouble,
I will deliver him and honor him.
With long life I will satisfy him
and show him my salvation."

Psalm 92

A psalm. A song. For the Sabbath day.

It is good to praise the LORD
and make music to your name, O Most High,

proclaiming your love in the morning
and your faithfulness at night,

to the music of the ten-stringed lyre
and the melody of the harp.

For you make me glad by your deeds, LORD;
I sing for joy at what your hands have done.

How great are your works, LORD,
how profound your thoughts!

Senseless people do not know,
fools do not understand,

that though the wicked spring up like grass
and all evildoers flourish,
they will be destroyed forever.

But you, LORD, are forever exalted.

For surely your enemies, LORD,
surely your enemies will perish;
all evildoers will be scattered.

You have exalted my horn like that
of a wild ox;
fine oils have been poured on me.

My eyes have seen the defeat
of my adversaries;
my ears have heard the rout of my
wicked foes.

The righteous will flourish like a palm tree,
they will grow like a cedar of Lebanon;

planted in the house of the LORD,
they will flourish in the courts of our God.

They will still bear fruit in old age,
they will stay fresh and green,

proclaiming, "The LORD is upright;
he is my Rock, and there is no wickedness
in him."

Psalm 93

The LORD reigns, he is robed in majesty;
the LORD is robed in majesty and armed with strength;
indeed, the world is established, firm and secure.

Your throne was established long ago;
you are from all eternity.

The seas have lifted up, LORD,
the seas have lifted up their voice;
the seas have lifted up their pounding waves.

Mightier than the thunder of the great waters,
mightier than the breakers of the sea —
the LORD on high is mighty.

Your statutes, LORD, stand firm;
holiness adorns your house
for endless days.

Psalm 94

The LORD is a God who avenges.
O God who avenges, shine forth.

Rise up, Judge of the earth;
pay back to the proud what they deserve.

How long, LORD, will the wicked,
how long will the wicked be jubilant?

They pour out arrogant words;
all the evildoers are full of boasting.

They crush your people, LORD;
they oppress your inheritance.

They slay the widow and the foreigner;
they murder the fatherless.

They say, "The LORD does not see;
the God of Jacob takes no notice."

Take notice, you senseless ones among the people;
you fools, when will you become wise?

Does he who fashioned the ear not hear?
Does he who formed the eye not see?

Does he who disciplines nations not punish?
Does he who teaches mankind lack knowledge?

The Lord knows all human plans;
he knows that they are futile.

Blessed is the one you discipline, Lord,
the one you teach from your law;

you grant them relief from days of trouble,
till a pit is dug for the wicked.

For the Lord will not reject his people;
he will never forsake his inheritance.

Judgment will again be founded on righteousness,
and all the upright in heart will follow it.

Who will rise up for me against the wicked?
Who will take a stand for me against evildoers?

Unless the Lord had given me help,
I would soon have dwelt in the silence of death.

When I said, "My foot is slipping,"
your unfailing love, Lord, supported me.

When anxiety was great within me,
your consolation brought me joy.

Can a corrupt throne be allied with you—
a throne that brings on misery by its decrees?

The wicked band together against the righteous
and condemn the innocent to death.

But the Lord has become my fortress,
and my God the rock in whom I take refuge.

He will repay them for their sins
and destroy them for their wickedness;
the Lord our God will destroy them.

Psalm 95

Come, let us sing for joy to the Lord;
let us shout aloud to the Rock of our salvation.

Let us come before him with thanksgiving
and extol him with music and song.

For the Lord is the great God,
the great King above all gods.

In his hand are the depths of the earth,
and the mountain peaks belong to him.

The sea is his, for he made it,
and his hands formed the dry land.

Come, let us bow down in worship,
let us kneel before the LORD our Maker;

for he is our God
and we are the people of his pasture,
the flock under his care.

Today, if only you would hear his voice,

"Do not harden your hearts as you did at Meribah,
as you did that day at Massah in the wilderness,

where your ancestors tested me;
they tried me, though they had seen what I did.

For forty years I was angry with that generation;
I said, 'They are a people whose hearts go astray,
and they have not known my ways.'

So I declared on oath in my anger,
'They shall never enter my rest.'"

Psalm 96

Sing to the LORD a new song;
sing to the LORD, all the earth.
Sing to the LORD, praise his name;
proclaim his salvation day after day.

Declare his glory among the nations,
his marvelous deeds among all peoples.

For great is the LORD and most worthy of praise;
he is to be feared above all gods.

For all the gods of the nations are idols,
but the LORD made the heavens.

Splendor and majesty are before him;
strength and glory are in his sanctuary.

Ascribe to the LORD, all you families of nations,
ascribe to the LORD glory and strength.

Ascribe to the LORD the glory due his name;
bring an offering and come into his courts.

Worship the LORD in the splendor of his holiness;
tremble before him, all the earth.

Say among the nations, "The Lord reigns."
The world is firmly established, it cannot be moved;
he will judge the peoples with equity.

Let the heavens rejoice, let the earth be glad;
let the sea resound, and all that is in it.

Let the fields be jubilant, and everything in them;
let all the trees of the forest sing for joy.

Let all creation rejoice before the Lord, for he comes,
he comes to judge the earth.

He will judge the world in righteousness
and the peoples in his faithfulness.

Psalm 97

The Lord reigns, let the earth be glad;
let the distant shores rejoice.

Clouds and thick darkness surround him;
righteousness and justice are the foundation
     of his throne.

Fire goes before him
and consumes his foes on every side.

His lightning lights up the world;
the earth sees and trembles.

The mountains melt like wax before the Lord,
before the Lord of all the earth.

The heavens proclaim his righteousness,
and all peoples see his glory.

All who worship images are put to shame,
those who boast in idols—
worship him, all you gods!

Zion hears and rejoices
and the villages of Judah are glad
because of your judgments, Lord.

For you, Lord, are the Most High over
     all the earth;
you are exalted far above all gods.

Let those who love the Lord hate evil,
for he guards the lives of his faithful ones
and delivers them from the hand of the wicked.

Light shines on the righteous
and joy on the upright in heart.

Rejoice in the LORD, you who are righteous,
and praise his holy name.

Psalm 98

A psalm.

Sing to the LORD a new song,
for he has done marvelous things;

his right hand and his holy arm
have worked salvation for him.

The LORD has made his salvation known
and revealed his righteousness to the nations.

He has remembered his love
and his faithfulness to Israel;

all the ends of the earth have seen
the salvation of our God.

Shout for joy to the LORD, all the earth,
burst into jubilant song with music;

make music to the LORD with the harp,
with the harp and the sound of singing,

with trumpets and the blast of the
      ram's horn —
shout for joy before the LORD, the King.

Let the sea resound, and everything in it,
the world, and all who live in it.

Let the rivers clap their hands,
let the mountains sing together for joy;

let them sing before the LORD,
for he comes to judge the earth.

He will judge the world in righteousness
and the peoples with equity.

Psalm 99

The LORD reigns,
let the nations tremble;

he sits enthroned between the cherubim,
let the earth shake.

Great is the LORD in Zion;
he is exalted over all the nations.

Let them praise your great and awesome name—
he is holy.

The King is mighty, he loves justice—
you have established equity;

in Jacob you have done
what is just and right.

Exalt the LORD our God
and worship at his footstool;
he is holy.

Moses and Aaron were among his priests,
Samuel was among those who called
on his name;

they called on the LORD
and he answered them.

He spoke to them from the pillar of cloud;
they kept his statutes and the decrees
he gave them.

LORD our God,
you answered them;

you were to Israel a forgiving God,
though you punished their misdeeds.

Exalt the LORD our God
and worship at his holy mountain,
for the LORD our God is holy.

Psalm 100

A psalm. For giving grateful praise.

Shout for joy to the LORD, all the earth.
Worship the LORD with gladness;
come before him with joyful songs.

Know that the LORD is God.
It is he who made us, and we are his;
we are his people, the sheep of his pasture.

Enter his gates with thanksgiving
and his courts with praise;
give thanks to him and praise his name.

For the Lord is good and his love endures
      forever;
his faithfulness continues through
      all generations.

Of David. A psalm.

I will sing of your love and justice;
to you, Lord, I will sing praise.

I will be careful to lead a blameless life—
when will you come to me?

I will conduct the affairs of my house
with a blameless heart.

I will not look with approval
on anything that is vile.

I hate what faithless people do;
I will have no part in it.

The perverse of heart shall be far from me;
I will have nothing to do with what is evil.

Whoever slanders their neighbor in secret,
I will put to silence;

whoever has haughty eyes and a proud heart,
I will not tolerate.

My eyes will be on the faithful
      in the land,
that they may dwell with me;

the one whose walk is blameless
will minister to me.

No one who practices deceit
will dwell in my house;

no one who speaks falsely
will stand in my presence.

Every morning I will put to silence
all the wicked in the land;

I will cut off every evildoer
from the city of the Lord.

Psalm 102

A prayer of an afflicted person who has grown weak and pours out a lament before the LORD.

Hear my prayer, LORD;
let my cry for help come to you.

Do not hide your face from me
when I am in distress.

Turn your ear to me;
when I call, answer me quickly.

For my days vanish like smoke;
my bones burn like glowing embers.

My heart is blighted and withered like grass;
I forget to eat my food.

In my distress I groan aloud
and am reduced to skin and bones.

I am like a desert owl,
like an owl among the ruins.

I lie awake; I have become
like a bird alone on a roof.

All day long my enemies taunt me;
those who rail against me use my name as a curse.

For I eat ashes as my food
and mingle my drink with tears

because of your great wrath,
for you have taken me up and thrown me aside.

My days are like the evening shadow;
I wither away like grass.

But you, LORD, sit enthroned forever;
your renown endures through all generations.

You will arise and have compassion on Zion,
for it is time to show favor to her;
the appointed time has come.

For her stones are dear to your servants;
her very dust moves them to pity.

The nations will fear the name of the LORD,
all the kings of the earth will revere your glory.

For the LORD will rebuild Zion
and appear in his glory.

He will respond to the prayer of the destitute;
he will not despise their plea.

Let this be written for a future generation,
that a people not yet created may praise the LORD:

"The LORD looked down from his sanctuary on high,
from heaven he viewed the earth,

to hear the groans of the prisoners
and release those condemned to death."

So the name of the LORD will be declared in Zion
and his praise in Jerusalem

when the peoples and the kingdoms
assemble to worship the LORD.

In the course of my life he broke my strength;
he cut short my days.

So I said:

"Do not take me away, my God, in the midst of my days;
your years go on through all generations.

In the beginning you laid the foundations of the earth,
and the heavens are the work of your hands.

They will perish, but you remain;
they will all wear out like a garment.

Like clothing you will change them
and they will be discarded.

But you remain the same,
and your years will never end.

The children of your servants will live in
your presence;
their descendants will be established
before you."

Psalm 103

Of David.

Praise the LORD, my soul;
all my inmost being, praise his holy name.

Praise the LORD, my soul,
and forget not all his benefits —

who forgives all your sins
and heals all your diseases,

who redeems your life from the pit
and crowns you with love and compassion,

who satisfies your desires with good things
so that your youth is renewed like the eagle's.

The LORD works righteousness
and justice for all the oppressed.

He made known his ways to Moses,
his deeds to the people of Israel:

The LORD is compassionate and gracious,
slow to anger, abounding in love.

He will not always accuse,
nor will he harbor his anger forever;

he does not treat us as our sins deserve
or repay us according to our iniquities.

For as high as the heavens are above the earth,
so great is his love for those who fear him;

as far as the east is from the west,
so far has he removed our transgressions from us.

As a father has compassion on his children,
so the LORD has compassion on those who fear him;

for he knows how we are formed,
he remembers that we are dust.

The life of mortals is like grass,
they flourish like a flower of the field;

the wind blows over it and it is gone,
and its place remembers it no more.

But from everlasting to everlasting
the LORD's love is with those who fear him,
and his righteousness with their children's
　　　children—

with those who keep his covenant
and remember to obey his precepts.

The LORD has established his throne in heaven,
and his kingdom rules over all.

Praise the LORD, you his angels,
you mighty ones who do his bidding,
who obey his word.

Praise the LORD, all his heavenly hosts,
you his servants who do his will.

Praise the LORD, all his works
everywhere in his dominion.

Praise the LORD, my soul.

Psalm 104

Praise the LORD, my soul.

LORD my God, you are very great;
you are clothed with splendor and majesty.

The LORD wraps himself in light as with a garment;
he stretches out the heavens like a tent
and lays the beams of his upper chambers on their
waters.
He makes the clouds his chariot
and rides on the wings of the wind.
He makes winds his messengers,
flames of fire his servants.

He set the earth on its foundations;
it can never be moved.
You covered it with the watery depths as with
a garment;
the waters stood above the mountains.
But at your rebuke the waters fled,
at the sound of your thunder they took
to flight;
they flowed over the mountains,
they went down into the valleys,
to the place you assigned for them.
You set a boundary they cannot cross;
never again will they cover the earth.

He makes springs pour water into the ravines;
it flows between the mountains.
They give water to all the beasts of the field;
the wild donkeys quench their thirst.
The birds of the sky nest by the waters;
they sing among the branches.

He waters the mountains from his upper chambers;
the land is satisfied by the fruit of his work.

He makes grass grow for the cattle,
and plants for people to cultivate—
bringing forth food from the earth:

wine that gladdens human hearts,
oil to make their faces shine,
and bread that sustains their hearts.

The trees of the LORD are well watered,
the cedars of Lebanon that he planted.

There the birds make their nests;
the stork has its home in the junipers.

The high mountains belong to the wild goats;
the crags are a refuge for the hyrax.

He made the moon to mark the seasons,
and the sun knows when to go down.

You bring darkness, it becomes night,
and all the beasts of the forest prowl.

The lions roar for their prey
and seek their food from God.

The sun rises, and they steal away;
they return and lie down in their dens.

Then people go out to their work,
to their labor until evening.

How many are your works, LORD!
In wisdom you made them all;
the earth is full of your creatures.

There is the sea, vast and spacious,
teeming with creatures beyond number—
living things both large and small.

There the ships go to and fro,
and Leviathan, which you formed to frolic there.

All creatures look to you
to give them their food at the proper time.

When you give it to them,
they gather it up;

when you open your hand,
they are satisfied with good things.

When you hide your face,
they are terrified;

when you take away their breath,
they die and return to the dust.

When you send your Spirit,
they are created,
and you renew the face of the ground.

May the glory of the Lord endure forever;
may the Lord rejoice in his works—

he who looks at the earth, and it trembles,
who touches the mountains, and they smoke.

I will sing to the Lord all my life;
I will sing praise to my God as long as I live.

May my meditation be pleasing to him,
as I rejoice in the Lord.

But may sinners vanish from the earth
and the wicked be no more.

Praise the Lord, my soul.

Praise the Lord.

Psalm 105

Give praise to the Lord, proclaim his name;
make known among the nations what
he has done.

Sing to him, sing praise to him;
tell of all his wonderful acts.

Glory in his holy name;
let the hearts of those who seek the Lord rejoice.

Look to the Lord and his strength;
seek his face always.

Remember the wonders he has done,
his miracles, and the judgments he pronounced,

you his servants, the descendants
of Abraham,
his chosen ones, the children of Jacob.

He is the Lord our God;
his judgments are in all the earth.

He remembers his covenant forever,
the promise he made, for a thousand generations,

the covenant he made with Abraham,
the oath he swore to Isaac.

He confirmed it to Jacob as a decree,
to Israel as an everlasting covenant:

"To you I will give the land of Canaan
as the portion you will inherit."

When they were but few in number,
few indeed, and strangers in it,

they wandered from nation to nation,
from one kingdom to another.

He allowed no one to oppress them;
for their sake he rebuked kings:

"Do not touch my anointed ones;
do my prophets no harm."

He called down famine on the land
and destroyed all their supplies of food;

and he sent a man before them—
Joseph, sold as a slave.

They bruised his feet with shackles,
his neck was put in irons,

till what he foretold came to pass,
till the word of the LORD proved him true.

The king sent and released him,
the ruler of peoples set him free.

He made him master of his household,
ruler over all he possessed,

to instruct his princes as he pleased
and teach his elders wisdom.

Then Israel entered Egypt;
Jacob resided as a foreigner in the land of Ham.

The LORD made his people very fruitful;
he made them too numerous for their foes,

whose hearts he turned to hate his people,
to conspire against his servants.

He sent Moses his servant,
and Aaron, whom he had chosen.

They performed his signs among them,
his wonders in the land of Ham.

He sent darkness and made the land dark—
for had they not rebelled against his words?

He turned their waters into blood,
causing their fish to die.

Their land teemed with frogs,
which went up into the bedrooms
of their rulers.

He spoke, and there came swarms of flies,
and gnats throughout their country.

He turned their rain into hail,
with lightning throughout their land;

he struck down their vines and fig trees
and shattered the trees of their country.

He spoke, and the locusts came,
grasshoppers without number;

they ate up every green thing in their land,
ate up the produce of their soil.

Then he struck down all the firstborn
in their land,
the firstfruits of all their manhood.

He brought out Israel, laden with silver and gold,
and from among their tribes no one faltered.

Egypt was glad when they left,
because dread of Israel had fallen on them.

He spread out a cloud as a covering,
and a fire to give light at night.

They asked, and he brought them quail;
he fed them well with the bread of heaven.

He opened the rock, and water gushed out;
it flowed like a river in the desert.

For he remembered his holy promise
given to his servant Abraham.

He brought out his people with rejoicing,
his chosen ones with shouts of joy;

he gave them the lands of the nations,
and they fell heir to what others had toiled for—

that they might keep his precepts
and observe his laws.

Praise the Lord.

Praise the Lord.

Give thanks to the Lord, for he is good;
his love endures forever.

Who can proclaim the mighty acts of the Lord
or fully declare his praise?
Blessed are those who act justly,
who always do what is right.

Remember me, Lord, when you show favor to your
people,
come to my aid when you save them,

that I may enjoy the prosperity of your chosen ones,
that I may share in the joy of your nation
and join your inheritance in giving praise.

We have sinned, even as our ancestors did;
we have done wrong and acted wickedly.

When our ancestors were in Egypt,
they gave no thought to your miracles;

they did not remember your many kindnesses,
and they rebelled by the sea, the Red Sea.

Yet he saved them for his name's sake,
to make his mighty power known.

He rebuked the Red Sea, and it dried up;
he led them through the depths as through a desert.

He saved them from the hand of the foe;
from the hand of the enemy he redeemed them.

The waters covered their adversaries;
not one of them survived.

Then they believed his promises
and sang his praise.

But they soon forgot what he had done
and did not wait for his plan to unfold.

In the desert they gave in to their craving;
in the wilderness they put God to the test.

So he gave them what they asked for,
but sent a wasting disease among them.

In the camp they grew envious of Moses
and of Aaron, who was consecrated to the LORD.

The earth opened up and swallowed Dathan;
it buried the company of Abiram.

Fire blazed among their followers;
a flame consumed the wicked.

At Horeb they made a calf
and worshiped an idol cast from metal.

They exchanged their glorious God
for an image of a bull, which eats grass.

They forgot the God who saved them,
who had done great things in Egypt,

miracles in the land of Ham
and awesome deeds by the Red Sea.

So he said he would destroy them—
had not Moses, his chosen one,

stood in the breach before him
to keep his wrath from destroying them.

Then they despised the pleasant land;
they did not believe his promise.

They grumbled in their tents
and did not obey the LORD.

So he swore to them with uplifted hand
that he would make them fall in the wilderness,

make their descendants fall among the nations
and scatter them throughout the lands.

They yoked themselves to the Baal of Peor
and ate sacrifices offered to lifeless gods;

they aroused the LORD's anger by their wicked deeds,
and a plague broke out among them.

But Phinehas stood up and intervened,
and the plague was checked.

This was credited to him as righteousness
for endless generations to come.

By the waters of Meribah they angered
the LORD,
and trouble came to Moses because of them;
for they rebelled against the Spirit of God,
and rash words came from Moses' lips.

They did not destroy the peoples
as the LORD had commanded them,
but they mingled with the nations
and adopted their customs.
They worshiped their idols,
which became a snare to them.
They sacrificed their sons
and their daughters to false gods.
They shed innocent blood,
the blood of their sons and daughters,
whom they sacrificed to the idols of Canaan,
and the land was desecrated by their blood.
They defiled themselves by what they did;
by their deeds they prostituted themselves.

Therefore the LORD was angry with his people
and abhorred his inheritance.
He gave them into the hands of the nations,
and their foes ruled over them.
Their enemies oppressed them
and subjected them to their power.
Many times he delivered them,
but they were bent on rebellion
and they wasted away in their sin.
Yet he took note of their distress
when he heard their cry;
for their sake he remembered his covenant
and out of his great love he relented.
He caused all who held them captive
to show them mercy.

Save us, LORD our God,
and gather us from the nations,
that we may give thanks to your holy name
and glory in your praise.

Praise be to the Lord, the God of Israel,
from everlasting to everlasting.

Let all the people say, "Amen!"

Praise the Lord.

BOOK V

Psalms 107 – 150

Psalm 107

Give thanks to the Lord, for he is good;
his love endures forever.

Let the redeemed of the Lord tell their story —
those he redeemed from the hand of the foe,

those he gathered from the lands,
from east and west, from north and south.

Some wandered in desert wastelands,
finding no way to a city where they could settle.

They were hungry and thirsty,
and their lives ebbed away.

Then they cried out to the Lord in their trouble,
and he delivered them from their distress.

He led them by a straight way
to a city where they could settle.

Let them give thanks to the Lord for his unfailing love
and his wonderful deeds for mankind,

for he satisfies the thirsty
and fills the hungry with good things.

Some sat in darkness, in utter darkness,
prisoners suffering in iron chains,

because they rebelled against God's commands
and despised the plans of the Most High.

So he subjected them to bitter labor;
they stumbled, and there was no one to help.

Then they cried to the LORD in their trouble,
and he saved them from their distress.

He brought them out of darkness, the utter darkness,
and broke away their chains.

Let them give thanks to the LORD for his unfailing love
and his wonderful deeds for mankind,

for he breaks down gates of bronze
and cuts through bars of iron.

Some became fools through their rebellious ways
and suffered affliction because of their iniquities.

They loathed all food
and drew near the gates of death.

Then they cried to the LORD in their trouble,
and he saved them from their distress.

He sent out his word and healed them;
he rescued them from the grave.

Let them give thanks to the LORD for his unfailing love
and his wonderful deeds for mankind.

Let them sacrifice thank offerings
and tell of his works with songs of joy.

Some went out on the sea in ships;
they were merchants on the mighty waters.

They saw the works of the LORD,
his wonderful deeds in the deep.

For he spoke and stirred up a tempest
that lifted high the waves.

They mounted up to the heavens and went down
to the depths;
in their peril their courage melted away.

They reeled and staggered like drunkards;
they were at their wits' end.

Then they cried out to the LORD in their trouble,
and he brought them out of their distress.

He stilled the storm to a whisper;
the waves of the sea were hushed.

They were glad when it grew calm,
and he guided them to their desired haven.

Let them give thanks to the LORD for his unfailing love
and his wonderful deeds for mankind.

Let them exalt him in the assembly of the people
and praise him in the council of the elders.

He turned rivers into a desert,
flowing springs into thirsty ground,
and fruitful land into a salt waste,
because of the wickedness of those who lived there.

He turned the desert into pools of water
and the parched ground into flowing springs;

there he brought the hungry to live,
and they founded a city where they could settle.

They sowed fields and planted vineyards
that yielded a fruitful harvest;

he blessed them, and their numbers greatly increased,
and he did not let their herds diminish.

Then their numbers decreased, and they
were humbled
by oppression, calamity and sorrow;

he who pours contempt on nobles
made them wander in a trackless waste.

But he lifted the needy out of their affliction
and increased their families like flocks.

The upright see and rejoice,
but all the wicked shut their mouths.

Let the one who is wise heed these things
and ponder the loving deeds of the LORD.

Psalm 108

A song. A psalm of David.

My heart, O God, is steadfast;
I will sing and make music with all my soul.

Awake, harp and lyre!
I will awaken the dawn.

I will praise you, LORD, among the nations;
I will sing of you among the peoples.

For great is your love, higher than the heavens;
your faithfulness reaches to the skies.

Be exalted, O God, above the heavens;
let your glory be over all the earth.

Save us and help us with your right hand,
that those you love may be delivered.

God has spoken from his sanctuary:
"In triumph I will parcel out Shechem
and measure off the Valley of Sukkoth.

Gilead is mine, Manasseh is mine;
Ephraim is my helmet,
Judah is my scepter.

Moab is my washbasin,
on Edom I toss my sandal;
over Philistia I shout in triumph."

Who will bring me to the fortified city?
Who will lead me to Edom?

Is it not you, God, you who have rejected us
and no longer go out with our armies?

Give us aid against the enemy,
for human help is worthless.

With God we will gain the victory,
and he will trample down our enemies.

Psalm 109

For the director of music. Of David. A psalm.

My God, whom I praise,
do not remain silent,

for people who are wicked and deceitful
have opened their mouths against me;
they have spoken against me with lying
tongues.

With words of hatred they surround me;
they attack me without cause.

In return for my friendship they accuse me,
but I am a man of prayer.

They repay me evil for good,
and hatred for my friendship.

Appoint someone evil to oppose my enemy;
let an accuser stand at his right hand.

When he is tried, let him be found guilty,
and may his prayers condemn him.

May his days be few;
may another take his place of leadership.

May his children be fatherless
and his wife a widow.

May his children be wandering beggars;
may they be driven from their ruined homes.

May a creditor seize all he has;
may strangers plunder the fruits of his labor.

May no one extend kindness to him
or take pity on his fatherless children.

May his descendants be cut off,
their names blotted out from the next generation.

May the iniquity of his fathers be remembered
    before the Lord;
may the sin of his mother never be blotted out.

May their sins always remain before the Lord,
that he may blot out their name from the earth.

For he never thought of doing a kindness,
but hounded to death the poor
and the needy and the brokenhearted.

He loved to pronounce a curse —
may it come back on him.

He found no pleasure in blessing —
may it be far from him.

He wore cursing as his garment;
it entered into his body like water,
into his bones like oil.

May it be like a cloak wrapped about him,
like a belt tied forever around him.

May this be the Lord's payment
    to my accusers,
to those who speak evil of me.

But you, Sovereign Lord,
help me for your name's sake;
out of the goodness of your love, deliver me.

For I am poor and needy,
and my heart is wounded within me.

I fade away like an evening shadow;
I am shaken off like a locust.

My knees give way from fasting;
my body is thin and gaunt.

I am an object of scorn to my accusers;
when they see me, they shake their heads.

Help me, Lord my God;
save me according to your unfailing love.

Let them know that it is your hand,
that you, Lord, have done it.

While they curse, may you bless;
may those who attack me be put to shame,
but may your servant rejoice.

May my accusers be clothed with disgrace
and wrapped in shame as in a cloak.

With my mouth I will greatly extol the Lord;
in the great throng of worshipers I will praise him.

For he stands at the right hand of the needy,
to save their lives from those who would
condemn them.

Psalm 110

Of David. A psalm.

The Lord says to my lord:

"Sit at my right hand
until I make your enemies
a footstool for your feet."

The Lord will extend your mighty scepter
from Zion, saying,
"Rule in the midst of your enemies!"

Your troops will be willing
on your day of battle.

Arrayed in holy splendor,
your young men will come to you
like dew from the morning's womb.

The Lord has sworn
and will not change his mind:

"You are a priest forever,
in the order of Melchizedek."

The Lord is at your right hand;
he will crush kings on the day of his wrath.

He will judge the nations, heaping up the dead
and crushing the rulers of the whole earth.

He will drink from a brook along the way,
and so he will lift his head high.

Psalm 111

Praise the Lord.

I will extol the Lord with all my heart
in the council of the upright and in the assembly.

Great are the works of the Lord;
they are pondered by all who delight in them.

Glorious and majestic are his deeds,
and his righteousness endures forever.

He has caused his wonders to be remembered;
the Lord is gracious and compassionate.

He provides food for those who fear him;
he remembers his covenant forever.

He has shown his people the power of his works,
giving them the lands of other nations.

The works of his hands are faithful and just;
all his precepts are trustworthy.

They are established for ever and ever,
enacted in faithfulness and uprightness.

He provided redemption for his people;
he ordained his covenant forever—
holy and awesome is his name.

The fear of the Lord is the beginning of wisdom;
all who follow his precepts have good
understanding.
To him belongs eternal praise.

Psalm 112

Praise the Lord.

Blessed are those who fear the Lord,
who find great delight in his commands.

Their children will be mighty in the land;
the generation of the upright will be blessed.

Wealth and riches are in their houses,
and their righteousness endures forever.

Even in darkness light dawns for the upright,
for those who are gracious and compassionate
and righteous.

Good will come to those who are generous
and lend freely,
who conduct their affairs with justice.

Surely the righteous will never be shaken;
they will be remembered forever.

They will have no fear of bad news;
their hearts are steadfast, trusting in the Lord.

Their hearts are secure, they will have no fear;
in the end they will look in triumph on their foes.

They have freely scattered their gifts to the poor,
their righteousness endures forever;
their horn will be lifted high in honor.

The wicked will see and be vexed,
they will gnash their teeth and waste away;
the longings of the wicked will come to nothing.

Psalm 113

Praise the Lord.

Praise the Lord, you his servants;
praise the name of the Lord.

Let the name of the Lord be praised,
both now and forevermore.

From the rising of the sun to the place where it sets,
the name of the Lord is to be praised.

The Lord is exalted over all the nations,
his glory above the heavens.

Who is like the Lord our God,
the One who sits enthroned on high,

who stoops down to look
on the heavens and the earth?

He raises the poor from the dust
and lifts the needy from the ash heap;

he seats them with princes,
with the princes of his people.

He settles the childless woman in her home
as a happy mother of children.

Praise the LORD.

Psalm 114

When Israel came out of Egypt,
Jacob from a people of foreign tongue,

Judah became God's sanctuary,
Israel his dominion.

The sea looked and fled,
the Jordan turned back;

the mountains leaped like rams,
the hills like lambs.

Why was it, sea, that you fled?
Why, Jordan, did you turn back?

Why, mountains, did you leap like rams,
you hills, like lambs?

Tremble, earth, at the presence of the Lord,
at the presence of the God of Jacob,

who turned the rock into a pool,
the hard rock into springs of water.

Psalm 115

Not to us, LORD, not to us
but to your name be the glory,
because of your love and faithfulness.

Why do the nations say,
"Where is their God?"

Our God is in heaven;
he does whatever pleases him.

But their idols are silver and gold,
made by human hands.

They have mouths, but cannot speak,
eyes, but cannot see.

They have ears, but cannot hear,
noses, but cannot smell.

They have hands, but cannot feel,
feet, but cannot walk,
nor can they utter a sound with their throats.

Those who make them will be like them,
and so will all who trust in them.

All you Israelites, trust in the Lord—
he is their help and shield.

House of Aaron, trust in the Lord—
he is their help and shield.

You who fear him, trust in the Lord—
he is their help and shield.

The Lord remembers us and will bless us:
He will bless his people Israel,
he will bless the house of Aaron,

he will bless those who fear the Lord—
small and great alike.

May the Lord cause you to flourish,
both you and your children.

May you be blessed by the Lord,
the Maker of heaven and earth.

The highest heavens belong to the Lord,
but the earth he has given to mankind.

It is not the dead who praise the Lord,
those who go down to the place of silence;

it is we who extol the Lord,
both now and forevermore.

Praise the Lord.

Psalm 116

I love the Lord, for he heard my voice;
he heard my cry for mercy.

Because he turned his ear to me,
I will call on him as long as I live.

The cords of death entangled me,
the anguish of the grave came over me;
I was overcome by distress and sorrow.

Then I called on the name of the LORD:
"LORD, save me!"

The LORD is gracious and righteous;
our God is full of compassion.

The LORD protects the unwary;
when I was brought low, he saved me.

Return to your rest, my soul,
for the LORD has been good to you.

For you, LORD, have delivered me
    from death,
my eyes from tears,
my feet from stumbling,

that I may walk before the LORD
in the land of the living.

I trusted in the LORD when I said,
"I am greatly afflicted";

in my alarm I said,
"Everyone is a liar."

What shall I return to the LORD
for all his goodness to me?

I will lift up the cup of salvation
and call on the name of the LORD.

I will fulfill my vows to the LORD
in the presence of all his people.

Precious in the sight of the LORD
is the death of his faithful servants.

Truly I am your servant, LORD;
I serve you just as my mother did;
you have freed me from my chains.

I will sacrifice a thank offering to you
and call on the name of the LORD.

I will fulfill my vows to the LORD
in the presence of all his people,

in the courts of the house of the Lord —
in your midst, Jerusalem.

Praise the Lord.

Psalm 117

Praise the Lord, all you nations;
extol him, all you peoples.

For great is his love toward us,
and the faithfulness of the Lord endures forever.

Praise the Lord.

Psalm 118

Give thanks to the Lord, for he is good;
his love endures forever.

Let Israel say:
"His love endures forever."

Let the house of Aaron say:
"His love endures forever."

Let those who fear the Lord say:
"His love endures forever."

When hard pressed, I cried to the Lord;
he brought me into a spacious place.

The Lord is with me; I will not be afraid.
What can mere mortals do to me?

The Lord is with me; he is my helper.
I look in triumph on my enemies.

It is better to take refuge in the Lord
than to trust in humans.

It is better to take refuge in the Lord
than to trust in princes.

All the nations surrounded me,
but in the name of the Lord I cut them down.

They surrounded me on every side,
but in the name of the Lord I cut them down.

They swarmed around me like bees,
but they were consumed as quickly as burning thorns;
in the name of the Lord I cut them down.

I was pushed back and about to fall,
but the Lord helped me.

The Lord is my strength and my defense;
he has become my salvation.

Shouts of joy and victory
resound in the tents of the righteous:

"The Lord's right hand has done mighty things!
The Lord's right hand is lifted high;
the Lord's right hand has done mighty things!"

I will not die but live,
and will proclaim what the Lord has done.

The Lord has chastened me severely,
but he has not given me over to death.

Open for me the gates of the righteous;
I will enter and give thanks to the Lord.

This is the gate of the Lord
through which the righteous may enter.

I will give you thanks, for you answered me;
you have become my salvation.

The stone the builders rejected
has become the cornerstone;

the Lord has done this,
and it is marvelous in our eyes.

The Lord has done it this very day;
let us rejoice today and be glad.

Lord, save us!
Lord, grant us success!

Blessed is he who comes in the name of the Lord.
From the house of the Lord we bless you.

The Lord is God,
and he has made his light shine on us.

With boughs in hand, join in the festal procession
up to the horns of the altar.

You are my God, and I will praise you;
you are my God, and I will exalt you.

Give thanks to the Lord, for he is good;
his love endures forever.

Psalm 119

Blessed are those whose ways are blameless,
who walk according to the law of the Lord.

Blessed are those who keep his statutes
and seek him with all their heart—

they do no wrong
but follow his ways.

You have laid down precepts
that are to be fully obeyed.

Oh, that my ways were steadfast
in obeying your decrees!

Then I would not be put to shame
when I consider all your commands.

I will praise you with an upright heart
as I learn your righteous laws.

I will obey your decrees;
do not utterly forsake me.

How can a young person stay on the path of purity?
By living according to your word.

I seek you with all my heart;
do not let me stray from your commands.

I have hidden your word in my heart
that I might not sin against you.

Praise be to you, Lord;
teach me your decrees.

With my lips I recount
all the laws that come from your mouth.

I rejoice in following your statutes
as one rejoices in great riches.

I meditate on your precepts
and consider your ways.

I delight in your decrees;
I will not neglect your word.

Be good to your servant while I live,
that I may obey your word.

Open my eyes that I may see
wonderful things in your law.

I am a stranger on earth;
do not hide your commands from me.

My soul is consumed with longing
for your laws at all times.

You rebuke the arrogant, who are accursed,
those who stray from your commands.

Remove from me their scorn and contempt,
for I keep your statutes.

Though rulers sit together and slander me,
your servant will meditate on your decrees.

Your statutes are my delight;
they are my counselors.

I am laid low in the dust;
preserve my life according to your word.

I gave an account of my ways and you answered me;
teach me your decrees.

Cause me to understand the way of your precepts,
that I may meditate on your wonderful deeds.

My soul is weary with sorrow;
strengthen me according to your word.

Keep me from deceitful ways;
be gracious to me and teach me your law.

I have chosen the way of faithfulness;
I have set my heart on your laws.

I hold fast to your statutes, Lord;
do not let me be put to shame.

I run in the path of your commands,
for you have broadened my understanding.

Teach me, Lord, the way of your decrees,
that I may follow it to the end.

Give me understanding, so that I may keep your law
and obey it with all my heart.

Direct me in the path of your commands,
for there I find delight.

Turn my heart toward your statutes
and not toward selfish gain.

Turn my eyes away from worthless things;
preserve my life according to your word.

Fulfill your promise to your servant,
so that you may be feared.

Take away the disgrace I dread,
for your laws are good.

How I long for your precepts!
In your righteousness preserve my life.

May your unfailing love come to me, Lord,
your salvation, according to your promise;

then I can answer anyone who taunts me,
for I trust in your word.

Never take your word of truth from my mouth,
for I have put my hope in your laws.

I will always obey your law,
for ever and ever.

I will walk about in freedom,
for I have sought out your precepts.

I will speak of your statutes before kings
and will not be put to shame,

for I delight in your commands
because I love them.

I reach out for your commands, which I love,
that I may meditate on your decrees.

Remember your word to your servant,
for you have given me hope.

My comfort in my suffering is this:
Your promise preserves my life.

The arrogant mock me unmercifully,
but I do not turn from your law.

I remember, Lord, your ancient laws,
and I find comfort in them.

Indignation grips me because of the wicked,
who have forsaken your law.

Your decrees are the theme of my song
wherever I lodge.

In the night, Lord, I remember your name,
that I may keep your law.

This has been my practice:
I obey your precepts.

You are my portion, LORD;
I have promised to obey your words.

I have sought your face with all my heart;
be gracious to me according to your promise.

I have considered my ways
and have turned my steps to your statutes.

I will hasten and not delay
to obey your commands.

Though the wicked bind me with ropes,
I will not forget your law.

At midnight I rise to give you thanks
for your righteous laws.

I am a friend to all who fear you,
to all who follow your precepts.

The earth is filled with your love, LORD;
teach me your decrees.

Do good to your servant
according to your word, LORD.

Teach me knowledge and good judgment,
for I trust your commands.

Before I was afflicted I went astray,
but now I obey your word.

You are good, and what you do is good;
teach me your decrees.

Though the arrogant have smeared me with lies,
I keep your precepts with all my heart.

Their hearts are callous and unfeeling,
but I delight in your law.

It was good for me to be afflicted
so that I might learn your decrees.

The law from your mouth is more precious to me
than thousands of pieces of silver and gold.

Your hands made me and formed me;
give me understanding to learn your commands.

May those who fear you rejoice when they see me,
for I have put my hope in your word.

I know, LORD, that your laws are righteous,
and that in faithfulness you have afflicted me.

May your unfailing love be my comfort,
according to your promise to your servant.

Let your compassion come to me that I may live,
for your law is my delight.

May the arrogant be put to shame for wronging me
    without cause;
but I will meditate on your precepts.

May those who fear you turn to me,
those who understand your statutes.

May I wholeheartedly follow your decrees,
that I may not be put to shame.

My soul faints with longing for your salvation,
but I have put my hope in your word.

My eyes fail, looking for your promise;
I say, "When will you comfort me?"

Though I am like a wineskin in the smoke,
I do not forget your decrees.

How long must your servant wait?
When will you punish my persecutors?

The arrogant dig pits to trap me,
contrary to your law.

All your commands are trustworthy;
help me, for I am being persecuted without cause.

They almost wiped me from the earth,
but I have not forsaken your precepts.

In your unfailing love preserve my life,
that I may obey the statutes of your mouth.

Your word, Lord, is eternal;
it stands firm in the heavens.

Your faithfulness continues through all generations;
you established the earth, and it endures.

Your laws endure to this day,
for all things serve you.

If your law had not been my delight,
I would have perished in my affliction.

I will never forget your precepts,
for by them you have preserved my life.

Save me, for I am yours;
I have sought out your precepts.

The wicked are waiting to destroy me,
but I will ponder your statutes.

To all perfection I see a limit,
but your commands are boundless.

Oh, how I love your law!
I meditate on it all day long.

Your commands are always with me
and make me wiser than my enemies.

I have more insight than all my teachers,
for I meditate on your statutes.

I have more understanding than the elders,
for I obey your precepts.

I have kept my feet from every evil path
so that I might obey your word.

I have not departed from your laws,
for you yourself have taught me.

How sweet are your words to my taste,
sweeter than honey to my mouth!

I gain understanding from your precepts;
therefore I hate every wrong path.

Your word is a lamp for my feet,
a light on my path.

I have taken an oath and confirmed it,
that I will follow your righteous laws.

I have suffered much;
preserve my life, Lord, according to your word.

Accept, Lord, the willing praise of my mouth,
and teach me your laws.

Though I constantly take my life in my hands,
I will not forget your law.

The wicked have set a snare for me,
but I have not strayed from your precepts.

Your statutes are my heritage forever;
they are the joy of my heart.

My heart is set on keeping your decrees
to the very end.

I hate double-minded people,
but I love your law.

You are my refuge and my shield;
I have put my hope in your word.

Away from me, you evildoers,
that I may keep the commands of my God!

Sustain me, my God, according to your promise,
     and I will live;
do not let my hopes be dashed.

Uphold me, and I will be delivered;
I will always have regard for your decrees.

You reject all who stray from your decrees,
for their delusions come to nothing.

All the wicked of the earth you discard like dross;
therefore I love your statutes.

My flesh trembles in fear of you;
I stand in awe of your laws.

I have done what is righteous and just;
do not leave me to my oppressors.

Ensure your servant's well-being;
do not let the arrogant oppress me.

My eyes fail, looking for your salvation,
looking for your righteous promise.

Deal with your servant according to your love
and teach me your decrees.

I am your servant; give me discernment
that I may understand your statutes.

It is time for you to act, Lord;
your law is being broken.

Because I love your commands
more than gold, more than pure gold,

and because I consider all your precepts right,
I hate every wrong path.

Your statutes are wonderful;
therefore I obey them.

The unfolding of your words gives light;
it gives understanding to the simple.

I open my mouth and pant,
longing for your commands.

Turn to me and have mercy on me,
as you always do to those who love your name.

Direct my footsteps according to your word;
let no sin rule over me.

Redeem me from human oppression,
that I may obey your precepts.

Make your face shine on your servant
and teach me your decrees.

Streams of tears flow from my eyes,
for your law is not obeyed.

You are righteous, Lord,
and your laws are right.

The statutes you have laid down are righteous;
they are fully trustworthy.

My zeal wears me out,
for my enemies ignore your words.

Your promises have been thoroughly tested,
and your servant loves them.

Though I am lowly and despised,
I do not forget your precepts.

Your righteousness is everlasting
and your law is true.

Trouble and distress have come upon me,
but your commands give me delight.

Your statutes are always righteous;
give me understanding that I may live.

I call with all my heart; answer me, Lord,
and I will obey your decrees.

I call out to you; save me
and I will keep your statutes.

I rise before dawn and cry for help;
I have put my hope in your word.

My eyes stay open through the watches of the night,
that I may meditate on your promises.

Hear my voice in accordance with your love;
preserve my life, Lord, according to your laws.

Those who devise wicked schemes are near,
but they are far from your law.

Yet you are near, Lord,
and all your commands are true.

Long ago I learned from your statutes
that you established them to last forever.

Look on my suffering and deliver me,
for I have not forgotten your law.

Defend my cause and redeem me;
preserve my life according to your promise.

Salvation is far from the wicked,
for they do not seek out your decrees.

Your compassion, LORD, is great;
preserve my life according to your laws.

Many are the foes who persecute me,
but I have not turned from your statutes.

I look on the faithless with loathing,
for they do not obey your word.

See how I love your precepts;
preserve my life, LORD, in accordance with your love.

All your words are true;
all your righteous laws are eternal.

Rulers persecute me without cause,
but my heart trembles at your word.

I rejoice in your promise
like one who finds great spoil.

I hate and detest falsehood
but I love your law.

Seven times a day I praise you
for your righteous laws.

Great peace have those who love your law,
and nothing can make them stumble.

I wait for your salvation, LORD,
and I follow your commands.

I obey your statutes,
for I love them greatly.

I obey your precepts and your statutes,
for all my ways are known to you.

May my cry come before you, LORD;
give me understanding according to your word.

May my supplication come before you;
deliver me according to your promise.

May my lips overflow with praise,
for you teach me your decrees.

May my tongue sing of your word,
for all your commands are righteous.

May your hand be ready to help me,
for I have chosen your precepts.

I long for your salvation, Lord,
and your law gives me delight.

Let me live that I may praise you,
and may your laws sustain me.

I have strayed like a lost sheep.
Seek your servant,
for I have not forgotten your commands.

Psalm 120

A song of ascents.

I call on the Lord in my distress,
and he answers me.

Save me, Lord,
from lying lips
and from deceitful tongues.

What will he do to you,
and what more besides,
you deceitful tongue?

He will punish you with a warrior's
    sharp arrows,
with burning coals of the broom bush.

Woe to me that I dwell in Meshek,
that I live among the tents of Kedar!

Too long have I lived
among those who hate peace.

I am for peace;
but when I speak, they are for war.

Psalm 121

A song of ascents.

I lift up my eyes to the mountains—
where does my help come from?

My help comes from the LORD,
the Maker of heaven and earth.

He will not let your foot slip—
he who watches over you will not slumber;
indeed, he who watches over Israel
will neither slumber nor sleep.

The LORD watches over you—
the LORD is your shade at your right hand;
the sun will not harm you by day,
nor the moon by night.

The LORD will keep you from all harm—
he will watch over your life;
the LORD will watch over your coming and going
both now and forevermore.

Psalm 122

A song of ascents. Of David.

I rejoiced with those who said to me,
"Let us go to the house of the LORD."
Our feet are standing
in your gates, Jerusalem.

Jerusalem is built like a city
that is closely compacted together.
That is where the tribes go up—
the tribes of the LORD—
to praise the name of the LORD
according to the statute given to Israel.
There stand the thrones for judgment,
the thrones of the house of David.

Pray for the peace of Jerusalem:
"May those who love you be secure.
May there be peace within your walls
and security within your citadels."
For the sake of my family and friends,
I will say, "Peace be within you."
For the sake of the house of the LORD our God,
I will seek your prosperity.

Psalm 123

A song of ascents.

I lift up my eyes to you,
   to you who sit enthroned in heaven.
As the eyes of slaves look to the hand
      of their master,
as the eyes of a female slave look to the hand
      of her mistress,
so our eyes look to the Lord our God,
   till he shows us his mercy.

Have mercy on us, Lord, have mercy on us,
   for we have endured no end of contempt.
We have endured no end
   of ridicule from the arrogant,
   of contempt from the proud.

Psalm 124

A song of ascents. Of David.

If the Lord had not been on our side—
   let Israel say—
if the Lord had not been on our side
   when people attacked us,
they would have swallowed us alive
   when their anger flared against us;
the flood would have engulfed us,
   the torrent would have swept over us,
the raging waters
   would have swept us away.

Praise be to the Lord,
   who has not let us be torn by their teeth.
We have escaped like a bird
   from the fowler's snare;
the snare has been broken,
   and we have escaped.
Our help is in the name of the Lord,
   the Maker of heaven and earth.

Psalm 125

A song of ascents.

Those who trust in the LORD are like Mount Zion,
which cannot be shaken but endures forever.

As the mountains surround Jerusalem,
so the LORD surrounds his people
both now and forevermore.

The scepter of the wicked will not remain
over the land allotted to the righteous,

for then the righteous might use
their hands to do evil.

LORD, do good to those who are good,
to those who are upright in heart.

But those who turn to crooked ways
the LORD will banish with the evildoers.

Peace be on Israel.

Psalm 126

A song of ascents.

When the LORD restored the fortunes of Zion,
we were like those who dreamed.

Our mouths were filled with laughter,
our tongues with songs of joy.

Then it was said among the nations,
"The LORD has done great things for them."

The LORD has done great things for us,
and we are filled with joy.

Restore our fortunes, LORD,
like streams in the Negev.

Those who sow with tears
will reap with songs of joy.

Those who go out weeping,
carrying seed to sow,

will return with songs of joy,
carrying sheaves with them.

A song of ascents. Of Solomon.

Unless the Lord builds the house,
the builders labor in vain.
Unless the Lord watches over the city,
the guards stand watch in vain.
In vain you rise early
and stay up late,
toiling for food to eat —
for he grants sleep to those he loves.

Children are a heritage from the Lord,
offspring a reward from him.
Like arrows in the hands of a warrior
are children born in one's youth.
Blessed is the man
whose quiver is full of them.
They will not be put to shame
when they contend with their opponents in court.

A song of ascents.

Blessed are all who fear the Lord,
who walk in obedience to him.
You will eat the fruit of your labor;
blessings and prosperity will be yours.
Your wife will be like a fruitful vine
within your house;
your children will be like olive shoots
around your table.
Yes, this will be the blessing
for the man who fears the Lord.

May the Lord bless you from Zion;
may you see the prosperity of Jerusalem
all the days of your life.
May you live to see your children's children —
peace be on Israel.

Psalm 129

A song of ascents.

"They have greatly oppressed me from my youth,"
let Israel say;
"they have greatly oppressed me from my youth,
but they have not gained the victory over me.

Plowmen have plowed my back
and made their furrows long.
But the Lord is righteous;
he has cut me free from the cords of the wicked."

May all who hate Zion
be turned back in shame.
May they be like grass on the roof,
which withers before it can grow;

a reaper cannot fill his hands with it,
nor one who gathers fill his arms.
May those who pass by not say to them,
"The blessing of the Lord be on you;
we bless you in the name of the Lord."

Psalm 130

A song of ascents.

Out of the depths I cry to you, Lord;
Lord, hear my voice.
Let your ears be attentive
to my cry for mercy.

If you, Lord, kept a record of sins,
Lord, who could stand?
But with you there is forgiveness,
so that we can, with reverence, serve you.

I wait for the Lord, my whole being waits,
and in his word I put my hope.
I wait for the Lord
more than watchmen wait for the morning,
more than watchmen wait for the morning.

Israel, put your hope in the LORD,
for with the LORD is unfailing love
and with him is full redemption.
He himself will redeem Israel
from all their sins.

Psalm 131

A song of ascents. Of David.

My heart is not proud, LORD,
my eyes are not haughty;
I do not concern myself with great matters
or things too wonderful for me.

But I have calmed and quieted myself,
I am like a weaned child with its mother;
like a weaned child I am content.

Israel, put your hope in the LORD
both now and forevermore.

Psalm 132

A song of ascents.

LORD, remember David
and all his self-denial.

He swore an oath to the LORD,
he made a vow to the Mighty One of Jacob:

"I will not enter my house
or go to my bed,

I will allow no sleep to my eyes
or slumber to my eyelids,

till I find a place for the LORD,
a dwelling for the Mighty One of Jacob."

We heard it in Ephrathah,
we came upon it in the fields of Jaar:

"Let us go to his dwelling place,
let us worship at his footstool, saying,

'Arise, LORD, and come to your resting place,
you and the ark of your might.

May your priests be clothed with your righteousness;
may your faithful people sing for joy.' "

For the sake of your servant David,
do not reject your anointed one.

The Lord swore an oath to David,
a sure oath he will not revoke:
"One of your own descendants
I will place on your throne.

If your sons keep my covenant
and the statutes I teach them,

then their sons will sit
on your throne for ever and ever."

For the Lord has chosen Zion,
he has desired it for his dwelling, saying,

"This is my resting place for ever and ever;
here I will sit enthroned, for I have desired it.

I will bless her with abundant provisions;
her poor I will satisfy with food.

I will clothe her priests with salvation,
and her faithful people will ever sing for joy.

"Here I will make a horn grow for David
and set up a lamp for my anointed one.

I will clothe his enemies with shame,
but his head will be adorned with a radiant crown."

Psalm 133

A song of ascents. Of David.

How good and pleasant it is
when God's people live together in unity!

It is like precious oil poured on the head,
running down on the beard,

running down on Aaron's beard,
down on the collar of his robe.

It is as if the dew of Hermon
were falling on Mount Zion.

For there the Lord bestows his blessing,
even life forevermore.

Psalm 134

A song of ascents.

Praise the Lord, all you servants of the Lord
who minister by night in the house of the Lord.
Lift up your hands in the sanctuary
and praise the Lord.

May the Lord bless you from Zion,
he who is the Maker of heaven and earth.

Psalm 135

Praise the Lord.

Praise the name of the Lord;
praise him, you servants of the Lord,
you who minister in the house of the Lord,
in the courts of the house of our God.

Praise the Lord, for the Lord is good;
sing praise to his name, for that is pleasant.
For the Lord has chosen Jacob to be his own,
Israel to be his treasured possession.

I know that the Lord is great,
that our Lord is greater than all gods.
The Lord does whatever pleases him,
in the heavens and on the earth,
in the seas and all their depths.

He makes clouds rise from the ends of the earth;
he sends lightning with the rain
and brings out the wind from his storehouses.

He struck down the firstborn of Egypt,
the firstborn of people and animals.
He sent his signs and wonders into your midst, Egypt,
against Pharaoh and all his servants.
He struck down many nations
and killed mighty kings—
Sihon king of the Amorites,
Og king of Bashan,
and all the kings of Canaan—

and he gave their land as an inheritance,
an inheritance to his people Israel.

Your name, Lord, endures forever,
your renown, Lord, through all generations.

For the Lord will vindicate his people
and have compassion on his servants.

The idols of the nations are silver and gold,
made by human hands.

They have mouths, but cannot speak,
eyes, but cannot see.

They have ears, but cannot hear,
nor is there breath in their mouths.

Those who make them will be like them,
and so will all who trust in them.

All you Israelites, praise the Lord;
house of Aaron, praise the Lord;

house of Levi, praise the Lord;
you who fear him, praise the Lord.

Praise be to the Lord from Zion,
to him who dwells in Jerusalem.

Praise the Lord.

Psalm 136

Give thanks to the Lord, for he is good.
His love endures forever.

Give thanks to the God of gods.
His love endures forever.

Give thanks to the Lord of lords:
His love endures forever.

to him who alone does great wonders,
His love endures forever.

who by his understanding made the heavens,
His love endures forever.

who spread out the earth upon the waters,
His love endures forever.

who made the great lights—
His love endures forever.

the sun to govern the day,
His love endures forever.

the moon and stars to govern the night;
His love endures forever.

to him who struck down the firstborn of Egypt
His love endures forever.

and brought Israel out from among them
His love endures forever.

with a mighty hand and outstretched arm;
His love endures forever.

to him who divided the Red Sea asunder
His love endures forever.

and brought Israel through the midst of it,
His love endures forever.

but swept Pharaoh and his army into
the Red Sea;
His love endures forever.

to him who led his people through
the wilderness;
His love endures forever.

to him who struck down great kings,
His love endures forever.

and killed mighty kings —
His love endures forever.

Sihon king of the Amorites
His love endures forever.

and Og king of Bashan —
His love endures forever.

and gave their land as an inheritance,
His love endures forever.

an inheritance to his servant Israel.
His love endures forever.

He remembered us in our low estate
His love endures forever.

and freed us from our enemies.
His love endures forever.

He gives food to every creature.
His love endures forever.

Give thanks to the God of heaven.
His love endures forever.

Psalm 137

By the rivers of Babylon we sat and wept
when we remembered Zion.

There on the poplars
we hung our harps,

for there our captors asked us for songs,
our tormentors demanded songs of joy;
they said, "Sing us one of the songs of Zion!"

How can we sing the songs of the LORD
while in a foreign land?

If I forget you, Jerusalem,
may my right hand forget its skill.

May my tongue cling to the roof of my mouth
if I do not remember you,

if I do not consider Jerusalem
my highest joy.

Remember, LORD, what the Edomites did
on the day Jerusalem fell.

"Tear it down," they cried,
"tear it down to its foundations!"

Daughter Babylon, doomed to destruction,
happy is the one who repays you
according to what you have done to us.

Happy is the one who seizes your infants
and dashes them against the rocks.

Psalm 138

Of David.

I will praise you, LORD, with all my heart;
before the "gods" I will sing your praise.

I will bow down toward your holy temple
and will praise your name
for your unfailing love and your faithfulness,

for you have so exalted your solemn decree
that it surpasses your fame.

When I called, you answered me;
you greatly emboldened me.

May all the kings of the earth praise you, Lord,
when they hear what you have decreed.

May they sing of the ways of the Lord,
for the glory of the Lord is great.

Though the Lord is exalted, he looks kindly on the lowly;
though lofty, he sees them from afar.

Though I walk in the midst of trouble,
you preserve my life.

You stretch out your hand against the anger of my foes;
with your right hand you save me.

The Lord will vindicate me;
your love, Lord, endures forever—
do not abandon the works of your hands.

Psalm 139

For the director of music. Of David. A psalm.

You have searched me, Lord,
and you know me.

You know when I sit and when I rise;
you perceive my thoughts from afar.

You discern my going out and my lying down;
you are familiar with all my ways.

Before a word is on my tongue
you, Lord, know it completely.

You hem me in behind and before,
and you lay your hand upon me.

Such knowledge is too wonderful for me,
too lofty for me to attain.

Where can I go from your Spirit?
Where can I flee from your presence?

If I go up to the heavens, you are there;
if I make my bed in the depths, you are there.

If I rise on the wings of the dawn,
if I settle on the far side of the sea,

even there your hand will guide me,
your right hand will hold me fast.

If I say, "Surely the darkness will hide me
and the light become night around me,"

even the darkness will not be dark to you;
the night will shine like the day,
for darkness is as light to you.

For you created my inmost being;
you knit me together in my mother's womb.

I praise you because I am fearfully and wonderfully made;
your works are wonderful,
I know that full well.

My frame was not hidden from you
when I was made in the secret place,
when I was woven together in the depths of the earth.

Your eyes saw my unformed body;
all the days ordained for me were written in your book
before one of them came to be.

How precious to me are your thoughts, God!
How vast is the sum of them!

Were I to count them,
they would outnumber the grains of sand—
when I awake, I am still with you.

If only you, God, would slay the wicked!
Away from me, you who are bloodthirsty!

They speak of you with evil intent;
your adversaries misuse your name.

Do I not hate those who hate you, Lord,
and abhor those who are in rebellion against you?

I have nothing but hatred for them;
I count them my enemies.

Search me, God, and know my heart;
test me and know my anxious thoughts.

See if there is any offensive way in me,
and lead me in the way everlasting.

Psalm 140

For the director of music. A psalm of David.

Rescue me, Lord, from evildoers;
protect me from the violent,

who devise evil plans in their hearts
and stir up war every day.

They make their tongues as sharp as a serpent's;
the poison of vipers is on their lips.

Keep me safe, Lord, from the hands of the wicked;
protect me from the violent,
who devise ways to trip my feet.

The arrogant have hidden a snare for me;
they have spread out the cords of their net
and have set traps for me along my path.

I say to the Lord, "You are my God."
Hear, Lord, my cry for mercy.

Sovereign Lord, my strong deliverer,
you shield my head in the day of battle.

Do not grant the wicked their desires, Lord;
do not let their plans succeed.

Those who surround me proudly rear their heads;
may the mischief of their lips engulf them.

May burning coals fall on them;
may they be thrown into the fire,
into miry pits, never to rise.

May slanderers not be established in the land;
may disaster hunt down the violent.

I know that the Lord secures justice for the poor
and upholds the cause of the needy.

Surely the righteous will praise your name,
and the upright will live in your presence.

Psalm 141

A psalm of David.

I call to you, Lord, come quickly to me;
hear me when I call to you.

May my prayer be set before you like incense;
may the lifting up of my hands be like the evening
    sacrifice.

Set a guard over my mouth, Lord;
keep watch over the door of my lips.

Do not let my heart be drawn to what is evil
so that I take part in wicked deeds

along with those who are evildoers;
do not let me eat their delicacies.

Let a righteous man strike me — that is a kindness;
let him rebuke me — that is oil on my head.
My head will not refuse it,
for my prayer will still be against the deeds
    of evildoers.

Their rulers will be thrown down from the cliffs,
and the wicked will learn that my words were well
    spoken.
They will say, "As one plows and breaks up the earth,
so our bones have been scattered at the mouth
    of the grave."

But my eyes are fixed on you, Sovereign Lord;
in you I take refuge — do not give me over to death.
Keep me safe from the traps set by evildoers,
from the snares they have laid for me.
Let the wicked fall into their own nets,
while I pass by in safety.

Psalm 142

A maskil of David. When he was in the cave. A prayer.

I cry aloud to the Lord;
I lift up my voice to the Lord for mercy.
I pour out before him my complaint;
before him I tell my trouble.

When my spirit grows faint within me,
it is you who watch over my way.
In the path where I walk
people have hidden a snare for me.
Look and see, there is no one at my right hand;
no one is concerned for me.
I have no refuge;
no one cares for my life.

I cry to you, Lord;
I say, "You are my refuge,
my portion in the land of the living."

Listen to my cry,
for I am in desperate need;

rescue me from those who pursue me,
for they are too strong for me.

Set me free from my prison,
that I may praise your name.

Then the righteous will gather about me
because of your goodness to me.

Psalm 143

A psalm of David.

LORD, hear my prayer,
listen to my cry for mercy;

in your faithfulness and righteousness
come to my relief.

Do not bring your servant into judgment,
for no one living is righteous before you.

The enemy pursues me,
he crushes me to the ground;

he makes me dwell in the darkness
like those long dead.

So my spirit grows faint within me;
my heart within me is dismayed.

I remember the days of long ago;
I meditate on all your works
and consider what your hands have done.

I spread out my hands to you;
I thirst for you like a parched land.

Answer me quickly, LORD;
my spirit fails.

Do not hide your face from me
or I will be like those who go down to the pit.

Let the morning bring me word of your
unfailing love,
for I have put my trust in you.

Show me the way I should go,
for to you I entrust my life.

Rescue me from my enemies, LORD,
for I hide myself in you.

Teach me to do your will,
for you are my God;

may your good Spirit
lead me on level ground.

For your name's sake, Lord, preserve my life;
in your righteousness, bring me out of trouble.

In your unfailing love, silence my enemies;
destroy all my foes,
for I am your servant.

Psalm 144

Of David.

Praise be to the Lord my Rock,
who trains my hands for war,
my fingers for battle.

He is my loving God and my fortress,
my stronghold and my deliverer,

my shield, in whom I take refuge,
who subdues peoples under me.

Lord, what are human beings that you care for them,
mere mortals that you think of them?

They are like a breath;
their days are like a fleeting shadow.

Part your heavens, Lord, and come down;
touch the mountains, so that they smoke.

Send forth lightning and scatter the enemy;
shoot your arrows and rout them.

Reach down your hand from on high;
deliver me and rescue me

from the mighty waters,
from the hands of foreigners

whose mouths are full of lies,
whose right hands are deceitful.

I will sing a new song to you, my God;
on the ten-stringed lyre I will make music to you,

to the One who gives victory to kings,
who delivers his servant David.

From the deadly sword deliver me;
rescue me from the hands of foreigners

whose mouths are full of lies,
whose right hands are deceitful.

Then our sons in their youth
will be like well-nurtured plants,

and our daughters will be like pillars
carved to adorn a palace.

Our barns will be filled
with every kind of provision.

Our sheep will increase by thousands,
by tens of thousands in our fields;
our oxen will draw heavy loads.

There will be no breaching of walls,
no going into captivity,
no cry of distress in our streets.

Blessed is the people of whom this is true;
blessed is the people whose God is the LORD.

Psalm 145

A psalm of praise. Of David.

I will exalt you, my God the King;
I will praise your name for ever and ever.

Every day I will praise you
and extol your name for ever and ever.

Great is the LORD and most worthy of praise;
his greatness no one can fathom.

One generation commends your works to another;
they tell of your mighty acts.

They speak of the glorious splendor of your majesty —
and I will meditate on your wonderful works.

They tell of the power of your awesome works —
and I will proclaim your great deeds.

They celebrate your abundant goodness
and joyfully sing of your righteousness.

The LORD is gracious and compassionate,
slow to anger and rich in love.

The Lord is good to all;
he has compassion on all he has made.

All your works praise you, Lord;
your faithful people extol you.

They tell of the glory of your kingdom
and speak of your might,

so that all people may know of your mighty acts
and the glorious splendor of your kingdom.

Your kingdom is an everlasting kingdom,
and your dominion endures through all generations.

The Lord is trustworthy in all he promises
and faithful in all he does.

The Lord upholds all who fall
and lifts up all who are bowed down.

The eyes of all look to you,
and you give them their food at the proper time.

You open your hand
and satisfy the desires of every living thing.

The Lord is righteous in all his ways
and faithful in all he does.

The Lord is near to all who call on him,
to all who call on him in truth.

He fulfills the desires of those who fear him;
he hears their cry and saves them.

The Lord watches over all who love him,
but all the wicked he will destroy.

My mouth will speak in praise of the Lord.
Let every creature praise his holy name
for ever and ever.

Psalm 146

Praise the Lord.

Praise the Lord, my soul.

I will praise the Lord all my life;
I will sing praise to my God as long as I live.

Do not put your trust in princes,
in human beings, who cannot save.

When their spirit departs, they return
    to the ground;
on that very day their plans come to nothing.

Blessed are those whose help is the God of Jacob,
whose hope is in the LORD their God.

He is the Maker of heaven and earth,
the sea, and everything in them—
he remains faithful forever.

He upholds the cause of the oppressed
and gives food to the hungry.

The LORD sets prisoners free,
the LORD gives sight to the blind,
the LORD lifts up those who are bowed down,
the LORD loves the righteous.

The LORD watches over the foreigner
and sustains the fatherless and the widow,
but he frustrates the ways of the wicked.

The LORD reigns forever,
your God, O Zion, for all generations.

Praise the LORD.

Psalm 147

Praise the LORD.

How good it is to sing praises to our God,
how pleasant and fitting to praise him!

The LORD builds up Jerusalem;
he gathers the exiles of Israel.

He heals the brokenhearted
and binds up their wounds.

He determines the number of the stars
and calls them each by name.

Great is our Lord and mighty in power;
his understanding has no limit.

The LORD sustains the humble
but casts the wicked to the ground.

Sing to the LORD with grateful praise;
make music to our God on the harp.

He covers the sky with clouds;
he supplies the earth with rain
and makes grass grow on the hills.

He provides food for the cattle
and for the young ravens when they call.

His pleasure is not in the strength
 of the horse,
nor his delight in the legs of the warrior;

the LORD delights in those who fear him,
who put their hope in his unfailing love.

Extol the LORD, Jerusalem;
praise your God, Zion.

He strengthens the bars of your gates
and blesses your people within you.

He grants peace to your borders
and satisfies you with the finest of wheat.

He sends his command to the earth;
his word runs swiftly.

He spreads the snow like wool
and scatters the frost like ashes.

He hurls down his hail like pebbles.
Who can withstand his icy blast?

He sends his word and melts them;
he stirs up his breezes, and the waters flow.

He has revealed his word to Jacob,
his laws and decrees to Israel.

He has done this for no other nation;
they do not know his laws.

Praise the LORD.

Psalm 148

Praise the LORD.

Praise the LORD from the heavens;
praise him in the heights above.

Praise him, all his angels;
praise him, all his heavenly hosts.

Praise him, sun and moon;
  praise him, all you shining stars.

Praise him, you highest heavens
  and you waters above the skies.

Let them praise the name of the LORD,
  for at his command they were created,

and he established them for ever and ever—
  he issued a decree that will never pass away.

Praise the LORD from the earth,
  you great sea creatures and all ocean depths,

lightning and hail, snow and clouds,
  stormy winds that do his bidding,

you mountains and all hills,
  fruit trees and all cedars,

wild animals and all cattle,
  small creatures and flying birds,

kings of the earth and all nations,
  you princes and all rulers on earth,

young men and women,
  old men and children.

Let them praise the name of the LORD,
  for his name alone is exalted;
  his splendor is above the earth and the heavens.

And he has raised up for his people a horn,
  the praise of all his faithful servants,
  of Israel, the people close to his heart.

Praise the LORD.

Psalm 149

Praise the LORD.

Sing to the LORD a new song,
  his praise in the assembly of his faithful people.

Let Israel rejoice in their Maker;
  let the people of Zion be glad in their King.

Let them praise his name with dancing
  and make music to him with timbrel and harp.

For the LORD takes delight in his people;
he crowns the humble with victory.

Let his faithful people rejoice in this honor
and sing for joy on their beds.

May the praise of God be in their mouths
and a double-edged sword in their hands,

to inflict vengeance on the nations
and punishment on the peoples,

to bind their kings with fetters,
their nobles with shackles of iron,

to carry out the sentence written against them—
this is the glory of all his faithful people.

Praise the LORD.

Psalm 150

Praise the LORD.

Praise God in his sanctuary;
praise him in his mighty heavens.

Praise him for his acts of power;
praise him for his surpassing greatness.

Praise him with the sounding of the trumpet,
praise him with the harp and lyre,

praise him with timbrel and dancing,
praise him with the strings and pipe,

praise him with the clash of cymbals,
praise him with resounding cymbals.

Let everything that has breath praise the LORD.

Praise the LORD.

INVITATION TO
LAMENTATIONS

When Jerusalem was conquered by the Babylonians and much of its population was deported, some of its citizens were left behind, living in terrible conditions in and around the shattered city. To express their sorrow, shame and grief over the destruction of their beloved home, they wrote songs about its desolation and about the sufferings they were witnessing and experiencing. Five of these songs have been preserved for us in the book of Lamentations. The authors' names aren't given, but tradition ascribes them to Jeremiah. Through these songs, we witness people of faith putting into words their struggle to understand how God could allow such suffering and devastation.

These songs follow a particular pattern. Each has 22 stanzas. In the first, second and fourth songs, the stanzas begin with the 22 letters of the Hebrew alphabet in consecutive order. The third song is structured almost identically, except that every line in each stanza begins with the same letter. In the fifth song, the stanzas don't start with letters in alphabetical order, but there are still 22 stanzas.

In some of the songs the city of Jerusalem, often referred to as *Zion* or *Daughter Zion*, breaks into the description of its destruction and speaks on its own behalf. And in some of the songs, the poet looks up from the city to heaven and cries out to God for mercy. Jerusalem's destruction would seem to have derailed God's entire plan of redemption. What could his people expect God to do next? There are only a few expressions of hope, but these are placed in the center of the book, to give them extra weight and importance in a situation where they're badly needed. Overall, this collection of laments also serves to remind us that expressing anguish over a broken, fallen world is a legitimate part of the biblical drama.

LAMENTATIONS

How deserted lies the city,
once so full of people!
How like a widow is she,
who once was great among the nations!
She who was queen among the provinces
has now become a slave.

Bitterly she weeps at night,
tears are on her cheeks.
Among all her lovers
there is no one to comfort her.
All her friends have betrayed her;
they have become her enemies.

After affliction and harsh labor,
Judah has gone into exile.
She dwells among the nations;
she finds no resting place.
All who pursue her have overtaken her
in the midst of her distress.

The roads to Zion mourn,
for no one comes to her appointed festivals.
All her gateways are desolate,
her priests groan,
her young women grieve,
and she is in bitter anguish.

Her foes have become her masters;
her enemies are at ease.
The Lord has brought her grief
because of her many sins.

Her children have gone into exile,
captive before the foe.

All the splendor has departed
from Daughter Zion.
Her princes are like deer
that find no pasture;
in weakness they have fled
before the pursuer.

In the days of her affliction and wandering
Jerusalem remembers all the treasures
that were hers in days of old.
When her people fell into enemy hands,
there was no one to help her.
Her enemies looked at her
and laughed at her destruction.

Jerusalem has sinned greatly
and so has become unclean.
All who honored her despise her,
for they have all seen her naked;
she herself groans
and turns away.

Her filthiness clung to her skirts;
she did not consider her future.
Her fall was astounding;
there was none to comfort her.
"Look, Lord, on my affliction,
for the enemy has triumphed."

The enemy laid hands
on all her treasures;
she saw pagan nations
enter her sanctuary —
those you had forbidden
to enter your assembly.

All her people groan
as they search for bread;
they barter their treasures for food
to keep themselves alive.

"Look, Lord, and consider,
for I am despised."

"Is it nothing to you, all you who pass by?
Look around and see.

Is any suffering like my suffering
that was inflicted on me,

that the Lord brought on me
in the day of his fierce anger?

"From on high he sent fire,
sent it down into my bones.

He spread a net for my feet
and turned me back.

He made me desolate,
faint all the day long.

"My sins have been bound into a yoke;
by his hands they were woven together.

They have been hung on my neck,
and the Lord has sapped my strength.

He has given me into the hands
of those I cannot withstand.

"The Lord has rejected
all the warriors in my midst;

he has summoned an army against me
to crush my young men.

In his winepress the Lord has trampled
Virgin Daughter Judah.

"This is why I weep
and my eyes overflow with tears.

No one is near to comfort me,
no one to restore my spirit.

My children are destitute
because the enemy has prevailed."

Zion stretches out her hands,
but there is no one to comfort her.

The Lord has decreed for Jacob
that his neighbors become his foes;

Jerusalem has become
an unclean thing among them.

"The LORD is righteous,
yet I rebelled against his command.
Listen, all you peoples;
look on my suffering.
My young men and young women
have gone into exile.

"I called to my allies
but they betrayed me.
My priests and my elders
perished in the city
while they searched for food
to keep themselves alive.

"See, LORD, how distressed I am!
I am in torment within,
and in my heart I am disturbed,
for I have been most rebellious.
Outside, the sword bereaves;
inside, there is only death.

"People have heard my groaning,
but there is no one to comfort me.
All my enemies have heard of my distress;
they rejoice at what you have done.
May you bring the day you have announced
so they may become like me.

"Let all their wickedness come before you;
deal with them
as you have dealt with me
because of all my sins.
My groans are many
and my heart is faint."

How the Lord has covered Daughter Zion
with the cloud of his anger!
He has hurled down the splendor of Israel
from heaven to earth;

he has not remembered his footstool
in the day of his anger.

Without pity the Lord has swallowed up
all the dwellings of Jacob;
in his wrath he has torn down
the strongholds of Daughter Judah.
He has brought her kingdom and its princes
down to the ground in dishonor.

In fierce anger he has cut off
every horn of Israel.
He has withdrawn his right hand
at the approach of the enemy.
He has burned in Jacob like a flaming fire
that consumes everything around it.

Like an enemy he has strung his bow;
his right hand is ready.
Like a foe he has slain
all who were pleasing to the eye;
he has poured out his wrath like fire
on the tent of Daughter Zion.

The Lord is like an enemy;
he has swallowed up Israel.
He has swallowed up all her palaces
and destroyed her strongholds.
He has multiplied mourning and lamentation
for Daughter Judah.

He has laid waste his dwelling like a garden;
he has destroyed his place of meeting.
The Lord has made Zion forget
her appointed festivals and her Sabbaths;
in his fierce anger he has spurned
both king and priest.

The Lord has rejected his altar
and abandoned his sanctuary.
He has given the walls of her palaces
into the hands of the enemy;

they have raised a shout in the house
      of the Lᴏʀᴅ
as on the day of an appointed festival.

The Lᴏʀᴅ determined to tear down
the wall around Daughter Zion.

He stretched out a measuring line
and did not withhold his hand from destroying.

He made ramparts and walls lament;
together they wasted away.

Her gates have sunk into the ground;
their bars he has broken and destroyed.

Her king and her princes are exiled
      among the nations,
the law is no more,

and her prophets no longer find
visions from the Lᴏʀᴅ.

The elders of Daughter Zion
sit on the ground in silence;

they have sprinkled dust on their heads
and put on sackcloth.

The young women of Jerusalem
have bowed their heads to the ground.

My eyes fail from weeping,
I am in torment within;

my heart is poured out on the ground
because my people are destroyed,

because children and infants faint
in the streets of the city.

They say to their mothers,
"Where is bread and wine?"

as they faint like the wounded
in the streets of the city,

as their lives ebb away
in their mothers' arms.

What can I say for you?
With what can I compare you,
Daughter Jerusalem?

To what can I liken you,
that I may comfort you,
Virgin Daughter Zion?

Your wound is as deep as the sea.
Who can heal you?

The visions of your prophets
were false and worthless;

they did not expose your sin
to ward off your captivity.

The prophecies they gave you
were false and misleading.

All who pass your way
clap their hands at you;

they scoff and shake their heads
at Daughter Jerusalem:

"Is this the city that was called
the perfection of beauty,
the joy of the whole earth?"

All your enemies open their mouths
wide against you;

they scoff and gnash their teeth
and say, "We have swallowed her up.

This is the day we have waited for;
we have lived to see it."

The Lord has done what he planned;
he has fulfilled his word,
which he decreed long ago.

He has overthrown you without pity,
he has let the enemy gloat over you,
he has exalted the horn of your foes.

The hearts of the people
cry out to the Lord.

You walls of Daughter Zion,
let your tears flow like a river
day and night;

give yourself no relief,
your eyes no rest.

Arise, cry out in the night,
as the watches of the night begin;
pour out your heart like water
in the presence of the Lord.
Lift up your hands to him
for the lives of your children,
who faint from hunger
at every street corner.

"Look, Lord, and consider:
Whom have you ever treated like this?
Should women eat their offspring,
the children they have cared for?
Should priest and prophet be killed
in the sanctuary of the Lord?

"Young and old lie together
in the dust of the streets;
my young men and young women
have fallen by the sword.
You have slain them in the day of your anger;
you have slaughtered them without pity.

"As you summon to a feast day,
so you summoned against me terrors on every side.
In the day of the Lord's anger
no one escaped or survived;
those I cared for and reared
my enemy has destroyed."

I am the man who has seen affliction
by the rod of the Lord's wrath.
He has driven me away and made me walk
in darkness rather than light;
indeed, he has turned his hand against me
again and again, all day long.

He has made my skin and my flesh grow old
and has broken my bones.
He has besieged me and surrounded me
with bitterness and hardship.

He has made me dwell in darkness
like those long dead.

He has walled me in so I cannot escape;
he has weighed me down with chains.

Even when I call out or cry for help,
he shuts out my prayer.

He has barred my way with blocks of stone;
he has made my paths crooked.

Like a bear lying in wait,
like a lion in hiding,

he dragged me from the path and mangled me
and left me without help.

He drew his bow
and made me the target for his arrows.

He pierced my heart
with arrows from his quiver.

I became the laughingstock of all my people;
they mock me in song all day long.

He has filled me with bitter herbs
and given me gall to drink.

He has broken my teeth with gravel;
he has trampled me in the dust.

I have been deprived of peace;
I have forgotten what prosperity is.

So I say, "My splendor is gone
and all that I had hoped from the LORD."

I remember my affliction and my wandering,
the bitterness and the gall.

I well remember them,
and my soul is downcast within me.

Yet this I call to mind
and therefore I have hope:

Because of the LORD's great love we
are not consumed,
for his compassions never fail.

They are new every morning;
great is your faithfulness.

I say to myself, "The LORD is my portion;
therefore I will wait for him."

The LORD is good to those whose hope is in him,
to the one who seeks him;

it is good to wait quietly
for the salvation of the LORD.

It is good for a man to bear the yoke
while he is young.

Let him sit alone in silence,
for the LORD has laid it on him.

Let him bury his face in the dust—
there may yet be hope.

Let him offer his cheek to one who would
strike him,
and let him be filled with disgrace.

For no one is cast off
by the Lord forever.

Though he brings grief, he will show compassion,
so great is his unfailing love.

For he does not willingly bring affliction
or grief to anyone.

To crush underfoot
all prisoners in the land,

to deny people their rights
before the Most High,

to deprive them of justice—
would not the Lord see such things?

Who can speak and have it happen
if the Lord has not decreed it?

Is it not from the mouth of the Most High
that both calamities and good things come?

Why should the living complain
when punished for their sins?

Let us examine our ways and test them,
and let us return to the LORD.

Let us lift up our hearts and our hands
to God in heaven, and say:

"We have sinned and rebelled
and you have not forgiven.

"You have covered yourself with anger
        and pursued us;
you have slain without pity.

You have covered yourself with a cloud
so that no prayer can get through.

You have made us scum and refuse
among the nations.

"All our enemies have opened their mouths
wide against us.

We have suffered terror and pitfalls,
ruin and destruction."

Streams of tears flow from my eyes
because my people are destroyed.

My eyes will flow unceasingly,
without relief,

until the Lord looks down
from heaven and sees.

What I see brings grief to my soul
because of all the women of my city.

Those who were my enemies without cause
hunted me like a bird.

They tried to end my life in a pit
and threw stones at me;

the waters closed over my head,
and I thought I was about to perish.

I called on your name, Lord,
from the depths of the pit.

You heard my plea: "Do not close your ears
to my cry for relief."

You came near when I called you,
and you said, "Do not fear."

You, Lord, took up my case;
you redeemed my life.

Lord, you have seen the wrong done to me.
Uphold my cause!

You have seen the depth of their
  vengeance,
all their plots against me.

LORD, you have heard their insults,
all their plots against me —

what my enemies whisper and mutter
against me all day long.

Look at them! Sitting or standing,
they mock me in their songs.

Pay them back what they deserve, LORD,
for what their hands have done.

Put a veil over their hearts,
and may your curse be on them!

Pursue them in anger and destroy them
from under the heavens of the LORD.

How the gold has lost its luster,
the fine gold become dull!
The sacred gems are scattered
at every street corner.

How the precious children of Zion,
once worth their weight in gold,

are now considered as pots of clay,
the work of a potter's hands!

Even jackals offer their breasts
to nurse their young,

but my people have become heartless
like ostriches in the desert.

Because of thirst the infant's tongue
sticks to the roof of its mouth;

the children beg for bread,
but no one gives it to them.

Those who once ate delicacies
are destitute in the streets.

Those brought up in royal purple
now lie on ash heaps.

The punishment of my people
is greater than that of Sodom,

which was overthrown in a moment
without a hand turned to help her.

Their princes were brighter than snow
and whiter than milk,

their bodies more ruddy than rubies,
their appearance like lapis lazuli.

But now they are blacker than soot;
they are not recognized in the streets.

Their skin has shriveled on their bones;
it has become as dry as a stick.

Those killed by the sword are better off
than those who die of famine;

racked with hunger, they waste away
for lack of food from the field.

With their own hands compassionate women
have cooked their own children,

who became their food
when my people were destroyed.

The Lord has given full vent to his wrath;
he has poured out his fierce anger.

He kindled a fire in Zion
that consumed her foundations.

The kings of the earth did not believe,
nor did any of the peoples of the world,

that enemies and foes could enter
the gates of Jerusalem.

But it happened because of the sins of her prophets
and the iniquities of her priests,

who shed within her
the blood of the righteous.

Now they grope through the streets
as if they were blind.

They are so defiled with blood
that no one dares to touch their garments.

"Go away! You are unclean!" people cry to them.
"Away! Away! Don't touch us!"

When they flee and wander about,
people among the nations say,
"They can stay here no longer."

The Lord himself has scattered them;
he no longer watches over them.

The priests are shown no honor,
the elders no favor.

Moreover, our eyes failed,
looking in vain for help;

from our towers we watched
for a nation that could not save us.

People stalked us at every step,
so we could not walk in our streets.

Our end was near, our days were numbered,
for our end had come.

Our pursuers were swifter
than eagles in the sky;

they chased us over the mountains
and lay in wait for us in the desert.

The Lord's anointed, our very life breath,
was caught in their traps.

We thought that under his shadow
we would live among the nations.

Rejoice and be glad, Daughter Edom,
you who live in the land of Uz.

But to you also the cup will be passed;
you will be drunk and stripped naked.

Your punishment will end, Daughter Zion;
he will not prolong your exile.

But he will punish your sin, Daughter Edom,
and expose your wickedness.

Remember, Lord, what has happened to us;
look, and see our disgrace.

Our inheritance has been turned over to strangers,
our homes to foreigners.

We have become fatherless,
our mothers are widows.

We must buy the water we drink;
our wood can be had only at a price.

Those who pursue us are at our heels;
we are weary and find no rest.

We submitted to Egypt and Assyria
to get enough bread.

Our ancestors sinned and are no more,
and we bear their punishment.

Slaves rule over us,
and there is no one to free us from their hands.

We get our bread at the risk of our lives
because of the sword in the desert.

Our skin is hot as an oven,
feverish from hunger.

Women have been violated in Zion,
and virgins in the towns of Judah.

Princes have been hung up by their hands;
elders are shown no respect.

Young men toil at the millstones;
boys stagger under loads of wood.

The elders are gone from the city gate;
the young men have stopped their music.

Joy is gone from our hearts;
our dancing has turned to mourning.

The crown has fallen from our head.
Woe to us, for we have sinned!

Because of this our hearts are faint,
because of these things our eyes grow dim

for Mount Zion, which lies desolate,
with jackals prowling over it.

You, Lord, reign forever;
your throne endures from generation
        to generation.

Why do you always forget us?
Why do you forsake us so long?

Restore us to yourself, Lᴏʀᴅ, that we
    may return;
renew our days as of old

unless you have utterly rejected us
and are angry with us beyond measure.

INVITATION TO
SONG OF SONGS

At traditional wedding celebrations in some parts of the Middle East, the bride and groom are cast in the roles of a king and queen. They sing to one another and the guests sing in their honor. The festivities include love songs along with special songs that praise the physical beauty of the bride and the handsomeness of the groom. This custom appears to have a long history. It seems to be reflected in the anthology of wedding songs that has been included in the Bible, which we know as the Song of Songs.

The songs in this collection have been arranged in such a way as to tell the story of the courtship of a man and woman, of their marriage (described as a royal wedding) and its consummation, and of the beginning of their new life together. The collection begins with a short introduction, and then it recounts six episodes in their relationship as it develops. At the end of each episode there's typically a reference to the *friends* of the man and woman. This may refer to the guests at their wedding who are helping them celebrate. These friends seem to be singing some of the songs that tell the couple's story, because at one point there's an exchange between them and the bride. In several places the bride addresses a specific group of these friends as the *daughters of Jerusalem*, probably meaning her yet-to-be-married female friends. It's not clear at every point in the collection who's speaking, but in most places we can get a good idea of who the speaker is from what they're saying and who they're speaking to.

The collection bears the title *Solomon's Song of Songs*. This can be taken to mean that Solomon, the son of David and third king of Israel, was the author of its individual songs. In this case he was likely also the person who brought them together in their present form. Since Solomon was renowned as a composer of songs, this is one good possibility. However, the phrase could also be a reference to the way that the collection, in its third main episode, refers to Solomon as the kind of glorious king the groom represents in the eyes of the bride and the guests. In that case, the individual songs may have been the work of many different composers over several centuries. They would have been used repeatedly in marriage celebrations and eventually gathered together, just as the psalms were collected after years of use in worship. In either case, the collection as a whole celebrates the delights of married love and the beauty of the human body, using vivid imagery drawn from the natural world, to show that both of these things are an integral part of the creation that God declared *very good*.

Song of Songs

S olomon's Song of Songs.

Let him kiss me with the kisses of his mouth—
for your love is more delightful than wine.

Pleasing is the fragrance of your perfumes;
your name is like perfume poured out.
No wonder the young women love you!

Take me away with you—let us hurry!
Let the king bring me into his chambers.

We rejoice and delight in you;
we will praise your love more than wine.

How right they are to adore you!

Dark am I, yet lovely,
daughters of Jerusalem,

dark like the tents of Kedar,
like the tent curtains of Solomon.

Do not stare at me because I am dark,
because I am darkened by the sun.

My mother's sons were angry with me
and made me take care of the vineyards;
my own vineyard I had to neglect.

T ell me, you whom I love,
where you graze your flock
and where you rest your sheep at midday.

Why should I be like a veiled woman
beside the flocks of your friends?

If you do not know, most beautiful of women,
follow the tracks of the sheep

and graze your young goats
by the tents of the shepherds.

I liken you, my darling, to a mare
among Pharaoh's chariot horses.
Your cheeks are beautiful with earrings,
your neck with strings of jewels.
We will make you earrings of gold,
studded with silver.

While the king was at his table,
my perfume spread its fragrance.
My beloved is to me a sachet of myrrh
resting between my breasts.
My beloved is to me a cluster of henna blossoms
from the vineyards of En Gedi.

How beautiful you are, my darling!
Oh, how beautiful!
Your eyes are doves.

How handsome you are, my beloved!
Oh, how charming!
And our bed is verdant.

The beams of our house are cedars;
our rafters are firs.

I am a rose of Sharon,
a lily of the valleys.

Like a lily among thorns
is my darling among the young women.

Like an apple tree among the trees
    of the forest
is my beloved among the young men.
I delight to sit in his shade,
and his fruit is sweet to my taste.
Let him lead me to the banquet hall,
and let his banner over me be love.
Strengthen me with raisins,
refresh me with apples,
for I am faint with love.

His left arm is under my head,
and his right arm embraces me.

Daughters of Jerusalem, I charge you
by the gazelles and by the does of the field:

Do not arouse or awaken love
until it so desires.

L isten! My beloved!
Look! Here he comes,

leaping across the mountains,
bounding over the hills.

My beloved is like a gazelle or a young stag.
Look! There he stands behind our wall,

gazing through the windows,
peering through the lattice.

My beloved spoke and said to me,
"Arise, my darling,
my beautiful one, come with me.

See! The winter is past;
the rains are over and gone.

Flowers appear on the earth;
the season of singing has come,

the cooing of doves
is heard in our land.

The fig tree forms its early fruit;
the blossoming vines spread their fragrance.

Arise, come, my darling;
my beautiful one, come with me."

My dove in the clefts of the rock,
in the hiding places on the mountainside,

show me your face,
let me hear your voice;

for your voice is sweet,
and your face is lovely.

Catch for us the foxes,
the little foxes

that ruin the vineyards,
our vineyards that are in bloom.

My beloved is mine and I am his;
he browses among the lilies.

Until the day breaks
and the shadows flee,

turn, my beloved,
and be like a gazelle

or like a young stag
on the rugged hills.

All night long on my bed
I looked for the one my heart loves;
I looked for him but did not find him.

I will get up now and go about the city,
through its streets and squares;

I will search for the one my heart loves.
So I looked for him but did not find him.

The watchmen found me
as they made their rounds in the city.
"Have you seen the one my heart loves?"

Scarcely had I passed them
when I found the one my heart loves.

I held him and would not let him go
till I had brought him to my mother's house,
to the room of the one who conceived me.

Daughters of Jerusalem, I charge you
by the gazelles and by the does of the field:

Do not arouse or awaken love
until it so desires.

W ho is this coming up from the wilderness
like a column of smoke,

perfumed with myrrh and incense
made from all the spices of the merchant?

Look! It is Solomon's carriage,
escorted by sixty warriors,
the noblest of Israel,

all of them wearing the sword,
all experienced in battle,

each with his sword at his side,
prepared for the terrors of the night.

King Solomon made for himself the carriage;
he made it of wood from Lebanon.

Its posts he made of silver,
its base of gold.

Its seat was upholstered with purple,
its interior inlaid with love.

Daughters of Jerusalem, come out,
and look, you daughters of Zion.

Look on King Solomon wearing a crown,
the crown with which his mother crowned him

on the day of his wedding,
the day his heart rejoiced.

How beautiful you are, my darling!
Oh, how beautiful!
Your eyes behind your veil are doves.

Your hair is like a flock of goats
descending from the hills of Gilead.

Your teeth are like a flock of sheep just
        shorn,
coming up from the washing.

Each has its twin;
not one of them is alone.

Your lips are like a scarlet ribbon;
your mouth is lovely.

Your temples behind your veil
are like the halves of a pomegranate.

Your neck is like the tower of David,
built with courses of stone;

on it hang a thousand shields,
all of them shields of warriors.

Your breasts are like two fawns,
like twin fawns of a gazelle
that browse among the lilies.

Until the day breaks
and the shadows flee,

I will go to the mountain of myrrh
and to the hill of incense.

You are altogether beautiful, my darling;
there is no flaw in you.

Come with me from Lebanon, my bride,
come with me from Lebanon.

Descend from the crest of Amana,
from the top of Senir, the summit of Hermon,

from the lions' dens
and the mountain haunts of leopards.

You have stolen my heart, my sister, my bride;
you have stolen my heart

with one glance of your eyes,
with one jewel of your necklace.

How delightful is your love, my sister, my bride!
How much more pleasing is your love than wine,

and the fragrance of your perfume
more than any spice!

Your lips drop sweetness as the honeycomb, my bride;
milk and honey are under your tongue.

The fragrance of your garments
is like the fragrance of Lebanon.

You are a garden locked up, my sister, my bride;
you are a spring enclosed, a sealed fountain.

Your plants are an orchard of pomegranates
with choice fruits,
with henna and nard,
nard and saffron,
calamus and cinnamon,
with every kind of incense tree,
with myrrh and aloes
and all the finest spices.

You are a garden fountain,
a well of flowing water
streaming down from Lebanon.

Awake, north wind,
and come, south wind!
Blow on my garden,
that its fragrance may spread everywhere.
Let my beloved come into his garden
and taste its choice fruits.

I have come into my garden, my sister, my bride;
I have gathered my myrrh with my spice.

I have eaten my honeycomb and my honey;
I have drunk my wine and my milk.

Eat, friends, and drink;
drink your fill of love.

I slept but my heart was awake.
Listen! My beloved is knocking:

"Open to me, my sister, my darling,
my dove, my flawless one.

My head is drenched with dew,
my hair with the dampness of the night."

I have taken off my robe—
must I put it on again?

I have washed my feet—
must I soil them again?

My beloved thrust his hand through
the latch-opening;
my heart began to pound for him.

I arose to open for my beloved,
and my hands dripped with myrrh,

my fingers with flowing myrrh,
on the handles of the bolt.

I opened for my beloved,
but my beloved had left; he was gone.
My heart sank at his departure.

I looked for him but did not find him.
I called him but he did not answer.

The watchmen found me
as they made their rounds in the city.

They beat me, they bruised me;
they took away my cloak,
those watchmen of the walls!

Daughters of Jerusalem, I charge you—
if you find my beloved,

what will you tell him?
Tell him I am faint with love.

How is your beloved better than others,
most beautiful of women?

How is your beloved better than others,
that you so charge us?

My beloved is radiant and ruddy,
outstanding among ten thousand.

His head is purest gold;
his hair is wavy
and black as a raven.

His eyes are like doves
by the water streams,

washed in milk,
mounted like jewels.

His cheeks are like beds of spice
yielding perfume.

His lips are like lilies
dripping with myrrh.

His arms are rods of gold
set with topaz.

His body is like polished ivory
decorated with lapis lazuli.

His legs are pillars of marble
set on bases of pure gold.

His appearance is like Lebanon,
choice as its cedars.

His mouth is sweetness itself;
he is altogether lovely.

This is my beloved, this is my friend,
daughters of Jerusalem.

Where has your beloved gone,
most beautiful of women?

Which way did your beloved turn,
that we may look for him with you?

My beloved has gone down to his garden,
to the beds of spices,

to browse in the gardens
and to gather lilies.

I am my beloved's and my beloved
is mine;
he browses among the lilies.

You are as beautiful as Tirzah, my darling,
as lovely as Jerusalem,
as majestic as troops with banners.

Turn your eyes from me;
they overwhelm me.

Your hair is like a flock of goats
descending from Gilead.

Your teeth are like a flock of sheep
coming up from the washing.

Each has its twin,
not one of them is missing.

Your temples behind your veil
are like the halves of a pomegranate.

Sixty queens there may be,
and eighty concubines,
and virgins beyond number;

but my dove, my perfect one, is unique,
the only daughter of her mother,
the favorite of the one who bore her.

The young women saw her and called her blessed;
the queens and concubines praised her.

Who is this that appears like the dawn,
fair as the moon, bright as the sun,
majestic as the stars in procession?

I went down to the grove of nut trees
to look at the new growth in the valley,

to see if the vines had budded
or the pomegranates were in bloom.

Before I realized it,
my desire set me among the royal chariots
    of my people.

Come back, come back, O Shulammite;
come back, come back, that we may
    gaze on you!

Why would you gaze on the Shulammite
as on the dance of Mahanaim?

How beautiful your sandaled feet,
O prince's daughter!

Your graceful legs are like jewels,
the work of an artist's hands.

Your navel is a rounded goblet
that never lacks blended wine.

Your waist is a mound of wheat
encircled by lilies.

Your breasts are like two fawns,
like twin fawns of a gazelle.

Your neck is like an ivory tower.

Your eyes are the pools of Heshbon
by the gate of Bath Rabbim.

Your nose is like the tower of Lebanon
looking toward Damascus.

Your head crowns you like Mount Carmel.
Your hair is like royal tapestry;
the king is held captive by its tresses.

How beautiful you are and how pleasing,
my love, with your delights!

Your stature is like that of the palm,
and your breasts like clusters of fruit.

I said, "I will climb the palm tree;
I will take hold of its fruit."

May your breasts be like clusters of grapes
        on the vine,
the fragrance of your breath like apples,
and your mouth like the best wine.

May the wine go straight to my beloved,
flowing gently over lips and teeth.

I belong to my beloved,
and his desire is for me.

Come, my beloved, let us go to the countryside,
let us spend the night in the villages.

Let us go early to the vineyards
to see if the vines have budded,

if their blossoms have opened,
and if the pomegranates are in bloom—
there I will give you my love.

The mandrakes send out their fragrance,
and at our door is every delicacy,

both new and old,
that I have stored up for you, my beloved.

If only you were to me like a brother,
who was nursed at my mother's breasts!

Then, if I found you outside,
I would kiss you,
and no one would despise me.

I would lead you
and bring you to my mother's house—
she who has taught me.

I would give you spiced wine to drink,
the nectar of my pomegranates.

His left arm is under my head
and his right arm embraces me.

Daughters of Jerusalem, I charge you:
Do not arouse or awaken love
until it so desires.

Who is this coming up from the wilderness
leaning on her beloved?

Under the apple tree I roused you;
there your mother conceived you,
there she who was in labor gave you birth.

Place me like a seal over your heart,
like a seal on your arm;

for love is as strong as death,
its jealousy unyielding as the grave.

It burns like blazing fire,
like a mighty flame.

Many waters cannot quench love;
rivers cannot sweep it away.

If one were to give
all the wealth of one's house for love,
it would be utterly scorned.

We have a little sister,
and her breasts are not yet grown.

What shall we do for our sister
on the day she is spoken for?

If she is a wall,
we will build towers of silver on her.

If she is a door,
we will enclose her with panels of cedar.

I am a wall,
and my breasts are like towers.

Thus I have become in his eyes
like one bringing contentment.

Solomon had a vineyard in Baal Hamon;
he let out his vineyard to tenants.

Each was to bring for its fruit
a thousand shekels of silver.

But my own vineyard is mine to give;
the thousand shekels are for you, Solomon,
and two hundred are for those who tend its fruit.

You who dwell in the gardens
with friends in attendance,
let me hear your voice!

Come away, my beloved,
and be like a gazelle

or like a young stag
on the spice-laden mountains.

INVITATION TO
PROVERBS

The people of Israel understood that God would speak to them through a variety of means. They expected to hear from God as their priests taught and interpreted the law of Moses, and as their prophets brought the word of the LORD to warn and exhort them. But they also recognized that God would speak to them through the lessons of everyday experience. The Creator God had made an orderly world, and its order could be discerned by reflection on life. The lessons distilled from experience were captured in compact, memorable sayings, called proverbs, passed down to Israel from the wisest of their ancestors. A collection of such sayings is found among Israel's sacred books. We know it today as the book of Proverbs.

Solomon, the son of David and the third king of Israel, was renowned for his wisdom. He's named at the beginning of this book as the source of its proverbs, and he's indeed responsible for most of them. But the book also contains the collected sayings of several other wise and godly teachers of the ancient world.

: The book begins with a short explanation of its contents and purpose (p. 211). Its *proverbs* and *parables* and *sayings* and *riddles* are all designed to help people avoid life's most common pitfalls and find the path that leads to prosperity, security and well-being. The book insists that we start on this path by embracing the *fear of the LORD*. (*Fear* here doesn't mean to be afraid, but rather refers to the awe and respect that leads to following God's ways.)

: The book then presents a series of exhortations, spoken as if from father to son, which are intended to impart the wisdom of preceding generations to the rising one (pp. 212-225). These exhortations warn against dangers such as banditry, adultery and laziness, and commend the benefits of wisdom. After the first and last exhortations, wisdom itself, personified as a woman, calls out to the simple, inviting them to grow in knowledge. This section ends by presenting a contrast between two banquets, one hosted by Wisdom and the other by Folly. This illustrates that each person must choose one of these "banquets" in life.

: The first collection of the proverbs of Solomon follows (pp. 225-250). These aren't exhortations to do one thing or avoid another, but rather observations of the way things are. Listeners must draw for themselves the lesson they imply about how to live. While the preceding exhortations contain many longer poetic passages, these proverbs are pithy sayings consisting of two halves each. In the first part of this collection, these two half-lines typically draw a contrast. In the second part of the collection, the second half of the proverb often restates the meaning of the first, or extends it in some way. Nevertheless, the message is consistent throughout the whole collection: as people cultivate qualities such as diligence, self-control, thrift, generosity, fairness and gracious speech, positive consequences will follow and negative ones will be avoided. There are 375 proverbs in this collection, corresponding to the numerical value of Solomon's name in Hebrew. (Hebrew letters were also used as numbers, so words had a value equal to the sum of their letters.)

: The book of Proverbs next presents two collections of the "sayings of the wise" (pp. 250-255). The first collection includes thirty sayings, while the second is a short supplemental set. Although these sayings present the same basic teaching as the shorter proverbs of Solomon, most of them have several lines, typically in the form of exhortations.

: The second collection of proverbs from Solomon comes next, introduced with an explanation that these were *compiled by the men of Hezekiah king of Judah* (pp. 255-264). There are 130 proverbs in this collection, matching the numerical value of Hezekiah's name in Hebrew. Like those in the first collection of Solomon's proverbs, these are mostly short observations with implied lessons, although some of the sayings in the first part of this collection are longer and written as exhortations. The second part of the collection consists of single-line sayings that contrast the behavior of the righteous and the wicked. The distinction between these two kinds of people is drawn directly in proverbs near the beginning, middle and end of this part.

: The book then concludes with brief collections of sayings from two other wise figures, Agur and Lemuel (pp. 264-268). Lemuel's words finish with a poem whose 22 parts begin with the consecutive letters of the Hebrew alphabet. In this poem the character qualities that have been praised throughout the book are given a final practical illustration in a description of an ideal wife. This poem concludes that *a woman who fears the Lord is to be praised*. Thus this complex book, built from diverse collections of sayings, presents a consistent message throughout: *the fear of the Lord is the beginning of knowledge.*

Proverbs

The proverbs of Solomon son of David, king of Israel:

for gaining wisdom and instruction;
for understanding words of insight;

for receiving instruction in prudent behavior,
doing what is right and just and fair;

for giving prudence to those who are simple,
knowledge and discretion to the young—

let the wise listen and add to their learning,
and let the discerning get guidance—

for understanding proverbs and parables,
the sayings and riddles of the wise.

The fear of the Lord is the beginning of knowledge,
but fools despise wisdom and instruction.

Listen, my son, to your father's instruction
and do not forsake your mother's teaching.

They are a garland to grace your head
and a chain to adorn your neck.

My son, if sinful men entice you,
do not give in to them.

If they say, "Come along with us;
let's lie in wait for innocent blood,
let's ambush some harmless soul;

let's swallow them alive, like the grave,
and whole, like those who go down to the pit;

we will get all sorts of valuable things
and fill our houses with plunder;

cast lots with us;
we will all share the loot"—

my son, do not go along with them,
do not set foot on their paths;

for their feet rush into evil,
they are swift to shed blood.

How useless to spread a net
where every bird can see it!

These men lie in wait for their own blood;
they ambush only themselves!

Such are the paths of all who go after ill-gotten gain;
it takes away the life of those who get it.

Out in the open wisdom calls aloud,
she raises her voice in the public square;

on top of the wall she cries out,
at the city gate she makes her speech:

"How long will you who are simple love your simple
    ways?
How long will mockers delight in mockery
and fools hate knowledge?

Repent at my rebuke!
Then I will pour out my thoughts to you,
I will make known to you my teachings.

But since you refuse to listen when I call
and no one pays attention when I stretch out my hand,

since you disregard all my advice
and do not accept my rebuke,

I in turn will laugh when disaster strikes you;
I will mock when calamity overtakes you —

when calamity overtakes you like a storm,
when disaster sweeps over you like a whirlwind,
when distress and trouble overwhelm you.

"Then they will call to me but I will not answer;
they will look for me but will not find me,

since they hated knowledge
and did not choose to fear the LORD.

Since they would not accept my advice
and spurned my rebuke,

they will eat the fruit of their ways
and be filled with the fruit of their schemes.

For the waywardness of the simple will kill them,
and the complacency of fools will destroy them;

but whoever listens to me will live in safety
and be at ease, without fear of harm."

My son, if you accept my words
and store up my commands within you,

turning your ear to wisdom
and applying your heart to understanding—

indeed, if you call out for insight
and cry aloud for understanding,

and if you look for it as for silver
and search for it as for hidden treasure,

then you will understand the fear of the Lord
and find the knowledge of God.

For the Lord gives wisdom;
from his mouth come knowledge and understanding.

He holds success in store for the upright,
he is a shield to those whose walk is blameless,

for he guards the course of the just
and protects the way of his faithful ones.

Then you will understand what is right and just
and fair—every good path.

For wisdom will enter your heart,
and knowledge will be pleasant to your soul.

Discretion will protect you,
and understanding will guard you.

Wisdom will save you from the ways of wicked men,
from men whose words are perverse,

who have left the straight paths
to walk in dark ways,

who delight in doing wrong
and rejoice in the perverseness of evil,

whose paths are crooked
and who are devious in their ways.

Wisdom will save you also from the adulterous woman,
from the wayward woman with her seductive words,

who has left the partner of her youth
and ignored the covenant she made before God.

Surely her house leads down to death
and her paths to the spirits of the dead.

None who go to her return
or attain the paths of life.

Thus you will walk in the ways of the good
and keep to the paths of the righteous.

For the upright will live in the land,
and the blameless will remain in it;

but the wicked will be cut off from the land,
and the unfaithful will be torn from it.

My son, do not forget my teaching,
but keep my commands in your heart,

for they will prolong your life many years
and bring you peace and prosperity.

Let love and faithfulness never leave you;
bind them around your neck,
write them on the tablet of your heart.

Then you will win favor and a good name
in the sight of God and man.

Trust in the LORD with all your heart
and lean not on your own understanding;

in all your ways submit to him,
and he will make your paths straight.

Do not be wise in your own eyes;
fear the LORD and shun evil.

This will bring health to your body
and nourishment to your bones.

Honor the LORD with your wealth,
with the firstfruits of all your crops;

then your barns will be filled to overflowing,
and your vats will brim over with new wine.

My son, do not despise the LORD's discipline,
and do not resent his rebuke,

because the Lord disciplines those he loves,
as a father the son he delights in.

Blessed are those who find wisdom,
those who gain understanding,

for she is more profitable than silver
and yields better returns than gold.

She is more precious than rubies;
nothing you desire can compare with her.

Long life is in her right hand;
in her left hand are riches and honor.

Her ways are pleasant ways,
and all her paths are peace.

She is a tree of life to those who take hold of her;
those who hold her fast will be blessed.

By wisdom the Lord laid the earth's foundations,
by understanding he set the heavens in place;

by his knowledge the watery depths were divided,
and the clouds let drop the dew.

My son, do not let wisdom and understanding
out of your sight,
preserve sound judgment and discretion;

they will be life for you,
an ornament to grace your neck.

Then you will go on your way in safety,
and your foot will not stumble.

When you lie down, you will not be afraid;
when you lie down, your sleep will be sweet.

Have no fear of sudden disaster
or of the ruin that overtakes the wicked,

for the Lord will be at your side
and will keep your foot from being snared.

Do not withhold good from those to whom it is due,
when it is in your power to act.

Do not say to your neighbor,
"Come back tomorrow and I'll give it to you" —
when you already have it with you.

Do not plot harm against your neighbor,
who lives trustfully near you.

Do not accuse anyone for no reason—
when they have done you no harm.

Do not envy the violent
or choose any of their ways.

For the Lord detests the perverse
but takes the upright into his confidence.

The Lord's curse is on the house of the wicked,
but he blesses the home of the righteous.

He mocks proud mockers
but shows favor to the humble and oppressed.

The wise inherit honor,
but fools get only shame.

Listen, my sons, to a father's instruction;
pay attention and gain understanding.

I give you sound learning,
so do not forsake my teaching.

For I too was a son to my father,
still tender, and cherished by my mother.

Then he taught me, and he said to me,
"Take hold of my words with all your heart;
keep my commands, and you will live.

Get wisdom, get understanding;
do not forget my words or turn away from them.

Do not forsake wisdom, and she will protect you;
love her, and she will watch over you.

The beginning of wisdom is this: Get wisdom.
Though it cost all you have, get understanding.

Cherish her, and she will exalt you;
embrace her, and she will honor you.

She will give you a garland to grace your head
and present you with a glorious crown."

Listen, my son, accept what I say,
and the years of your life will be many.

I instruct you in the way of wisdom
and lead you along straight paths.

When you walk, your steps will not be hampered;
when you run, you will not stumble.

Hold on to instruction, do not let it go;
guard it well, for it is your life.

Do not set foot on the path of the wicked
or walk in the way of evildoers.

Avoid it, do not travel on it;
turn from it and go on your way.

For they cannot rest until they do evil;
they are robbed of sleep till they make someone
    stumble.

They eat the bread of wickedness
and drink the wine of violence.

The path of the righteous is like the morning sun,
shining ever brighter till the full light of day.

But the way of the wicked is like deep darkness;
they do not know what makes them stumble.

My son, pay attention to what I say;
turn your ear to my words.

Do not let them out of your sight,
keep them within your heart;

for they are life to those who find them
and health to one's whole body.

Above all else, guard your heart,
for everything you do flows from it.

Keep your mouth free of perversity;
keep corrupt talk far from your lips.

Let your eyes look straight ahead;
fix your gaze directly before you.

Give careful thought to the paths for your feet
and be steadfast in all your ways.

Do not turn to the right or the left;
keep your foot from evil.

My son, pay attention to my wisdom,
turn your ear to my words of insight,

that you may maintain discretion
and your lips may preserve knowledge.

For the lips of the adulterous woman drip honey,
and her speech is smoother than oil;

but in the end she is bitter as gall,
sharp as a double-edged sword.

Her feet go down to death;
her steps lead straight to the grave.

She gives no thought to the way of life;
her paths wander aimlessly, but she does
    not know it.

Now then, my sons, listen to me;
do not turn aside from what I say.

Keep to a path far from her,
do not go near the door of her house,

lest you lose your honor to others
and your dignity to one who is cruel,

lest strangers feast on your wealth
and your toil enrich the house of another.

At the end of your life you will groan,
when your flesh and body are spent.

You will say, "How I hated discipline!
How my heart spurned correction!

I would not obey my teachers
or turn my ear to my instructors.

And I was soon in serious trouble
in the assembly of God's people."

Drink water from your own cistern,
running water from your own well.

Should your springs overflow in the streets,
your streams of water in the public squares?

Let them be yours alone,
never to be shared with strangers.

May your fountain be blessed,
and may you rejoice in the wife of your youth.

A loving doe, a graceful deer —
may her breasts satisfy you always,
may you ever be intoxicated with her love.

Why, my son, be intoxicated with another man's wife?
Why embrace the bosom of a wayward woman?

For your ways are in full view of the LORD,
and he examines all your paths.

The evil deeds of the wicked ensnare them;
the cords of their sins hold them fast.

For lack of discipline they will die,
led astray by their own great folly.

My son, if you have put up security for your
      neighbor,
if you have shaken hands in pledge for a stranger,

you have been trapped by what you said,
ensnared by the words of your mouth.

So do this, my son, to free yourself,
since you have fallen into your neighbor's hands:

Go — to the point of exhaustion —
and give your neighbor no rest!

Allow no sleep to your eyes,
no slumber to your eyelids.

Free yourself, like a gazelle from the hand
      of the hunter,
like a bird from the snare of the fowler.

Go to the ant, you sluggard;
consider its ways and be wise!

It has no commander,
no overseer or ruler,

yet it stores its provisions in summer
and gathers its food at harvest.

How long will you lie there, you sluggard?
When will you get up from your sleep?

A little sleep, a little slumber,
a little folding of the hands to rest —

and poverty will come on you like a thief
and scarcity like an armed man.

A troublemaker and a villain,
who goes about with a corrupt mouth,
who winks maliciously with his eye,
signals with his feet
and motions with his fingers,
who plots evil with deceit in his heart —
he always stirs up conflict.

Therefore disaster will overtake him in an instant;
he will suddenly be destroyed—without remedy.

There are six things the LORD hates,
seven that are detestable to him:
haughty eyes,
a lying tongue,
hands that shed innocent blood,
a heart that devises wicked schemes,
feet that are quick to rush into evil,
a false witness who pours out lies
and a person who stirs up conflict in
    the community.

My son, keep your father's command
and do not forsake your mother's teaching.

Bind them always on your heart;
fasten them around your neck.

When you walk, they will guide you;
when you sleep, they will watch over you;
when you awake, they will speak to you.

For this command is a lamp,
this teaching is a light,

and correction and instruction
are the way to life,

keeping you from your neighbor's wife,
from the smooth talk of a wayward woman.

Do not lust in your heart after her beauty
or let her captivate you with her eyes.

For a prostitute can be had for a loaf of bread,
but another man's wife preys on your very life.

Can a man scoop fire into his lap
without his clothes being burned?

Can a man walk on hot coals
without his feet being scorched?

So is he who sleeps with another man's wife;
no one who touches her will go unpunished.

People do not despise a thief if he steals
to satisfy his hunger when he is starving.

Yet if he is caught, he must pay sevenfold,
though it costs him all the wealth of his house.

But a man who commits adultery has no sense;
whoever does so destroys himself.

Blows and disgrace are his lot,
and his shame will never be wiped away.

For jealousy arouses a husband's fury,
and he will show no mercy when he takes revenge.

He will not accept any compensation;
he will refuse a bribe, however great it is.

My son, keep my words
and store up my commands within you.

Keep my commands and you will live;
guard my teachings as the apple of your eye.

Bind them on your fingers;
write them on the tablet of your heart.

Say to wisdom, "You are my sister,"
and to insight, "You are my relative."

They will keep you from the adulterous woman,
from the wayward woman with her
    seductive words.

At the window of my house
I looked down through the lattice.

I saw among the simple,
I noticed among the young men,
a youth who had no sense.

He was going down the street near her corner,
walking along in the direction of her house

at twilight, as the day was fading,
as the dark of night set in.

Then out came a woman to meet him,
dressed like a prostitute and with
    crafty intent.

(She is unruly and defiant,
her feet never stay at home;

now in the street, now in the squares,
at every corner she lurks.)

She took hold of him and kissed him
and with a brazen face she said:

"Today I fulfilled my vows,
and I have food from my fellowship offering at home.

So I came out to meet you;
I looked for you and have found you!

I have covered my bed
with colored linens from Egypt.

I have perfumed my bed
with myrrh, aloes and cinnamon.

Come, let's drink deeply of love till morning;
let's enjoy ourselves with love!

My husband is not at home;
he has gone on a long journey.

He took his purse filled with money
and will not be home till full moon."

With persuasive words she led him astray;
she seduced him with her smooth talk.

All at once he followed her
like an ox going to the slaughter,

like a deer stepping into a noose
till an arrow pierces his liver,

like a bird darting into a snare,
little knowing it will cost him his life.

Now then, my sons, listen to me;
pay attention to what I say.

Do not let your heart turn to her ways
or stray into her paths.

Many are the victims she has brought down;
her slain are a mighty throng.

Her house is a highway to the grave,
leading down to the chambers of death.

Does not wisdom call out?
Does not understanding raise her voice?

At the highest point along the way,
where the paths meet, she takes her stand;

beside the gate leading into the city,
at the entrance, she cries aloud:

"To you, O people, I call out;
I raise my voice to all mankind.

You who are simple, gain prudence;
you who are foolish, set your hearts on it.

Listen, for I have trustworthy things to say;
I open my lips to speak what is right.

My mouth speaks what is true,
for my lips detest wickedness.

All the words of my mouth are just;
none of them is crooked or perverse.

To the discerning all of them are right;
they are upright to those who have found knowledge.

Choose my instruction instead of silver,
knowledge rather than choice gold,

for wisdom is more precious than rubies,
and nothing you desire can compare with her.

"I, wisdom, dwell together with prudence;
I possess knowledge and discretion.

To fear the Lord is to hate evil;
I hate pride and arrogance,
evil behavior and perverse speech.

Counsel and sound judgment are mine;
I have insight, I have power.

By me kings reign
and rulers issue decrees that are just;

by me princes govern,
and nobles—all who rule on earth.

I love those who love me,
and those who seek me find me.

With me are riches and honor,
enduring wealth and prosperity.

My fruit is better than fine gold;
what I yield surpasses choice silver.

I walk in the way of righteousness,
along the paths of justice,

bestowing a rich inheritance on those who love me
and making their treasuries full.

"The LORD brought me forth as the first of his works,
before his deeds of old;
I was formed long ages ago,
at the very beginning, when the world came to be.

When there were no watery depths, I was given birth,
when there were no springs overflowing with water;
before the mountains were settled in place,
before the hills, I was given birth,
before he made the world or its fields
or any of the dust of the earth.

I was there when he set the heavens in place,
when he marked out the horizon on the face
of the deep,
when he established the clouds above
and fixed securely the fountains of the deep,
when he gave the sea its boundary
so the waters would not overstep his command,
and when he marked out the foundations of the earth.
Then I was constantly at his side.

I was filled with delight day after day,
rejoicing always in his presence,
rejoicing in his whole world
and delighting in mankind.

"Now then, my children, listen to me;
blessed are those who keep my ways.

Listen to my instruction and be wise;
do not disregard it.

Blessed are those who listen to me,
watching daily at my doors,
waiting at my doorway.

For those who find me find life
and receive favor from the LORD.

But those who fail to find me harm themselves;
all who hate me love death."

Wisdom has built her house;
she has set up its seven pillars.
She has prepared her meat and mixed her wine;
she has also set her table.

She has sent out her servants, and she calls
from the highest point of the city,
"Let all who are simple come to my house!"

To those who have no sense she says,
"Come, eat my food
and drink the wine I have mixed.

Leave your simple ways and you will live;
walk in the way of insight."

Whoever corrects a mocker invites insults;
whoever rebukes the wicked incurs abuse.

Do not rebuke mockers or they will hate you;
rebuke the wise and they will love you.

Instruct the wise and they will be wiser still;
teach the righteous and they will add to their learning.

The fear of the Lord is the beginning of wisdom,
and knowledge of the Holy One is understanding.

For through wisdom your days will be many,
and years will be added to your life.

If you are wise, your wisdom will reward you;
if you are a mocker, you alone will suffer.

Folly is an unruly woman;
she is simple and knows nothing.

She sits at the door of her house,
on a seat at the highest point of the city,

calling out to those who pass by,
who go straight on their way,
"Let all who are simple come to my house!"

To those who have no sense she says,
"Stolen water is sweet;
food eaten in secret is delicious!"

But little do they know that the dead are there,
that her guests are deep in the realm of the dead.

T he proverbs of Solomon:

A wise son brings joy to his father,
but a foolish son brings grief to his mother.

Ill-gotten treasures have no lasting value,
but righteousness delivers from death.

The Lord does not let the righteous go hungry,
but he thwarts the craving of the wicked.

Lazy hands make for poverty,
but diligent hands bring wealth.

He who gathers crops in summer is a prudent son,
but he who sleeps during harvest is a disgraceful son.

Blessings crown the head of the righteous,
but violence overwhelms the mouth of the wicked.

The name of the righteous is used in blessings,
but the name of the wicked will rot.

The wise in heart accept commands,
but a chattering fool comes to ruin.

Whoever walks in integrity walks securely,
but whoever takes crooked paths will be
found out.

Whoever winks maliciously causes grief,
and a chattering fool comes to ruin.

The mouth of the righteous is a fountain of life,
but the mouth of the wicked conceals violence.

Hatred stirs up conflict,
but love covers over all wrongs.

Wisdom is found on the lips of the discerning,
but a rod is for the back of one who has no sense.

The wise store up knowledge,
but the mouth of a fool invites ruin.

The wealth of the rich is their fortified city,
but poverty is the ruin of the poor.

The wages of the righteous is life,
but the earnings of the wicked are sin and death.

Whoever heeds discipline shows the way to life,
but whoever ignores correction leads others astray.

Whoever conceals hatred with lying lips
and spreads slander is a fool.

Sin is not ended by multiplying words,
but the prudent hold their tongues.

The tongue of the righteous is choice silver,
but the heart of the wicked is of little value.

The lips of the righteous nourish many,
but fools die for lack of sense.

The blessing of the Lord brings wealth,
without painful toil for it.

A fool finds pleasure in wicked schemes,
but a person of understanding delights in wisdom.

What the wicked dread will overtake them;
what the righteous desire will be granted.

When the storm has swept by, the wicked are gone,
but the righteous stand firm forever.

As vinegar to the teeth and smoke to the eyes,
so are sluggards to those who send them.

The fear of the Lord adds length to life,
but the years of the wicked are cut short.

The prospect of the righteous is joy,
but the hopes of the wicked come to nothing.

The way of the Lord is a refuge for the blameless,
but it is the ruin of those who do evil.

The righteous will never be uprooted,
but the wicked will not remain in the land.

From the mouth of the righteous comes the fruit of
     wisdom,
but a perverse tongue will be silenced.

The lips of the righteous know what finds favor,
but the mouth of the wicked only what is perverse.

The Lord detests dishonest scales,
but accurate weights find favor with him.

When pride comes, then comes disgrace,
but with humility comes wisdom.

The integrity of the upright guides them,
but the unfaithful are destroyed by their duplicity.

Wealth is worthless in the day of wrath,
but righteousness delivers from death.

The righteousness of the blameless makes their paths
straight,
but the wicked are brought down by their own
wickedness.

The righteousness of the upright delivers them,
but the unfaithful are trapped by evil desires.

Hopes placed in mortals die with them;
all the promise of their power comes to nothing.

The righteous person is rescued from trouble,
and it falls on the wicked instead.

With their mouths the godless destroy their neighbors,
but through knowledge the righteous escape.

When the righteous prosper, the city rejoices;
when the wicked perish, there are shouts of joy.

Through the blessing of the upright a city is exalted,
but by the mouth of the wicked it is destroyed.

Whoever derides their neighbor has no sense,
but the one who has understanding holds their tongue.

A gossip betrays a confidence,
but a trustworthy person keeps a secret.

For lack of guidance a nation falls,
but victory is won through many advisers.

Whoever puts up security for a stranger will surely
suffer,
but whoever refuses to shake hands in pledge is safe.

A kindhearted woman gains honor,
but ruthless men gain only wealth.

Those who are kind benefit themselves,
but the cruel bring ruin on themselves.

A wicked person earns deceptive wages,
but the one who sows righteousness reaps
a sure reward.

Truly the righteous attain life,
but whoever pursues evil finds death.

The LORD detests those whose hearts are perverse,
but he delights in those whose ways are blameless.

Be sure of this: The wicked will not go unpunished,
but those who are righteous will go free.

Like a gold ring in a pig's snout
is a beautiful woman who shows no discretion.

The desire of the righteous ends only in good,
but the hope of the wicked only in wrath.

One person gives freely, yet gains even more;
another withholds unduly, but comes to poverty.

A generous person will prosper;
whoever refreshes others will be refreshed.

People curse the one who hoards grain,
but they pray God's blessing on the one who is willing
to sell.

Whoever seeks good finds favor,
but evil comes to one who searches for it.

Those who trust in their riches will fall,
but the righteous will thrive like a green leaf.

Whoever brings ruin on their family will inherit
only wind,
and the fool will be servant to the wise.

The fruit of the righteous is a tree of life,
and the one who is wise saves lives.

If the righteous receive their due on earth,
how much more the ungodly and the sinner!

Whoever loves discipline loves knowledge,
but whoever hates correction is stupid.

Good people obtain favor from the LORD,
but he condemns those who devise wicked schemes.

No one can be established through wickedness,
but the righteous cannot be uprooted.

A wife of noble character is her husband's crown,
but a disgraceful wife is like decay in his bones.

The plans of the righteous are just,
but the advice of the wicked is deceitful.

The words of the wicked lie in wait for blood,
but the speech of the upright rescues them.

The wicked are overthrown and are no more,
but the house of the righteous stands firm.

A person is praised according to their prudence,
and one with a warped mind is despised.

Better to be a nobody and yet have a servant
than pretend to be somebody and have no food.

The righteous care for the needs of their animals,
but the kindest acts of the wicked are cruel.

Those who work their land will have abundant food,
but those who chase fantasies have no sense.

The wicked desire the stronghold of evildoers,
but the root of the righteous endures.

Evildoers are trapped by their sinful talk,
and so the innocent escape trouble.

From the fruit of their lips people are filled with good
things,
and the work of their hands brings them reward.

The way of fools seems right to them,
but the wise listen to advice.

Fools show their annoyance at once,
but the prudent overlook an insult.

An honest witness tells the truth,
but a false witness tells lies.

The words of the reckless pierce like swords,
but the tongue of the wise brings healing.

Truthful lips endure forever,
but a lying tongue lasts only a moment.

Deceit is in the hearts of those who plot evil,
but those who promote peace have joy.

No harm overtakes the righteous,
but the wicked have their fill of trouble.

The LORD detests lying lips,
but he delights in people who are trustworthy.

The prudent keep their knowledge to themselves,
but a fool's heart blurts out folly.

Diligent hands will rule,
but laziness ends in forced labor.

Anxiety weighs down the heart,
but a kind word cheers it up.

The righteous choose their friends carefully,
but the way of the wicked leads them astray.

The lazy do not roast any game,
but the diligent feed on the riches of the hunt.

In the way of righteousness there is life;
along that path is immortality.

A wise son heeds his father's instruction,
but a mocker does not respond to rebukes.

From the fruit of their lips people enjoy good things,
but the unfaithful have an appetite for violence.

Those who guard their lips preserve their lives,
but those who speak rashly will come to ruin.

A sluggard's appetite is never filled,
but the desires of the diligent are fully satisfied.

The righteous hate what is false,
but the wicked make themselves a stench
and bring shame on themselves.

Righteousness guards the person of integrity,
but wickedness overthrows the sinner.

One person pretends to be rich, yet has nothing;
another pretends to be poor, yet has great wealth.

A person's riches may ransom their life,
but the poor cannot respond to threatening rebukes.

The light of the righteous shines brightly,
but the lamp of the wicked is snuffed out.

Where there is strife, there is pride,
but wisdom is found in those who take advice.

Dishonest money dwindles away,
but whoever gathers money little by little makes
    it grow.

Hope deferred makes the heart sick,
but a longing fulfilled is a tree of life.

Whoever scorns instruction will pay for it,
but whoever respects a command is rewarded.

The teaching of the wise is a fountain of life,
turning a person from the snares of death.

Good judgment wins favor,
but the way of the unfaithful leads to their
    destruction.

All who are prudent act with knowledge,
but fools expose their folly.

A wicked messenger falls into trouble,
but a trustworthy envoy brings healing.

Whoever disregards discipline comes to poverty
    and shame,
but whoever heeds correction is honored.

A longing fulfilled is sweet to the soul,
but fools detest turning from evil.

Walk with the wise and become wise,
for a companion of fools suffers harm.

Trouble pursues the sinner,
but the righteous are rewarded with good things.

A good person leaves an inheritance for their children's
children,
but a sinner's wealth is stored up for the righteous.

An unplowed field produces food for the poor,
but injustice sweeps it away.

Whoever spares the rod hates their children,
but the one who loves their children is careful to
discipline them.

The righteous eat to their hearts' content,
but the stomach of the wicked goes hungry.

The wise woman builds her house,
but with her own hands the foolish one tears hers down.

Whoever fears the LORD walks uprightly,
but those who despise him are devious in their ways.

A fool's mouth lashes out with pride,
but the lips of the wise protect them.

Where there are no oxen, the manger is empty,
but from the strength of an ox come abundant harvests.

An honest witness does not deceive,
but a false witness pours out lies.

The mocker seeks wisdom and finds none,
but knowledge comes easily to the discerning.

Stay away from a fool,
for you will not find knowledge on their lips.

The wisdom of the prudent is to give thought
to their ways,
but the folly of fools is deception.

Fools mock at making amends for sin,
but goodwill is found among the upright.

Each heart knows its own bitterness,
and no one else can share its joy.

The house of the wicked will be destroyed,
but the tent of the upright will flourish.

There is a way that appears to be right,
but in the end it leads to death.

Even in laughter the heart may ache,
and rejoicing may end in grief.

The faithless will be fully repaid for their ways,
and the good rewarded for theirs.

The simple believe anything,
but the prudent give thought to their steps.

The wise fear the LORD and shun evil,
but a fool is hotheaded and yet feels secure.

A quick-tempered person does foolish things,
and the one who devises evil schemes is hated.

The simple inherit folly,
but the prudent are crowned with knowledge.

Evildoers will bow down in the presence of the good,
and the wicked at the gates of the righteous.

The poor are shunned even by their neighbors,
but the rich have many friends.

It is a sin to despise one's neighbor,
but blessed is the one who is kind to the needy.

Do not those who plot evil go astray?
But those who plan what is good find love and
    faithfulness.

All hard work brings a profit,
but mere talk leads only to poverty.

The wealth of the wise is their crown,
but the folly of fools yields folly.

A truthful witness saves lives,
but a false witness is deceitful.

Whoever fears the Lord has a secure fortress,
and for their children it will be a refuge.

The fear of the Lord is a fountain of life,
turning a person from the snares of death.

A large population is a king's glory,
but without subjects a prince is ruined.

Whoever is patient has great understanding,
but one who is quick-tempered displays folly.

A heart at peace gives life to the body,
but envy rots the bones.

Whoever oppresses the poor shows contempt for their
    Maker,
but whoever is kind to the needy honors God.

When calamity comes, the wicked are brought down,
but even in death the righteous seek refuge in God.

Wisdom reposes in the heart of the discerning
and even among fools she lets herself be known.

Righteousness exalts a nation,
but sin condemns any people.

A king delights in a wise servant,
but a shameful servant arouses his fury.

A gentle answer turns away wrath,
but a harsh word stirs up anger.

The tongue of the wise adorns knowledge,
but the mouth of the fool gushes folly.

The eyes of the Lord are everywhere,
keeping watch on the wicked and the good.

The soothing tongue is a tree of life,
but a perverse tongue crushes the spirit.

A fool spurns a parent's discipline,
but whoever heeds correction shows prudence.

The house of the righteous contains great treasure,
but the income of the wicked brings ruin.

The lips of the wise spread knowledge,
but the hearts of fools are not upright.

The LORD detests the sacrifice of the wicked,
but the prayer of the upright pleases him.

The LORD detests the way of the wicked,
but he loves those who pursue righteousness.

Stern discipline awaits anyone who leaves the path;
the one who hates correction will die.

Death and Destruction lie open before the LORD—
how much more do human hearts!

Mockers resent correction,
so they avoid the wise.

A happy heart makes the face cheerful,
but heartache crushes the spirit.

The discerning heart seeks knowledge,
but the mouth of a fool feeds on folly.

All the days of the oppressed are wretched,
but the cheerful heart has a continual feast.

Better a little with the fear of the LORD
than great wealth with turmoil.

Better a small serving of vegetables with love
than a fattened calf with hatred.

A hot-tempered person stirs up conflict,
but the one who is patient calms a quarrel.

The way of the sluggard is blocked with thorns,
but the path of the upright is a highway.

A wise son brings joy to his father,
but a foolish man despises his mother.

Folly brings joy to one who has no sense,
but whoever has understanding keeps
    a straight course.

Plans fail for lack of counsel,
but with many advisers they succeed.

A person finds joy in giving an apt reply—
and how good is a timely word!

The path of life leads upward for the prudent
to keep them from going down to the realm of the dead.

The Lord tears down the house of the proud,
but he sets the widow's boundary stones in place.

The Lord detests the thoughts of the wicked,
but gracious words are pure in his sight.

The greedy bring ruin to their households,
but the one who hates bribes will live.

The heart of the righteous weighs its answers,
but the mouth of the wicked gushes evil.

The Lord is far from the wicked,
but he hears the prayer of the righteous.

Light in a messenger's eyes brings joy to the heart,
and good news gives health to the bones.

Whoever heeds life-giving correction
will be at home among the wise.

Those who disregard discipline despise themselves,
but the one who heeds correction gains
        understanding.

Wisdom's instruction is to fear the Lord,
and humility comes before honor.

To humans belong the plans of the heart,
but from the Lord comes the proper answer of the
        tongue.

All a person's ways seem pure to them,
but motives are weighed by the Lord.

Commit to the Lord whatever you do,
and he will establish your plans.

The Lord works out everything to its proper end—
even the wicked for a day of disaster.

The Lord detests all the proud of heart.
Be sure of this: They will not go unpunished.

Through love and faithfulness sin is atoned for;
through the fear of the Lord evil is avoided.

When the Lord takes pleasure in anyone's way,
he causes their enemies to make peace with them.

Better a little with righteousness
than much gain with injustice.

In their hearts humans plan their course,
but the Lord establishes their steps.

The lips of a king speak as an oracle,
and his mouth does not betray justice.

Honest scales and balances belong to the Lord;
all the weights in the bag are of his making.

Kings detest wrongdoing,
for a throne is established through righteousness.

Kings take pleasure in honest lips;
they value the one who speaks what is right.

A king's wrath is a messenger of death,
but the wise will appease it.

When a king's face brightens, it means life;
his favor is like a rain cloud in spring.

How much better to get wisdom than gold,
to get insight rather than silver!

The highway of the upright avoids evil;
those who guard their ways preserve their lives.

Pride goes before destruction,
a haughty spirit before a fall.

Better to be lowly in spirit along with the oppressed
than to share plunder with the proud.

Whoever gives heed to instruction prospers,
and blessed is the one who trusts in the Lord.

The wise in heart are called discerning,
and gracious words promote instruction.

Prudence is a fountain of life to the prudent,
but folly brings punishment to fools.

The hearts of the wise make their mouths prudent,
and their lips promote instruction.

Gracious words are a honeycomb,
sweet to the soul and healing to the bones.

There is a way that appears to be right,
but in the end it leads to death.

The appetite of laborers works for them;
their hunger drives them on.

A scoundrel plots evil,
and on their lips it is like a scorching fire.

A perverse person stirs up conflict,
and a gossip separates close friends.

A violent person entices their neighbor
and leads them down a path that is not good.

Whoever winks with their eye is plotting perversity;
whoever purses their lips is bent on evil.

Gray hair is a crown of splendor;
it is attained in the way of righteousness.

Better a patient person than a warrior,
one with self-control than one who takes a city.

The lot is cast into the lap,
but its every decision is from the Lord.

Better a dry crust with peace and quiet
than a house full of feasting, with strife.

A prudent servant will rule over a disgraceful son
and will share the inheritance as one of the family.

The crucible for silver and the furnace for gold,
but the Lord tests the heart.

A wicked person listens to deceitful lips;
a liar pays attention to a destructive tongue.

Whoever mocks the poor shows contempt for their
        Maker;
whoever gloats over disaster will not go unpunished.

Children's children are a crown to the aged,
and parents are the pride of their children.

Eloquent lips are unsuited to a godless fool —
how much worse lying lips to a ruler!

A bribe is seen as a charm by the one who gives it;
they think success will come at every turn.

Whoever would foster love covers over an offense,
but whoever repeats the matter separates close friends.

A rebuke impresses a discerning person
more than a hundred lashes a fool.

Evildoers foster rebellion against God;
the messenger of death will be sent against them.

Better to meet a bear robbed of her cubs
than a fool bent on folly.

Evil will never leave the house
of one who pays back evil for good.

Starting a quarrel is like breaching a dam;
so drop the matter before a dispute breaks out.

Acquitting the guilty and condemning the innocent —
the Lord detests them both.

Why should fools have money in hand to buy wisdom,
when they are not able to understand it?

A friend loves at all times,
and a brother is born for a time of adversity.

One who has no sense shakes hands in pledge
and puts up security for a neighbor.

Whoever loves a quarrel loves sin;
whoever builds a high gate invites destruction.

One whose heart is corrupt does not prosper;
one whose tongue is perverse falls into trouble.

To have a fool for a child brings grief;
there is no joy for the parent of a godless fool.

A cheerful heart is good medicine,
but a crushed spirit dries up the bones.

The wicked accept bribes in secret
to pervert the course of justice.

A discerning person keeps wisdom in view,
but a fool's eyes wander to the ends of the earth.

A foolish son brings grief to his father
and bitterness to the mother who bore him.

If imposing a fine on the innocent is not good,
surely to flog honest officials is not right.

The one who has knowledge uses words with restraint,
and whoever has understanding is even-tempered.

Even fools are thought wise if they keep silent,
and discerning if they hold their tongues.

An unfriendly person pursues selfish ends
and against all sound judgment starts quarrels.

Fools find no pleasure in understanding
but delight in airing their own opinions.

When wickedness comes, so does contempt,
and with shame comes reproach.

The words of the mouth are deep waters,
but the fountain of wisdom is a rushing stream.

It is not good to be partial to the wicked
and so deprive the innocent of justice.

The lips of fools bring them strife,
and their mouths invite a beating.

The mouths of fools are their undoing,
and their lips are a snare to their very lives.

The words of a gossip are like choice morsels;
they go down to the inmost parts.

One who is slack in his work
is brother to one who destroys.

The name of the LORD is a fortified tower;
the righteous run to it and are safe.

The wealth of the rich is their fortified city;
they imagine it a wall too high to scale.

Before a downfall the heart is haughty,
but humility comes before honor.

To answer before listening—
that is folly and shame.

The human spirit can endure in sickness,
but a crushed spirit who can bear?

The heart of the discerning acquires knowledge,
for the ears of the wise seek it out.

A gift opens the way
and ushers the giver into the presence
        of the great.

In a lawsuit the first to speak seems right,
until someone comes forward and cross-examines.

Casting the lot settles disputes
and keeps strong opponents apart.

A brother wronged is more unyielding than
        a fortified city;
disputes are like the barred gates of a citadel.

From the fruit of their mouth a person's stomach is
        filled;
with the harvest of their lips they are satisfied.

The tongue has the power of life and death,
and those who love it will eat its fruit.

He who finds a wife finds what is good
and receives favor from the LORD.

The poor plead for mercy,
but the rich answer harshly.

One who has unreliable friends soon comes to ruin,
but there is a friend who sticks closer than a brother.

Better the poor whose walk is blameless
than a fool whose lips are perverse.

Desire without knowledge is not good—
how much more will hasty feet miss the way!

A person's own folly leads to their ruin,
yet their heart rages against the LORD.

Wealth attracts many friends,
but even the closest friend of the poor person deserts
them.

A false witness will not go unpunished,
and whoever pours out lies will not go free.

Many curry favor with a ruler,
and everyone is the friend of one who gives gifts.

The poor are shunned by all their relatives—
how much more do their friends avoid them!
Though the poor pursue them with pleading,
they are nowhere to be found.

The one who gets wisdom loves life;
the one who cherishes understanding will soon prosper.

A false witness will not go unpunished,
and whoever pours out lies will perish.

It is not fitting for a fool to live in luxury—
how much worse for a slave to rule over princes!

A person's wisdom yields patience;
it is to one's glory to overlook an offense.

A king's rage is like the roar of a lion,
but his favor is like dew on the grass.

A foolish child is a father's ruin,
and a quarrelsome wife is like

the constant dripping of a leaky roof.

Houses and wealth are inherited from parents,
but a prudent wife is from the LORD.

Laziness brings on deep sleep,
and the shiftless go hungry.

Whoever keeps commandments keeps their life,
but whoever shows contempt for their ways will die.

Whoever is kind to the poor lends to the LORD,
and he will reward them for what they have done.

Discipline your children, for in that there is hope;
do not be a willing party to their death.

A hot-tempered person must pay the penalty;
rescue them, and you will have to do it again.

Listen to advice and accept discipline,
and at the end you will be counted among the wise.

Many are the plans in a person's heart,
but it is the LORD's purpose that prevails.

What a person desires is unfailing love;
better to be poor than a liar.

The fear of the LORD leads to life;
then one rests content, untouched by trouble.

A sluggard buries his hand in the dish;
he will not even bring it back to his mouth!

Flog a mocker, and the simple will learn prudence;
rebuke the discerning, and they will gain knowledge.

Whoever robs their father and drives out
     their mother
is a child who brings shame and disgrace.

Stop listening to instruction, my son,
and you will stray from the words of knowledge.

A corrupt witness mocks at justice,
and the mouth of the wicked gulps down evil.

Penalties are prepared for mockers,
and beatings for the backs of fools.

Wine is a mocker and beer a brawler;
whoever is led astray by them is not wise.

A king's wrath strikes terror like the roar of a lion;
those who anger him forfeit their lives.

It is to one's honor to avoid strife,
but every fool is quick to quarrel.

Sluggards do not plow in season;
so at harvest time they look but find nothing.

The purposes of a person's heart are deep waters,
but one who has insight draws them out.

Many claim to have unfailing love,
but a faithful person who can find?

The righteous lead blameless lives;
blessed are their children after them.

When a king sits on his throne to judge,
he winnows out all evil with his eyes.

Who can say, "I have kept my heart pure;
I am clean and without sin"?

Differing weights and differing measures—
the Lord detests them both.

Even small children are known by their actions,
so is their conduct really pure and upright?

Ears that hear and eyes that see—
the Lord has made them both.

Do not love sleep or you will grow poor;
stay awake and you will have food to spare.

"It's no good, it's no good!" says the buyer—
then goes off and boasts about the purchase.

Gold there is, and rubies in abundance,
but lips that speak knowledge are a rare jewel.

Take the garment of one who puts up security
    for a stranger;
hold it in pledge if it is done for an outsider.

Food gained by fraud tastes sweet,
but one ends up with a mouth full of gravel.

Plans are established by seeking advice;
so if you wage war, obtain guidance.

A gossip betrays a confidence;
so avoid anyone who talks too much.

If someone curses their father or mother,
their lamp will be snuffed out in pitch darkness.

An inheritance claimed too soon
will not be blessed at the end.

Do not say, "I'll pay you back for this wrong!"
Wait for the Lord, and he will avenge you.

The Lord detests differing weights,
and dishonest scales do not please him.

A person's steps are directed by the Lord.
How then can anyone understand their own way?

It is a trap to dedicate something rashly
and only later to consider one's vows.

A wise king winnows out the wicked;
he drives the threshing wheel over them.

The human spirit is the lamp of the Lord
that sheds light on one's inmost being.

Love and faithfulness keep a king safe;
through love his throne is made secure.

The glory of young men is their strength,
gray hair the splendor of the old.

Blows and wounds scrub away evil,
and beatings purge the inmost being.

In the Lord's hand the king's heart is a stream of water
that he channels toward all who please him.

A person may think their own ways are right,
but the LORD weighs the heart.

To do what is right and just
is more acceptable to the LORD than sacrifice.

Haughty eyes and a proud heart—
the unplowed field of the wicked—produce sin.

The plans of the diligent lead to profit
as surely as haste leads to poverty.

A fortune made by a lying tongue
is a fleeting vapor and a deadly snare.

The violence of the wicked will drag them away,
for they refuse to do what is right.

The way of the guilty is devious,
but the conduct of the innocent is upright.

Better to live on a corner of the roof
than share a house with a quarrelsome wife.

The wicked crave evil;
their neighbors get no mercy from them.

When a mocker is punished, the simple gain wisdom;
by paying attention to the wise they get knowledge.

The Righteous One takes note of the house
of the wicked
and brings the wicked to ruin.

Whoever shuts their ears to the cry of the poor
will also cry out and not be answered.

A gift given in secret soothes anger,
and a bribe concealed in the cloak pacifies great wrath.

When justice is done, it brings joy to the righteous
but terror to evildoers.

Whoever strays from the path of prudence
comes to rest in the company of the dead.

Whoever loves pleasure will become poor;
whoever loves wine and olive oil will never be rich.

The wicked become a ransom for the righteous,
and the unfaithful for the upright.

Better to live in a desert
than with a quarrelsome and nagging wife.

The wise store up choice food and olive oil,
but fools gulp theirs down.

Whoever pursues righteousness and love
finds life, prosperity and honor.

One who is wise can go up against the city of the mighty
and pull down the stronghold in which they trust.

Those who guard their mouths and their tongues
keep themselves from calamity.

The proud and arrogant person—"Mocker" is his
        name—
behaves with insolent fury.

The craving of a sluggard will be the death of him,
because his hands refuse to work.
All day long he craves for more,
but the righteous give without sparing.

The sacrifice of the wicked is detestable—
how much more so when brought with evil intent!

A false witness will perish,
but a careful listener will testify successfully.

The wicked put up a bold front,
but the upright give thought to their ways.

There is no wisdom, no insight, no plan
that can succeed against the Lord.

The horse is made ready for the day of battle,
but victory rests with the Lord.

A good name is more desirable than great riches;
to be esteemed is better than silver or gold.

Rich and poor have this in common:
The Lord is the Maker of them all.

The prudent see danger and take refuge,
but the simple keep going and pay the penalty.

Humility is the fear of the LORD;
its wages are riches and honor and life.

In the paths of the wicked are snares and pitfalls,
but those who would preserve their life stay
    far from them.

Start children off on the way they should go,
and even when they are old they will not turn
    from it.

The rich rule over the poor,
and the borrower is slave to the lender.

Whoever sows injustice reaps calamity,
and the rod they wield in fury will be broken.

The generous will themselves be blessed,
for they share their food with the poor.

Drive out the mocker, and out goes strife;
quarrels and insults are ended.

One who loves a pure heart and who speaks
    with grace
will have the king for a friend.

The eyes of the LORD keep watch over knowledge,
but he frustrates the words of the unfaithful.

The sluggard says, "There's a lion outside!
I'll be killed in the public square!"

The mouth of an adulterous woman is
    a deep pit;
a man who is under the LORD's wrath falls
    into it.

Folly is bound up in the heart of a child,
but the rod of discipline will drive it far away.

One who oppresses the poor to increase his wealth
and one who gives gifts to the rich—both come
    to poverty.

P ay attention and turn your ear to the sayings
of the wise;
apply your heart to what I teach,

for it is pleasing when you keep them
in your heart
and have all of them ready on your lips.

So that your trust may be in the LORD,
I teach you today, even you.

Have I not written thirty sayings for you,
sayings of counsel and knowledge,

teaching you to be honest and to speak the truth,
so that you bring back truthful reports
to those you serve?

Do not exploit the poor because they are poor
and do not crush the needy in court,

for the LORD will take up their case
and will exact life for life.

Do not make friends with a hot-tempered person,
do not associate with one easily angered,

or you may learn their ways
and get yourself ensnared.

Do not be one who shakes hands in pledge
or puts up security for debts;

if you lack the means to pay,
your very bed will be snatched from under you.

Do not move an ancient boundary stone
set up by your ancestors.

Do you see someone skilled in their work?
They will serve before kings;
they will not serve before officials of low rank.

When you sit to dine with a ruler,
note well what is before you,

and put a knife to your throat
if you are given to gluttony.

Do not crave his delicacies,
for that food is deceptive.

Do not wear yourself out to get rich;
do not trust your own cleverness.
Cast but a glance at riches, and they are gone,
for they will surely sprout wings
and fly off to the sky like an eagle.

Do not eat the food of a begrudging host,
do not crave his delicacies;
for he is the kind of person
who is always thinking about the cost.
"Eat and drink," he says to you,
but his heart is not with you.
You will vomit up the little you have eaten
and will have wasted your compliments.

Do not speak to fools,
for they will scorn your prudent words.

Do not move an ancient boundary stone
or encroach on the fields of the fatherless,
for their Defender is strong;
he will take up their case against you.

Apply your heart to instruction
and your ears to words of knowledge.

Do not withhold discipline from a child;
if you punish them with the rod, they will not die.
Punish them with the rod
and save them from death.

My son, if your heart is wise,
then my heart will be glad indeed;
my inmost being will rejoice
when your lips speak what is right.

Do not let your heart envy sinners,
but always be zealous for the fear of the LORD.
There is surely a future hope for you,
and your hope will not be cut off.

Listen, my son, and be wise,
and set your heart on the right path:

Do not join those who drink too much wine
or gorge themselves on meat,

for drunkards and gluttons become poor,
and drowsiness clothes them in rags.

Listen to your father, who gave you life,
and do not despise your mother when she is old.

Buy the truth and do not sell it—
wisdom, instruction and insight as well.

The father of a righteous child has great joy;
a man who fathers a wise son rejoices in him.

May your father and mother rejoice;
may she who gave you birth be joyful!

My son, give me your heart
and let your eyes delight in my ways,

for an adulterous woman is a deep pit,
and a wayward wife is a narrow well.

Like a bandit she lies in wait
and multiplies the unfaithful among men.

Who has woe? Who has sorrow?
Who has strife? Who has complaints?
Who has needless bruises? Who has bloodshot eyes?

Those who linger over wine,
who go to sample bowls of mixed wine.

Do not gaze at wine when it is red,
when it sparkles in the cup,
when it goes down smoothly!

In the end it bites like a snake
and poisons like a viper.

Your eyes will see strange sights,
and your mind will imagine confusing things.

You will be like one sleeping on the high seas,
lying on top of the rigging.

"They hit me," you will say, "but I'm not hurt!
They beat me, but I don't feel it!

When will I wake up
so I can find another drink?"

Do not envy the wicked,
do not desire their company;

for their hearts plot violence,
and their lips talk about making trouble.

By wisdom a house is built,
and through understanding it is established;

through knowledge its rooms are filled
with rare and beautiful treasures.

The wise prevail through great power,
and those who have knowledge muster their strength.

Surely you need guidance to wage war,
and victory is won through many advisers.

Wisdom is too high for fools;
in the assembly at the gate they must not open
their mouths.

Whoever plots evil
will be known as a schemer.

The schemes of folly are sin,
and people detest a mocker.

If you falter in a time of trouble,
how small is your strength!

Rescue those being led away to death;
hold back those staggering toward slaughter.

If you say, "But we knew nothing about this,"
does not he who weighs the heart perceive it?

Does not he who guards your life know it?
Will he not repay everyone according to what
they have done?

Eat honey, my son, for it is good;
honey from the comb is sweet to your taste.

Know also that wisdom is like honey for you:
If you find it, there is a future hope for you,
and your hope will not be cut off.

Do not lurk like a thief near the house
of the righteous,
do not plunder their dwelling place;

for though the righteous fall seven times,
        they rise again,
but the wicked stumble when calamity strikes.

Do not gloat when your enemy falls;
when they stumble, do not let your heart rejoice,

or the LORD will see and disapprove
and turn his wrath away from them.

Do not fret because of evildoers
or be envious of the wicked,

for the evildoer has no future hope,
and the lamp of the wicked will be snuffed out.

Fear the LORD and the king, my son,
and do not join with rebellious officials,

for those two will send sudden destruction on them,
and who knows what calamities they can bring?

These also are sayings of the wise:

To show partiality in judging is not good:

Whoever says to the guilty, "You are innocent,"
will be cursed by peoples and denounced by nations.

But it will go well with those who convict
        the guilty,
and rich blessing will come on them.

An honest answer
is like a kiss on the lips.

Put your outdoor work in order
and get your fields ready;
after that, build your house.

Do not testify against your neighbor without cause—
would you use your lips to mislead?

Do not say, "I'll do to them as they have done to me;
I'll pay them back for what they did."

I went past the field of a sluggard,
past the vineyard of someone who has no sense;

thorns had come up everywhere,
the ground was covered with weeds,
and the stone wall was in ruins.

I applied my heart to what I observed
and learned a lesson from what I saw:

A little sleep, a little slumber,
a little folding of the hands to rest —

and poverty will come on you like a thief
and scarcity like an armed man.

These are more proverbs of Solomon, compiled by the men of
Hezekiah king of Judah:

It is the glory of God to conceal a matter;
to search out a matter is the glory of kings.

As the heavens are high and the earth is deep,
so the hearts of kings are unsearchable.

Remove the dross from the silver,
and a silversmith can produce a vessel;

remove wicked officials from the king's presence,
and his throne will be established through
righteousness.

Do not exalt yourself in the king's presence,
and do not claim a place among his great men;

it is better for him to say to you, "Come up here,"
than for him to humiliate you before his nobles.

What you have seen with your eyes
do not bring hastily to court,

for what will you do in the end
if your neighbor puts you to shame?

If you take your neighbor to court,
do not betray another's confidence,

or the one who hears it may shame you
and the charge against you will stand.

Like apples of gold in settings of silver
is a ruling rightly given.

Like an earring of gold or an ornament of fine gold
is the rebuke of a wise judge to a listening ear.

Like a snow-cooled drink at harvest time
is a trustworthy messenger to the one who sends him;
he refreshes the spirit of his master.

Like clouds and wind without rain
is one who boasts of gifts never given.

Through patience a ruler can be persuaded,
and a gentle tongue can break a bone.

If you find honey, eat just enough—
too much of it, and you will vomit.

Seldom set foot in your neighbor's house—
too much of you, and they will hate you.

Like a club or a sword or a sharp arrow
is one who gives false testimony against a neighbor.

Like a broken tooth or a lame foot
is reliance on the unfaithful in a time of trouble.

Like one who takes away a garment on a cold day,
or like vinegar poured on a wound,
is one who sings songs to a heavy heart.

If your enemy is hungry, give him food to eat;
if he is thirsty, give him water to drink.

In doing this, you will heap burning coals on his head,
and the LORD will reward you.

Like a north wind that brings unexpected rain
is a sly tongue—which provokes a horrified look.

Better to live on a corner of the roof
than share a house with a quarrelsome wife.

Like cold water to a weary soul
is good news from a distant land.

Like a muddied spring or a polluted well
are the righteous who give way to the wicked.

It is not good to eat too much honey,
nor is it honorable to search out matters that
    are too deep.

Like a city whose walls are broken through
is a person who lacks self-control.

Like snow in summer or rain in harvest,
honor is not fitting for a fool.

Like a fluttering sparrow or a darting swallow,
an undeserved curse does not come to rest.

A whip for the horse, a bridle for the donkey,
and a rod for the backs of fools!

Do not answer a fool according to his folly,
or you yourself will be just like him.

Answer a fool according to his folly,
or he will be wise in his own eyes.

Sending a message by the hands of a fool
is like cutting off one's feet or drinking poison.

Like the useless legs of one who is lame
is a proverb in the mouth of a fool.

Like tying a stone in a sling
is the giving of honor to a fool.

Like a thornbush in a drunkard's hand
is a proverb in the mouth of a fool.

Like an archer who wounds at random
is one who hires a fool or any passer-by.

As a dog returns to its vomit,
so fools repeat their folly.

Do you see a person wise in their own eyes?
There is more hope for a fool than for them.

A sluggard says, "There's a lion in the road,
a fierce lion roaming the streets!"

As a door turns on its hinges,
so a sluggard turns on his bed.

A sluggard buries his hand in the dish;
he is too lazy to bring it back to his mouth.

A sluggard is wiser in his own eyes
than seven people who answer discreetly.

Like one who grabs a stray dog by the ears
is someone who rushes into a quarrel not their own.

Like a maniac shooting
flaming arrows of death

is one who deceives their neighbor
and says, "I was only joking!"

Without wood a fire goes out;
without a gossip a quarrel dies down.

As charcoal to embers and as wood to fire,
so is a quarrelsome person for kindling strife.

The words of a gossip are like choice morsels;
they go down to the inmost parts.

Like a coating of silver dross on earthenware
are fervent lips with an evil heart.

Enemies disguise themselves with their lips,
but in their hearts they harbor deceit.

Though their speech is charming, do not believe them,
for seven abominations fill their hearts.

Their malice may be concealed by deception,
but their wickedness will be exposed in the assembly.

Whoever digs a pit will fall into it;
if someone rolls a stone, it will roll back on them.

A lying tongue hates those it hurts,
and a flattering mouth works ruin.

Do not boast about tomorrow,
for you do not know what a day may bring.

Let someone else praise you, and not your
    own mouth;
an outsider, and not your own lips.

Stone is heavy and sand a burden,
but a fool's provocation is heavier than both.

Anger is cruel and fury overwhelming,
but who can stand before jealousy?

Better is open rebuke
than hidden love.

Wounds from a friend can be trusted,
but an enemy multiplies kisses.

One who is full loathes honey from the comb,
but to the hungry even what is bitter tastes sweet.

Like a bird that flees its nest
is anyone who flees from home.

Perfume and incense bring joy to the heart,
and the pleasantness of a friend
springs from their heartfelt advice.

Do not forsake your friend or a friend of your family,
and do not go to your relative's house when disaster
    strikes you —
better a neighbor nearby than a relative far away.

Be wise, my son, and bring joy to my heart;
then I can answer anyone who treats me with
    contempt.

The prudent see danger and take refuge,
but the simple keep going and pay the penalty.

Take the garment of one who puts up security for a
    stranger;
hold it in pledge if it is done for an outsider.

If anyone loudly blesses their neighbor early in the
    morning,
it will be taken as a curse.

A quarrelsome wife is like the dripping
of a leaky roof in a rainstorm;
restraining her is like restraining the wind
or grasping oil with the hand.

As iron sharpens iron,
so one person sharpens another.

The one who guards a fig tree will eat its fruit,
and whoever protects their master will be honored.

As water reflects the face,
so one's life reflects the heart.

Death and Destruction are never satisfied,
and neither are human eyes.

The crucible for silver and the furnace for gold,
but people are tested by their praise.

Though you grind a fool in a mortar,
grinding them like grain with a pestle,
you will not remove their folly from them.

Be sure you know the condition of your flocks,
give careful attention to your herds;

for riches do not endure forever,
and a crown is not secure for all generations.

When the hay is removed and new growth appears
and the grass from the hills is gathered in,

the lambs will provide you with clothing,
and the goats with the price of a field.

You will have plenty of goats' milk to feed
    your family
and to nourish your female servants.

The wicked flee though no one pursues,
but the righteous are as bold as a lion.

When a country is rebellious, it has many rulers,
but a ruler with discernment and knowledge
    maintains order.

A ruler who oppresses the poor
is like a driving rain that leaves no crops.

Those who forsake instruction praise the wicked,
but those who heed it resist them.

Evildoers do not understand what is right,
but those who seek the Lord understand it fully.

Better the poor whose walk is blameless
than the rich whose ways are perverse.

A discerning son heeds instruction,
but a companion of gluttons disgraces his father.

Whoever increases wealth by taking interest or profit
    from the poor
amasses it for another, who will be kind to the poor.

If anyone turns a deaf ear to my instruction,
even their prayers are detestable.

Whoever leads the upright along an evil path
will fall into their own trap,
but the blameless will receive a good inheritance.

The rich are wise in their own eyes;
one who is poor and discerning sees how deluded they
　　are.

When the righteous triumph, there is great elation;
but when the wicked rise to power, people go into
　　hiding.

Whoever conceals their sins does not prosper,
but the one who confesses and renounces them
　　finds mercy.

Blessed is the one who always trembles before God,
but whoever hardens their heart falls into trouble.

Like a roaring lion or a charging bear
is a wicked ruler over a helpless people.

A tyrannical ruler practices extortion,
but one who hates ill-gotten gain will enjoy a long reign.

Anyone tormented by the guilt of murder
will seek refuge in the grave;
let no one hold them back.

The one whose walk is blameless is kept safe,
but the one whose ways are perverse will fall into the pit.

Those who work their land will have abundant food,
but those who chase fantasies will have their fill of
　　poverty.

A faithful person will be richly blessed,
but one eager to get rich will not go unpunished.

To show partiality is not good —
yet a person will do wrong for a piece of bread.

The stingy are eager to get rich
and are unaware that poverty awaits them.

Whoever rebukes a person will in the end gain favor
rather than one who has a flattering tongue.

Whoever robs their father or mother
and says, "It's not wrong,"
is partner to one who destroys.

The greedy stir up conflict,
but those who trust in the LORD will prosper.

Those who trust in themselves are fools,
but those who walk in wisdom are kept safe.

Those who give to the poor will lack nothing,
but those who close their eyes to them receive
        many curses.

When the wicked rise to power, people go into hiding;
but when the wicked perish, the righteous thrive.

Whoever remains stiff-necked after many rebukes
will suddenly be destroyed—without remedy.

When the righteous thrive, the people rejoice;
when the wicked rule, the people groan.

A man who loves wisdom brings joy to his father,
but a companion of prostitutes squanders
        his wealth.

By justice a king gives a country stability,
but those who are greedy for bribes tear it down.

Those who flatter their neighbors
are spreading nets for their feet.

Evildoers are snared by their own sin,
but the righteous shout for joy and are glad.

The righteous care about justice for the poor,
but the wicked have no such concern.

Mockers stir up a city,
but the wise turn away anger.

If a wise person goes to court with a fool,
the fool rages and scoffs, and there is no peace.

The bloodthirsty hate a person of integrity
and seek to kill the upright.

Fools give full vent to their rage,
but the wise bring calm in the end.

If a ruler listens to lies,
all his officials become wicked.

The poor and the oppressor have this in common:
The LORD gives sight to the eyes of both.

If a king judges the poor with fairness,
his throne will be established forever.

A rod and a reprimand impart wisdom,
but a child left undisciplined disgraces its mother.

When the wicked thrive, so does sin,
but the righteous will see their downfall.

Discipline your children, and they will give you peace;
they will bring you the delights you desire.

Where there is no revelation, people cast off restraint;
but blessed is the one who heeds wisdom's instruction.

Servants cannot be corrected by mere words;
though they understand, they will not respond.

Do you see someone who speaks in haste?
There is more hope for a fool than for them.

A servant pampered from youth
will turn out to be insolent.

An angry person stirs up conflict,
and a hot-tempered person commits many sins.

Pride brings a person low,
but the lowly in spirit gain honor.

The accomplices of thieves are their own enemies;
they are put under oath and dare not testify.

Fear of man will prove to be a snare,
but whoever trusts in the LORD is kept safe.

Many seek an audience with a ruler,
but it is from the LORD that one gets justice.

The righteous detest the dishonest;
the wicked detest the upright.

The sayings of Agur son of Jakeh—an inspired utterance.

This man's utterance to Ithiel:

"I am weary, God,
but I can prevail.

Surely I am only a brute, not a man;
I do not have human understanding.

I have not learned wisdom,
nor have I attained to the knowledge of the Holy One.

Who has gone up to heaven and come down?
Whose hands have gathered up the wind?

Who has wrapped up the waters in a cloak?
Who has established all the ends of the earth?

What is his name, and what is the name of his son?
Surely you know!

"Every word of God is flawless;
he is a shield to those who take refuge in him.

Do not add to his words,
or he will rebuke you and prove you a liar.

"Two things I ask of you, LORD;
do not refuse me before I die:

Keep falsehood and lies far from me;
give me neither poverty nor riches,
but give me only my daily bread.

Otherwise, I may have too much and disown you
and say, 'Who is the LORD?'

Or I may become poor and steal,
and so dishonor the name of my God.

"Do not slander a servant to their master,
or they will curse you, and you will pay for it.

"There are those who curse their fathers
and do not bless their mothers;

those who are pure in their own eyes
and yet are not cleansed of their filth;

those whose eyes are ever so haughty,
whose glances are so disdainful;

those whose teeth are swords
and whose jaws are set with knives

to devour the poor from the earth
and the needy from among mankind.

"The leech has two daughters.
'Give! Give!' they cry.

"There are three things that are never satisfied,
four that never say, 'Enough!':

the grave, the barren womb,
land, which is never satisfied with water,
and fire, which never says, 'Enough!'

"The eye that mocks a father,
that scorns an aged mother,

will be pecked out by the ravens of the valley,
will be eaten by the vultures.

"There are three things that are too amazing for me,
four that I do not understand:

the way of an eagle in the sky,
the way of a snake on a rock,

the way of a ship on the high seas,
and the way of a man with a young woman.

"This is the way of an adulterous woman:
She eats and wipes her mouth
and says, 'I've done nothing wrong.'

"Under three things the earth trembles,
under four it cannot bear up:

a servant who becomes king,
a godless fool who gets plenty to eat,

a contemptible woman who gets married,
and a servant who displaces her mistress.

"Four things on earth are small,
yet they are extremely wise:

Ants are creatures of little strength,
yet they store up their food in the summer;

hyraxes are creatures of little power,
yet they make their home in the crags;

locusts have no king,
yet they advance together in ranks;

a lizard can be caught with the hand,
yet it is found in kings' palaces.

"There are three things that are stately
in their stride,
four that move with stately bearing:

a lion, mighty among beasts,
who retreats before nothing;

a strutting rooster, a he-goat,
and a king secure against revolt.

"If you play the fool and exalt yourself,
or if you plan evil,
clap your hand over your mouth!

For as churning cream produces butter,
and as twisting the nose produces blood,
so stirring up anger produces strife."

T he sayings of King Lemuel — an inspired utterance his mother
taught him.

Listen, my son! Listen, son of my womb!
Listen, my son, the answer to my prayers!

Do not spend your strength on women,
your vigor on those who ruin kings.

It is not for kings, Lemuel —
it is not for kings to drink wine,
not for rulers to crave beer,

lest they drink and forget what has been decreed,
and deprive all the oppressed of their rights.

Let beer be for those who are perishing,
wine for those who are in anguish!

Let them drink and forget their poverty
and remember their misery no more.

Speak up for those who cannot speak for themselves,
for the rights of all who are destitute.

Speak up and judge fairly;
defend the rights of the poor and needy.

A wife of noble character who can find?
She is worth far more than rubies.

Her husband has full confidence in her
and lacks nothing of value.

She brings him good, not harm,
all the days of her life.

She selects wool and flax
and works with eager hands.

She is like the merchant ships,
bringing her food from afar.

She gets up while it is still night;
she provides food for her family
and portions for her female servants.

She considers a field and buys it;
out of her earnings she plants a vineyard.

She sets about her work vigorously;
her arms are strong for her tasks.

She sees that her trading is profitable,
and her lamp does not go out at night.

In her hand she holds the distaff
and grasps the spindle with her fingers.

She opens her arms to the poor
and extends her hands to the needy.

When it snows, she has no fear for her household;
for all of them are clothed in scarlet.

She makes coverings for her bed;
she is clothed in fine linen and purple.

Her husband is respected at the city gate,
where he takes his seat among the elders
of the land.

She makes linen garments and sells them,
and supplies the merchants with sashes.

She is clothed with strength and dignity;
she can laugh at the days to come.

She speaks with wisdom,
and faithful instruction is on her tongue.

She watches over the affairs of her household
and does not eat the bread of idleness.

Her children arise and call her blessed;
her husband also, and he praises her:

"Many women do noble things,
but you surpass them all."

Charm is deceptive, and beauty is fleeting;
but a woman who fears the LORD is to be praised.

Honor her for all that her hands have done,
and let her works bring her praise at the city gate.

INVITATION TO
ECCLESIASTES

The word Ecclesiastes is a Greek translation of the Hebrew title *Qoholeth* that the author of this book adopts. It's translated here as *Teacher*. The term likely refers to "someone who addresses an assembly." This book is therefore the collected words of a "teacher" or "preacher," just as a note at the end informs us: *Not only was the Teacher wise, but he also imparted knowledge to the people. He pondered and searched out and set in order many proverbs.* The Teacher describes himself as having been *king over Israel in Jerusalem*, and the editor introduces him with the title *son of David*. Both of these mean that he was in the royal line of Judah. He isn't identified further, and while tradition identifies him with Solomon, who was renowned for his wisdom, it's appropriate to leave this cloak of anonymity in place. After all, the Teacher warns us not to make fame our life's pursuit: *Even those yet to come will not be remembered by those who follow them.*

The words of the Teacher himself begin and end with the declaration, *Meaningless! Meaningless! Everything is meaningless!* As we discover from the teachings in the rest of the book, this phrase warns us that all of the rewards we work for and count on in life are uncertain, fleeting and ultimately unsatisfying. They're not a dependable source of enduring meaning. The Teacher pursues this insight, and the problem it poses for living, in a long discourse that shifts back and forth between autobiography and exhortation. The words of the Teacher are provocative and unsettling, and the editor who presents them explains that they will serve as *goads* to prod readers out of their complacent assumptions about life and make them re-examine the course they've chosen.

Ecclesiastes is essentially a long series of individual reflections that make observations and draw conclusions about various aspects of life as we know it on earth. These are gathered into seven larger reflections that all lead to the same conclusion: *a person can do nothing better than to eat and drink and find satisfaction in their own toil.* This means that people shouldn't sacrifice present joys for rewards that are fleeting and uncertain. Instead, they should find work that they enjoy while they're doing it, and be sure not to miss the simple joys that life always has to offer. While this larger "reflection" pattern provides a loose structure for the book as a whole, the discourse is nevertheless intentionally repetitive, almost rambling, alternating between poetry and prose. This form is designed to mirror the book's description of life, which it symbolizes in its opening speech by the wind: *round and round it goes, ever returning on its course.*

The basic issue addressed in the book is the futility that commonly reveals itself in how things turn out in life. It's true, the Teacher says, that there are joys and satisfactions that the uncertainty of life often does not threaten. These include finding joy in one's daily work, as well as in friendship and marriage. But when he says that *what is crooked cannot be straightened*, he reminds us that something has intruded into our world and made it wrong somehow. *Under the sun*, where we all live, there are no guarantees about the results of our efforts. This fits right into the larger Jewish story told in the rest of the Scriptures. Setting things right again is what this bigger drama is about. The Teacher, however, does not tell us about God's attempts at straightening out the world. He is content in the end to inform us that God is still sovereign over all things and that it's our duty to follow his ways for living, for he *will bring every deed into judgment.*

ECCLESIASTES

T he words of the Teacher, son of David, king in Jerusalem:

"Meaningless! Meaningless!"
  says the Teacher.
  "Utterly meaningless!
  Everything is meaningless."

What do people gain from all their labors
  at which they toil under the sun?

Generations come and generations go,
  but the earth remains forever.
The sun rises and the sun sets,
  and hurries back to where it rises.
The wind blows to the south
  and turns to the north;
round and round it goes,
  ever returning on its course.
All streams flow into the sea,
  yet the sea is never full.
To the place the streams come from,
  there they return again.
All things are wearisome,
  more than one can say.
The eye never has enough of seeing,
  nor the ear its fill of hearing.
What has been will be again,
  what has been done will be done again;
there is nothing new under the sun.

Is there anything of which one can say,
"Look! This is something new"?

It was here already, long ago;
it was here before our time.

No one remembers the former generations,
and even those yet to come

will not be remembered
by those who follow them.

I, the Teacher, was king over Israel in Jerusalem. I applied my mind to study and to explore by wisdom all that is done under the heavens. What a heavy burden God has laid on mankind! I have seen all the things that are done under the sun; all of them are meaningless, a chasing after the wind.

What is crooked cannot be straightened;
what is lacking cannot be counted.

I said to myself, "Look, I have increased in wisdom more than anyone who has ruled over Jerusalem before me; I have experienced much of wisdom and knowledge." Then I applied myself to the understanding of wisdom, and also of madness and folly, but I learned that this, too, is a chasing after the wind.

For with much wisdom comes much sorrow;
the more knowledge, the more grief.

I said to myself, "Come now, I will test you with pleasure to find out what is good." But that also proved to be meaningless. "Laughter," I said, "is madness. And what does pleasure accomplish?" I tried cheering myself with wine, and embracing folly—my mind still guiding me with wisdom. I wanted to see what was good for people to do under the heavens during the few days of their lives.

I undertook great projects: I built houses for myself and planted vineyards. I made gardens and parks and planted all kinds of fruit trees in them. I made reservoirs to water groves of flourishing trees. I bought male and female slaves and had other slaves who were born in my house. I also owned more herds and flocks than anyone in Jerusalem before me. I amassed silver and gold for myself, and the treasure of kings and provinces. I acquired male and female singers, and a harem as well — the delights of a man's heart. I became greater by far than anyone in Jerusalem before me. In all this my wisdom stayed with me.

> I denied myself nothing my eyes desired;
> I refused my heart no pleasure.

> My heart took delight in all my labor,
> and this was the reward for all my toil.

> Yet when I surveyed all that my hands had done
> and what I had toiled to achieve,

> everything was meaningless, a chasing after the wind;
> nothing was gained under the sun.

> Then I turned my thoughts to consider wisdom,
> and also madness and folly.

> What more can the king's successor do
> than what has already been done?

> I saw that wisdom is better than folly,
> just as light is better than darkness.

> The wise have eyes in their heads,
> while the fool walks in the darkness;

> but I came to realize
> that the same fate overtakes them both.

Then I said to myself,

> "The fate of the fool will overtake me also.
> What then do I gain by being wise?"

> I said to myself,
> "This too is meaningless."

> For the wise, like the fool, will not be long remembered;
> the days have already come when both have been
> forgotten.

> Like the fool, the wise too must die!

So I hated life, because the work that is done under the sun was grievous to me. All of it is meaningless, a chasing after the wind. I hated all the things I had toiled for under the sun, because I must leave them to the one who comes after me. And who knows whether that person will be wise or foolish? Yet they will have control over all the fruit of my toil into which I have poured my effort and skill under the sun. This too is meaningless. So my heart began to despair over all my toilsome labor under the sun. For a person may labor with wisdom, knowledge and skill, and then they must leave all they own to another who has not toiled for it. This too is meaningless and a great misfortune. What do people get for all the toil and anxious striving with which they labor under the sun? All their days their work is grief and pain; even at night their minds do not rest. This too is meaningless.

A person can do nothing better than to eat and drink and find satisfaction in their own toil. This too, I see, is from the hand of God, for without him, who can eat or find enjoyment? To the person who pleases him, God gives wisdom, knowledge and happiness, but to the sinner he gives the task of gathering and storing up wealth to hand it over to the one who pleases God. This too is meaningless, a chasing after the wind.

T here is a time for everything,
and a season for every activity under the heavens:

a time to be born and a time to die,
a time to plant and a time to uproot,
a time to kill and a time to heal,
a time to tear down and a time to build,
a time to weep and a time to laugh,
a time to mourn and a time to dance,
a time to scatter stones and a time to gather them,
a time to embrace and a time to refrain from embracing,
a time to search and a time to give up,
a time to keep and a time to throw away,
a time to tear and a time to mend,
a time to be silent and a time to speak,
a time to love and a time to hate,
a time for war and a time for peace.

W hat do workers gain from their toil? I have seen the burden God has laid on the human race. He has made everything beautiful in its time. He has also set eternity in the human heart; yet no one can fathom what God has done from beginning to end. I know that there is nothing better for people than to be happy and to do good while they live. That each of them may eat and drink, and find satisfaction in all their toil — this is the gift of God. I know that everything God does will endure forever; nothing can be added to it and nothing taken from it. God does it so that people will fear him.

> Whatever is has already been,
> and what will be has been before;
> and God will call the past to account.

And I saw something else under the sun:

> In the place of judgment — wickedness was there,
> in the place of justice — wickedness was there.

I said to myself,

> "God will bring into judgment
> both the righteous and the wicked,
> for there will be a time for every activity,
> a time to judge every deed."

I also said to myself, "As for humans, God tests them so that they may see that they are like the animals. Surely the fate of human beings is like that of the animals; the same fate awaits them both: As one dies, so dies the other. All have the same breath; humans have no advantage over animals. Everything is meaningless. All go to the same place; all come from dust, and to dust all return. Who knows if the human spirit rises upward and if the spirit of the animal goes down into the earth?"

So I saw that there is nothing better for a person than to enjoy their work, because that is their lot. For who can bring them to see what will happen after them?

Again I looked and saw all the oppression that was taking place under the sun:

> I saw the tears of the oppressed —
> and they have no comforter;
> power was on the side of their oppressors —
> and they have no comforter.
>
> And I declared that the dead,
> who had already died,
> are happier than the living,
> who are still alive.

But better than both
is the one who has never been born,

who has not seen the evil
that is done under the sun.

And I saw that all toil and all achievement spring from one person's envy of another. This too is meaningless, a chasing after the wind.

Fools fold their hands
and ruin themselves.

Better one handful with tranquillity
than two handfuls with toil
and chasing after the wind.

Again I saw something meaningless under the sun:

There was a man all alone;
he had neither son nor brother.

There was no end to his toil,
yet his eyes were not content with his wealth.

"For whom am I toiling," he asked,
"and why am I depriving myself of enjoyment?"

This too is meaningless—
a miserable business!

Two are better than one,
because they have a good return for their labor:

If either of them falls down,
one can help the other up.

But pity anyone who falls
and has no one to help them up.

Also, if two lie down together, they will keep warm.
But how can one keep warm alone?

Though one may be overpowered,
two can defend themselves.

A cord of three strands is not quickly broken.

Better a poor but wise youth than an old but foolish king who no longer knows how to heed a warning. The youth may have come from prison to the kingship, or he may have been born in poverty within his kingdom. I saw that all who lived and walked under the sun followed the youth, the king's successor. There was no end to all the people who were before them. But those who came later were not pleased with the successor. This too is meaningless, a chasing after the wind.

Guard your steps when you go to the house of God. Go near to listen rather than to offer the sacrifice of fools, who do not know that they do wrong.

> Do not be quick with your mouth,
> do not be hasty in your heart
> to utter anything before God.

> God is in heaven
> and you are on earth,
> so let your words be few.

> A dream comes when there are many cares,
> and many words mark the speech of a fool.

When you make a vow to God, do not delay to fulfill it. He has no pleasure in fools; fulfill your vow. It is better not to make a vow than to make one and not fulfill it. Do not let your mouth lead you into sin. And do not protest to the temple messenger, "My vow was a mistake." Why should God be angry at what you say and destroy the work of your hands? Much dreaming and many words are meaningless. Therefore fear God.

If you see the poor oppressed in a district, and justice and rights denied, do not be surprised at such things; for one official is eyed by a higher one, and over them both are others higher still. The increase from the land is taken by all; the king himself profits from the fields.

> Whoever loves money never has enough;
> whoever loves wealth is never satisfied with their
>   income.
> This too is meaningless.

> As goods increase,
> so do those who consume them.

> And what benefit are they to the owners
> except to feast their eyes on them?

> The sleep of a laborer is sweet,
> whether they eat little or much,

but as for the rich, their abundance
permits them no sleep.

I have seen a grievous evil under the sun:

wealth hoarded to the harm of its owners,
or wealth lost through some misfortune,
so that when they have children
there is nothing left for them to inherit.
Everyone comes naked from their mother's womb,
and as everyone comes, so they depart.
They take nothing from their toil
that they can carry in their hands.

This too is a grievous evil:

As everyone comes, so they depart,
and what do they gain,
since they toil for the wind?
All their days they eat in darkness,
with great frustration, affliction and anger.

This is what I have observed to be good: that it is appropriate
for a person to eat, to drink and to find satisfaction in their toilsome labor under the sun during the few days of life God has giv-
en them — for this is their lot. Moreover, when God gives someone
wealth and possessions, and the ability to enjoy them, to accept
their lot and be happy in their toil — this is a gift of God. They seldom reflect on the days of their life, because God keeps them occupied with gladness of heart.

I have seen another evil under the sun, and it weighs heavily on
mankind: God gives some people wealth, possessions and honor,
so that they lack nothing their hearts desire, but God does not grant
them the ability to enjoy them, and strangers enjoy them instead.
This is meaningless, a grievous evil.

A man may have a hundred children and live many years; yet
no matter how long he lives, if he cannot enjoy his prosperity and
does not receive proper burial, I say that a stillborn child is better
off than he. It comes without meaning, it departs in darkness, and

in darkness its name is shrouded. Though it never saw the sun or knew anything, it has more rest than does that man — even if he lives a thousand years twice over but fails to enjoy his prosperity. Do not all go to the same place?

> Everyone's toil is for their mouth,
> yet their appetite is never satisfied.

> What advantage have the wise over fools?

> What do the poor gain
> by knowing how to conduct themselves
>   before others?

> Better what the eye sees
> than the roving of the appetite.

> This too is meaningless,
> a chasing after the wind.

> Whatever exists has already been named,
> and what humanity is has been known;

> no one can contend
> with someone who is stronger.

> The more the words,
> the less the meaning,
> and how does that profit anyone?

For who knows what is good for a person in life, during the few and meaningless days they pass through like a shadow? Who can tell them what will happen under the sun after they are gone?

> A good name is better than fine perfume,
> and the day of death better than the day of birth.

> It is better to go to a house of mourning
> than to go to a house of feasting,

> for death is the destiny of everyone;
> the living should take this to heart.

> Frustration is better than laughter,
> because a sad face is good for the heart.

> The heart of the wise is in the house of mourning,
> but the heart of fools is in the house of pleasure.

> It is better to heed the rebuke of a wise person
> than to listen to the song of fools.

Like the crackling of thorns under the pot,
so is the laughter of fools.
This too is meaningless.

Extortion turns a wise person into a fool,
and a bribe corrupts the heart.

The end of a matter is better than its beginning,
and patience is better than pride.

Do not be quickly provoked in your spirit,
for anger resides in the lap of fools.

Do not say, "Why were the old days better than these?"
For it is not wise to ask such questions.

Wisdom, like an inheritance, is a good thing
and benefits those who see the sun.

Wisdom is a shelter
as money is a shelter,

but the advantage of knowledge is this:
Wisdom preserves those who have it.

Consider what God has done:

Who can straighten
what he has made crooked?

When times are good, be happy;
but when times are bad, consider this:

God has made the one
as well as the other.

Therefore, no one can discover
anything about their future.

In this meaningless life of mine I have seen both of these:

the righteous perishing in their righteousness,
and the wicked living long in their wickedness.

Do not be overrighteous,
neither be overwise —
why destroy yourself?

Do not be overwicked,
and do not be a fool —
why die before your time?

It is good to grasp the one
and not let go of the other.
Whoever fears God will avoid all extremes.

Wisdom makes one wise person more powerful
than ten rulers in a city.

Indeed, there is no one on earth who is righteous,
no one who does what is right and never sins.

Do not pay attention to every word people say,
or you may hear your servant cursing you —

for you know in your heart
that many times you yourself have cursed others.

All this I tested by wisdom and I said,

"I am determined to be wise" —
but this was beyond me.

Whatever exists is far off and most profound —
who can discover it?

So I turned my mind to understand,
to investigate and to search out wisdom and
the scheme of things

and to understand the stupidity of wickedness
and the madness of folly.

I find more bitter than death
the woman who is a snare,

whose heart is a trap
and whose hands are chains.

The man who pleases God will escape her,
but the sinner she will ensnare.

"Look," says the Teacher, "this is what I have discovered:

"Adding one thing to another to discover the scheme
of things —
while I was still searching
but not finding —

I found one upright man among a thousand,
but not one upright woman among them all.

This only have I found:
God created mankind upright,
but they have gone in search of many schemes."

Who is like the wise?
Who knows the explanation of things?

A person's wisdom brightens their face
and changes its hard appearance.

Obey the king's command, I say, because you took an oath before God. Do not be in a hurry to leave the king's presence. Do not stand up for a bad cause, for he will do whatever he pleases. Since a king's word is supreme, who can say to him, "What are you doing?"

Whoever obeys his command will come to no harm,
and the wise heart will know the proper time and
procedure.

For there is a proper time and procedure for
every matter,
though a person may be weighed down by misery.

Since no one knows the future,
who can tell someone else what is to come?

As no one has power over the wind to contain it,
so no one has power over the time of their death.

As no one is discharged in time of war,
so wickedness will not release those who practice it.

All this I saw, as I applied my mind to everything done under the sun. There is a time when a man lords it over others to his own hurt. Then too, I saw the wicked buried—those who used to come and go from the holy place and receive praise in the city where they did this. This too is meaningless.

When the sentence for a crime is not quickly carried out, people's hearts are filled with schemes to do wrong. Although a wicked person who commits a hundred crimes may live a long time, I know that it will go better with those who fear God, who are reverent before him. Yet because the wicked do not fear God, it will not go well with them, and their days will not lengthen like a shadow.

There is something else meaningless that occurs on earth: the righteous who get what the wicked deserve, and the wicked who get what the righteous deserve. This too, I say, is meaningless. So I commend the enjoyment of life, because there is nothing better for a person under the sun than to eat and drink and be glad. Then joy will accompany them in their toil all the days of the life God has given them under the sun.

When I applied my mind to know wisdom and to observe the labor that is done on earth—people getting no sleep day or night— then I saw all that God has done. No one can comprehend what goes on under the sun. Despite all their efforts to search it out, no one can discover its meaning. Even if the wise claim they know, they cannot really comprehend it.

So I reflected on all this and concluded that the righteous and the wise and what they do are in God's hands, but no one knows whether love or hate awaits them. All share a common destiny—the righteous and the wicked, the good and the bad, the clean and the unclean, those who offer sacrifices and those who do not.

> As it is with the good,
> so with the sinful;
>
> as it is with those who take oaths,
> so with those who are afraid to take them.

This is the evil in everything that happens under the sun: The same destiny overtakes all. The hearts of people, moreover, are full of evil and there is madness in their hearts while they live, and afterward they join the dead. Anyone who is among the living has hope—even a live dog is better off than a dead lion!

> For the living know that they will die,
> but the dead know nothing;
>
> they have no further reward,
> and even their name is forgotten.
>
> Their love, their hate
> and their jealousy have long since vanished;
>
> never again will they have a part
> in anything that happens under the sun.

Go, eat your food with gladness, and drink your wine with a joyful heart, for God has already approved what you do. Always be clothed in white, and always anoint your head with oil. Enjoy life with your wife, whom you love, all the days of this meaningless life that God has given you under the sun—all your meaningless days. For this is your lot in life and in your toilsome labor under the sun. Whatever your hand finds to do, do it with all your might, for in the realm of the dead, where you are going, there is neither working nor planning nor knowledge nor wisdom.

I have seen something else under the sun:

> The race is not to the swift
> or the battle to the strong,
>
> nor does food come to the wise
> or wealth to the brilliant
> or favor to the learned;
>
> but time and chance happen to them all.

Moreover, no one knows when their hour will come:

> As fish are caught in a cruel net,
> or birds are taken in a snare,
>
> so people are trapped by evil times
> that fall unexpectedly upon them.

I also saw under the sun this example of wisdom that greatly impressed me: There was once a small city with only a few people in it. And a powerful king came against it, surrounded it and built huge siege works against it. Now there lived in that city a man poor but wise, and he saved the city by his wisdom. But nobody remembered that poor man. So I said, "Wisdom is better than strength." But the poor man's wisdom is despised, and his words are no longer heeded.

> The quiet words of the wise are more
>   to be heeded
> than the shouts of a ruler of fools.
>
> Wisdom is better than weapons of war,
> but one sinner destroys much good.
>
> As dead flies give perfume a bad smell,
> so a little folly outweighs wisdom and honor.
>
> The heart of the wise inclines to the right,
> but the heart of the fool to the left.
>
> Even as fools walk along the road,
> they lack sense
> and show everyone how stupid they are.

If a ruler's anger rises against you,
do not leave your post;
calmness can lay great offenses to rest.

There is an evil I have seen under the sun,
the sort of error that arises from a ruler:

Fools are put in many high positions,
while the rich occupy the low ones.

I have seen slaves on horseback,
while princes go on foot like slaves.

Whoever digs a pit may fall into it;
whoever breaks through a wall may be bitten
    by a snake.

Whoever quarries stones may be injured by them;
whoever splits logs may be endangered by them.

If the ax is dull
and its edge unsharpened,

more strength is needed,
but skill will bring success.

If a snake bites before it is charmed,
the charmer receives no fee.

Words from the mouth of the wise are gracious,
but fools are consumed by their own lips.

At the beginning their words are folly;
at the end they are wicked madness —
and fools multiply words.

No one knows what is coming —
who can tell someone else what will happen
    after them?

The toil of fools wearies them;
they do not know the way to town.

Woe to the land whose king was a servant
and whose princes feast in the morning.

Blessed is the land whose king is of noble birth
and whose princes eat at a proper time —
for strength and not for drunkenness.

Through laziness, the rafters sag;
because of idle hands, the house leaks.

A feast is made for laughter,
wine makes life merry,
and money is the answer for everything.

Do not revile the king even in your thoughts,
or curse the rich in your bedroom,
because a bird in the sky may carry your words,
and a bird on the wing may report what
you say.

Ship your grain across the sea;
after many days you may receive a return.
Invest in seven ventures, yes, in eight;
you do not know what disaster may come
upon the land.

If clouds are full of water,
they pour rain on the earth.
Whether a tree falls to the south or to the north,
in the place where it falls, there it will lie.
Whoever watches the wind will not plant;
whoever looks at the clouds will not reap.

As you do not know the path of the wind,
or how the body is formed in a mother's womb,
so you cannot understand the work of God,
the Maker of all things.

Sow your seed in the morning,
and at evening let your hands not be idle,
for you do not know which will succeed,
whether this or that,
or whether both will do equally well.

Light is sweet,
and it pleases the eyes to see the sun.
However many years anyone may live,
let them enjoy them all.

But let them remember the days of darkness,
for there will be many.
Everything to come is meaningless.

You who are young, be happy while you are young,
and let your heart give you joy in the days of your youth.

Follow the ways of your heart
and whatever your eyes see,

but know that for all these things
God will bring you into judgment.

So then, banish anxiety from your heart
and cast off the troubles of your body,
for youth and vigor are meaningless.

Remember your Creator
in the days of your youth,
before the days of trouble come
and the years approach when you will say,
"I find no pleasure in them" —

before the sun and the light
and the moon and the stars grow dark,
and the clouds return after the rain;

when the keepers of the house tremble,
and the strong men stoop,

when the grinders cease because they are few,
and those looking through the windows grow dim;

when the doors to the street are closed
and the sound of grinding fades;

when people rise up at the sound of birds,
but all their songs grow faint;

when people are afraid of heights
and of dangers in the streets;

when the almond tree blossoms
and the grasshopper drags itself along
and desire no longer is stirred.

Then people go to their eternal home
and mourners go about the streets.

Remember him — before the silver cord is severed,
and the golden bowl is broken;

before the pitcher is shattered at the spring,
and the wheel broken at the well,

and the dust returns to the ground it came from,
and the spirit returns to God who gave it.

"Meaningless! Meaningless!" says the Teacher.
"Everything is meaningless!"

Not only was the Teacher wise, but he also imparted knowledge to the people. He pondered and searched out and set in order many proverbs. The Teacher searched to find just the right words, and what he wrote was upright and true.

The words of the wise are like goads, their collected sayings like firmly embedded nails — given by one shepherd. Be warned, my son, of anything in addition to them.

Of making many books there is no end, and much study wearies the body.

Now all has been heard;
here is the conclusion of the matter:

Fear God and keep his commandments,
for this is the duty of all mankind.

For God will bring every deed into judgment,
including every hidden thing,
whether it is good or evil.

INVITATION TO
JOB

Among the books of wisdom literature in the Bible, Proverbs describes how living right and cultivating godly character will generally lead to success, prosperity and well-being. The book of Ecclesiastes complements this teaching by warning that none of these rewards are actually guaranteed to anyone, since a kind of "crookedness" has come into our world. The book of Job goes a step further, exploring the situation of righteous people who not only aren't rewarded, but who actively suffer, through no fault of their own. It explores their situation by using a literary form that's well-attested in the literature of the international wisdom tradition, an extended conversation among people who take turns giving poetic speeches.

The book begins by introducing its central character, Job, as a man who was *blameless and upright; he feared God and shunned evil*. It then gives us a glimpse into the councils of heaven, where "the adversary" (the term is *satan* in Hebrew, but here it is as much a title as a name) points out an apparent problem with God's moral government of the universe. If goodness is always rewarded, how can it be known whether anyone is ever good out of pure love for God, rather than out of a desire for reward? In other words, even though this challenge eventually leads into detailed discussions of the "problem of evil"— why do people suffer in a universe governed by a good God, and how should they respond when they do?—the book is originally about the "problem of good." Can genuine goodness exist and be recognized? To test this, God allows the adversary to bring loss, sorrow and suffering into Job's life. The adversary tells God that Job *will surely curse you to your face.* Job struggles in this story, but he doesn't turn away from God.

Nevertheless, Job has a great many questions. He raises them in an exchange of speeches with his three friends Eliphaz, Bildad and Zophar, who come to sympathize with him and comfort him. Unfortunately, their rigid view of the moral universe keeps them from offering much sympathy or comfort. They're all convinced that goodness is invariably rewarded in this world and wrongdoing is inevitably punished, so they decide that Job's sufferings must be the consequence of something he's done wrong. They try, gently at first but then more insistently, to persuade him of this. In his replies to their speeches, Job acknowledges that what they say is generally true, but he insists that his case is an exception. God has brought suffering into his life for inexplicable reasons.

The friends speak in turn, always in the same order, and in eloquent poetry. However, they don't go three full rounds of debate before they apparently have nothing left to say. Job is then allowed to speak his piece, which he does even more eloquently than they do, insisting to the end that he's done nothing wrong and deserves a hearing before God. A new character then joins the conversation, a younger man named Elihu. He has kept quiet in deference to his elders, but he now challenges Job when he sees that the three friends have no answer for him. Elihu suggests, over the course of four poetic speeches (to which Job does not reply), that God may sometimes cause the righteous to suffer in order to warn them when they're tempted to do wrong. This is a slightly milder version of the friends' argument, and it amplifies the overall discussion. But it still doesn't address Job's actual situation. However, Job will soon get the hearing he desires. In his final speech Elihu describes God's greatness by what seems to be an analogy to a gathering storm. But it turns out that the storm is real, and it's bringing God to speak with Job in person.

As God addresses Job, he doesn't explain that by remaining loyal, despite having many questions and offering many protests, he's been showing that genuine goodness is possible. If God gave Job this explanation, it would ruin the whole test. Instead, God challenges Job's presumption that he, as a finite human, can understand how the universe should be run, and that he can complain knowledgeably when this isn't done to his liking. By appealing to his own work in creating, sustaining and caring for the creation, God presents his own infinite power and wisdom. In a second speech, God then contrastingly demonstrates the limits of human power by comparing people to two great beasts, *Behemoth* and *Leviathan*.

Job responds to these speeches by withdrawing his demand to state his case before God and by humbly acknowledging the limits of his own understanding. God then rebukes the three friends, who are guilty of far worse presumption than Job. As the book closes, God blesses Job with twice as much as he had before. These blessings, it is now recognized, are not a direct reward for good behavior, but rather an expression of the generosity and care of the same God who *cuts a channel for the torrents of rain . . . to satisfy a desolate wasteland* and who *provides food for the raven when its young cry out*.

The book of Job speaks to a universal question, and so it contains few specific references that indicate precisely when and where it was written. In the end, however, a precise date may not be necessary or even desirable. It's clear that the book's intention is to dispute the position of the three friends. Overconfident reductions of God's moral government to easy formulas can be found in every age. Eliphaz, Bildad and Zophar live on among us, and within us. And so to all of us, God still asks out of the whirlwind, *Where were you when I laid the earth's foundation?*

JOB

I n the land of Uz there lived a man whose name was Job. This man was blameless and upright; he feared God and shunned evil. He had seven sons and three daughters, and he owned seven thousand sheep, three thousand camels, five hundred yoke of oxen and five hundred donkeys, and had a large number of servants. He was the greatest man among all the people of the East.

His sons used to hold feasts in their homes on their birthdays, and they would invite their three sisters to eat and drink with them. When a period of feasting had run its course, Job would make arrangements for them to be purified. Early in the morning he would sacrifice a burnt offering for each of them, thinking, "Perhaps my children have sinned and cursed God in their hearts." This was Job's regular custom.

One day the angels came to present themselves before the LORD, and Satan also came with them. The LORD said to Satan, "Where have you come from?"

Satan answered the LORD, "From roaming throughout the earth, going back and forth on it."

Then the LORD said to Satan, "Have you considered my servant Job? There is no one on earth like him; he is blameless and upright, a man who fears God and shuns evil."

"Does Job fear God for nothing?" Satan replied. "Have you not put a hedge around him and his household and everything he has? You have blessed the work of his hands, so that his flocks and herds are spread throughout the land. But now stretch out your hand and strike everything he has, and he will surely curse you to your face."

The LORD said to Satan, "Very well, then, everything he has is in your power, but on the man himself do not lay a finger."

Then Satan went out from the presence of the LORD.

One day when Job's sons and daughters were feasting and drinking wine at the oldest brother's house, a messenger came to Job and said, "The oxen were plowing and the donkeys were grazing nearby, and the Sabeans attacked and made off with them. They put the servants to the sword, and I am the only one who has escaped to tell you!"

While he was still speaking, another messenger came and said, "The fire of God fell from the heavens and burned up the sheep and the servants, and I am the only one who has escaped to tell you!"

While he was still speaking, another messenger came and said, "The Chaldeans formed three raiding parties and swept down on your camels and made off with them. They put the servants to the sword, and I am the only one who has escaped to tell you!"

While he was still speaking, yet another messenger came and said, "Your sons and daughters were feasting and drinking wine at the oldest brother's house, when suddenly a mighty wind swept in from the desert and struck the four corners of the house. It collapsed on them and they are dead, and I am the only one who has escaped to tell you!"

At this, Job got up and tore his robe and shaved his head. Then he fell to the ground in worship and said:

> "Naked I came from my mother's womb,
>   and naked I will depart.
>
> The Lord gave and the Lord has taken away;
>   may the name of the Lord be praised."

In all this, Job did not sin by charging God with wrongdoing.

On another day the angels came to present themselves before the Lord, and Satan also came with them to present himself before him. And the Lord said to Satan, "Where have you come from?"

Satan answered the Lord, "From roaming throughout the earth, going back and forth on it."

Then the Lord said to Satan, "Have you considered my servant Job? There is no one on earth like him; he is blameless and upright, a man who fears God and shuns evil. And he still maintains his integrity, though you incited me against him to ruin him without any reason."

"Skin for skin!" Satan replied. "A man will give all he has for his own life. But now stretch out your hand and strike his flesh and bones, and he will surely curse you to your face."

The Lord said to Satan, "Very well, then, he is in your hands; but you must spare his life."

So Satan went out from the presence of the Lord and afflicted Job with painful sores from the soles of his feet to the crown of his head. Then Job took a piece of broken pottery and scraped himself with it as he sat among the ashes.

His wife said to him, "Are you still maintaining your integrity? Curse God and die!"

He replied, "You are talking like a foolish woman. Shall we accept good from God, and not trouble?"

In all this, Job did not sin in what he said.

When Job's three friends, Eliphaz the Temanite, Bildad the Shuhite and Zophar the Naamathite, heard about all the troubles that had come upon him, they set out from their homes and met together by agreement to go and sympathize with him and comfort him. When they saw him from a distance, they could hardly recognize him; they began to weep aloud, and they tore their robes and sprinkled dust on their heads. Then they sat on the ground with him for seven days and seven nights. No one said a word to him, because they saw how great his suffering was.

After this, Job opened his mouth and cursed the day of his birth. He said:

"May the day of my birth perish,
and the night that said, 'A boy is conceived!'

That day — may it turn to darkness;
may God above not care about it;
may no light shine on it.

May gloom and utter darkness claim it
        once more;
may a cloud settle over it;
may blackness overwhelm it.

That night — may thick darkness seize it;
may it not be included among the days
        of the year
nor be entered in any of the months.

May that night be barren;
may no shout of joy be heard in it.

May those who curse days curse that day,
those who are ready to rouse Leviathan.

May its morning stars become dark;
may it wait for daylight in vain

and not see the first rays of dawn,

for it did not shut the doors of the womb
      on me
to hide trouble from my eyes.

"Why did I not perish at birth,
and die as I came from the womb?

Why were there knees to receive me
and breasts that I might be nursed?

For now I would be lying down in peace;
I would be asleep and at rest

with kings and rulers of the earth,
who built for themselves places now lying
      in ruins,

with princes who had gold,
who filled their houses with silver.

Or why was I not hidden away in the ground
      like a stillborn child,
like an infant who never saw the light of day?

There the wicked cease from turmoil,
and there the weary are at rest.

Captives also enjoy their ease;
they no longer hear the slave driver's shout.

The small and the great are there,
and the slaves are freed from their owners.

"Why is light given to those in misery,
and life to the bitter of soul,

to those who long for death that does not come,
who search for it more than for hidden treasure,

who are filled with gladness
and rejoice when they reach the grave?

Why is life given to a man
whose way is hidden,
whom God has hedged in?

For sighing has become my daily food;
my groans pour out like water.

What I feared has come upon me;
what I dreaded has happened to me.

I have no peace, no quietness;
I have no rest, but only turmoil."

Then Eliphaz the Temanite replied:

"If someone ventures a word with you, will you be
      impatient?
But who can keep from speaking?

Think how you have instructed many,
how you have strengthened feeble hands.

Your words have supported those who stumbled;
you have strengthened faltering knees.

But now trouble comes to you, and you are
      discouraged;
it strikes you, and you are dismayed.

Should not your piety be your confidence
and your blameless ways your hope?

"Consider now: Who, being innocent, has
      ever perished?
Where were the upright ever destroyed?

As I have observed, those who plow evil
and those who sow trouble reap it.

At the breath of God they perish;
at the blast of his anger they are no more.

The lions may roar and growl,
yet the teeth of the great lions are broken.

The lion perishes for lack of prey,
and the cubs of the lioness are scattered.

"A word was secretly brought to me,
my ears caught a whisper of it.

Amid disquieting dreams in the night,
when deep sleep falls on people,

fear and trembling seized me
and made all my bones shake.

A spirit glided past my face,
and the hair on my body stood on end.

It stopped,
but I could not tell what it was.

A form stood before my eyes,
and I heard a hushed voice:

'Can a mortal be more righteous than God?
Can even a strong man be more pure than
     his Maker?

If God places no trust in his servants,
if he charges his angels with error,

how much more those who live in houses of clay,
whose foundations are in the dust,
who are crushed more readily than a moth!

Between dawn and dusk they are broken to pieces;
unnoticed, they perish forever.

Are not the cords of their tent pulled up,
so that they die without wisdom?'

"Call if you will, but who will answer you?
To which of the holy ones will you turn?

Resentment kills a fool,
and envy slays the simple.

I myself have seen a fool taking root,
but suddenly his house was cursed.

His children are far from safety,
crushed in court without a defender.

The hungry consume his harvest,
taking it even from among thorns,
and the thirsty pant after his wealth.

For hardship does not spring from the soil,
nor does trouble sprout from the ground.

Yet man is born to trouble
as surely as sparks fly upward.

"But if I were you, I would appeal to God;
I would lay my cause before him.

He performs wonders that cannot be fathomed,
miracles that cannot be counted.

He provides rain for the earth;
he sends water on the countryside.

The lowly he sets on high,
and those who mourn are lifted to safety.

He thwarts the plans of the crafty,
so that their hands achieve no success.

He catches the wise in their craftiness,
and the schemes of the wily are swept away.

Darkness comes upon them in the daytime;
at noon they grope as in the night.

He saves the needy from the sword in their
mouth;
he saves them from the clutches of the powerful.

So the poor have hope,
and injustice shuts its mouth.

"Blessed is the one whom God corrects;
so do not despise the discipline of the Almighty.

For he wounds, but he also binds up;
he injures, but his hands also heal.

From six calamities he will rescue you;
in seven no harm will touch you.

In famine he will deliver you from death,
and in battle from the stroke of the sword.

You will be protected from the lash of the tongue,
and need not fear when destruction comes.

You will laugh at destruction and famine,
and need not fear the wild animals.

For you will have a covenant with the stones
of the field,
and the wild animals will be at peace with you.

You will know that your tent is secure;
you will take stock of your property and find
nothing missing.

You will know that your children will be many,
and your descendants like the grass of the earth.

You will come to the grave in full vigor,
like sheaves gathered in season.

"We have examined this, and it is true.
So hear it and apply it to yourself."

Then Job replied:

"If only my anguish could be weighed
and all my misery be placed on the scales!

It would surely outweigh the sand of the seas —
no wonder my words have been impetuous.

The arrows of the Almighty are in me,
my spirit drinks in their poison;
God's terrors are marshaled against me.

Does a wild donkey bray when it has grass,
or an ox bellow when it has fodder?

Is tasteless food eaten without salt,
or is there flavor in the sap of the mallow?

I refuse to touch it;
such food makes me ill.

"Oh, that I might have my request,
that God would grant what I hope for,

that God would be willing to crush me,
to let loose his hand and cut off my life!

Then I would still have this consolation —
my joy in unrelenting pain —
that I had not denied the words of the Holy One.

"What strength do I have, that I should still hope?
What prospects, that I should be patient?

Do I have the strength of stone?
Is my flesh bronze?

Do I have any power to help myself,
now that success has been driven from me?

"Anyone who withholds kindness from a friend
forsakes the fear of the Almighty.

But my brothers are as undependable as intermittent
streams,
as the streams that overflow

when darkened by thawing ice
and swollen with melting snow,

but that stop flowing in the dry season,
and in the heat vanish from their channels.

Caravans turn aside from their routes;
they go off into the wasteland and perish.

The caravans of Tema look for water,
the traveling merchants of Sheba look in hope.

They are distressed, because they had been
confident;
they arrive there, only to be disappointed.

Now you too have proved to be of no help;
you see something dreadful and are afraid.

Have I ever said, 'Give something on my behalf,
pay a ransom for me from your wealth,

deliver me from the hand of the enemy,
rescue me from the clutches of the ruthless'?

"Teach me, and I will be quiet;
show me where I have been wrong.

How painful are honest words!
But what do your arguments prove?

Do you mean to correct what I say,
and treat my desperate words as wind?

You would even cast lots for the fatherless
and barter away your friend.

"But now be so kind as to look at me.
Would I lie to your face?

Relent, do not be unjust;
reconsider, for my integrity is at stake.

Is there any wickedness on my lips?
Can my mouth not discern malice?

"Do not mortals have hard service on earth?
Are not their days like those of hired laborers?

Like a slave longing for the evening shadows,
or a hired laborer waiting to be paid,

so I have been allotted months of futility,
and nights of misery have been assigned to me.

When I lie down I think, 'How long before I get up?'
The night drags on, and I toss and turn until dawn.

My body is clothed with worms and scabs,
my skin is broken and festering.

"My days are swifter than a weaver's shuttle,
and they come to an end without hope.

Remember, O God, that my life is but a breath;
my eyes will never see happiness again.

The eye that now sees me will see me no longer;
you will look for me, but I will be no more.

As a cloud vanishes and is gone,
so one who goes down to the grave does not return.

He will never come to his house again;
his place will know him no more.

"Therefore I will not keep silent;
I will speak out in the anguish of my spirit,
I will complain in the bitterness of my soul.

Am I the sea, or the monster of the deep,
that you put me under guard?

When I think my bed will comfort me
and my couch will ease my complaint,

even then you frighten me with dreams
and terrify me with visions,

so that I prefer strangling and death,
rather than this body of mine.

I despise my life; I would not live forever.
Let me alone; my days have no meaning.

"What is mankind that you make so much of them,
that you give them so much attention,

that you examine them every morning
and test them every moment?

Will you never look away from me,
or let me alone even for an instant?

If I have sinned, what have I done to you,
you who see everything we do?

Why have you made me your target?
Have I become a burden to you?

Why do you not pardon my offenses
and forgive my sins?

For I will soon lie down in the dust;
you will search for me, but I will be no more."

Then Bildad the Shuhite replied:

"How long will you say such things?
Your words are a blustering wind.

Does God pervert justice?
Does the Almighty pervert what is right?

When your children sinned against him,
he gave them over to the penalty of their sin.

But if you will seek God earnestly
and plead with the Almighty,

if you are pure and upright,
even now he will rouse himself on your behalf
and restore you to your prosperous state.

Your beginnings will seem humble,
so prosperous will your future be.

"Ask the former generation
and find out what their ancestors learned,

for we were born only yesterday and know
     nothing,
and our days on earth are but a shadow.

Will they not instruct you and tell you?
Will they not bring forth words from their
     understanding?

Can papyrus grow tall where there is no marsh?
Can reeds thrive without water?

While still growing and uncut,
they wither more quickly than grass.

Such is the destiny of all who forget God;
so perishes the hope of the godless.

What they trust in is fragile;
what they rely on is a spider's web.

They lean on the web, but it gives way;
they cling to it, but it does not hold.

They are like a well-watered plant in the sunshine,
spreading its shoots over the garden;

it entwines its roots around a pile of rocks
and looks for a place among the stones.

But when it is torn from its spot,
that place disowns it and says, 'I never saw you.'

Surely its life withers away,
and from the soil other plants grow.

"Surely God does not reject one who is blameless
or strengthen the hands of evildoers.

He will yet fill your mouth with laughter
and your lips with shouts of joy.

Your enemies will be clothed in shame,
and the tents of the wicked will be no more."

Then Job replied:

"Indeed, I know that this is true.
But how can mere mortals prove their innocence before
　　God?

Though they wished to dispute with him,
they could not answer him one time out of a thousand.

His wisdom is profound, his power is vast.
Who has resisted him and come out unscathed?

He moves mountains without their knowing it
and overturns them in his anger.

He shakes the earth from its place
and makes its pillars tremble.

He speaks to the sun and it does not shine;
he seals off the light of the stars.

He alone stretches out the heavens
and treads on the waves of the sea.

He is the Maker of the Bear and Orion,
the Pleiades and the constellations of the south.

He performs wonders that cannot be fathomed,
miracles that cannot be counted.

When he passes me, I cannot see him;
when he goes by, I cannot perceive him.

If he snatches away, who can stop him?
Who can say to him, 'What are you doing?'

God does not restrain his anger;
even the cohorts of Rahab cowered at his feet.

"How then can I dispute with him?
How can I find words to argue with him?

Though I were innocent, I could not answer him;
I could only plead with my Judge for mercy.

Even if I summoned him and he responded,
I do not believe he would give me a hearing.

He would crush me with a storm
and multiply my wounds for no reason.

He would not let me catch my breath
but would overwhelm me with misery.

If it is a matter of strength, he is mighty!
And if it is a matter of justice, who can challenge him?

Even if I were innocent, my mouth would
     condemn me;
if I were blameless, it would pronounce me guilty.

"Although I am blameless,
I have no concern for myself;
I despise my own life.

It is all the same; that is why I say,
'He destroys both the blameless and the wicked.'

When a scourge brings sudden death,
he mocks the despair of the innocent.

When a land falls into the hands of the wicked,
he blindfolds its judges.
If it is not he, then who is it?

"My days are swifter than a runner;
they fly away without a glimpse of joy.

They skim past like boats of papyrus,
like eagles swooping down on their prey.

If I say, 'I will forget my complaint,
I will change my expression, and smile,'

I still dread all my sufferings,
for I know you will not hold me innocent.

Since I am already found guilty,
why should I struggle in vain?

Even if I washed myself with soap
and my hands with cleansing powder,

you would plunge me into a slime pit
so that even my clothes would detest me.

"He is not a mere mortal like me that I might
     answer him,
that we might confront each other in court.

If only there were someone to mediate between us,
someone to bring us together,

someone to remove God's rod from me,
so that his terror would frighten me no more.

Then I would speak up without fear of him,
but as it now stands with me, I cannot.

"I loathe my very life;
therefore I will give free rein to my complaint
and speak out in the bitterness of my soul.

I say to God: Do not declare me guilty,
but tell me what charges you have against me.

Does it please you to oppress me,
to spurn the work of your hands,
while you smile on the plans of the wicked?

Do you have eyes of flesh?
Do you see as a mortal sees?

Are your days like those of a mortal
or your years like those of a strong man,

that you must search out my faults
and probe after my sin —

though you know that I am not guilty
and that no one can rescue me from your hand?

"Your hands shaped me and made me.
Will you now turn and destroy me?

Remember that you molded me like clay.
Will you now turn me to dust again?

Did you not pour me out like milk
and curdle me like cheese,

clothe me with skin and flesh
and knit me together with bones and sinews?

You gave me life and showed me kindness,
and in your providence watched over my spirit.

"But this is what you concealed in your heart,
and I know that this was in your mind:

If I sinned, you would be watching me
and would not let my offense go unpunished.

If I am guilty — woe to me!
Even if I am innocent, I cannot lift my head,

for I am full of shame
and drowned in my affliction.

If I hold my head high, you stalk me like a lion
and again display your awesome power against me.

You bring new witnesses against me
and increase your anger toward me;
your forces come against me wave upon wave.

"Why then did you bring me out of the womb?
I wish I had died before any eye saw me.

If only I had never come into being,
or had been carried straight from the womb
   to the grave!

Are not my few days almost over?
Turn away from me so I can have a moment's joy

before I go to the place of no return,
to the land of gloom and utter darkness,

to the land of deepest night,
of utter darkness and disorder,
where even the light is like darkness."

Then Zophar the Naamathite replied:

"Are all these words to go unanswered?
Is this talker to be vindicated?

Will your idle talk reduce others to silence?
Will no one rebuke you when you mock?

You say to God, 'My beliefs are flawless
and I am pure in your sight.'

Oh, how I wish that God would speak,
that he would open his lips against you

and disclose to you the secrets of wisdom,
for true wisdom has two sides.
Know this: God has even forgotten some of your sin.

"Can you fathom the mysteries of God?
Can you probe the limits of the Almighty?

They are higher than the heavens above —
   what can you do?
They are deeper than the depths below —
   what can you know?

Their measure is longer than the earth
and wider than the sea.

"If he comes along and confines you in prison
and convenes a court, who can oppose him?

Surely he recognizes deceivers;
and when he sees evil, does he not take note?

But the witless can no more become wise
than a wild donkey's colt can be born human.

"Yet if you devote your heart to him
and stretch out your hands to him,

if you put away the sin that is in your hand
and allow no evil to dwell in your tent,

then, free of fault, you will lift up your face;
you will stand firm and without fear.

You will surely forget your trouble,
recalling it only as waters gone by.

Life will be brighter than noonday,
and darkness will become like morning.

You will be secure, because there is hope;
you will look about you and take your rest in safety.

You will lie down, with no one to make you afraid,
and many will court your favor.

But the eyes of the wicked will fail,
and escape will elude them;
their hope will become a dying gasp."

Then Job replied:

"Doubtless you are the only people who matter,
and wisdom will die with you!

But I have a mind as well as you;
I am not inferior to you.
Who does not know all these things?

"I have become a laughingstock to my friends,
though I called on God and he answered—
a mere laughingstock, though righteous and
      blameless!

Those who are at ease have contempt for misfortune
as the fate of those whose feet are slipping.

The tents of marauders are undisturbed,
and those who provoke God are secure—
those God has in his hand.

"But ask the animals, and they will teach you,
or the birds in the sky, and they will tell you;

or speak to the earth, and it will teach you,
or let the fish in the sea inform you.

Which of all these does not know
that the hand of the Lord has done this?

In his hand is the life of every creature
and the breath of all mankind.

Does not the ear test words
as the tongue tastes food?

Is not wisdom found among the aged?
Does not long life bring understanding?

"To God belong wisdom and power;
counsel and understanding are his.

What he tears down cannot be rebuilt;
those he imprisons cannot be released.

If he holds back the waters, there is drought;
if he lets them loose, they devastate the land.

To him belong strength and insight;
both deceived and deceiver are his.

He leads rulers away stripped
and makes fools of judges.

He takes off the shackles put on by kings
and ties a loincloth around their waist.

He leads priests away stripped
and overthrows officials long established.

He silences the lips of trusted advisers
and takes away the discernment of elders.

He pours contempt on nobles
and disarms the mighty.

He reveals the deep things of darkness
and brings utter darkness into the light.

He makes nations great, and destroys them;
he enlarges nations, and disperses them.

He deprives the leaders of the earth of their reason;
he makes them wander in a trackless waste.

They grope in darkness with no light;
he makes them stagger like drunkards.

"My eyes have seen all this,
my ears have heard and understood it.

What you know, I also know;
I am not inferior to you.

But I desire to speak to the Almighty
and to argue my case with God.

You, however, smear me with lies;
you are worthless physicians, all of you!

If only you would be altogether silent!
For you, that would be wisdom.

Hear now my argument;
listen to the pleas of my lips.

Will you speak wickedly on God's behalf?
Will you speak deceitfully for him?

Will you show him partiality?
Will you argue the case for God?

Would it turn out well if he examined you?
Could you deceive him as you might deceive
    a mortal?

He would surely call you to account
if you secretly showed partiality.

Would not his splendor terrify you?
Would not the dread of him fall on you?

Your maxims are proverbs of ashes;
your defenses are defenses of clay.

"Keep silent and let me speak;
then let come to me what may.

Why do I put myself in jeopardy
and take my life in my hands?

Though he slay me, yet will I hope in him;
I will surely defend my ways to his face.

Indeed, this will turn out for my deliverance,
for no godless person would dare come before him!

Listen carefully to what I say;
let my words ring in your ears.

Now that I have prepared my case,
I know I will be vindicated.

Can anyone bring charges against me?
If so, I will be silent and die.

"Only grant me these two things, God,
and then I will not hide from you:

Withdraw your hand far from me,
and stop frightening me with your terrors.

Then summon me and I will answer,
or let me speak, and you reply to me.

How many wrongs and sins have I committed?
Show me my offense and my sin.

Why do you hide your face
and consider me your enemy?

Will you torment a windblown leaf?
Will you chase after dry chaff?

For you write down bitter things against me
and make me reap the sins of my youth.

You fasten my feet in shackles;
you keep close watch on all my paths
by putting marks on the soles of my feet.

"So man wastes away like something rotten,
like a garment eaten by moths.

"Mortals, born of woman,
are of few days and full of trouble.

They spring up like flowers and wither away;
like fleeting shadows, they do not endure.

Do you fix your eye on them?
Will you bring them before you for judgment?

Who can bring what is pure from the impure?
No one!

A person's days are determined;
you have decreed the number of his months
and have set limits he cannot exceed.

So look away from him and let him alone,
till he has put in his time like a hired laborer.

"At least there is hope for a tree:
If it is cut down, it will sprout again,
and its new shoots will not fail.

Its roots may grow old in the ground
and its stump die in the soil,

yet at the scent of water it will bud
and put forth shoots like a plant.

But a man dies and is laid low;
he breathes his last and is no more.

As the water of a lake dries up
or a riverbed becomes parched and dry,

so he lies down and does not rise;
till the heavens are no more, people will not awake
or be roused from their sleep.

"If only you would hide me in the grave
and conceal me till your anger has passed!
If only you would set me a time
and then remember me!

If someone dies, will they live again?
All the days of my hard service
I will wait for my renewal to come.
You will call and I will answer you;
you will long for the creature your hands have made.

Surely then you will count my steps
but not keep track of my sin.
My offenses will be sealed up in a bag;
you will cover over my sin.

"But as a mountain erodes and crumbles
and as a rock is moved from its place,

as water wears away stones
and torrents wash away the soil,
so you destroy a person's hope.

You overpower them once for all, and they are gone;
you change their countenance and send them away.

If their children are honored, they do not know it;
if their offspring are brought low, they do not see it.

They feel but the pain of their own bodies
and mourn only for themselves."

Then Eliphaz the Temanite replied:

"Would a wise person answer with empty notions
or fill their belly with the hot east wind?

Would they argue with useless words,
with speeches that have no value?

But you even undermine piety
and hinder devotion to God.

Your sin prompts your mouth;
you adopt the tongue of the crafty.

Your own mouth condemns you, not mine;
your own lips testify against you.

"Are you the first man ever born?
Were you brought forth before the hills?

Do you listen in on God's council?
Do you have a monopoly on wisdom?

What do you know that we do not know?
What insights do you have that we do not have?

The gray-haired and the aged are on our side,
men even older than your father.

Are God's consolations not enough for you,
words spoken gently to you?

Why has your heart carried you away,
and why do your eyes flash,

so that you vent your rage against God
and pour out such words from your mouth?

"What are mortals, that they could be pure,
or those born of woman, that they could be righteous?

If God places no trust in his holy ones,
if even the heavens are not pure in his eyes,

how much less mortals, who are vile and corrupt,
who drink up evil like water!

"Listen to me and I will explain to you;
let me tell you what I have seen,

what the wise have declared,
hiding nothing received from their ancestors

(to whom alone the land was given
when no foreigners moved among them):

All his days the wicked man suffers torment,
the ruthless man through all the years stored up for him.

Terrifying sounds fill his ears;
when all seems well, marauders attack him.

He despairs of escaping the realm of darkness;
he is marked for the sword.

He wanders about for food like a vulture;
he knows the day of darkness is at hand.

Distress and anguish fill him with terror;
troubles overwhelm him, like a king poised
    to attack,

because he shakes his fist at God
and vaunts himself against the Almighty,

defiantly charging against him
with a thick, strong shield.

"Though his face is covered with fat
and his waist bulges with flesh,

he will inhabit ruined towns
and houses where no one lives,
houses crumbling to rubble.

He will no longer be rich and his wealth
    will not endure,
nor will his possessions spread over the land.

He will not escape the darkness;
a flame will wither his shoots,
and the breath of God's mouth will carry him away.

Let him not deceive himself by trusting what is
    worthless,
for he will get nothing in return.

Before his time he will wither,
and his branches will not flourish.

He will be like a vine stripped of its unripe grapes,
like an olive tree shedding its blossoms.

For the company of the godless will be barren,
and fire will consume the tents of those
    who love bribes.

They conceive trouble and give birth to evil;
their womb fashions deceit."

Then Job replied:

"I have heard many things like these;
you are miserable comforters, all of you!

Will your long-winded speeches never end?
What ails you that you keep on arguing?

I also could speak like you,
if you were in my place;

I could make fine speeches against you
and shake my head at you.

But my mouth would encourage you;
comfort from my lips would bring you relief.

"Yet if I speak, my pain is not relieved;
and if I refrain, it does not go away.

Surely, God, you have worn me out;
you have devastated my entire household.

You have shriveled me up—and it has become a witness;
my gauntness rises up and testifies against me.

God assails me and tears me in his anger
and gnashes his teeth at me;
my opponent fastens on me his piercing eyes.

People open their mouths to jeer at me;
they strike my cheek in scorn
and unite together against me.

God has turned me over to the ungodly
and thrown me into the clutches of the wicked.

All was well with me, but he shattered me;
he seized me by the neck and crushed me.

He has made me his target;
his archers surround me.

Without pity, he pierces my kidneys
and spills my gall on the ground.

Again and again he bursts upon me;
he rushes at me like a warrior.

"I have sewed sackcloth over my skin
and buried my brow in the dust.

My face is red with weeping,
dark shadows ring my eyes;

yet my hands have been free of violence
and my prayer is pure.

"Earth, do not cover my blood;
may my cry never be laid to rest!

Even now my witness is in heaven;
my advocate is on high.

My intercessor is my friend
as my eyes pour out tears to God;

on behalf of a man he pleads with God
as one pleads for a friend.

"Only a few years will pass
before I take the path of no return.

My spirit is broken,
my days are cut short,
the grave awaits me.

Surely mockers surround me;
my eyes must dwell on their hostility.

"Give me, O God, the pledge you demand.
Who else will put up security for me?

You have closed their minds to understanding;
therefore you will not let them triumph.

If anyone denounces their friends for reward,
the eyes of their children will fail.

"God has made me a byword to everyone,
a man in whose face people spit.

My eyes have grown dim with grief;
my whole frame is but a shadow.

The upright are appalled at this;
the innocent are aroused against the ungodly.

Nevertheless, the righteous will hold to their ways,
and those with clean hands will grow stronger.

"But come on, all of you, try again!
I will not find a wise man among you.

My days have passed, my plans are shattered.
Yet the desires of my heart

turn night into day;
in the face of the darkness light is near.

If the only home I hope for is the grave,
if I spread out my bed in the realm of darkness,

if I say to corruption, 'You are my father,'
and to the worm, 'My mother' or 'My sister,'

where then is my hope—
who can see any hope for me?

Will it go down to the gates of death?
Will we descend together into the dust?"

Then Bildad the Shuhite replied:

"When will you end these speeches?
Be sensible, and then we can talk.

Why are we regarded as cattle
and considered stupid in your sight?

You who tear yourself to pieces in your anger,
is the earth to be abandoned for your sake?
Or must the rocks be moved from their place?

"The lamp of a wicked man is snuffed out;
the flame of his fire stops burning.

The light in his tent becomes dark;
the lamp beside him goes out.

The vigor of his step is weakened;
his own schemes throw him down.

His feet thrust him into a net;
he wanders into its mesh.

A trap seizes him by the heel;
a snare holds him fast.

A noose is hidden for him on the ground;
a trap lies in his path.

Terrors startle him on every side
and dog his every step.

Calamity is hungry for him;
disaster is ready for him when he falls.

It eats away parts of his skin;
death's firstborn devours his limbs.

He is torn from the security of his tent
and marched off to the king of terrors.

Fire resides in his tent;
burning sulfur is scattered over his dwelling.

His roots dry up below
and his branches wither above.

The memory of him perishes from the earth;
he has no name in the land.

He is driven from light into the realm of darkness
and is banished from the world.

He has no offspring or descendants among his people,
no survivor where once he lived.

People of the west are appalled at his fate;
those of the east are seized with horror.

Surely such is the dwelling of an evil man;
such is the place of one who does not know God."

Then Job replied:

"How long will you torment me
and crush me with words?

Ten times now you have reproached me;
shamelessly you attack me.

If it is true that I have gone astray,
my error remains my concern alone.

If indeed you would exalt yourselves above me
and use my humiliation against me,

then know that God has wronged me
and drawn his net around me.

"Though I cry, 'Violence!' I get no response;
though I call for help, there is no justice.

He has blocked my way so I cannot pass;
he has shrouded my paths in darkness.

He has stripped me of my honor
and removed the crown from my head.

He tears me down on every side till I am gone;
he uproots my hope like a tree.

His anger burns against me;
he counts me among his enemies.

His troops advance in force;
they build a siege ramp against me
and encamp around my tent.

"He has alienated my family from me;
my acquaintances are completely estranged from me.

My relatives have gone away;
my closest friends have forgotten me.

My guests and my female servants count me a foreigner;
they look on me as on a stranger.

I summon my servant, but he does not answer,
though I beg him with my own mouth.

My breath is offensive to my wife;
I am loathsome to my own family.

Even the little boys scorn me;
when I appear, they ridicule me.

All my intimate friends detest me;
those I love have turned against me.

I am nothing but skin and bones;
I have escaped only by the skin of my teeth.

"Have pity on me, my friends, have pity,
for the hand of God has struck me.

Why do you pursue me as God does?
Will you never get enough of my flesh?

"Oh, that my words were recorded,
that they were written on a scroll,

that they were inscribed with an iron tool on lead,
or engraved in rock forever!

I know that my redeemer lives,
and that in the end he will stand on the earth.

And after my skin has been destroyed,
yet in my flesh I will see God;

I myself will see him
with my own eyes—I, and not another.
How my heart yearns within me!

"If you say, 'How we will hound him,
since the root of the trouble lies in him,'

you should fear the sword yourselves;
for wrath will bring punishment by the sword,
and then you will know that there is judgment."

Then Zophar the Naamathite replied:

"My troubled thoughts prompt me to answer
because I am greatly disturbed.

I hear a rebuke that dishonors me,
and my understanding inspires me to reply.

"Surely you know how it has been from of old,
ever since mankind was placed on the earth,

that the mirth of the wicked is brief,
the joy of the godless lasts but a moment.

Though the pride of the godless person reaches to the
      heavens
and his head touches the clouds,

he will perish forever, like his own dung;
those who have seen him will say, 'Where is he?'

Like a dream he flies away, no more to be found,
banished like a vision of the night.

The eye that saw him will not see him again;
his place will look on him no more.

His children must make amends to the poor;
his own hands must give back his wealth.

The youthful vigor that fills his bones
will lie with him in the dust.

"Though evil is sweet in his mouth
and he hides it under his tongue,

though he cannot bear to let it go
and lets it linger in his mouth,

yet his food will turn sour in his stomach;
it will become the venom of serpents within him.

He will spit out the riches he swallowed;
God will make his stomach vomit them up.

He will suck the poison of serpents;
the fangs of an adder will kill him.

He will not enjoy the streams,
the rivers flowing with honey and cream.

What he toiled for he must give back uneaten;
he will not enjoy the profit from his trading.

For he has oppressed the poor and left them destitute;
he has seized houses he did not build.

"Surely he will have no respite from his craving;
he cannot save himself by his treasure.

Nothing is left for him to devour;
his prosperity will not endure.

In the midst of his plenty, distress will overtake him;
the full force of misery will come upon him.

When he has filled his belly,
God will vent his burning anger against him
and rain down his blows on him.

Though he flees from an iron weapon,
a bronze-tipped arrow pierces him.

He pulls it out of his back,
the gleaming point out of his liver.

Terrors will come over him;
total darkness lies in wait for his treasures.

A fire unfanned will consume him
and devour what is left in his tent.

The heavens will expose his guilt;
the earth will rise up against him.

A flood will carry off his house,
rushing waters on the day of God's wrath.

Such is the fate God allots the wicked,
the heritage appointed for them by God."

Then Job replied:

"Listen carefully to my words;
let this be the consolation you give me.

Bear with me while I speak,
and after I have spoken, mock on.

"Is my complaint directed to a human being?
Why should I not be impatient?

Look at me and be appalled;
clap your hand over your mouth.

When I think about this, I am terrified;
trembling seizes my body.

Why do the wicked live on,
growing old and increasing in power?

They see their children established around them,
their offspring before their eyes.

Their homes are safe and free from fear;
the rod of God is not on them.

Their bulls never fail to breed;
their cows calve and do not miscarry.

They send forth their children as a flock;
their little ones dance about.

They sing to the music of timbrel and lyre;
they make merry to the sound of the pipe.

They spend their years in prosperity
and go down to the grave in peace.

Yet they say to God, 'Leave us alone!
We have no desire to know your ways.

Who is the Almighty, that we should serve him?
What would we gain by praying to him?'

But their prosperity is not in their own hands,
so I stand aloof from the plans of the wicked.

"Yet how often is the lamp of the wicked snuffed out?
How often does calamity come upon them,
the fate God allots in his anger?

How often are they like straw before the wind,
like chaff swept away by a gale?

It is said, 'God stores up the punishment of the wicked
for their children.'
Let him repay the wicked, so that they themselves will
experience it!

Let their own eyes see their destruction;
let them drink the cup of the wrath of the Almighty.

For what do they care about the families they leave
behind
when their allotted months come to an end?

"Can anyone teach knowledge to God,
since he judges even the highest?

One person dies in full vigor,
completely secure and at ease,

well nourished in body,
bones rich with marrow.

Another dies in bitterness of soul,
never having enjoyed anything good.

Side by side they lie in the dust,
and worms cover them both.

"I know full well what you are thinking,
the schemes by which you would wrong me.

You say, 'Where now is the house of the great,
the tents where the wicked lived?'

Have you never questioned those who travel?
Have you paid no regard to their accounts —

that the wicked are spared from the day of calamity,
that they are delivered from the day of wrath?

Who denounces their conduct to their face?
Who repays them for what they have done?

They are carried to the grave,
and watch is kept over their tombs.

The soil in the valley is sweet to them;
everyone follows after them,
and a countless throng goes before them.

"So how can you console me with your nonsense?
Nothing is left of your answers but falsehood!"

Then Eliphaz the Temanite replied:

"Can a man be of benefit to God?
Can even a wise person benefit him?

What pleasure would it give the Almighty if you were
righteous?
What would he gain if your ways were blameless?

"Is it for your piety that he rebukes you
and brings charges against you?

Is not your wickedness great?
Are not your sins endless?

You demanded security from your relatives for no
reason;
you stripped people of their clothing, leaving them
naked.

You gave no water to the weary
and you withheld food from the hungry,

though you were a powerful man, owning land —
an honored man, living on it.

And you sent widows away empty-handed
and broke the strength of the fatherless.

That is why snares are all around you,
why sudden peril terrifies you,

why it is so dark you cannot see,
and why a flood of water covers you.

"Is not God in the heights of heaven?
And see how lofty are the highest stars!

Yet you say, 'What does God know?
Does he judge through such darkness?

Thick clouds veil him, so he does not see us
as he goes about in the vaulted heavens.'

Will you keep to the old path
that the wicked have trod?

They were carried off before their time,
their foundations washed away by a flood.

They said to God, 'Leave us alone!
What can the Almighty do to us?'

Yet it was he who filled their houses with good things,
so I stand aloof from the plans of the wicked.

The righteous see their ruin and rejoice;
the innocent mock them, saying,

'Surely our foes are destroyed,
and fire devours their wealth.'

"Submit to God and be at peace with him;
in this way prosperity will come to you.

Accept instruction from his mouth
and lay up his words in your heart.

If you return to the Almighty, you will be restored:
If you remove wickedness far from your tent

and assign your nuggets to the dust,
your gold of Ophir to the rocks in the ravines,

then the Almighty will be your gold,
the choicest silver for you.

Surely then you will find delight in the Almighty
and will lift up your face to God.

You will pray to him, and he will hear you,
and you will fulfill your vows.

What you decide on will be done,
and light will shine on your ways.

When people are brought low and you say, 'Lift them up!'
then he will save the downcast.

He will deliver even one who is not innocent,
who will be delivered through the cleanness of your
hands."

Then Job replied:

"Even today my complaint is bitter;
his hand is heavy in spite of my groaning.

If only I knew where to find him;
if only I could go to his dwelling!

I would state my case before him
and fill my mouth with arguments.

I would find out what he would answer me,
and consider what he would say to me.

Would he vigorously oppose me?
No, he would not press charges against me.

There the upright can establish their innocence before
him,
and there I would be delivered forever from my judge.

"But if I go to the east, he is not there;
if I go to the west, I do not find him.

When he is at work in the north, I do not see him;
when he turns to the south, I catch no glimpse of him.

But he knows the way that I take;
when he has tested me, I will come forth as gold.

My feet have closely followed his steps;
I have kept to his way without turning aside.

I have not departed from the commands of his lips;
I have treasured the words of his mouth more than my
daily bread.

"But he stands alone, and who can oppose him?
He does whatever he pleases.

He carries out his decree against me,
and many such plans he still has in store.

That is why I am terrified before him;
when I think of all this, I fear him.

God has made my heart faint;
the Almighty has terrified me.

Yet I am not silenced by the darkness,
by the thick darkness that covers my face.

"Why does the Almighty not set times
for judgment?
Why must those who know him look in vain
for such days?

There are those who move boundary stones;
they pasture flocks they have stolen.

They drive away the orphan's donkey
and take the widow's ox in pledge.

They thrust the needy from the path
and force all the poor of the land into hiding.

Like wild donkeys in the desert,
the poor go about their labor of foraging food;
the wasteland provides food for their children.

They gather fodder in the fields
and glean in the vineyards of the wicked.

Lacking clothes, they spend the night naked;
they have nothing to cover themselves in the cold.

They are drenched by mountain rains
and hug the rocks for lack of shelter.

The fatherless child is snatched from the breast;
the infant of the poor is seized for a debt.

Lacking clothes, they go about naked;
they carry the sheaves, but still go hungry.

They crush olives among the terraces;
they tread the winepresses, yet suffer thirst.

The groans of the dying rise from the city,
and the souls of the wounded cry out for help.
But God charges no one with wrongdoing.

"There are those who rebel against the light,
who do not know its ways
or stay in its paths.

When daylight is gone, the murderer rises up,
kills the poor and needy,
and in the night steals forth like a thief.

The eye of the adulterer watches for dusk;
he thinks, 'No eye will see me,'
and he keeps his face concealed.

In the dark, thieves break into houses,
but by day they shut themselves in;
they want nothing to do with the light.

For all of them, midnight is their morning;
they make friends with the terrors of darkness.

"Yet they are foam on the surface of the water;
their portion of the land is cursed,
so that no one goes to the vineyards.

As heat and drought snatch away the melted snow,
so the grave snatches away those who have sinned.

The womb forgets them,
the worm feasts on them;

the wicked are no longer remembered
but are broken like a tree.

They prey on the barren and childless woman,
and to the widow they show no kindness.

But God drags away the mighty by his power;
though they become established, they have
        no assurance of life.

He may let them rest in a feeling of security,
but his eyes are on their ways.

For a little while they are exalted, and then
        they are gone;
they are brought low and gathered up like all others;
they are cut off like heads of grain.

"If this is not so, who can prove me false
and reduce my words to nothing?"

Then Bildad the Shuhite replied:

"Dominion and awe belong to God;
he establishes order in the heights of heaven.

Can his forces be numbered?
On whom does his light not rise?

How then can a mortal be righteous before God?
How can one born of woman be pure?

If even the moon is not bright
and the stars are not pure in his eyes,

how much less a mortal, who is but a maggot—
a human being, who is only a worm!"

Then Job replied:

"How you have helped the powerless!
How you have saved the arm that is feeble!

What advice you have offered to one without wisdom!
And what great insight you have displayed!

Who has helped you utter these words?
And whose spirit spoke from your mouth?

"The dead are in deep anguish,
those beneath the waters and all that live in them.

The realm of the dead is naked before God;
Destruction lies uncovered.

He spreads out the northern skies over empty space;
he suspends the earth over nothing.

He wraps up the waters in his clouds,
yet the clouds do not burst under their weight.

He covers the face of the full moon,
spreading his clouds over it.

He marks out the horizon on the face of the waters
for a boundary between light and darkness.

The pillars of the heavens quake,
aghast at his rebuke.

By his power he churned up the sea;
by his wisdom he cut Rahab to pieces.

By his breath the skies became fair;
his hand pierced the gliding serpent.

And these are but the outer fringe of his works;
how faint the whisper we hear of him!
Who then can understand the thunder
of his power?"

And Job continued his discourse:

"As surely as God lives, who has denied me justice,
the Almighty, who has made my life bitter,

as long as I have life within me,
the breath of God in my nostrils,

my lips will not say anything wicked,
and my tongue will not utter lies.

I will never admit you are in the right;
till I die, I will not deny my integrity.

I will maintain my innocence and never let go of it;
my conscience will not reproach me as long as I live.

"May my enemy be like the wicked,
my adversary like the unjust!

For what hope have the godless when they are cut off,
when God takes away their life?

Does God listen to their cry
when distress comes upon them?

Will they find delight in the Almighty?
Will they call on God at all times?

"I will teach you about the power of God;
the ways of the Almighty I will not conceal.

You have all seen this yourselves.
Why then this meaningless talk?

"Here is the fate God allots to the wicked,
the heritage a ruthless man receives from the Almighty:

However many his children, their fate is the sword;
his offspring will never have enough to eat.

The plague will bury those who survive him,
and their widows will not weep for them.

Though he heaps up silver like dust
and clothes like piles of clay,

what he lays up the righteous will wear,
and the innocent will divide his silver.

The house he builds is like a moth's cocoon,
like a hut made by a watchman.

He lies down wealthy, but will do so no more;
when he opens his eyes, all is gone.

Terrors overtake him like a flood;
a tempest snatches him away in the night.

The east wind carries him off, and he is gone;
it sweeps him out of his place.

It hurls itself against him without mercy
as he flees headlong from its power.

It claps its hands in derision
and hisses him out of his place."

There is a mine for silver
and a place where gold is refined.

Iron is taken from the earth,
and copper is smelted from ore.

Mortals put an end to the darkness;
they search out the farthest recesses
for ore in the blackest darkness.

Far from human dwellings they cut a shaft,
in places untouched by human feet;
far from other people they dangle and sway.

The earth, from which food comes,
is transformed below as by fire;

lapis lazuli comes from its rocks,
and its dust contains nuggets of gold.

No bird of prey knows that hidden path,
no falcon's eye has seen it.

Proud beasts do not set foot on it,
and no lion prowls there.

People assault the flinty rock with their hands
and lay bare the roots of the mountains.

They tunnel through the rock;
their eyes see all its treasures.

They search the sources of the rivers
and bring hidden things to light.

But where can wisdom be found?
Where does understanding dwell?

No mortal comprehends its worth;
it cannot be found in the land of the living.

The deep says, "It is not in me";
the sea says, "It is not with me."

It cannot be bought with the finest gold,
nor can its price be weighed out in silver.

It cannot be bought with the gold of Ophir,
with precious onyx or lapis lazuli.

Neither gold nor crystal can compare with it,
nor can it be had for jewels of gold.

Coral and jasper are not worthy of mention;
the price of wisdom is beyond rubies.

The topaz of Cush cannot compare with it;
it cannot be bought with pure gold.

Where then does wisdom come from?
Where does understanding dwell?

It is hidden from the eyes of every living thing,
concealed even from the birds in the sky.

Destruction and Death say,
"Only a rumor of it has reached our ears."

God understands the way to it
and he alone knows where it dwells,

for he views the ends of the earth
and sees everything under the heavens.

When he established the force of the wind
and measured out the waters,

when he made a decree for the rain
and a path for the thunderstorm,

then he looked at wisdom and appraised it;
he confirmed it and tested it.

And he said to the human race,
"The fear of the Lord—that is wisdom,
and to shun evil is understanding."

Job continued his discourse:

"How I long for the months gone by,
for the days when God watched over me,

when his lamp shone on my head
and by his light I walked through darkness!

Oh, for the days when I was in my prime,
when God's intimate friendship blessed my house,

when the Almighty was still with me
and my children were around me,

when my path was drenched with cream
and the rock poured out for me streams
of olive oil.

"When I went to the gate of the city
and took my seat in the public square,

the young men saw me and stepped aside
and the old men rose to their feet;

the chief men refrained from speaking
and covered their mouths with their hands;

the voices of the nobles were hushed,
and their tongues stuck to the roof of their mouths.

Whoever heard me spoke well of me,
and those who saw me commended me,

because I rescued the poor who cried for help,
and the fatherless who had none to assist them.

The one who was dying blessed me;
I made the widow's heart sing.

I put on righteousness as my clothing;
justice was my robe and my turban.

I was eyes to the blind
and feet to the lame.

I was a father to the needy;
I took up the case of the stranger.

I broke the fangs of the wicked
and snatched the victims from their teeth.

"I thought, 'I will die in my own house,
my days as numerous as the grains of sand.

My roots will reach to the water,
and the dew will lie all night on my branches.

My glory will not fade;
the bow will be ever new in my hand.'

"People listened to me expectantly,
waiting in silence for my counsel.

After I had spoken, they spoke no more;
my words fell gently on their ears.

They waited for me as for showers
and drank in my words as the spring rain.

When I smiled at them, they scarcely believed it;
the light of my face was precious to them.

I chose the way for them and sat as their chief;
I dwelt as a king among his troops;
I was like one who comforts mourners.

"But now they mock me,
men younger than I,

whose fathers I would have disdained
to put with my sheep dogs.

Of what use was the strength of their hands to me,
since their vigor had gone from them?

Haggard from want and hunger,
they roamed the parched land
in desolate wastelands at night.

In the brush they gathered salt herbs,
and their food was the root of the broom bush.

They were banished from human society,
shouted at as if they were thieves.

They were forced to live in the dry stream beds,
among the rocks and in holes in the ground.

They brayed among the bushes
and huddled in the undergrowth.

A base and nameless brood,
they were driven out of the land.

"And now those young men mock me in song;
I have become a byword among them.

They detest me and keep their distance;
they do not hesitate to spit in my face.

Now that God has unstrung my bow and
    afflicted me,
they throw off restraint in my presence.

On my right the tribe attacks;
they lay snares for my feet,
they build their siege ramps against me.

They break up my road;
they succeed in destroying me.
'No one can help him,' they say.

They advance as through a gaping breach;
amid the ruins they come rolling in.

Terrors overwhelm me;
my dignity is driven away as by the wind,
my safety vanishes like a cloud.

"And now my life ebbs away;
days of suffering grip me.

Night pierces my bones;
my gnawing pains never rest.

In his great power God becomes like clothing to me;
he binds me like the neck of my garment.

He throws me into the mud,
and I am reduced to dust and ashes.

"I cry out to you, God, but you do not answer;
I stand up, but you merely look at me.

You turn on me ruthlessly;
with the might of your hand you attack me.

You snatch me up and drive me before the wind;
you toss me about in the storm.

I know you will bring me down to death,
to the place appointed for all the living.

"Surely no one lays a hand on a broken man
when he cries for help in his distress.

Have I not wept for those in trouble?
Has not my soul grieved for the poor?

Yet when I hoped for good, evil came;
when I looked for light, then came darkness.

The churning inside me never stops;
days of suffering confront me.

I go about blackened, but not by the sun;
I stand up in the assembly and cry for help.

I have become a brother of jackals,
a companion of owls.

My skin grows black and peels;
my body burns with fever.

My lyre is tuned to mourning,
and my pipe to the sound of wailing.

"I made a covenant with my eyes
not to look lustfully at a young woman.

For what is our lot from God above,
our heritage from the Almighty on high?

Is it not ruin for the wicked,
disaster for those who do wrong?

Does he not see my ways
and count my every step?

"If I have walked with falsehood
or my foot has hurried after deceit—

let God weigh me in honest scales
and he will know that I am blameless—

if my steps have turned from the path,
if my heart has been led by my eyes,
or if my hands have been defiled,

then may others eat what I have sown,
and may my crops be uprooted.

"If my heart has been enticed by a woman,
or if I have lurked at my neighbor's door,

then may my wife grind another man's grain,
and may other men sleep with her.

For that would have been wicked,
a sin to be judged.

It is a fire that burns to Destruction;
it would have uprooted my harvest.

"If I have denied justice to any of my servants,
whether male or female,
when they had a grievance against me,

what will I do when God confronts me?
What will I answer when called to account?

Did not he who made me in the womb make them?
Did not the same one form us both within our mothers?

"If I have denied the desires of the poor
or let the eyes of the widow grow weary,

if I have kept my bread to myself,
not sharing it with the fatherless—

but from my youth I reared them as a father would,
and from my birth I guided the widow—

if I have seen anyone perishing for lack of clothing,
or the needy without garments,

and their hearts did not bless me
for warming them with the fleece from my sheep,

if I have raised my hand against the fatherless,
knowing that I had influence in court,

then let my arm fall from the shoulder,
let it be broken off at the joint.

For I dreaded destruction from God,
and for fear of his splendor I could not
    do such things.

"If I have put my trust in gold
or said to pure gold, 'You are my security,'

if I have rejoiced over my great wealth,
the fortune my hands had gained,

if I have regarded the sun in its radiance
or the moon moving in splendor,

so that my heart was secretly enticed
and my hand offered them a kiss of homage,

then these also would be sins to be judged,
for I would have been unfaithful to God
    on high.

"If I have rejoiced at my enemy's misfortune
or gloated over the trouble that came to him —

I have not allowed my mouth to sin
by invoking a curse against their life —

if those of my household have never said,
'Who has not been filled with Job's meat?' —

but no stranger had to spend the night
    in the street,
for my door was always open to the traveler —

if I have concealed my sin as people do,
by hiding my guilt in my heart

because I so feared the crowd
and so dreaded the contempt of the clans
that I kept silent and would not go outside —

("Oh, that I had someone to hear me!
I sign now my defense — let the Almighty
    answer me;
let my accuser put his indictment in writing.

Surely I would wear it on my shoulder,
I would put it on like a crown.

I would give him an account of my every step;
I would present it to him as to a ruler.) —

"if my land cries out against me
and all its furrows are wet with tears,

if I have devoured its yield without payment
or broken the spirit of its tenants,

then let briers come up instead of wheat
and stinkweed instead of barley."

The words of Job are ended.

S o these three men stopped answering Job, because he was righteous in his own eyes. But Elihu son of Barakel the Buzite, of the
family of Ram, became very angry with Job for justifying himself
rather than God. He was also angry with the three friends, because
they had found no way to refute Job, and yet had condemned him.
Now Elihu had waited before speaking to Job because they were
older than he. But when he saw that the three men had nothing
more to say, his anger was aroused.

So Elihu son of Barakel the Buzite said:

"I am young in years,
and you are old;

that is why I was fearful,
not daring to tell you what I know.

I thought, 'Age should speak;
advanced years should teach wisdom.'

But it is the spirit in a person,
the breath of the Almighty, that gives them
understanding.

It is not only the old who are wise,
not only the aged who understand what is right.

"Therefore I say: Listen to me;
I too will tell you what I know.

I waited while you spoke,
I listened to your reasoning;

while you were searching for words,
I gave you my full attention.

But not one of you has proved Job wrong;
none of you has answered his arguments.

Do not say, 'We have found wisdom;
let God, not a man, refute him.'

But Job has not marshaled his words against me,
and I will not answer him with your arguments.

"They are dismayed and have no more to say;
words have failed them.

Must I wait, now that they are silent,
now that they stand there with no reply?

I too will have my say;
I too will tell what I know.

For I am full of words,
and the spirit within me compels me;

inside I am like bottled-up wine,
like new wineskins ready to burst.

I must speak and find relief;
I must open my lips and reply.

I will show no partiality,
nor will I flatter anyone;

for if I were skilled in flattery,
my Maker would soon take me away.

"But now, Job, listen to my words;
pay attention to everything I say.

I am about to open my mouth;
my words are on the tip of my tongue.

My words come from an upright heart;
my lips sincerely speak what I know.

The Spirit of God has made me;
the breath of the Almighty gives me life.

Answer me then, if you can;
stand up and argue your case before me.

I am the same as you in God's sight;
I too am a piece of clay.

No fear of me should alarm you,
nor should my hand be heavy on you.

"But you have said in my hearing—
I heard the very words—

'I am pure, I have done no wrong;
I am clean and free from sin.

Yet God has found fault with me;
he considers me his enemy.

He fastens my feet in shackles;
he keeps close watch on all my paths.'

"But I tell you, in this you are not right,
for God is greater than any mortal.

Why do you complain to him
that he responds to no one's words?

For God does speak — now one way, now another —
though no one perceives it.

In a dream, in a vision of the night,
when deep sleep falls on people
as they slumber in their beds,

he may speak in their ears
and terrify them with warnings,

to turn them from wrongdoing
and keep them from pride,

to preserve them from the pit,
their lives from perishing by the sword.

"Or someone may be chastened on a bed of pain
with constant distress in their bones,

so that their body finds food repulsive
and their soul loathes the choicest meal.

Their flesh wastes away to nothing,
and their bones, once hidden, now stick out.

They draw near to the pit,
and their life to the messengers of death.

Yet if there is an angel at their side,
a messenger, one out of a thousand,
sent to tell them how to be upright,

and he is gracious to that person and says to God,
'Spare them from going down to the pit;
I have found a ransom for them —

let their flesh be renewed like a child's;
let them be restored as in the days of their youth' —

then that person can pray to God and find favor
    with him,
they will see God's face and shout for joy;
he will restore them to full well-being.

And they will go to others and say,
'I have sinned, I have perverted what is right,
but I did not get what I deserved.

God has delivered me from going down to the pit,
and I shall live to enjoy the light of life.'

"God does all these things to a person—
twice, even three times—

to turn them back from the pit,
that the light of life may shine on them.

"Pay attention, Job, and listen to me;
be silent, and I will speak.

If you have anything to say, answer me;
speak up, for I want to vindicate you.

But if not, then listen to me;
be silent, and I will teach you wisdom."

Then Elihu said:

"Hear my words, you wise men;
listen to me, you men of learning.

For the ear tests words
as the tongue tastes food.

Let us discern for ourselves what is right;
let us learn together what is good.

"Job says, 'I am innocent,
but God denies me justice.

Although I am right,
I am considered a liar;

although I am guiltless,
his arrow inflicts an incurable wound.'

Is there anyone like Job,
who drinks scorn like water?

He keeps company with evildoers;
he associates with the wicked.

For he says, 'There is no profit
in trying to please God.'

"So listen to me, you men of understanding.
Far be it from God to do evil,
from the Almighty to do wrong.

He repays everyone for what they have done;
he brings on them what their conduct deserves.

It is unthinkable that God would do wrong,
that the Almighty would pervert justice.

Who appointed him over the earth?
Who put him in charge of the whole world?

If it were his intention
and he withdrew his spirit and breath,

all humanity would perish together
and mankind would return to the dust.

"If you have understanding, hear this;
listen to what I say.

Can someone who hates justice govern?
Will you condemn the just and mighty One?

Is he not the One who says to kings, 'You are
      worthless,'
and to nobles, 'You are wicked,'

who shows no partiality to princes
and does not favor the rich over the poor,
for they are all the work of his hands?

They die in an instant, in the middle of the night;
the people are shaken and they pass away;
the mighty are removed without human hand.

"His eyes are on the ways of mortals;
he sees their every step.

There is no deep shadow, no utter darkness,
where evildoers can hide.

God has no need to examine people further,
that they should come before him for judgment.

Without inquiry he shatters the mighty
and sets up others in their place.

Because he takes note of their deeds,
he overthrows them in the night and they
      are crushed.

He punishes them for their wickedness
where everyone can see them,

because they turned from following him
and had no regard for any of his ways.

They caused the cry of the poor to come
      before him,
so that he heard the cry of the needy.

But if he remains silent, who can condemn him?
If he hides his face, who can see him?

Yet he is over individual and nation alike,
to keep the godless from ruling,
from laying snares for the people.

"Suppose someone says to God,
'I am guilty but will offend no more.

Teach me what I cannot see;
if I have done wrong, I will not do so again.'

Should God then reward you on your terms,
when you refuse to repent?

You must decide, not I;
so tell me what you know.

"Men of understanding declare,
wise men who hear me say to me,

'Job speaks without knowledge;
his words lack insight.'

Oh, that Job might be tested to the utmost
for answering like a wicked man!

To his sin he adds rebellion;
scornfully he claps his hands among us
and multiplies his words against God."

Then Elihu said:

"Do you think this is just?
You say, 'I am in the right, not God.'

Yet you ask him, 'What profit is it to me,
and what do I gain by not sinning?'

"I would like to reply to you
and to your friends with you.

Look up at the heavens and see;
gaze at the clouds so high above you.

If you sin, how does that affect him?
If your sins are many, what does that do to him?

If you are righteous, what do you give to him,
or what does he receive from your hand?

Your wickedness only affects humans like yourself,
and your righteousness only other people.

"People cry out under a load of oppression;
they plead for relief from the arm of the powerful.

But no one says, 'Where is God my Maker,
who gives songs in the night,

who teaches us more than he teaches the beasts
of the earth

and makes us wiser than the birds in the sky?'

He does not answer when people cry out
because of the arrogance of the wicked.

Indeed, God does not listen to their empty plea;
the Almighty pays no attention to it.

How much less, then, will he listen
when you say that you do not see him,

that your case is before him
and you must wait for him,

and further, that his anger never punishes
and he does not take the least notice of wickedness.

So Job opens his mouth with empty talk;
without knowledge he multiplies words."

Elihu continued:

"Bear with me a little longer and I will show you
that there is more to be said in God's behalf.

I get my knowledge from afar;
I will ascribe justice to my Maker.

Be assured that my words are not false;
one who has perfect knowledge is with you.

"God is mighty, but despises no one;
he is mighty, and firm in his purpose.

He does not keep the wicked alive
but gives the afflicted their rights.

He does not take his eyes off the righteous;
he enthrones them with kings
and exalts them forever.

But if people are bound in chains,
held fast by cords of affliction,

he tells them what they have done —
that they have sinned arrogantly.

He makes them listen to correction
and commands them to repent of their evil.

If they obey and serve him,
they will spend the rest of their days in prosperity
and their years in contentment.

But if they do not listen,
they will perish by the sword
and die without knowledge.

"The godless in heart harbor resentment;
even when he fetters them, they do not cry for help.

They die in their youth,
among male prostitutes of the shrines.

But those who suffer he delivers in their suffering;
he speaks to them in their affliction.

"He is wooing you from the jaws of distress
to a spacious place free from restriction,
to the comfort of your table laden with choice food.

But now you are laden with the judgment due the
        wicked;
judgment and justice have taken hold of you.

Be careful that no one entices you by riches;
do not let a large bribe turn you aside.

Would your wealth or even all your mighty efforts
sustain you so you would not be in distress?

Do not long for the night,
to drag people away from their homes.

Beware of turning to evil,
which you seem to prefer to affliction.

"God is exalted in his power.
Who is a teacher like him?

Who has prescribed his ways for him,
or said to him, 'You have done wrong'?

Remember to extol his work,
which people have praised in song.

All humanity has seen it;
mortals gaze on it from afar.

How great is God — beyond our understanding!
The number of his years is past finding out.

"He draws up the drops of water,
which distill as rain to the streams;
the clouds pour down their moisture
and abundant showers fall on mankind.

Who can understand how he spreads out the clouds,
how he thunders from his pavilion?

See how he scatters his lightning about him,
bathing the depths of the sea.

This is the way he governs the nations
and provides food in abundance.

He fills his hands with lightning
and commands it to strike its mark.

His thunder announces the coming storm;
even the cattle make known its approach.

"At this my heart pounds
and leaps from its place.

Listen! Listen to the roar of his voice,
to the rumbling that comes from his mouth.

He unleashes his lightning beneath the whole heaven
and sends it to the ends of the earth.

After that comes the sound of his roar;
he thunders with his majestic voice.

When his voice resounds,
he holds nothing back.

God's voice thunders in marvelous ways;
he does great things beyond our understanding.

He says to the snow, 'Fall on the earth,'
and to the rain shower, 'Be a mighty downpour.'

So that everyone he has made may know his work,
he stops all people from their labor.

The animals take cover;
they remain in their dens.

The tempest comes out from its chamber,
the cold from the driving winds.

The breath of God produces ice,
and the broad waters become frozen.

He loads the clouds with moisture;
he scatters his lightning through them.

At his direction they swirl around
over the face of the whole earth
to do whatever he commands them.

He brings the clouds to punish people,
or to water his earth and show his love.

"Listen to this, Job;
stop and consider God's wonders.

Do you know how God controls the clouds
and makes his lightning flash?

Do you know how the clouds hang poised,
those wonders of him who has perfect knowledge?

You who swelter in your clothes
when the land lies hushed under the south wind,

can you join him in spreading out the skies,
hard as a mirror of cast bronze?

"Tell us what we should say to him;
we cannot draw up our case because of our
darkness.

Should he be told that I want to speak?
Would anyone ask to be swallowed up?

Now no one can look at the sun,
bright as it is in the skies
after the wind has swept them clean.

Out of the north he comes in golden splendor;
God comes in awesome majesty.

The Almighty is beyond our reach and exalted
in power;
in his justice and great righteousness, he does
not oppress.

Therefore, people revere him,
for does he not have regard for all the wise in heart?"

Then the Lord spoke to Job out of the storm. He said:

"Who is this that obscures my plans
with words without knowledge?

Brace yourself like a man;
I will question you,
and you shall answer me.

"Where were you when I laid the earth's foundation?
Tell me, if you understand.

Who marked off its dimensions? Surely you know!
Who stretched a measuring line across it?

On what were its footings set,
or who laid its cornerstone—

while the morning stars sang together
and all the angels shouted for joy?

"Who shut up the sea behind doors
when it burst forth from the womb,

when I made the clouds its garment
and wrapped it in thick darkness,

when I fixed limits for it
and set its doors and bars in place,

when I said, 'This far you may come and no farther;
here is where your proud waves halt'?

"Have you ever given orders to the morning,
or shown the dawn its place,

that it might take the earth by the edges
and shake the wicked out of it?

The earth takes shape like clay under a seal;
its features stand out like those of a garment.

The wicked are denied their light,
and their upraised arm is broken.

"Have you journeyed to the springs of the sea
or walked in the recesses of the deep?

Have the gates of death been shown to you?
Have you seen the gates of the deepest darkness?

Have you comprehended the vast expanses
of the earth?
Tell me, if you know all this.

"What is the way to the abode of light?
And where does darkness reside?

Can you take them to their places?
Do you know the paths to their dwellings?

Surely you know, for you were already born!
You have lived so many years!

"Have you entered the storehouses of the snow
　　or seen the storehouses of the hail,

which I reserve for times of trouble,
　　for days of war and battle?

What is the way to the place where the lightning is
　　　　dispersed,
or the place where the east winds are scattered
　　　　over the earth?

Who cuts a channel for the torrents of rain,
　　and a path for the thunderstorm,

to water a land where no one lives,
　　an uninhabited desert,

to satisfy a desolate wasteland
　　and make it sprout with grass?

Does the rain have a father?
　　Who fathers the drops of dew?

From whose womb comes the ice?
　　Who gives birth to the frost from the heavens

when the waters become hard as stone,
　　when the surface of the deep is frozen?

"Can you bind the chains of the Pleiades?
　　Can you loosen Orion's belt?

Can you bring forth the constellations in their seasons
　　or lead out the Bear with its cubs?

Do you know the laws of the heavens?
　　Can you set up God's dominion over the earth?

"Can you raise your voice to the clouds
　　and cover yourself with a flood of water?

Do you send the lightning bolts on their way?
　　Do they report to you, 'Here we are'?

Who gives the ibis wisdom
　　or gives the rooster understanding?

Who has the wisdom to count the clouds?
　　Who can tip over the water jars of the heavens

when the dust becomes hard
　　and the clods of earth stick together?

"Do you hunt the prey for the lioness
　　and satisfy the hunger of the lions

when they crouch in their dens
or lie in wait in a thicket?

Who provides food for the raven
when its young cry out to God
and wander about for lack of food?

"Do you know when the mountain goats
          give birth?
Do you watch when the doe bears her fawn?

Do you count the months till they bear?
Do you know the time they give birth?

They crouch down and bring forth their young;
their labor pains are ended.

Their young thrive and grow strong in
          the wilds;
they leave and do not return.

"Who let the wild donkey go free?
Who untied its ropes?

I gave it the wasteland as its home,
the salt flats as its habitat.

It laughs at the commotion in the town;
it does not hear a driver's shout.

It ranges the hills for its pasture
and searches for any green thing.

"Will the wild ox consent to serve you?
Will it stay by your manger at night?

Can you hold it to the furrow with a harness?
Will it till the valleys behind you?

Will you rely on it for its great strength?
Will you leave your heavy work to it?

Can you trust it to haul in your grain
and bring it to your threshing floor?

"The wings of the ostrich flap joyfully,
though they cannot compare
with the wings and feathers of the stork.

She lays her eggs on the ground
and lets them warm in the sand,

unmindful that a foot may crush them,
that some wild animal may trample them.

She treats her young harshly, as if they
    were not hers;
she cares not that her labor was in vain,

for God did not endow her with wisdom
or give her a share of good sense.

Yet when she spreads her feathers to run,
she laughs at horse and rider.

"Do you give the horse its strength
or clothe its neck with a flowing mane?

Do you make it leap like a locust,
striking terror with its proud snorting?

It paws fiercely, rejoicing in its strength,
and charges into the fray.

It laughs at fear, afraid of nothing;
it does not shy away from the sword.

The quiver rattles against its side,
along with the flashing spear and lance.

In frenzied excitement it eats up the ground;
it cannot stand still when the trumpet sounds.

At the blast of the trumpet it snorts, 'Aha!'
It catches the scent of battle from afar,
the shout of commanders and the battle cry.

"Does the hawk take flight by your wisdom
and spread its wings toward the south?

Does the eagle soar at your command
and build its nest on high?

It dwells on a cliff and stays there at night;
a rocky crag is its stronghold.

From there it looks for food;
its eyes detect it from afar.

Its young ones feast on blood,
and where the slain are, there it is."

The Lord said to Job:

"Will the one who contends with the Almighty
    correct him?
Let him who accuses God answer him!"

Then Job answered the LORD:

> "I am unworthy—how can I reply to you?
> I put my hand over my mouth.
>
> I spoke once, but I have no answer—
> twice, but I will say no more."

Then the LORD spoke to Job out of the storm:

> "Brace yourself like a man;
> I will question you,
> and you shall answer me.
>
> "Would you discredit my justice?
> Would you condemn me to justify yourself?
>
> Do you have an arm like God's,
> and can your voice thunder like his?
>
> Then adorn yourself with glory and splendor,
> and clothe yourself in honor and majesty.
>
> Unleash the fury of your wrath,
> look at all who are proud and bring them low,
>
> look at all who are proud and humble them,
> crush the wicked where they stand.
>
> Bury them all in the dust together;
> shroud their faces in the grave.
>
> Then I myself will admit to you
> that your own right hand can save you.
>
> "Look at Behemoth,
> which I made along with you
> and which feeds on grass like an ox.
>
> What strength it has in its loins,
> what power in the muscles of its belly!
>
> Its tail sways like a cedar;
> the sinews of its thighs are close-knit.
>
> Its bones are tubes of bronze,
> its limbs like rods of iron.
>
> It ranks first among the works of God,
> yet its Maker can approach it with
> his sword.

The hills bring it their produce,
and all the wild animals play nearby.

Under the lotus plants it lies,
hidden among the reeds in the marsh.

The lotuses conceal it in their shadow;
the poplars by the stream surround it.

A raging river does not alarm it;
it is secure, though the Jordan should surge against
      its mouth.

Can anyone capture it by the eyes,
or trap it and pierce its nose?

"Can you pull in Leviathan with a fishhook
or tie down its tongue with a rope?

Can you put a cord through its nose
or pierce its jaw with a hook?

Will it keep begging you for mercy?
Will it speak to you with gentle words?

Will it make an agreement with you
for you to take it as your slave for life?

Can you make a pet of it like a bird
or put it on a leash for the young women
      in your house?

Will traders barter for it?
Will they divide it up among the merchants?

Can you fill its hide with harpoons
or its head with fishing spears?

If you lay a hand on it,
you will remember the struggle and never
      do it again!

Any hope of subduing it is false;
the mere sight of it is overpowering.

No one is fierce enough to rouse it.
Who then is able to stand against me?

Who has a claim against me that I must pay?
Everything under heaven belongs to me.

"I will not fail to speak of Leviathan's limbs,
its strength and its graceful form.

Who can strip off its outer coat?
Who can penetrate its double coat of armor?

Who dares open the doors of its mouth,
ringed about with fearsome teeth?

Its back has rows of shields
tightly sealed together;

each is so close to the next
that no air can pass between.

They are joined fast to one another;
they cling together and cannot be parted.

Its snorting throws out flashes of light;
its eyes are like the rays of dawn.

Flames stream from its mouth;
sparks of fire shoot out.

Smoke pours from its nostrils
as from a boiling pot over burning reeds.

Its breath sets coals ablaze,
and flames dart from its mouth.

Strength resides in its neck;
dismay goes before it.

The folds of its flesh are tightly joined;
they are firm and immovable.

Its chest is hard as rock,
hard as a lower millstone.

When it rises up, the mighty are terrified;
they retreat before its thrashing.

The sword that reaches it has no effect,
nor does the spear or the dart or the javelin.

Iron it treats like straw
and bronze like rotten wood.

Arrows do not make it flee;
slingstones are like chaff to it.

A club seems to it but a piece of straw;
it laughs at the rattling of the lance.

Its undersides are jagged potsherds,
leaving a trail in the mud like a threshing sledge.

It makes the depths churn like a boiling caldron
and stirs up the sea like a pot of ointment.

It leaves a glistening wake behind it;
one would think the deep had white hair.

Nothing on earth is its equal—
a creature without fear.

> It looks down on all that are haughty;
> it is king over all that are proud."

Then Job replied to the LORD:

> "I know that you can do all things;
> no purpose of yours can be thwarted.
> You asked, 'Who is this that obscures my plans without
> knowledge?'
> Surely I spoke of things I did not understand,
> things too wonderful for me to know.

> "You said, 'Listen now, and I will speak;
> I will question you,
> and you shall answer me.'
> My ears had heard of you
> but now my eyes have seen you.

> Therefore I despise myself
> and repent in dust and ashes."

After the LORD had said these things to Job, he said to Eliphaz the Temanite, "I am angry with you and your two friends, because you have not spoken the truth about me, as my servant Job has. So now take seven bulls and seven rams and go to my servant Job and sacrifice a burnt offering for yourselves. My servant Job will pray for you, and I will accept his prayer and not deal with you according to your folly. You have not spoken the truth about me, as my servant Job has." So Eliphaz the Temanite, Bildad the Shuhite and Zophar the Naamathite did what the LORD told them; and the LORD accepted Job's prayer.

After Job had prayed for his friends, the LORD restored his fortunes and gave him twice as much as he had before. All his brothers and sisters and everyone who had known him before came and ate with him in his house. They comforted and consoled him over all the trouble the LORD had brought on him, and each one gave him a piece of silver and a gold ring.

The LORD blessed the latter part of Job's life more than the former part. He had fourteen thousand sheep, six thousand camels, a thousand yoke of oxen and a thousand donkeys. And he also had seven sons and three daughters. The first daughter he named Jemimah, the second Keziah and the third Keren-Happuch. Nowhere in all the land were there found women as beautiful as Job's daughters, and their father granted them an inheritance along with their brothers.

After this, Job lived a hundred and forty years; he saw his children and their children to the fourth generation. And so Job died, an old man and full of years.

CHRONICLES–EZRA–
NEHEMIAH

In the fifth century BC, the exiles from Judah were allowed to return to their homeland. It must have been difficult for them to see how they could still fulfill God's special purpose for them as a distinct nation. Their capital city and its temple had been destroyed; they were no longer ruled by their own king; many of them had married people from other nations; and foreigners had settled in many parts of the land. They may have thought they should still see themselves as scattered among the nations, and fulfill God's purposes by seeking the good of the foreign country they served. But the books of Chronicles, Ezra and Nehemiah speak a resounding "No!" to this way of thinking. Together they insist that the returned exiles can still provide a demonstration to the surrounding nations that their God is the only true God, if they'll once again form a distinct society, now to be centered in the worship of God in a rebuilt temple in Jerusalem. (These books are really one long book, telling a continuous story; one can see, for example, how the end of 2 Chronicles overlaps with the beginning of Ezra, p. 463.)

These books communicate their message by presenting a sweeping chronicle of Israel's national history, beginning with a long genealogy (ancestor list). Going all the way back to Adam, it situates the people of Israel among the nations, implicitly reminding them of their calling on behalf of all people even as it documents their credentials as a distinct people. Most of the genealogy is a record of the sons of Jacob (Israel) and their descendants. Special attention is given to Judah, the ancestor of the royal line of David, and to Levi, the ancestor of the priests and temple attendants. The genealogy follows these descendants down through the exile and return. At the end, it goes back to the list of Benjamin's descendants in order to introduce Saul, the first king of Israel.

This leads into the second main part of this national chronicle, a description of each of the kings who ruled in Jerusalem down to the time of the exile. David receives more attention than any other king, but even so, many details of his life known from other sources are left out. The history focuses essentially on his military campaigns and on his elaborate preparations for the temple in Jerusalem. The reason for this selection of material becomes clear when it's explained that David wasn't permitted to build the temple himself because he was a warrior. God wanted *a man of peace and rest* to build the temple, since it would be a place where people of all nations could come and pray. This honor therefore fell to David's son Solomon. The chronicle devotes more space to Solomon than to any other king besides David. It documents the splendors of his reign and describes how he built the temple. Afterwards it relates how the kingdom of Israel was divided, and it traces the fortunes of the Judean kings who continued to sit on the throne of David in Jerusalem. Most are treated briefly, because in general the kingdom declined under them as they turned away from God. Only those kings who showed concern for true worship and keeping God's law receive significant attention. By the end of this section, short accounts of briefly-reigning kings follow one another in rapid succession, ending with a report of the exile.

The final part of this national chronicle relates the experiences of the returned exiles. It lists the various groups of returning Judeans and describes how they overcame persistent opposition to rebuild the temple. The memoirs of Ezra, a leader of the second generation of returned Judeans, are then incorporated into the history. They relate how Ezra helped to create a distinct community by forbidding intermarriage with the surrounding nations. (It may actually have been Ezra himself who compiled the entire chronicle: he tells us that he *devoted himself to the study and observance of the Law of the Lord, and to teaching its decrees and laws in Israel.*) The memoirs of another leader of this second generation, Nehemiah, then follow. They describe how he was granted leave from his position in the court of the Persian emperor to direct the rebuilding of Jerusalem's walls. His memoirs are interrupted by a description of a great covenant renewal ceremony that he and Ezra led together. The history then concludes with the rest of Nehemiah's memoirs, which describe the dedication of Jerusalem's walls and some further reforms.

An important theme of the entire account—which can appropriately be called a temple history—is that pure worship must be offered on God's terms, not our own. And so the book continually insists that priests and temple assistants have the proper lineage and fulfill their prescribed duties. Kings must ensure that festivals such as Passover and Tabernacles are observed at the appropriate times. And above all, the temple of God must be in Jerusalem, the city God has chosen. Throughout the history there's a corresponding emphasis on being willing to provide gladly for the exact worship that God has asked for. Occasions when the people of Israel provided generously for the temple are recounted and celebrated.

The distinctive worship of the people of Israel defines their community and sets it apart from other nations. Paradoxically, however, it also invites people from those nations to join in serving the true God. This recounts Israel's founding purpose under their father Abraham. Even though the community has a concern for purity of lineage, it's defined essentially not by ethnicity, but by worship. It's therefore possible for people from all over the world to come and join in this worship. This additional important theme of the history may be summarized well in the words of one of Solomon's requests at the dedication of the temple: *As for the foreigner who does not belong to your people Israel but has come from a distant land because of your great name and your mighty hand and your outstretched arm—when they come and pray toward this temple, then hear from heaven, your dwelling place. Do whatever the foreigner asks of you, so that all the peoples of the earth may know your name and fear you, as do your own people Israel.* Chronicles–Ezra–Nehemiah recalls the returned Judeans to this special vocation: to enable all the peoples of the earth to know and serve the true God.

CHRONICLES–EZRA–NEHEMIAH

A dam, Seth, Enosh, Kenan, Mahalalel, Jared, Enoch, Methuse-
lah, Lamech, Noah.

The sons of Noah:
  Shem, Ham and Japheth.

The sons of Japheth:
  Gomer, Magog, Madai, Javan, Tubal, Meshek and Tiras.
The sons of Gomer:
  Ashkenaz, Riphath and Togarmah.
The sons of Javan:
  Elishah, Tarshish, the Kittites and the Rodanites.

The sons of Ham:
  Cush, Egypt, Put and Canaan.
The sons of Cush:
  Seba, Havilah, Sabta, Raamah and Sabteka.
The sons of Raamah:
  Sheba and Dedan.
Cush was the father of
  Nimrod, who became a mighty warrior on earth.
Egypt was the father of
  the Ludites, Anamites, Lehabites, Naphtuhites, Pathrusites,
  Kasluhites (from whom the Philistines came) and Caphtorites.
Canaan was the father of
  Sidon his firstborn, and of the Hittites, Jebusites, Amorites,
  Girgashites, Hivites, Arkites, Sinites, Arvadites, Zemarites
  and Hamathites.

The sons of Shem:
  Elam, Ashur, Arphaxad, Lud and Aram.
The sons of Aram:
  Uz, Hul, Gether and Meshek.
Arphaxad was the father of Shelah,
  and Shelah the father of Eber.

Two sons were born to Eber:
>One was named Peleg, because in his time the earth was divided; his brother was named Joktan.

Joktan was the father of
>Almodad, Sheleph, Hazarmaveth, Jerah, Hadoram, Uzal, Diklah, Obal, Abimael, Sheba, Ophir, Havilah and Jobab. All these were sons of Joktan.

>Shem, Arphaxad, Shelah,
>Eber, Peleg, Reu,
>Serug, Nahor, Terah
>and Abram (that is, Abraham).

T he sons of Abraham:
>Isaac and Ishmael.

These were their descendants:
>Nebaioth the firstborn of Ishmael, Kedar, Adbeel, Mibsam, Mishma, Dumah, Massa, Hadad, Tema, Jetur, Naphish and Kedemah. These were the sons of Ishmael.

The sons born to Keturah, Abraham's concubine:
>Zimran, Jokshan, Medan, Midian, Ishbak and Shuah.

The sons of Jokshan:
>Sheba and Dedan.

The sons of Midian:
>Ephah, Epher, Hanok, Abida and Eldaah.

All these were descendants of Keturah.

Abraham was the father of Isaac.

The sons of Isaac:
>Esau and Israel.

The sons of Esau:
>Eliphaz, Reuel, Jeush, Jalam and Korah.

The sons of Eliphaz:
>Teman, Omar, Zepho, Gatam and Kenaz;
>by Timna: Amalek.

The sons of Reuel:
>Nahath, Zerah, Shammah and Mizzah.

The sons of Seir:
>Lotan, Shobal, Zibeon, Anah, Dishon, Ezer and Dishan.

The sons of Lotan:
>Hori and Homam. Timna was Lotan's sister.

The sons of Shobal:
Alvan, Manahath, Ebal, Shepho and Onam.
The sons of Zibeon:
Aiah and Anah.
The son of Anah:
Dishon.
The sons of Dishon:
Hemdan, Eshban, Ithran and Keran.
The sons of Ezer:
Bilhan, Zaavan and Akan.
The sons of Dishan:
Uz and Aran.

These were the kings who reigned in Edom before any Israelite king reigned:
Bela son of Beor, whose city was named Dinhabah.
When Bela died, Jobab son of Zerah from Bozrah succeeded him as king.
When Jobab died, Husham from the land of the Temanites succeeded him as king.
When Husham died, Hadad son of Bedad, who defeated Midian in the country of Moab, succeeded him as king. His city was named Avith.
When Hadad died, Samlah from Masrekah succeeded him as king.
When Samlah died, Shaul from Rehoboth on the river succeeded him as king.
When Shaul died, Baal-Hanan son of Akbor succeeded him as king.
When Baal-Hanan died, Hadad succeeded him as king. His city was named Pau, and his wife's name was Mehetabel daughter of Matred, the daughter of Me-Zahab. Hadad also died.

The chiefs of Edom were:
Timna, Alvah, Jetheth, Oholibamah, Elah, Pinon, Kenaz, Teman, Mibzar, Magdiel and Iram. These were the chiefs of Edom.

T hese were the sons of Israel:
Reuben, Simeon, Levi, Judah, Issachar, Zebulun, Dan, Joseph, Benjamin, Naphtali, Gad and Asher.

The sons of Judah:

Er, Onan and Shelah. These three were born to him by a Canaanite woman, the daughter of Shua. Er, Judah's firstborn, was wicked in the LORD's sight; so the LORD put him to death. Judah's daughter-in-law Tamar bore Perez and Zerah to Judah. He had five sons in all.

The sons of Perez:

Hezron and Hamul.

The sons of Zerah:

Zimri, Ethan, Heman, Kalkol and Darda—five in all.

The son of Karmi:

Achar, who brought trouble on Israel by violating the ban on taking devoted things.

The son of Ethan:

Azariah.

The sons born to Hezron were:

Jerahmeel, Ram and Caleb.

Ram was the father of

Amminadab, and Amminadab the father of Nahshon, the leader of the people of Judah. Nahshon was the father of Salmon, Salmon the father of Boaz, Boaz the father of Obed and Obed the father of Jesse.

Jesse was the father of

Eliab his firstborn; the second son was Abinadab, the third Shimea, the fourth Nethanel, the fifth Raddai, the sixth Ozem and the seventh David. Their sisters were Zeruiah and Abigail. Zeruiah's three sons were Abishai, Joab and Asahel. Abigail was the mother of Amasa, whose father was Jether the Ishmaelite.

Caleb son of Hezron had children by his wife Azubah (and by Jerioth). These were her sons: Jesher, Shobab and Ardon. When Azubah died, Caleb married Ephrath, who bore him Hur. Hur was the father of Uri, and Uri the father of Bezalel. Later, Hezron, when he was sixty years old, married the daughter of Makir the father of Gilead. He made love to her, and she bore him Segub. Segub was the father of Jair, who controlled twenty-three towns in Gilead. (But Geshur and Aram captured Havvoth Jair, as well as Kenath with its surrounding settlements—sixty towns.) All these were descendants of Makir the father of Gilead.

After Hezron died in Caleb Ephrathah, Abijah the wife of Hezron bore him Ashhur the father of Tekoa.

The sons of Jerahmeel the firstborn of Hezron:
Ram his firstborn, Bunah, Oren, Ozem and Ahijah. Jerahmeel had another wife, whose name was Atarah; she was the mother of Onam.

The sons of Ram the firstborn of Jerahmeel:
Maaz, Jamin and Eker.

The sons of Onam:
Shammai and Jada.

The sons of Shammai:
Nadab and Abishur.

Abishur's wife was named Abihail, who bore him Ahban and Molid.

The sons of Nadab:
Seled and Appaim. Seled died without children.

The son of Appaim:
Ishi, who was the father of Sheshan.
Sheshan was the father of Ahlai.

The sons of Jada, Shammai's brother:
Jether and Jonathan. Jether died without children.

The sons of Jonathan:
Peleth and Zaza.

These were the descendants of Jerahmeel.

Sheshan had no sons—only daughters.
He had an Egyptian servant named Jarha. Sheshan gave his daughter in marriage to his servant Jarha, and she bore him Attai.

Attai was the father of Nathan,
Nathan the father of Zabad,
Zabad the father of Ephlal,
Ephlal the father of Obed,
Obed the father of Jehu,
Jehu the father of Azariah,
Azariah the father of Helez,
Helez the father of Eleasah,
Eleasah the father of Sismai,
Sismai the father of Shallum,
Shallum the father of Jekamiah,
and Jekamiah the father of Elishama.

The sons of Caleb the brother of Jerahmeel:
Mesha his firstborn, who was the father of Ziph, and his son Mareshah, who was the father of Hebron.

The sons of Hebron:
>   Korah, Tappuah, Rekem and Shema. Shema was the father
>   of Raham, and Raham the father of Jorkeam. Rekem was the
>   father of Shammai. The son of Shammai was Maon, and
>   Maon was the father of Beth Zur.

Caleb's concubine Ephah was the mother of Haran, Moza and
Gazez. Haran was the father of Gazez.

The sons of Jahdai:
>   Regem, Jotham, Geshan, Pelet, Ephah and Shaaph.

Caleb's concubine Maakah was the mother of Sheber and Tir-
hanah. She also gave birth to Shaaph the father of Madman-
nah and to Sheva the father of Makbenah and Gibea. Caleb's
daughter was Aksah. These were the descendants of Caleb.

The sons of Hur the firstborn of Ephrathah:
>   Shobal the father of Kiriath Jearim, Salma the father of
>   Bethlehem, and Hareph the father of Beth Gader.

The descendants of Shobal the father of Kiriath Jearim were:
>   Haroeh, half the Manahathites, and the clans of Kiriath Je-
>   arim: the Ithrites, Puthites, Shumathites and Mishraites.
>   From these descended the Zorathites and Eshtaolites.

The descendants of Salma:
>   Bethlehem, the Netophathites, Atroth Beth Joab, half the
>   Manahathites, the Zorites, and the clans of scribes who
>   lived at Jabez: the Tirathites, Shimeathites and Sucathites.
>   These are the Kenites who came from Hammath, the father
>   of the Rekabites.

These were the sons of David born to him in Hebron:
>   The firstborn was Amnon the son of Ahinoam of Jezreel;
>   the second, Daniel the son of Abigail of Carmel;
>   the third, Absalom the son of Maakah daughter of Talmai
>   king of Geshur;
>   the fourth, Adonijah the son of Haggith;
>   the fifth, Shephatiah the son of Abital;
>   and the sixth, Ithream, by his wife Eglah.
>   These six were born to David in Hebron, where he reigned
>   seven years and six months.

David reigned in Jerusalem thirty-three years, and these were the
children born to him there:
>   Shammua, Shobab, Nathan and Solomon. These four were by
>   Bathsheba daughter of Ammiel. There were also Ibhar, Eli-
>   shua, Eliphelet, Nogah, Nepheg, Japhia, Elishama, Eliada and
>   Eliphelet — nine in all. All these were the sons of David, be-
>   sides his sons by his concubines. And Tamar was their sister.

Solomon's son was Rehoboam,
   Abijah his son,
   Asa his son,
   Jehoshaphat his son,
   Jehoram his son,
   Ahaziah his son,
   Joash his son,
   Amaziah his son,
   Azariah his son,
   Jotham his son,
   Ahaz his son,
   Hezekiah his son,
   Manasseh his son,
   Amon his son,
   Josiah his son.
The sons of Josiah:
   Johanan the firstborn,
   Jehoiakim the second son,
   Zedekiah the third,
   Shallum the fourth.
The successors of Jehoiakim:
   Jehoiachin his son,
   and Zedekiah.

The descendants of Jehoiachin the captive:
   Shealtiel his son, Malkiram, Pedaiah, Shenazzar, Jekamiah,
   Hoshama and Nedabiah.
The sons of Pedaiah:
   Zerubbabel and Shimei.
The sons of Zerubbabel:
   Meshullam and Hananiah.
   Shelomith was their sister.
   There were also five others:
   Hashubah, Ohel, Berekiah, Hasadiah and Jushab-Hesed.
The descendants of Hananiah:
   Pelatiah and Jeshaiah, and the sons of Rephaiah, of Arnan,
   of Obadiah and of Shekaniah.
The descendants of Shekaniah:
   Shemaiah and his sons:
   Hattush, Igal, Bariah, Neariah and Shaphat — six in all.
The sons of Neariah:
   Elioenai, Hizkiah and Azrikam — three in all.
The sons of Elioenai:
   Hodaviah, Eliashib, Pelaiah, Akkub, Johanan, Delaiah and
   Anani — seven in all.

The descendants of Judah:
Perez, Hezron, Karmi, Hur and Shobal.

Reaiah son of Shobal was the father of Jahath, and Jahath the father of Ahumai and Lahad. These were the clans of the Zorathites.

These were the sons of Etam:
Jezreel, Ishma and Idbash. Their sister was named Hazzelelponi. Penuel was the father of Gedor, and Ezer the father of Hushah.

These were the descendants of Hur, the firstborn of Ephrathah and father of Bethlehem.

Ashhur the father of Tekoa had two wives, Helah and Naarah.

Naarah bore him Ahuzzam, Hepher, Temeni and Haahashtari. These were the descendants of Naarah.

The sons of Helah:
Zereth, Zohar, Ethnan, and Koz, who was the father of Anub and Hazzobebah and of the clans of Aharhel son of Harum.

Jabez was more honorable than his brothers. His mother had named him Jabez, saying, "I gave birth to him in pain." Jabez cried out to the God of Israel, "Oh, that you would bless me and enlarge my territory! Let your hand be with me, and keep me from harm so that I will be free from pain." And God granted his request.

Kelub, Shuhah's brother, was the father of Mehir, who was the father of Eshton. Eshton was the father of Beth Rapha, Paseah and Tehinnah the father of Ir Nahash. These were the men of Rekah.

The sons of Kenaz:
Othniel and Seraiah.

The sons of Othniel:
Hathath and Meonothai. Meonothai was the father of Ophrah.

Seraiah was the father of Joab,
the father of Ge Harashim. It was called this because its people were skilled workers.

The sons of Caleb son of Jephunneh:
Iru, Elah and Naam.

The son of Elah:
Kenaz.

The sons of Jehallelel:
Ziph, Ziphah, Tiria and Asarel.

The sons of Ezrah:
Jether, Mered, Epher and Jalon. One of Mered's wives gave birth to Miriam, Shammai and Ishbah the father of

Eshtemoa. (His wife from the tribe of Judah gave birth to Jered the father of Gedor, Heber the father of Soko, and Jekuthiel the father of Zanoah.) These were the children of Pharaoh's daughter Bithiah, whom Mered had married.

The sons of Hodiah's wife, the sister of Naham:

the father of Keilah the Garmite, and Eshtemoa the Maakathite.

The sons of Shimon:

Amnon, Rinnah, Ben-Hanan and Tilon.

The descendants of Ishi:

Zoheth and Ben-Zoheth.

The sons of Shelah son of Judah:

Er the father of Lekah, Laadah the father of Mareshah and the clans of the linen workers at Beth Ashbea, Jokim, the men of Kozeba, and Joash and Saraph, who ruled in Moab and Jashubi Lehem. (These records are from ancient times.) They were the potters who lived at Netaim and Gederah; they stayed there and worked for the king.

The descendants of Simeon:

Nemuel, Jamin, Jarib, Zerah and Shaul;

Shallum was Shaul's son, Mibsam his son and Mishma his son.

The descendants of Mishma:

Hammuel his son, Zakkur his son and Shimei his son.

Shimei had sixteen sons and six daughters, but his brothers did not have many children; so their entire clan did not become as numerous as the people of Judah. They lived in Beersheba, Moladah, Hazar Shual, Bilhah, Ezem, Tolad, Bethuel, Hormah, Ziklag, Beth Markaboth, Hazar Susim, Beth Biri and Shaaraim. These were their towns until the reign of David. Their surrounding villages were Etam, Ain, Rimmon, Token and Ashan — five towns — and all the villages around these towns as far as Baalath. These were their settlements. And they kept a genealogical record.

Meshobab, Jamlech, Joshah son of Amaziah, Joel, Jehu son of Joshibiah, the son of Seraiah, the son of Asiel, also Elioenai, Jaakobah, Jeshohaiah, Asaiah, Adiel, Jesimiel, Benaiah, and Ziza son of Shiphi, the son of Allon, the son of Jedaiah, the son of Shimri, the son of Shemaiah.

The men listed above by name were leaders of their clans. Their families increased greatly, and they went to the outskirts of Gedor to the east of the valley in search of pasture for their flocks.

They found rich, good pasture, and the land was spacious, peaceful and quiet. Some Hamites had lived there formerly.

The men whose names were listed came in the days of Hezekiah king of Judah. They attacked the Hamites in their dwellings and also the Meunites who were there and completely destroyed them, as is evident to this day. Then they settled in their place, because there was pasture for their flocks. And five hundred of these Simeonites, led by Pelatiah, Neariah, Rephaiah and Uzziel, the sons of Ishi, invaded the hill country of Seir. They killed the remaining Amalekites who had escaped, and they have lived there to this day.

The sons of Reuben the firstborn of Israel (he was the firstborn, but when he defiled his father's marriage bed, his rights as firstborn were given to the sons of Joseph son of Israel; so he could not be listed in the genealogical record in accordance with his birthright, and though Judah was the strongest of his brothers and a ruler came from him, the rights of the firstborn belonged to Joseph) — the sons of Reuben the firstborn of Israel:

Hanok, Pallu, Hezron and Karmi.

The descendants of Joel:

Shemaiah his son, Gog his son,
Shimei his son, Micah his son,
Reaiah his son, Baal his son,
and Beerah his son, whom Tiglath-Pileser king of Assyria took into exile. Beerah was a leader of the Reubenites.

Their relatives by clans, listed according to their genealogical records:

Jeiel the chief, Zechariah, and Bela son of Azaz, the son of Shema, the son of Joel. They settled in the area from Aroer to Nebo and Baal Meon. To the east they occupied the land up to the edge of the desert that extends to the Euphrates River, because their livestock had increased in Gilead.

During Saul's reign they waged war against the Hagrites, who were defeated at their hands; they occupied the dwellings of the Hagrites throughout the entire region east of Gilead.

The Gadites lived next to them in Bashan, as far as Salekah:

Joel was the chief, Shapham the second, then Janai and Shaphat, in Bashan.

Their relatives, by families, were:

Michael, Meshullam, Sheba, Jorai, Jakan, Zia and Eber — seven in all.

These were the sons of Abihail son of Huri, the son of Jaroah, the son of Gilead, the son of Michael, the son of Jeshishai, the son of Jahdo, the son of Buz.

Ahi son of Abdiel, the son of Guni, was head of their family.

The Gadites lived in Gilead, in Bashan and its outlying villages, and on all the pasturelands of Sharon as far as they extended.

All these were entered in the genealogical records during the reigns of Jotham king of Judah and Jeroboam king of Israel.

The Reubenites, the Gadites and the half-tribe of Manasseh had 44,760 men ready for military service — able-bodied men who could handle shield and sword, who could use a bow, and who were trained for battle. They waged war against the Hagrites, Jetur, Naphish and Nodab. They were helped in fighting them, and God delivered the Hagrites and all their allies into their hands, because they cried out to him during the battle. He answered their prayers, because they trusted in him. They seized the livestock of the Hagrites — fifty thousand camels, two hundred fifty thousand sheep and two thousand donkeys. They also took one hundred thousand people captive, and many others fell slain, because the battle was God's. And they occupied the land until the exile.

The people of the half-tribe of Manasseh were numerous; they settled in the land from Bashan to Baal Hermon, that is, to Senir (Mount Hermon).

These were the heads of their families: Epher, Ishi, Eliel, Azriel, Jeremiah, Hodaviah and Jahdiel. They were brave warriors, famous men, and heads of their families. But they were unfaithful to the God of their ancestors and prostituted themselves to the gods of the peoples of the land, whom God had destroyed before them. So the God of Israel stirred up the spirit of Pul king of Assyria (that is, Tiglath-Pileser king of Assyria), who took the Reubenites, the Gadites and the half-tribe of Manasseh into exile. He took them to Halah, Habor, Hara and the river of Gozan, where they are to this day.

The sons of Levi:
    Gershon, Kohath and Merari.
    The sons of Kohath:
    Amram, Izhar, Hebron and Uzziel.
    The children of Amram:
    Aaron, Moses and Miriam.

The sons of Aaron:
>Nadab, Abihu, Eleazar and Ithamar.
>Eleazar was the father of Phinehas,
>Phinehas the father of Abishua,
>Abishua the father of Bukki,
>Bukki the father of Uzzi,
>Uzzi the father of Zerahiah,
>Zerahiah the father of Meraioth,
>Meraioth the father of Amariah,
>Amariah the father of Ahitub,
>Ahitub the father of Zadok,
>Zadok the father of Ahimaaz,
>Ahimaaz the father of Azariah,
>Azariah the father of Johanan,
>Johanan the father of Azariah (it was he who served as priest
>in the temple Solomon built in Jerusalem),
>Azariah the father of Amariah,
>Amariah the father of Ahitub,
>Ahitub the father of Zadok,
>Zadok the father of Shallum,
>Shallum the father of Hilkiah,
>Hilkiah the father of Azariah,
>Azariah the father of Seraiah,
>and Seraiah the father of Jozadak.

Jozadak was deported when the Lord sent Judah and Jerusalem into exile by the hand of Nebuchadnezzar.

The sons of Levi:
>Gershon, Kohath and Merari.

These are the names of the sons of Gershon:
>Libni and Shimei.

The sons of Kohath:
>Amram, Izhar, Hebron and Uzziel.

The sons of Merari:
>Mahli and Mushi.

These are the clans of the Levites listed according to their fathers:

Of Gershon:
>Libni his son, Jahath his son,
>Zimmah his son, Joah his son,
>Iddo his son, Zerah his son
>and Jeatherai his son.

The descendants of Kohath:
>Amminadab his son, Korah his son,
>Assir his son, Elkanah his son,

Ebiasaph his son, Assir his son,
Tahath his son, Uriel his son,
Uzziah his son and Shaul his son.
The descendants of Elkanah:
Amasai, Ahimoth,
Elkanah his son, Zophai his son,
Nahath his son, Eliab his son,
Jeroham his son, Elkanah his son
and Samuel his son.
The sons of Samuel:
Joel the firstborn
and Abijah the second son.
The descendants of Merari:
Mahli, Libni his son,
Shimei his son, Uzzah his son,
Shimea his son, Haggiah his son
and Asaiah his son.

These are the men David put in charge of the music in the house of the LORD after the ark came to rest there. They ministered with music before the tabernacle, the tent of meeting, until Solomon built the temple of the LORD in Jerusalem. They performed their duties according to the regulations laid down for them.

Here are the men who served, together with their sons:
From the Kohathites:
Heman, the musician,
the son of Joel, the son of Samuel,
the son of Elkanah, the son of Jeroham,
the son of Eliel, the son of Toah,
the son of Zuph, the son of Elkanah,
the son of Mahath, the son of Amasai,
the son of Elkanah, the son of Joel,
the son of Azariah, the son of Zephaniah,
the son of Tahath, the son of Assir,
the son of Ebiasaph, the son of Korah,
the son of Izhar, the son of Kohath,
the son of Levi, the son of Israel;
and Heman's associate Asaph, who served at his right hand:
Asaph son of Berekiah, the son of Shimea,
the son of Michael, the son of Baaseiah,
the son of Malkijah, the son of Ethni,
the son of Zerah, the son of Adaiah,
the son of Ethan, the son of Zimmah,
the son of Shimei, the son of Jahath,
the son of Gershon, the son of Levi;

and from their associates, the Merarites, at his left hand:
    Ethan son of Kishi, the son of Abdi,
    the son of Malluk, the son of Hashabiah,
    the son of Amaziah, the son of Hilkiah,
    the son of Amzi, the son of Bani,
    the son of Shemer, the son of Mahli,
    the son of Mushi, the son of Merari,
    the son of Levi.

Their fellow Levites were assigned to all the other duties of the tabernacle, the house of God. But Aaron and his descendants were the ones who presented offerings on the altar of burnt offering and on the altar of incense in connection with all that was done in the Most Holy Place, making atonement for Israel, in accordance with all that Moses the servant of God had commanded.

These were the descendants of Aaron:
    Eleazar his son, Phinehas his son,
    Abishua his son, Bukki his son,
    Uzzi his son, Zerahiah his son,
    Meraioth his son, Amariah his son,
    Ahitub his son, Zadok his son
    and Ahimaaz his son.

These were the locations of their settlements allotted as their territory (they were assigned to the descendants of Aaron who were from the Kohathite clan, because the first lot was for them):
    They were given Hebron in Judah with its surrounding pasturelands. But the fields and villages around the city were given to Caleb son of Jephunneh.
    So the descendants of Aaron were given Hebron (a city of refuge), and Libnah, Jattir, Eshtemoa, Hilen, Debir, Ashan, Juttah and Beth Shemesh, together with their pasturelands. And from the tribe of Benjamin they were given Gibeon, Geba, Alemeth and Anathoth, together with their pasturelands.
    The total number of towns distributed among the Kohathite clans came to thirteen.
    The rest of Kohath's descendants were allotted ten towns from the clans of half the tribe of Manasseh.
    The descendants of Gershon, clan by clan, were allotted thirteen towns from the tribes of Issachar, Asher and Naphtali, and from the part of the tribe of Manasseh that is in Bashan.
    The descendants of Merari, clan by clan, were allotted twelve towns from the tribes of Reuben, Gad and Zebulun.
    So the Israelites gave the Levites these towns and their

pasturelands. From the tribes of Judah, Simeon and Benjamin they allotted the previously named towns.

Some of the Kohathite clans were given as their territory towns from the tribe of Ephraim.

In the hill country of Ephraim they were given Shechem (a city of refuge), and Gezer, Jokmeam, Beth Horon, Aijalon and Gath Rimmon, together with their pasturelands.

And from half the tribe of Manasseh the Israelites gave Aner and Bileam, together with their pasturelands, to the rest of the Kohathite clans.

The Gershonites received the following:
From the clan of the half-tribe of Manasseh
they received Golan in Bashan and also Ashtaroth, together with their pasturelands;
from the tribe of Issachar
they received Kedesh, Daberath, Ramoth and Anem, together with their pasturelands;
from the tribe of Asher
they received Mashal, Abdon, Hukok and Rehob, together with their pasturelands;
and from the tribe of Naphtali
they received Kedesh in Galilee, Hammon and Kiriathaim, together with their pasturelands.

The Merarites (the rest of the Levites) received the following:
From the tribe of Zebulun
they received Jokneam, Kartah, Rimmono and Tabor, together with their pasturelands;
from the tribe of Reuben across the Jordan east of Jericho
they received Bezer in the wilderness, Jahzah, Kedemoth and Mephaath, together with their pasturelands;
and from the tribe of Gad
they received Ramoth in Gilead, Mahanaim, Heshbon and Jazer, together with their pasturelands.

The sons of Issachar:
Tola, Puah, Jashub and Shimron—four in all.
The sons of Tola:
Uzzi, Rephaiah, Jeriel, Jahmai, Ibsam and Samuel—heads of their families. During the reign of David, the descendants of Tola listed as fighting men in their genealogy numbered 22,600.
The son of Uzzi:
Izrahiah.

The sons of Izrahiah:
> Michael, Obadiah, Joel and Ishiah. All five of them were
> chiefs. According to their family genealogy, they had 36,000
> men ready for battle, for they had many wives and children.
> The relatives who were fighting men belonging to all the clans
> of Issachar, as listed in their genealogy, were 87,000 in all.

Three sons of Benjamin:
> Bela, Beker and Jediael.

The sons of Bela:
> Ezbon, Uzzi, Uzziel, Jerimoth and Iri, heads of families —
> five in all. Their genealogical record listed 22,034 fighting
> men.

The sons of Beker:
> Zemirah, Joash, Eliezer, Elioenai, Omri, Jeremoth, Abijah,
> Anathoth and Alemeth. All these were the sons of Beker.
> Their genealogical record listed the heads of families and
> 20,200 fighting men.

The son of Jediael:
> Bilhan.

The sons of Bilhan:
> Jeush, Benjamin, Ehud, Kenaanah, Zethan, Tarshish and
> Ahishahar. All these sons of Jediael were heads of families.
> There were 17,200 fighting men ready to go out to war.

The Shuppites and Huppites were the descendants of Ir, and
the Hushites the descendants of Aher.

The sons of Naphtali:
> Jahziel, Guni, Jezer and Shillem — the descendants of Bil-
> hah.

The descendants of Manasseh:
> Asriel was his descendant through his Aramean concubine.
> She gave birth to Makir the father of Gilead. Makir took a wife
> from among the Huppites and Shuppites. His sister's name was
> Maakah.
>
> Another descendant was named Zelophehad, who had only
> daughters.
>
> Makir's wife Maakah gave birth to a son and named him Pe-
> resh. His brother was named Sheresh, and his sons were Ulam
> and Rakem.

The son of Ulam:
Bedan.
These were the sons of Gilead son of Makir, the son of Manasseh. His sister Hammoleketh gave birth to Ishhod, Abiezer and Mahlah.
The sons of Shemida were:
Ahian, Shechem, Likhi and Aniam.

The descendants of Ephraim:
Shuthelah, Bered his son,
Tahath his son, Eleadah his son,
Tahath his son, Zabad his son
and Shuthelah his son.
Ezer and Elead were killed by the native-born men of Gath, when they went down to seize their livestock. Their father Ephraim mourned for them many days, and his relatives came to comfort him. Then he made love to his wife again, and she became pregnant and gave birth to a son. He named him Beriah, because there had been misfortune in his family. His daughter was Sheerah, who built Lower and Upper Beth Horon as well as Uzzen Sheerah.
Rephah was his son, Resheph his son,
Telah his son, Tahan his son,
Ladan his son, Ammihud his son,
Elishama his son, Nun his son
and Joshua his son.
Their lands and settlements included Bethel and its surrounding villages, Naaran to the east, Gezer and its villages to the west, and Shechem and its villages all the way to Ayyah and its villages. Along the borders of Manasseh were Beth Shan, Taanach, Megiddo and Dor, together with their villages. The descendants of Joseph son of Israel lived in these towns.

The sons of Asher:
Imnah, Ishvah, Ishvi and Beriah. Their sister was Serah.
The sons of Beriah:
Heber and Malkiel, who was the father of Birzaith.
Heber was the father of Japhlet, Shomer and Hotham and of their sister Shua.
The sons of Japhlet:
Pasak, Bimhal and Ashvath.
These were Japhlet's sons.

The sons of Shomer:
    Ahi, Rohgah, Hubbah and Aram.
The sons of his brother Helem:
    Zophah, Imna, Shelesh and Amal.
The sons of Zophah:
    Suah, Harnepher, Shual, Beri, Imrah, Bezer, Hod, Shamma,
    Shilshah, Ithran and Beera.
The sons of Jether:
    Jephunneh, Pispah and Ara.
The sons of Ulla:
    Arah, Hanniel and Rizia.
    All these were descendants of Asher — heads of families,
choice men, brave warriors and outstanding leaders. The number
of men ready for battle, as listed in their genealogy, was 26,000.

Benjamin was the father of Bela his firstborn,
    Ashbel the second son, Aharah the third,
    Nohah the fourth and Rapha the fifth.
The sons of Bela were:
    Addar, Gera, Abihud, Abishua, Naaman, Ahoah, Gera, She-
    phuphan and Huram.
These were the descendants of Ehud, who were heads of fami-
    lies of those living in Geba and were deported to Manahath:
    Naaman, Ahijah, and Gera, who deported them and who
    was the father of Uzza and Ahihud.
Sons were born to Shaharaim in Moab after he had divorced
    his wives Hushim and Baara. By his wife Hodesh he had Jo-
    bab, Zibia, Mesha, Malkam, Jeuz, Sakia and Mirmah. These
    were his sons, heads of families. By Hushim he had Abitub
    and Elpaal.
The sons of Elpaal:
    Eber, Misham, Shemed (who built Ono and Lod with its sur-
    rounding villages), and Beriah and Shema, who were heads
    of families of those living in Aijalon and who drove out the
    inhabitants of Gath.
Ahio, Shashak, Jeremoth, Zebadiah, Arad, Eder, Michael, Ish-
    pah and Joha were the sons of Beriah.
Zebadiah, Meshullam, Hizki, Heber, Ishmerai, Izliah and Jobab
    were the sons of Elpaal.
Jakim, Zikri, Zabdi, Elienai, Zillethai, Eliel, Adaiah, Beraiah
    and Shimrath were the sons of Shimei.
Ishpan, Eber, Eliel, Abdon, Zikri, Hanan, Hananiah, Elam, An-
    thothijah, Iphdeiah and Penuel were the sons of Shashak.

Shamsherai, Shehariah, Athaliah, Jaareshiah, Elijah and Zikri
were the sons of Jeroham.

All these were heads of families, chiefs as listed in their genealogy, and they lived in Jerusalem.

Jeiel the father of Gibeon lived in Gibeon.

His wife's name was Maakah, and his firstborn son was Abdon, followed by Zur, Kish, Baal, Ner, Nadab, Gedor, Ahio,
Zeker and Mikloth, who was the father of Shimeah. They
too lived near their relatives in Jerusalem.

Ner was the father of Kish, Kish the father of Saul, and Saul the
father of Jonathan, Malki-Shua, Abinadab and Esh-Baal.

The son of Jonathan:

Merib-Baal, who was the father of Micah.

The sons of Micah:

Pithon, Melek, Tarea and Ahaz.

Ahaz was the father of Jehoaddah, Jehoaddah was the father
of Alemeth, Azmaveth and Zimri, and Zimri was the father
of Moza. Moza was the father of Binea; Raphah was his son,
Eleasah his son and Azel his son.

Azel had six sons, and these were their names:

Azrikam, Bokeru, Ishmael, Sheariah, Obadiah and Hanan.
All these were the sons of Azel.

The sons of his brother Eshek:

Ulam his firstborn, Jeush the second son and Eliphelet the
third. The sons of Ulam were brave warriors who could handle the bow. They had many sons and grandsons — 150 in
all.

All these were the descendants of Benjamin.

A ll Israel was listed in the genealogies recorded in the book of
the kings of Israel and Judah. They were taken captive to Babylon because of their unfaithfulness.

Now the first to resettle on their own property in their own
towns were some Israelites, priests, Levites and temple servants.

Those from Judah, from Benjamin, and from Ephraim and Manasseh who lived in Jerusalem were:

Uthai son of Ammihud, the son of Omri, the son of Imri, the
son of Bani, a descendant of Perez son of Judah.

Of the Shelanites:

Asaiah the firstborn and his sons.

Of the Zerahites:

Jeuel.

The people from Judah numbered 690.

Of the Benjamites:

Sallu son of Meshullam, the son of Hodaviah, the son of Hassenuah;

Ibneiah son of Jeroham; Elah son of Uzzi, the son of Mikri; and Meshullam son of Shephatiah, the son of Reuel, the son of Ibnijah.

The people from Benjamin, as listed in their genealogy, numbered 956. All these men were heads of their families.

Of the priests:

Jedaiah; Jehoiarib; Jakin;

Azariah son of Hilkiah, the son of Meshullam, the son of Zadok, the son of Meraioth, the son of Ahitub, the official in charge of the house of God;

Adaiah son of Jeroham, the son of Pashhur, the son of Malkijah; and Maasai son of Adiel, the son of Jahzerah, the son of Meshullam, the son of Meshillemith, the son of Immer.

The priests, who were heads of families, numbered 1,760. They were able men, responsible for ministering in the house of God.

Of the Levites:

Shemaiah son of Hasshub, the son of Azrikam, the son of Hashabiah, a Merarite; Bakbakkar, Heresh, Galal and Mattaniah son of Mika, the son of Zikri, the son of Asaph; Obadiah son of Shemaiah, the son of Galal, the son of Jeduthun; and Berekiah son of Asa, the son of Elkanah, who lived in the villages of the Netophathites.

The gatekeepers:

Shallum, Akkub, Talmon, Ahiman and their fellow Levites, Shallum their chief being stationed at the King's Gate on the east, up to the present time. These were the gatekeepers belonging to the camp of the Levites. Shallum son of Kore, the son of Ebiasaph, the son of Korah, and his fellow gatekeepers from his family (the Korahites) were responsible for guarding the thresholds of the tent just as their ancestors had been responsible for guarding the entrance to the dwelling of the LORD. In earlier times Phinehas son of Eleazar was the official in charge of the gatekeepers, and the LORD was with him. Zechariah son of Meshelemiah was the gatekeeper at the entrance to the tent of meeting.

Altogether, those chosen to be gatekeepers at the thresholds numbered 212. They were registered by genealogy in their villages. The gatekeepers had been assigned to their positions of trust by David and

Samuel the seer. They and their descendants were in charge of guarding the gates of the house of the LORD—the house called the tent of meeting. The gatekeepers were on the four sides: east, west, north and south. Their fellow Levites in their villages had to come from time to time and share their duties for seven-day periods. But the four principal gatekeepers, who were Levites, were entrusted with the responsibility for the rooms and treasuries in the house of God. They would spend the night stationed around the house of God, because they had to guard it; and they had charge of the key for opening it each morning.

Some of them were in charge of the articles used in the temple service; they counted them when they were brought in and when they were taken out. Others were assigned to take care of the furnishings and all the other articles of the sanctuary, as well as the special flour and wine, and the olive oil, incense and spices. But some of the priests took care of mixing the spices. A Levite named Mattithiah, the firstborn son of Shallum the Korahite, was entrusted with the responsibility for baking the offering bread. Some of the Kohathites, their fellow Levites, were in charge of preparing for every Sabbath the bread set out on the table.

Those who were musicians, heads of Levite families, stayed in the rooms of the temple and were exempt from other duties because they were responsible for the work day and night.

All these were heads of Levite families, chiefs as listed in their genealogy, and they lived in Jerusalem.

Jeiel the father of Gibeon lived in Gibeon.
His wife's name was Maakah, and his firstborn son was Abdon, followed by Zur, Kish, Baal, Ner, Nadab, Gedor, Ahio, Zechariah and Mikloth. Mikloth was the father of Shimeam. They too lived near their relatives in Jerusalem.
Ner was the father of Kish, Kish the father of Saul, and Saul the father of Jonathan, Malki-Shua, Abinadab and Esh-Baal.
The son of Jonathan:
Merib-Baal, who was the father of Micah.
The sons of Micah:
Pithon, Melek, Tahrea and Ahaz.
Ahaz was the father of Jadah, Jadah was the father of Alemeth, Azmaveth and Zimri, and Zimri was the father of Moza. Moza was the father of Binea; Rephaiah was his son, Eleasah his son and Azel his son.
Azel had six sons, and these were their names:
Azrikam, Bokeru, Ishmael, Sheariah, Obadiah and Hanan. These were the sons of Azel.

N ow the Philistines fought against Israel; the Israelites fled before them, and many fell dead on Mount Gilboa. The Philistines were in hot pursuit of Saul and his sons, and they killed his sons Jonathan, Abinadab and Malki-Shua. The fighting grew fierce around Saul, and when the archers overtook him, they wounded him.

Saul said to his armor-bearer, "Draw your sword and run me through, or these uncircumcised fellows will come and abuse me."

But his armor-bearer was terrified and would not do it; so Saul took his own sword and fell on it. When the armor-bearer saw that Saul was dead, he too fell on his sword and died. So Saul and his three sons died, and all his house died together.

When all the Israelites in the valley saw that the army had fled and that Saul and his sons had died, they abandoned their towns and fled. And the Philistines came and occupied them.

The next day, when the Philistines came to strip the dead, they found Saul and his sons fallen on Mount Gilboa. They stripped him and took his head and his armor, and sent messengers throughout the land of the Philistines to proclaim the news among their idols and their people. They put his armor in the temple of their gods and hung up his head in the temple of Dagon.

When all the inhabitants of Jabesh Gilead heard what the Philistines had done to Saul, all their valiant men went and took the bodies of Saul and his sons and brought them to Jabesh. Then they buried their bones under the great tree in Jabesh, and they fasted seven days.

Saul died because he was unfaithful to the LORD; he did not keep the word of the LORD and even consulted a medium for guidance, and did not inquire of the LORD. So the LORD put him to death and turned the kingdom over to David son of Jesse.

A ll Israel came together to David at Hebron and said, "We are your own flesh and blood. In the past, even while Saul was king, you were the one who led Israel on their military campaigns. And the LORD your God said to you, 'You will shepherd my people Israel, and you will become their ruler.'"

When all the elders of Israel had come to King David at Hebron, he made a covenant with them at Hebron before the LORD, and they anointed David king over Israel, as the LORD had promised through Samuel.

David and all the Israelites marched to Jerusalem (that is, Jebus). The Jebusites who lived there said to David, "You will not get in here." Nevertheless, David captured the fortress of Zion—which is the City of David.

David had said, "Whoever leads the attack on the Jebusites will become commander-in-chief." Joab son of Zeruiah went up first, and so he received the command.

David then took up residence in the fortress, and so it was called the City of David. He built up the city around it, from the terraces to the surrounding wall, while Joab restored the rest of the city. And David became more and more powerful, because the LORD Almighty was with him.

These were the chiefs of David's mighty warriors—they, together with all Israel, gave his kingship strong support to extend it over the whole land, as the LORD had promised—this is the list of David's mighty warriors:

Jashobeam, a Hakmonite, was chief of the officers; he raised his spear against three hundred men, whom he killed in one encounter.

Next to him was Eleazar son of Dodai the Ahohite, one of the three mighty warriors. He was with David at Pas Dammim when the Philistines gathered there for battle. At a place where there was a field full of barley, the troops fled from the Philistines. But they took their stand in the middle of the field. They defended it and struck the Philistines down, and the LORD brought about a great victory.

Three of the thirty chiefs came down to David to the rock at the cave of Adullam, while a band of Philistines was encamped in the Valley of Rephaim. At that time David was in the stronghold, and the Philistine garrison was at Bethlehem. David longed for water and said, "Oh, that someone would get me a drink of water from the well near the gate of Bethlehem!" So the Three broke through the Philistine lines, drew water from the well near the gate of Bethlehem and carried it back to David. But he refused to drink it; instead, he poured it out to the LORD. "God forbid that I should do this!" he said. "Should I drink the blood of these men who went at the risk of their lives?" Because they risked their lives to bring it back, David would not drink it.

Such were the exploits of the three mighty warriors.

Abishai the brother of Joab was chief of the Three. He raised his spear against three hundred men, whom he killed, and so he became as famous as the Three. He was doubly honored above the

Three and became their commander, even though he was not included among them.

Benaiah son of Jehoiada, a valiant fighter from Kabzeel, performed great exploits. He struck down Moab's two mightiest warriors. He also went down into a pit on a snowy day and killed a lion. And he struck down an Egyptian who was five cubits tall. Although the Egyptian had a spear like a weaver's rod in his hand, Benaiah went against him with a club. He snatched the spear from the Egyptian's hand and killed him with his own spear. Such were the exploits of Benaiah son of Jehoiada; he too was as famous as the three mighty warriors. He was held in greater honor than any of the Thirty, but he was not included among the Three. And David put him in charge of his bodyguard.

The mighty warriors were:
Asahel the brother of Joab,
Elhanan son of Dodo from Bethlehem,
Shammoth the Harorite,
Helez the Pelonite,
Ira son of Ikkesh from Tekoa,
Abiezer from Anathoth,
Sibbekai the Hushathite,
Ilai the Ahohite,
Maharai the Netophathite,
Heled son of Baanah the Netophathite,
Ithai son of Ribai from Gibeah in Benjamin,
Benaiah the Pirathonite,
Hurai from the ravines of Gaash,
Abiel the Arbathite,
Azmaveth the Baharumite,
Eliahba the Shaalbonite,
the sons of Hashem the Gizonite,
Jonathan son of Shagee the Hararite,
Ahiam son of Sakar the Hararite,
Eliphal son of Ur,
Hepher the Mekerathite,
Ahijah the Pelonite,
Hezro the Carmelite,
Naarai son of Ezbai,
Joel the brother of Nathan,
Mibhar son of Hagri,
Zelek the Ammonite,
Naharai the Berothite, the armor-bearer of Joab son of Zeruiah,
Ira the Ithrite,
Gareb the Ithrite,

Uriah the Hittite,
Zabad son of Ahlai,
Adina son of Shiza the Reubenite, who was chief of the Reubenites, and the thirty with him,
Hanan son of Maakah,
Joshaphat the Mithnite,
Uzzia the Ashterathite,
Shama and Jeiel the sons of Hotham the Aroerite,
Jediael son of Shimri,
his brother Joha the Tizite,
Eliel the Mahavite,
Jeribai and Joshaviah the sons of Elnaam,
Ithmah the Moabite,
Eliel, Obed and Jaasiel the Mezobaite.

These were the men who came to David at Ziklag, while he was banished from the presence of Saul son of Kish (they were among the warriors who helped him in battle; they were armed with bows and were able to shoot arrows or to sling stones right-handed or left-handed; they were relatives of Saul from the tribe of Benjamin):

Ahiezer their chief and Joash the sons of Shemaah the Gibeathite; Jeziel and Pelet the sons of Azmaveth; Berakah, Jehu the Anathothite, and Ishmaiah the Gibeonite, a mighty warrior among the Thirty, who was a leader of the Thirty; Jeremiah, Jahaziel, Johanan, Jozabad the Gederathite, Eluzai, Jerimoth, Bealiah, Shemariah and Shephatiah the Haruphite; Elkanah, Ishiah, Azarel, Joezer and Jashobeam the Korahites; and Joelah and Zebadiah the sons of Jeroham from Gedor.

Some Gadites defected to David at his stronghold in the wilderness. They were brave warriors, ready for battle and able to handle the shield and spear. Their faces were the faces of lions, and they were as swift as gazelles in the mountains.
Ezer was the chief,
Obadiah the second in command, Eliab the third,
Mishmannah the fourth, Jeremiah the fifth,
Attai the sixth, Eliel the seventh,
Johanan the eighth, Elzabad the ninth,
Jeremiah the tenth and Makbannai the eleventh.
These Gadites were army commanders; the least was a match for a hundred, and the greatest for a thousand. It was they who crossed the Jordan in the first month when it was overflowing all its banks, and they put to flight everyone living in the valleys, to the east and to the west.
Other Benjamites and some men from Judah also came to

David in his stronghold. David went out to meet them and said to them, "If you have come to me in peace to help me, I am ready for you to join me. But if you have come to betray me to my enemies when my hands are free from violence, may the God of our ancestors see it and judge you."

Then the Spirit came on Amasai, chief of the Thirty, and he said:

> "We are yours, David!
> We are with you, son of Jesse!
>
> Success, success to you,
> and success to those who help you,
> for your God will help you."

So David received them and made them leaders of his raiding bands.

Some of the tribe of Manasseh defected to David when he went with the Philistines to fight against Saul. (He and his men did not help the Philistines because, after consultation, their rulers sent him away. They said, "It will cost us our heads if he deserts to his master Saul.") When David went to Ziklag, these were the men of Manasseh who defected to him: Adnah, Jozabad, Jediael, Michael, Jozabad, Elihu and Zillethai, leaders of units of a thousand in Manasseh. They helped David against raiding bands, for all of them were brave warriors, and they were commanders in his army. Day after day men came to help David, until he had a great army, like the army of God.

These are the numbers of the men armed for battle who came to David at Hebron to turn Saul's kingdom over to him, as the LORD had said:

from Judah, carrying shield and spear — 6,800 armed for battle;

from Simeon, warriors ready for battle — 7,100;

from Levi — 4,600, including Jehoiada, leader of the family of Aaron, with 3,700 men, and Zadok, a brave young warrior, with 22 officers from his family;

from Benjamin, Saul's tribe — 3,000, most of whom had remained loyal to Saul's house until then;

from Ephraim, brave warriors, famous in their own clans — 20,800;

from half the tribe of Manasseh, designated by name to come and make David king — 18,000;

from Issachar, men who understood the times and knew what Israel should do — 200 chiefs, with all their relatives under their command;

from Zebulun, experienced soldiers prepared for battle with
every type of weapon, to help David with undivided loyalty — 50,000;

from Naphtali — 1,000 officers, together with 37,000 men carrying shields and spears;

from Dan, ready for battle — 28,600;

from Asher, experienced soldiers prepared for battle — 40,000;

and from east of the Jordan, from Reuben, Gad and the half-
tribe of Manasseh, armed with every type of weapon —
120,000.

All these were fighting men who volunteered to serve in the
ranks. They came to Hebron fully determined to make David king
over all Israel. All the rest of the Israelites were also of one mind
to make David king. The men spent three days there with David,
eating and drinking, for their families had supplied provisions for
them. Also, their neighbors from as far away as Issachar, Zebulun
and Naphtali came bringing food on donkeys, camels, mules and
oxen. There were plentiful supplies of flour, fig cakes, raisin cakes,
wine, olive oil, cattle and sheep, for there was joy in Israel.

David conferred with each of his officers, the commanders of thousands and commanders of hundreds. He then said to the whole assembly of Israel, "If it seems good to you and if it is the will of the
Lord our God, let us send word far and wide to the rest of our people
throughout the territories of Israel, and also to the priests and Levites who are with them in their towns and pasturelands, to come
and join us. Let us bring the ark of our God back to us, for we did not
inquire of it during the reign of Saul." The whole assembly agreed to
do this, because it seemed right to all the people.

So David assembled all Israel, from the Shihor River in Egypt
to Lebo Hamath, to bring the ark of God from Kiriath Jearim. David
and all Israel went to Baalah of Judah (Kiriath Jearim) to bring up
from there the ark of God the Lord, who is enthroned between the
cherubim — the ark that is called by the Name.

They moved the ark of God from Abinadab's house on a new
cart, with Uzzah and Ahio guiding it. David and all the Israelites
were celebrating with all their might before God, with songs and
with harps, lyres, timbrels, cymbals and trumpets.

When they came to the threshing floor of Kidon, Uzzah
reached out his hand to steady the ark, because the oxen stumbled.
The Lord's anger burned against Uzzah, and he struck him down
because he had put his hand on the ark. So he died there before God.

Then David was angry because the Lord's wrath had broken
out against Uzzah, and to this day that place is called Perez Uzzah.

David was afraid of God that day and asked, "How can I ever bring the ark of God to me?" He did not take the ark to be with him in the City of David. Instead, he took it to the house of Obed-Edom the Gittite. The ark of God remained with the family of Obed-Edom in his house for three months, and the LORD blessed his household and everything he had.

Now Hiram king of Tyre sent messengers to David, along with cedar logs, stonemasons and carpenters to build a palace for him. And David knew that the LORD had established him as king over Israel and that his kingdom had been highly exalted for the sake of his people Israel.

In Jerusalem David took more wives and became the father of more sons and daughters. These are the names of the children born to him there: Shammua, Shobab, Nathan, Solomon, Ibhar, Elishua, Elpelet, Nogah, Nepheg, Japhia, Elishama, Beeliada and Eliphelet.

When the Philistines heard that David had been anointed king over all Israel, they went up in full force to search for him, but David heard about it and went out to meet them. Now the Philistines had come and raided the Valley of Rephaim; so David inquired of God: "Shall I go and attack the Philistines? Will you deliver them into my hands?"

The LORD answered him, "Go, I will deliver them into your hands."

So David and his men went up to Baal Perazim, and there he defeated them. He said, "As waters break out, God has broken out against my enemies by my hand." So that place was called Baal Perazim. The Philistines had abandoned their gods there, and David gave orders to burn them in the fire.

Once more the Philistines raided the valley; so David inquired of God again, and God answered him, "Do not go directly after them, but circle around them and attack them in front of the poplar trees. As soon as you hear the sound of marching in the tops of the poplar trees, move out to battle, because that will mean God has gone out in front of you to strike the Philistine army." So David did as God commanded him, and they struck down the Philistine army, all the way from Gibeon to Gezer.

So David's fame spread throughout every land, and the LORD made all the nations fear him.

After David had constructed buildings for himself in the City of David, he prepared a place for the ark of God and pitched a tent for it. Then David said, "No one but the Levites may carry the ark of God, because the L ORD chose them to carry the ark of the L ORD and to minister before him forever."

David assembled all Israel in Jerusalem to bring up the ark of the L ORD to the place he had prepared for it. He called together the descendants of Aaron and the Levites:

From the descendants of Kohath,

Uriel the leader and 120 relatives;

from the descendants of Merari,

Asaiah the leader and 220 relatives;

from the descendants of Gershon,

Joel the leader and 130 relatives;

from the descendants of Elizaphan,

Shemaiah the leader and 200 relatives;

from the descendants of Hebron,

Eliel the leader and 80 relatives;

from the descendants of Uzziel,

Amminadab the leader and 112 relatives.

Then David summoned Zadok and Abiathar the priests, and Uriel, Asaiah, Joel, Shemaiah, Eliel and Amminadab the Levites. He said to them, "You are the heads of the Levitical families; you and your fellow Levites are to consecrate yourselves and bring up the ark of the L ORD, the God of Israel, to the place I have prepared for it. It was because you, the Levites, did not bring it up the first time that the L ORD our God broke out in anger against us. We did not inquire of him about how to do it in the prescribed way." So the priests and Levites consecrated themselves in order to bring up the ark of the L ORD, the God of Israel. And the Levites carried the ark of God with the poles on their shoulders, as Moses had commanded in accordance with the word of the L ORD.

David told the leaders of the Levites to appoint their fellow Levites as musicians to make a joyful sound with musical instruments: lyres, harps and cymbals.

So the Levites appointed Heman son of Joel; from his relatives, Asaph son of Berekiah; and from their relatives the Merarites, Ethan son of Kushaiah; and with them their relatives next in rank: Zechariah, Jaaziel, Shemiramoth, Jehiel, Unni, Eliab, Benaiah, Maaseiah, Mattithiah, Eliphelehu, Mikneiah, Obed-Edom and Jeiel, the gatekeepers.

The musicians Heman, Asaph and Ethan were to sound the bronze cymbals; Zechariah, Jaaziel, Shemiramoth, Jehiel, Unni, Eliab, Maaseiah and Benaiah were to play the lyres according to *alamoth*, and Mattithiah, Eliphelehu, Mikneiah, Obed-Edom, Jeiel and Azaziah were to play the harps, directing according to *sheminith*. Kenaniah the head Levite was in charge of the singing; that was his responsibility because he was skillful at it.

Berekiah and Elkanah were to be doorkeepers for the ark. Shebaniah, Joshaphat, Nethanel, Amasai, Zechariah, Benaiah and Eliezer the priests were to blow trumpets before the ark of God. Obed-Edom and Jehiah were also to be doorkeepers for the ark.

So David and the elders of Israel and the commanders of units of a thousand went to bring up the ark of the covenant of the LORD from the house of Obed-Edom, with rejoicing. Because God had helped the Levites who were carrying the ark of the covenant of the LORD, seven bulls and seven rams were sacrificed. Now David was clothed in a robe of fine linen, as were all the Levites who were carrying the ark, and as were the musicians, and Kenaniah, who was in charge of the singing of the choirs. David also wore a linen ephod. So all Israel brought up the ark of the covenant of the LORD with shouts, with the sounding of rams' horns and trumpets, and of cymbals, and the playing of lyres and harps.

As the ark of the covenant of the LORD was entering the City of David, Michal daughter of Saul watched from a window. And when she saw King David dancing and celebrating, she despised him in her heart.

They brought the ark of God and set it inside the tent that David had pitched for it, and they presented burnt offerings and fellowship offerings before God. After David had finished sacrificing the burnt offerings and fellowship offerings, he blessed the people in the name of the LORD. Then he gave a loaf of bread, a cake of dates and a cake of raisins to each Israelite man and woman.

He appointed some of the Levites to minister before the ark of the LORD, to extol, thank, and praise the LORD, the God of Israel: Asaph was the chief, and next to him in rank were Zechariah, then Jaaziel, Shemiramoth, Jehiel, Mattithiah, Eliab, Benaiah, Obed-Edom and Jeiel. They were to play the lyres and harps, Asaph was to sound the cymbals, and Benaiah and Jahaziel the priests were to blow the trumpets regularly before the ark of the covenant of God.

That day David first appointed Asaph and his associates to give praise to the LORD in this manner:

Give praise to the LORD, proclaim his name;
make known among the nations what he has done.

Sing to him, sing praise to him;
tell of all his wonderful acts.

Glory in his holy name;
let the hearts of those who seek the LORD rejoice.

Look to the LORD and his strength;
seek his face always.

Remember the wonders he has done,
his miracles, and the judgments he pronounced,

you his servants, the descendants of Israel,
his chosen ones, the children of Jacob.

He is the Lord our God;
his judgments are in all the earth.

He remembers his covenant forever,
the promise he made, for a thousand generations,

the covenant he made with Abraham,
the oath he swore to Isaac.

He confirmed it to Jacob as a decree,
to Israel as an everlasting covenant:

"To you I will give the land of Canaan
as the portion you will inherit."

When they were but few in number,
few indeed, and strangers in it,

they wandered from nation to nation,
from one kingdom to another.

He allowed no one to oppress them;
for their sake he rebuked kings:

"Do not touch my anointed ones;
do my prophets no harm."

Sing to the Lord, all the earth;
proclaim his salvation day after day.

Declare his glory among the nations,
his marvelous deeds among all peoples.

For great is the Lord and most worthy
of praise;
he is to be feared above all gods.

For all the gods of the nations are idols,
but the Lord made the heavens.

Splendor and majesty are before him;
strength and joy are in his dwelling place.

Ascribe to the Lord, all you families of nations,
ascribe to the Lord glory and strength.

Ascribe to the Lord the glory due his name;
bring an offering and come before him.

Worship the Lord in the splendor of his holiness.
Tremble before him, all the earth!
The world is firmly established; it cannot be moved.

Let the heavens rejoice, let the earth be glad;
let them say among the nations, "The Lord reigns!"

Let the sea resound, and all that is in it;
let the fields be jubilant, and everything in them!

Let the trees of the forest sing,
let them sing for joy before the Lord,
for he comes to judge the earth.

Give thanks to the Lord, for he is good;
his love endures forever.

Cry out, "Save us, God our Savior;
gather us and deliver us from the nations,

that we may give thanks to your holy name,
and glory in your praise."

Praise be to the Lord, the God of Israel,
from everlasting to everlasting.

Then all the people said "Amen" and "Praise the Lord."

David left Asaph and his associates before the ark of the covenant of the Lord to minister there regularly, according to each day's requirements. He also left Obed-Edom and his sixty-eight associates to minister with them. Obed-Edom son of Jeduthun, and also Hosah, were gatekeepers.

David left Zadok the priest and his fellow priests before the tabernacle of the Lord at the high place in Gibeon to present burnt offerings to the Lord on the altar of burnt offering regularly, morning and evening, in accordance with everything written in the Law of the Lord, which he had given Israel. With them were Heman and Jeduthun and the rest of those chosen and designated by name to give thanks to the Lord, "for his love endures forever." Heman and Jeduthun were responsible for the sounding of the trumpets and cymbals and for the playing of the other instruments for sacred song. The sons of Jeduthun were stationed at the gate.

Then all the people left, each for their own home, and David returned home to bless his family.

After David was settled in his palace, he said to Nathan the prophet, "Here I am, living in a house of cedar, while the ark of the covenant of the Lord is under a tent."

Nathan replied to David, "Whatever you have in mind, do it, for God is with you."

But that night the word of God came to Nathan, saying:

"Go and tell my servant David, 'This is what the Lord says: You are not the one to build me a house to dwell in. I have not dwelt in a house from the day I brought Israel up out of Egypt to this day. I have moved from one tent site to another, from one dwelling place to another. Wherever I have moved with all the Israelites, did I ever say to any of their leaders whom I commanded to shepherd my people, "Why have you not built me a house of cedar?"'

"Now then, tell my servant David, 'This is what the Lord Almighty says: I took you from the pasture, from tending the flock, and appointed you ruler over my people Israel. I have been with you wherever you have gone, and I have cut off all your enemies from before you. Now I will make your name like the names of the greatest men on earth. And I will provide a place for my people Israel and will plant them so that they can have a home of their own and no longer be disturbed. Wicked people will not oppress them anymore, as they did at the beginning and have done ever since the time I appointed leaders over my people Israel. I will also subdue all your enemies.

" 'I declare to you that the Lord will build a house for you: When your days are over and you go to be with your ancestors, I will raise up your offspring to succeed you, one of your own sons, and I will establish his kingdom. He is the one who will build a house for me, and I will establish his throne forever. I will be his father, and he will be my son. I will never take my love away from him, as I took it away from your predecessor. I will set him over my house and my kingdom forever; his throne will be established forever.' "

Nathan reported to David all the words of this entire revelation.

Then King David went in and sat before the Lord, and he said:

"Who am I, Lord God, and what is my family, that you have brought me this far? And as if this were not enough in your sight, my God, you have spoken about the future of the house of your servant. You, Lord God, have looked on me as though I were the most exalted of men.

"What more can David say to you for honoring your servant? For you know your servant, Lord. For the sake of your servant and according to your will, you have done this great thing and made known all these great promises.

"There is no one like you, Lord, and there is no God but you, as we have heard with our own ears. And who is like your people Israel — the one nation on earth whose God went out to redeem a people for himself, and to make a name for yourself, and to perform great and awesome wonders by driving out nations from before your people, whom you redeemed from Egypt? You made your people Israel your very own forever, and you, Lord, have become their God.

"And now, Lord, let the promise you have made concerning your servant and his house be established forever. Do as you promised, so that it will be established and that your name will be great forever. Then people will say, 'The Lord Almighty, the God over Israel, is Israel's God!' And the house of your servant David will be established before you.

"You, my God, have revealed to your servant that you will build a house for him. So your servant has found courage to pray to you. You, Lord, are God! You have promised these good things to your servant. Now you have been pleased to bless the house of your servant, that it may continue forever in your sight; for you, Lord, have blessed it, and it will be blessed forever."

In the course of time, David defeated the Philistines and subdued them, and he took Gath and its surrounding villages from the control of the Philistines.

David also defeated the Moabites, and they became subject to him and brought him tribute.

Moreover, David defeated Hadadezer king of Zobah, in the vicinity of Hamath, when he went to set up his monument at the Euphrates River. David captured a thousand of his chariots, seven thousand charioteers and twenty thousand foot soldiers. He hamstrung all but a hundred of the chariot horses.

When the Arameans of Damascus came to help Hadadezer king of Zobah, David struck down twenty-two thousand of them. He put garrisons in the Aramean kingdom of Damascus, and the Arameans became subject to him and brought him tribute. The Lord gave David victory wherever he went.

David took the gold shields carried by the officers of Hadadezer and brought them to Jerusalem. From Tebah and Kun, towns that belonged to Hadadezer, David took a great quantity of bronze, which Solomon used to make the bronze Sea, the pillars and various bronze articles.

When Tou king of Hamath heard that David had defeated the entire army of Hadadezer king of Zobah, he sent his son Hadoram to King David to greet him and congratulate him on his victory in battle over Hadadezer, who had been at war with Tou. Hadoram brought all kinds of articles of gold, of silver and of bronze.

King David dedicated these articles to the Lord, as he had done with the silver and gold he had taken from all these nations: Edom and Moab, the Ammonites and the Philistines, and Amalek.

Abishai son of Zeruiah struck down eighteen thousand Edomites in the Valley of Salt. He put garrisons in Edom, and all the Edomites became subject to David. The Lord gave David victory wherever he went.

David reigned over all Israel, doing what was just and right for all his people. Joab son of Zeruiah was over the army; Jehoshaphat son of Ahilud was recorder; Zadok son of Ahitub and Ahimelek son of Abiathar were priests; Shavsha was secretary; Benaiah son of Jehoiada was over the Kerethites and Pelethites; and David's sons were chief officials at the king's side.

In the course of time, Nahash king of the Ammonites died, and his son succeeded him as king. David thought, "I will show kindness to Hanun son of Nahash, because his father showed kindness to me." So David sent a delegation to express his sympathy to Hanun concerning his father.

When David's envoys came to Hanun in the land of the Ammonites to express sympathy to him, the Ammonite commanders said to Hanun, "Do you think David is honoring your father by sending envoys to you to express sympathy? Haven't his envoys come to you only to explore and spy out the country and overthrow it?" So Hanun seized David's envoys, shaved them, cut off their garments at the buttocks, and sent them away.

When someone came and told David about the men, he sent messengers to meet them, for they were greatly humiliated. The king said, "Stay at Jericho till your beards have grown, and then come back."

When the Ammonites realized that they had become obnoxious to David, Hanun and the Ammonites sent a thousand talents of silver to hire chariots and charioteers from Aram Naharaim, Aram Maakah and Zobah. They hired thirty-two thousand chariots and charioteers, as well as the king of Maakah with his troops, who came and camped near Medeba, while the Ammonites were mustered from their towns and moved out for battle.

On hearing this, David sent Joab out with the entire army of fighting men. The Ammonites came out and drew up in battle formation at the entrance to their city, while the kings who had come were by themselves in the open country.

Joab saw that there were battle lines in front of him and behind him; so he selected some of the best troops in Israel and deployed them against the Arameans. He put the rest of the men under the command of Abishai his brother, and they were deployed against the Ammonites. Joab said, "If the Arameans are too strong for me, then you are to rescue me; but if the Ammonites are too strong for you, then I will rescue you. Be strong, and let us fight bravely for our people and the cities of our God. The LORD will do what is good in his sight."

Then Joab and the troops with him advanced to fight the Arameans, and they fled before him. When the Ammonites realized that the Arameans were fleeing, they too fled before his brother Abishai and went inside the city. So Joab went back to Jerusalem.

After the Arameans saw that they had been routed by Israel, they sent messengers and had Arameans brought from beyond the Euphrates River, with Shophak the commander of Hadadezer's army leading them.

When David was told of this, he gathered all Israel and crossed the Jordan; he advanced against them and formed his battle lines opposite them. David formed his lines to meet the Arameans in battle, and they fought against him. But they fled before Israel, and David killed seven thousand of their charioteers and forty thousand of their foot soldiers. He also killed Shophak the commander of their army.

When the vassals of Hadadezer saw that they had been routed by Israel, they made peace with David and became subject to him.

So the Arameans were not willing to help the Ammonites anymore.

In the spring, at the time when kings go off to war, Joab led out the armed forces. He laid waste the land of the Ammonites and went to Rabbah and besieged it, but David remained in Jerusalem. Joab attacked Rabbah and left it in ruins. David took the crown from the head of their king — its weight was found to be a talent of gold, and it was set with precious stones — and it was placed on David's head. He took a great quantity of plunder from the city and brought out the people who were there, consigning them to labor with saws and with iron picks and axes. David did this to all the Ammonite towns. Then David and his entire army returned to Jerusalem.

In the course of time, war broke out with the Philistines, at Gezer. At that time Sibbekai the Hushathite killed Sippai, one of the descendants of the Rephaites, and the Philistines were subjugated.

In another battle with the Philistines, Elhanan son of Jair killed Lahmi the brother of Goliath the Gittite, who had a spear with a shaft like a weaver's rod.

In still another battle, which took place at Gath, there was a huge man with six fingers on each hand and six toes on each foot—twenty-four in all. He also was descended from Rapha. When he taunted Israel, Jonathan son of Shimea, David's brother, killed him.

These were descendants of Rapha in Gath, and they fell at the hands of David and his men.

Satan rose up against Israel and incited David to take a census of Israel. So David said to Joab and the commanders of the troops, "Go and count the Israelites from Beersheba to Dan. Then report back to me so that I may know how many there are."

But Joab replied, "May the LORD multiply his troops a hundred times over. My lord the king, are they not all my lord's subjects? Why does my lord want to do this? Why should he bring guilt on Israel?"

The king's word, however, overruled Joab; so Joab left and went throughout Israel and then came back to Jerusalem. Joab reported the number of the fighting men to David: In all Israel there were one million one hundred thousand men who could handle a sword, including four hundred and seventy thousand in Judah.

But Joab did not include Levi and Benjamin in the numbering, because the king's command was repulsive to him. This command was also evil in the sight of God; so he punished Israel.

Then David said to God, "I have sinned greatly by doing this. Now, I beg you, take away the guilt of your servant. I have done a very foolish thing."

The LORD said to Gad, David's seer, "Go and tell David, 'This is what the LORD says: I am giving you three options. Choose one of them for me to carry out against you.'"

So Gad went to David and said to him, "This is what the LORD says: 'Take your choice: three years of famine, three months of being swept away before your enemies, with their swords overtaking you, or three days of the sword of the LORD—days of plague in the land, with the angel of the LORD ravaging every part of Israel.' Now then, decide how I should answer the one who sent me."

David said to Gad, "I am in deep distress. Let me fall into the hands of the LORD, for his mercy is very great; but do not let me fall into human hands."

So the LORD sent a plague on Israel, and seventy thousand men of Israel fell dead. And God sent an angel to destroy Jerusalem. But as the angel was doing so, the LORD saw it and relented concerning the disaster and said to the angel who was destroying the people,

"Enough! Withdraw your hand." The angel of the Lord was then standing at the threshing floor of Araunah the Jebusite.

David looked up and saw the angel of the Lord standing between heaven and earth, with a drawn sword in his hand extended over Jerusalem. Then David and the elders, clothed in sackcloth, fell facedown.

David said to God, "Was it not I who ordered the fighting men to be counted? I, the shepherd, have sinned and done wrong. These are but sheep. What have they done? Lord my God, let your hand fall on me and my family, but do not let this plague remain on your people."

Then the angel of the Lord ordered Gad to tell David to go up and build an altar to the Lord on the threshing floor of Araunah the Jebusite. So David went up in obedience to the word that Gad had spoken in the name of the Lord.

While Araunah was threshing wheat, he turned and saw the angel; his four sons who were with him hid themselves. Then David approached, and when Araunah looked and saw him, he left the threshing floor and bowed down before David with his face to the ground.

David said to him, "Let me have the site of your threshing floor so I can build an altar to the Lord, that the plague on the people may be stopped. Sell it to me at the full price."

Araunah said to David, "Take it! Let my lord the king do whatever pleases him. Look, I will give the oxen for the burnt offerings, the threshing sledges for the wood, and the wheat for the grain offering. I will give all this."

But King David replied to Araunah, "No, I insist on paying the full price. I will not take for the Lord what is yours, or sacrifice a burnt offering that costs me nothing."

So David paid Araunah six hundred shekels of gold for the site. David built an altar to the Lord there and sacrificed burnt offerings and fellowship offerings. He called on the Lord, and the Lord answered him with fire from heaven on the altar of burnt offering.

Then the Lord spoke to the angel, and he put his sword back into its sheath. At that time, when David saw that the Lord had answered him on the threshing floor of Araunah the Jebusite, he offered sacrifices there. The tabernacle of the Lord, which Moses had made in the wilderness, and the altar of burnt offering were at that time on the high place at Gibeon. But David could not go before it to inquire of God, because he was afraid of the sword of the angel of the Lord.

Then David said, "The house of the Lord God is to be here, and also the altar of burnt offering for Israel."

So David gave orders to assemble the foreigners residing in Israel, and from among them he appointed stonecutters to prepare dressed stone for building the house of God. He provided a large amount of iron to make nails for the doors of the gateways and for the fittings, and more bronze than could be weighed. He also provided more cedar logs than could be counted, for the Sidonians and Tyrians had brought large numbers of them to David.

David said, "My son Solomon is young and inexperienced, and the house to be built for the Lord should be of great magnificence and fame and splendor in the sight of all the nations. Therefore I will make preparations for it." So David made extensive preparations before his death.

Then he called for his son Solomon and charged him to build a house for the Lord, the God of Israel. David said to Solomon: "My son, I had it in my heart to build a house for the Name of the Lord my God. But this word of the Lord came to me: 'You have shed much blood and have fought many wars. You are not to build a house for my Name, because you have shed much blood on the earth in my sight. But you will have a son who will be a man of peace and rest, and I will give him rest from all his enemies on every side. His name will be Solomon, and I will grant Israel peace and quiet during his reign. He is the one who will build a house for my Name. He will be my son, and I will be his father. And I will establish the throne of his kingdom over Israel forever.'

"Now, my son, the Lord be with you, and may you have success and build the house of the Lord your God, as he said you would. May the Lord give you discretion and understanding when he puts you in command over Israel, so that you may keep the law of the Lord your God. Then you will have success if you are careful to observe the decrees and laws that the Lord gave Moses for Israel. Be strong and courageous. Do not be afraid or discouraged.

"I have taken great pains to provide for the temple of the Lord a hundred thousand talents of gold, a million talents of silver, quantities of bronze and iron too great to be weighed, and wood and stone. And you may add to them. You have many workers: stonecutters, masons and carpenters, as well as those skilled in every kind of work in gold and silver, bronze and iron—craftsmen beyond number. Now begin the work, and the Lord be with you."

Then David ordered all the leaders of Israel to help his son Solomon. He said to them, "Is not the Lord your God with you? And has he not granted you rest on every side? For he has given the inhabitants of the land into my hands, and the land is subject to the Lord and to his people. Now devote your heart and soul to seeking the Lord your God. Begin to build the sanctuary of the Lord God, so that you may bring the ark of the covenant of the Lᴏʀᴅ and the sacred articles belonging to God into the temple that will be built for the Name of the Lᴏʀᴅ."

When David was old and full of years, he made his son Solomon king over Israel.

He also gathered together all the leaders of Israel, as well as the priests and Levites. The Levites thirty years old or more were counted, and the total number of men was thirty-eight thousand. David said, "Of these, twenty-four thousand are to be in charge of the work of the temple of the Lᴏʀᴅ and six thousand are to be officials and judges. Four thousand are to be gatekeepers and four thousand are to praise the Lᴏʀᴅ with the musical instruments I have provided for that purpose."

David separated the Levites into divisions corresponding to the sons of Levi: Gershon, Kohath and Merari.

Belonging to the Gershonites:
    Ladan and Shimei.
The sons of Ladan:
    Jehiel the first, Zetham and Joel—three in all.
The sons of Shimei:
    Shelomoth, Haziel and Haran—three in all.
    These were the heads of the families of Ladan.
And the sons of Shimei:
    Jahath, Ziza, Jeush and Beriah.
    These were the sons of Shimei—four in all.
    Jahath was the first and Ziza the second, but Jeush and Beriah did not have many sons; so they were counted as one family with one assignment.

The sons of Kohath:
    Amram, Izhar, Hebron and Uzziel—four in all.
The sons of Amram:
    Aaron and Moses.
    Aaron was set apart, he and his descendants forever, to consecrate the most holy things, to offer sacrifices before the Lᴏʀᴅ, to minister before him and to pronounce blessings in his name forever. The sons of Moses the man of God were counted as part of the tribe of Levi.
The sons of Moses:
    Gershom and Eliezer.
The descendants of Gershom:
    Shubael was the first.

The descendants of Eliezer:
Rehabiah was the first.
Eliezer had no other sons, but the sons of Rehabiah were very numerous.
The sons of Izhar:
Shelomith was the first.
The sons of Hebron:
Jeriah the first, Amariah the second, Jahaziel the third and Jekameam the fourth.
The sons of Uzziel:
Micah the first and Ishiah the second.

The sons of Merari:
Mahli and Mushi.
The sons of Mahli:
Eleazar and Kish.
Eleazar died without having sons: he had only daughters.
Their cousins, the sons of Kish, married them.
The sons of Mushi:
Mahli, Eder and Jerimoth — three in all.

These were the descendants of Levi by their families — the heads of families as they were registered under their names and counted individually, that is, the workers twenty years old or more who served in the temple of the LORD. For David had said, "Since the LORD, the God of Israel, has granted rest to his people and has come to dwell in Jerusalem forever, the Levites no longer need to carry the tabernacle or any of the articles used in its service." According to the last instructions of David, the Levites were counted from those twenty years old or more.

The duty of the Levites was to help Aaron's descendants in the service of the temple of the LORD: to be in charge of the courtyards, the side rooms, the purification of all sacred things and the performance of other duties at the house of God. They were in charge of the bread set out on the table, the special flour for the grain offerings, the thin loaves made without yeast, the baking and the mixing, and all measurements of quantity and size. They were also to stand every morning to thank and praise the LORD. They were to do the same in the evening and whenever burnt offerings were presented to the LORD on the Sabbaths, at the New Moon feasts and at the appointed festivals. They were to serve before the LORD regularly in the proper number and in the way prescribed for them.

And so the Levites carried out their responsibilities for the tent of meeting, for the Holy Place and, under their relatives the descendants of Aaron, for the service of the temple of the LORD.

These were the divisions of the descendants of Aaron:

The sons of Aaron were Nadab, Abihu, Eleazar and Ithamar. But Nadab and Abihu died before their father did, and they had no sons; so Eleazar and Ithamar served as the priests. With the help of Zadok a descendant of Eleazar and Ahimelek a descendant of Ithamar, David separated them into divisions for their appointed order of ministering. A larger number of leaders were found among Eleazar's descendants than among Ithamar's, and they were divided accordingly: sixteen heads of families from Eleazar's descendants and eight heads of families from Ithamar's descendants. They divided them impartially by casting lots, for there were officials of the sanctuary and officials of God among the descendants of both Eleazar and Ithamar.

The scribe Shemaiah son of Nethanel, a Levite, recorded their names in the presence of the king and of the officials: Zadok the priest, Ahimelek son of Abiathar and the heads of families of the priests and of the Levites — one family being taken from Eleazar and then one from Ithamar.

The first lot fell to Jehoiarib,
  the second to Jedaiah,
  the third to Harim,
  the fourth to Seorim,
  the fifth to Malkijah,
  the sixth to Mijamin,
  the seventh to Hakkoz,
  the eighth to Abijah,
  the ninth to Jeshua,
  the tenth to Shekaniah,
  the eleventh to Eliashib,
  the twelfth to Jakim,
  the thirteenth to Huppah,
  the fourteenth to Jeshebeab,
  the fifteenth to Bilgah,
  the sixteenth to Immer,
  the seventeenth to Hezir,
  the eighteenth to Happizzez,
  the nineteenth to Pethahiah,
  the twentieth to Jehezkel,
  the twenty-first to Jakin,
  the twenty-second to Gamul,
  the twenty-third to Delaiah
  and the twenty-fourth to Maaziah.

This was their appointed order of ministering when they entered the temple of the LORD, according to the regulations prescribed for them by their ancestor Aaron, as the Lord, the God of Israel, had commanded him.

As for the rest of the descendants of Levi:
    from the sons of Amram: Shubael;
        from the sons of Shubael: Jehdeiah.
        As for Rehabiah, from his sons:
        Ishiah was the first.
    From the Izharites: Shelomoth;
        from the sons of Shelomoth: Jahath.
    The sons of Hebron: Jeriah the first, Amariah the second,
        Jahaziel the third and Jekameam the fourth.
    The son of Uzziel: Micah;
        from the sons of Micah: Shamir.
        The brother of Micah: Ishiah;
        from the sons of Ishiah: Zechariah.
    The sons of Merari: Mahli and Mushi.
        The son of Jaaziah: Beno.
    The sons of Merari:
        from Jaaziah: Beno, Shoham, Zakkur and Ibri.
    From Mahli: Eleazar, who had no sons.
    From Kish: the son of Kish:
    Jerahmeel.
    And the sons of Mushi: Mahli, Eder and Jerimoth.

These were the Levites, according to their families. They also cast lots, just as their relatives the descendants of Aaron did, in the presence of King David and of Zadok, Ahimelek, and the heads of families of the priests and of the Levites. The families of the oldest brother were treated the same as those of the youngest.

David, together with the commanders of the army, set apart some of the sons of Asaph, Heman and Jeduthun for the ministry of prophesying, accompanied by harps, lyres and cymbals. Here is the list of the men who performed this service:

From the sons of Asaph:
    Zakkur, Joseph, Nethaniah and Asarelah. The sons of Asaph were under the supervision of Asaph, who prophesied under the king's supervision.
As for Jeduthun, from his sons:
    Gedaliah, Zeri, Jeshaiah, Shimei, Hashabiah and Mattithiah, six in all, under the supervision of their father Jeduthun, who prophesied, using the harp in thanking and praising the Lord.
As for Heman, from his sons:
    Bukkiah, Mattaniah, Uzziel, Shubael and Jerimoth; Hananiah, Hanani, Eliathah, Giddalti and Romamti-Ezer; Joshbekashah,

Mallothi, Hothir and Mahazioth. (All these were sons of Heman the king's seer. They were given him through the promises of God to exalt him. God gave Heman fourteen sons and three daughters.)

All these men were under the supervision of their father for the music of the temple of the LORD, with cymbals, lyres and harps, for the ministry at the house of God.

Asaph, Jeduthun and Heman were under the supervision of the king. Along with their relatives — all of them trained and skilled in music for the LORD — they numbered 288. Young and old alike, teacher as well as student, cast lots for their duties.

The first lot, which was for Asaph, fell to Joseph,
his sons and relatives 12
the second to Gedaliah,
him and his relatives and sons 12
the third to Zakkur,
his sons and relatives 12
the fourth to Izri,
his sons and relatives 12
the fifth to Nethaniah,
his sons and relatives 12
the sixth to Bukkiah,
his sons and relatives 12
the seventh to Jesarelah,
his sons and relatives 12
the eighth to Jeshaiah,
his sons and relatives 12
the ninth to Mattaniah,
his sons and relatives 12
the tenth to Shimei,
his sons and relatives 12
the eleventh to Azarel,
his sons and relatives 12
the twelfth to Hashabiah,
his sons and relatives 12
the thirteenth to Shubael,
his sons and relatives 12
the fourteenth to Mattithiah,
his sons and relatives 12
the fifteenth to Jerimoth,
his sons and relatives 12
the sixteenth to Hananiah,
his sons and relatives 12

the seventeenth to Joshbekashah,
 his sons and relatives   12
the eighteenth to Hanani,
 his sons and relatives   12
the nineteenth to Mallothi,
 his sons and relatives   12
the twentieth to Eliathah,
 his sons and relatives   12
the twenty-first to Hothir,
 his sons and relatives   12
the twenty-second to Giddalti,
 his sons and relatives   12
the twenty-third to Mahazioth,
 his sons and relatives   12
the twenty-fourth to Romamti-Ezer,
 his sons and relatives   12.

The divisions of the gatekeepers:

From the Korahites: Meshelemiah son of Kore, one of the sons
of Asaph.
Meshelemiah had sons:
 Zechariah the firstborn,
 Jediael the second,
 Zebadiah the third,
 Jathniel the fourth,
 Elam the fifth,
 Jehohanan the sixth
 and Eliehoenai the seventh.
Obed-Edom also had sons:
 Shemaiah the firstborn,
 Jehozabad the second,
 Joah the third,
 Sakar the fourth,
 Nethanel the fifth,
 Ammiel the sixth,
 Issachar the seventh
 and Peullethai the eighth.
 (For God had blessed Obed-Edom.)

Obed-Edom's son Shemaiah also had sons, who were leaders
in their father's family because they were very capable men.
The sons of Shemaiah: Othni, Rephael, Obed and Elzabad;
his relatives Elihu and Semakiah were also able men. All
these were descendants of Obed-Edom; they and their sons

and their relatives were capable men with the strength to do the work—descendants of Obed-Edom, 62 in all.

Meshelemiah had sons and relatives, who were able men—18 in all.

Hosah the Merarite had sons: Shimri the first (although he was not the firstborn, his father had appointed him the first), Hilkiah the second, Tabaliah the third and Zechariah the fourth. The sons and relatives of Hosah were 13 in all.

These divisions of the gatekeepers, through their leaders, had duties for ministering in the temple of the LORD, just as their relatives had. Lots were cast for each gate, according to their families, young and old alike.

The lot for the East Gate fell to Shelemiah. Then lots were cast for his son Zechariah, a wise counselor, and the lot for the North Gate fell to him. The lot for the South Gate fell to Obed-Edom, and the lot for the storehouse fell to his sons. The lots for the West Gate and the Shalleketh Gate on the upper road fell to Shuppim and Hosah.

Guard was alongside of guard: There were six Levites a day on the east, four a day on the north, four a day on the south and two at a time at the storehouse. As for the court to the west, there were four at the road and two at the court itself.

These were the divisions of the gatekeepers who were descendants of Korah and Merari.

Their fellow Levites were in charge of the treasuries of the house of God and the treasuries for the dedicated things.

The descendants of Ladan, who were Gershonites through Ladan and who were heads of families belonging to Ladan the Gershonite, were Jehieli, the sons of Jehieli, Zetham and his brother Joel. They were in charge of the treasuries of the temple of the LORD.

From the Amramites, the Izharites, the Hebronites and the Uzzielites:

Shubael, a descendant of Gershom son of Moses, was the official in charge of the treasuries. His relatives through Eliezer: Rehabiah his son, Jeshaiah his son, Joram his son, Zikri his son and Shelomith his son. Shelomith and his relatives were in charge of all the treasuries for the things dedicated by King David, by the heads of families who were the commanders of thousands and commanders of hundreds, and by the other army commanders. Some of the plunder taken in battle they dedicated for the repair of the temple of the LORD. And everything dedicated by Samuel the seer and by Saul son of Kish, Abner son of Ner and Joab son of Zeruiah, and all the other dedicated things were in the care of Shelomith and his relatives.

From the Izharites: Kenaniah and his sons were assigned duties away from the temple, as officials and judges over Israel.

From the Hebronites: Hashabiah and his relatives — seventeen hundred able men — were responsible in Israel west of the Jordan for all the work of the LORD and for the king's service. As for the Hebronites, Jeriah was their chief according to the genealogical records of their families. In the fortieth year of David's reign a search was made in the records, and capable men among the Hebronites were found at Jazer in Gilead. Jeriah had twenty-seven hundred relatives, who were able men and heads of families, and King David put them in charge of the Reubenites, the Gadites and the half-tribe of Manasseh for every matter pertaining to God and for the affairs of the king.

This is the list of the Israelites — heads of families, commanders of thousands and commanders of hundreds, and their officers, who served the king in all that concerned the army divisions that were on duty month by month throughout the year. Each division consisted of 24,000 men.

In charge of the first division, for the first month, was Jashobeam son of Zabdiel. There were 24,000 men in his division. He was a descendant of Perez and chief of all the army officers for the first month.

In charge of the division for the second month was Dodai the Ahohite; Mikloth was the leader of his division. There were 24,000 men in his division.

The third army commander, for the third month, was Benaiah son of Jehoiada the priest. He was chief and there were 24,000 men in his division. This was the Benaiah who was a mighty warrior among the Thirty and was over the Thirty. His son Ammizabad was in charge of his division.

The fourth, for the fourth month, was Asahel the brother of Joab; his son Zebadiah was his successor. There were 24,000 men in his division.

The fifth, for the fifth month, was the commander Shamhuth the Izrahite. There were 24,000 men in his division.

The sixth, for the sixth month, was Ira the son of Ikkesh the Tekoite. There were 24,000 men in his division.

The seventh, for the seventh month, was Helez the Pelonite, an Ephraimite. There were 24,000 men in his division.

The eighth, for the eighth month, was Sibbekai the Hushathite, a Zerahite. There were 24,000 men in his division.

The ninth, for the ninth month, was Abiezer the Anathothite, a Benjamite. There were 24,000 men in his division.

The tenth, for the tenth month, was Maharai the Netophathite, a Zerahite. There were 24,000 men in his division.

The eleventh, for the eleventh month, was Benaiah the Pirathonite, an Ephraimite. There were 24,000 men in his division.

The twelfth, for the twelfth month, was Heldai the Netophathite, from the family of Othniel. There were 24,000 men in his division.

The leaders of the tribes of Israel:

over the Reubenites: Eliezer son of Zikri;
over the Simeonites: Shephatiah son of Maakah;
over Levi: Hashabiah son of Kemuel;
over Aaron: Zadok;
over Judah: Elihu, a brother of David;
over Issachar: Omri son of Michael;
over Zebulun: Ishmaiah son of Obadiah;
over Naphtali: Jerimoth son of Azriel;
over the Ephraimites: Hoshea son of Azaziah;
over half the tribe of Manasseh: Joel son of Pedaiah;
over the half-tribe of Manasseh in Gilead: Iddo son of Zechariah;
over Benjamin: Jaasiel son of Abner;
over Dan: Azarel son of Jeroham.
These were the leaders of the tribes of Israel.

David did not take the number of the men twenty years old or less, because the LORD had promised to make Israel as numerous as the stars in the sky. Joab son of Zeruiah began to count the men but did not finish. God's wrath came on Israel on account of this numbering, and the number was not entered in the book of the annals of King David.

Azmaveth son of Adiel was in charge of the royal storehouses.

Jonathan son of Uzziah was in charge of the storehouses in the outlying districts, in the towns, the villages and the watchtowers.

Ezri son of Kelub was in charge of the workers who farmed the land.

Shimei the Ramathite was in charge of the vineyards.

Zabdi the Shiphmite was in charge of the produce of the vineyards for the wine vats.

Baal-Hanan the Gederite was in charge of the olive and sycamore-fig trees in the western foothills.

Joash was in charge of the supplies of olive oil.

Shitrai the Sharonite was in charge of the herds grazing in Sharon.

Shaphat son of Adlai was in charge of the herds in the valleys.
Obil the Ishmaelite was in charge of the camels.
Jehdeiah the Meronothite was in charge of the donkeys.
Jaziz the Hagrite was in charge of the flocks.
All these were the officials in charge of King David's property.

Jonathan, David's uncle, was a counselor, a man of insight and a scribe. Jehiel son of Hakmoni took care of the king's sons.
Ahithophel was the king's counselor.
Hushai the Arkite was the king's confidant. Ahithophel was succeeded by Jehoiada son of Benaiah and by Abiathar.
Joab was the commander of the royal army.

David summoned all the officials of Israel to assemble at Jerusalem: the officers over the tribes, the commanders of the divisions in the service of the king, the commanders of thousands and commanders of hundreds, and the officials in charge of all the property and livestock belonging to the king and his sons, together with the palace officials, the warriors and all the brave fighting men.

King David rose to his feet and said: "Listen to me, my fellow Israelites, my people. I had it in my heart to build a house as a place of rest for the ark of the covenant of the LORD, for the footstool of our God, and I made plans to build it. But God said to me, 'You are not to build a house for my Name, because you are a warrior and have shed blood.'

"Yet the LORD, the God of Israel, chose me from my whole family to be king over Israel forever. He chose Judah as leader, and from the tribe of Judah he chose my family, and from my father's sons he was pleased to make me king over all Israel. Of all my sons — and the LORD has given me many — he has chosen my son Solomon to sit on the throne of the kingdom of the LORD over Israel. He said to me: 'Solomon your son is the one who will build my house and my courts, for I have chosen him to be my son, and I will be his father. I will establish his kingdom forever if he is unswerving in carrying out my commands and laws, as is being done at this time.'

"So now I charge you in the sight of all Israel and of the assembly of the LORD, and in the hearing of our God: Be careful to follow all the commands of the LORD your God, that you may possess this good land and pass it on as an inheritance to your descendants forever.

"And you, my son Solomon, acknowledge the God of your father, and serve him with wholehearted devotion and with a willing mind, for the LORD searches every heart and understands every desire and every thought. If you seek him, he will be found by you; but if you forsake him, he will reject you forever. Consider now, for the LORD has chosen you to build a house as the sanctuary. Be strong and do the work."

Then David gave his son Solomon the plans for the portico of the temple, its buildings, its storerooms, its upper parts, its inner rooms and the place of atonement. He gave him the plans of all that the Spirit had put in his mind for the courts of the temple of the LORD and all the surrounding rooms, for the treasuries of the temple of God and for the treasuries for the dedicated things. He gave him instructions for the divisions of the priests and Levites, and for all the work of serving in the temple of the LORD, as well as for all the articles to be used in its service. He designated the weight of gold for all the gold articles to be used in various kinds of service, and the weight of silver for all the silver articles to be used in various kinds of service: the weight of gold for the gold lampstands and their lamps, with the weight for each lampstand and its lamps; and the weight of silver for each silver lampstand and its lamps, according to the use of each lampstand; the weight of gold for each table for consecrated bread; the weight of silver for the silver tables; the weight of pure gold for the forks, sprinkling bowls and pitchers; the weight of gold for each gold dish; the weight of silver for each silver dish; and the weight of the refined gold for the altar of incense. He also gave him the plan for the chariot, that is, the cherubim of gold that spread their wings and overshadow the ark of the covenant of the LORD.

"All this," David said, "I have in writing as a result of the LORD's hand on me, and he enabled me to understand all the details of the plan."

David also said to Solomon his son, "Be strong and courageous, and do the work. Do not be afraid or discouraged, for the LORD God, my God, is with you. He will not fail you or forsake you until all the work for the service of the temple of the LORD is finished. The divisions of the priests and Levites are ready for all the work on the temple of God, and every willing person skilled in any craft will help you in all the work. The officials and all the people will obey your every command."

Then King David said to the whole assembly: "My son Solomon, the one whom God has chosen, is young and inexperienced. The task is great, because this palatial structure is not for man but for the LORD God. With all my resources I have provided for the temple of my God—gold for the gold work, silver for the silver, bronze for the bronze, iron for the iron and wood for the wood, as well as onyx for the settings, turquoise, stones of various colors, and all kinds of fine stone and marble—all of these in large quantities. Besides, in my devotion to the temple of my God I now give my personal treasures

of gold and silver for the temple of my God, over and above everything I have provided for this holy temple: three thousand talents of
gold (gold of Ophir) and seven thousand talents of refined silver, for
the overlaying of the walls of the buildings, for the gold work and
the silver work, and for all the work to be done by the craftsmen.
Now, who is willing to consecrate themselves to the LORD today?"

Then the leaders of families, the officers of the tribes of Israel,
the commanders of thousands and commanders of hundreds, and
the officials in charge of the king's work gave willingly. They gave
toward the work on the temple of God five thousand talents and
ten thousand darics of gold, ten thousand talents of silver, eighteen thousand talents of bronze and a hundred thousand talents of
iron. Anyone who had precious stones gave them to the treasury of
the temple of the LORD in the custody of Jehiel the Gershonite. The
people rejoiced at the willing response of their leaders, for they had
given freely and wholeheartedly to the LORD. David the king also
rejoiced greatly.

David praised the LORD in the presence of the whole assembly, saying,

> "Praise be to you, LORD,
> the God of our father Israel,
> from everlasting to everlasting.

> Yours, LORD, is the greatness and the power
> and the glory and the majesty and the splendor,
> for everything in heaven and earth is yours.

> Yours, LORD, is the kingdom;
> you are exalted as head over all.

> Wealth and honor come from you;
> you are the ruler of all things.

> In your hands are strength and power
> to exalt and give strength to all.

> Now, our God, we give you thanks,
> and praise your glorious name.

"But who am I, and who are my people, that we should be able
to give as generously as this? Everything comes from you, and we
have given you only what comes from your hand. We are foreigners and strangers in your sight, as were all our ancestors. Our days
on earth are like a shadow, without hope. LORD our God, all this
abundance that we have provided for building you a temple for your
Holy Name comes from your hand, and all of it belongs to you. I
know, my God, that you test the heart and are pleased with integrity. All these things I have given willingly and with honest intent.

And now I have seen with joy how willingly your people who are here have given to you. LORD, the God of our fathers Abraham, Isaac and Israel, keep these desires and thoughts in the hearts of your people forever, and keep their hearts loyal to you. And give my son Solomon the wholehearted devotion to keep your commands, statutes and decrees and to do everything to build the palatial structure for which I have provided."

Then David said to the whole assembly, "Praise the LORD your God." So they all praised the LORD, the God of their fathers; they bowed down, prostrating themselves before the LORD and the king.

The next day they made sacrifices to the LORD and presented burnt offerings to him: a thousand bulls, a thousand rams and a thousand male lambs, together with their drink offerings, and other sacrifices in abundance for all Israel. They ate and drank with great joy in the presence of the LORD that day.

Then they acknowledged Solomon son of David as king a second time, anointing him before the LORD to be ruler and Zadok to be priest. So Solomon sat on the throne of the LORD as king in place of his father David. He prospered and all Israel obeyed him. All the officers and warriors, as well as all of King David's sons, pledged their submission to King Solomon.

The LORD highly exalted Solomon in the sight of all Israel and bestowed on him royal splendor such as no king over Israel ever had before.

David son of Jesse was king over all Israel. He ruled over Israel forty years — seven in Hebron and thirty-three in Jerusalem. He died at a good old age, having enjoyed long life, wealth and honor. His son Solomon succeeded him as king.

As for the events of King David's reign, from beginning to end, they are written in the records of Samuel the seer, the records of Nathan the prophet and the records of Gad the seer, together with the details of his reign and power, and the circumstances that surrounded him and Israel and the kingdoms of all the other lands.

S olomon son of David established himself firmly over his kingdom, for the LORD his God was with him and made him exceedingly great.

Then Solomon spoke to all Israel — to the commanders of thousands and commanders of hundreds, to the judges and to all the leaders in Israel, the heads of families — and Solomon and the whole assembly went to the high place at Gibeon, for God's tent of meeting was there, which Moses the LORD's servant had made in the wilderness. Now David had brought up the ark of God from Kiriath Jearim to the place he had prepared for it, because he had pitched a tent for it in Jerusalem. But the bronze altar that Bezalel son of Uri, the son of Hur, had made was in Gibeon in front of the tabernacle of the LORD; so Solomon and the assembly inquired of him there. Solomon went up to the bronze altar before the LORD in the tent of meeting and offered a thousand burnt offerings on it.

That night God appeared to Solomon and said to him, "Ask for whatever you want me to give you."

Solomon answered God, "You have shown great kindness to David my father and have made me king in his place. Now, LORD God, let your promise to my father David be confirmed, for you have made me king over a people who are as numerous as the dust of the earth. Give me wisdom and knowledge, that I may lead this people, for who is able to govern this great people of yours?"

God said to Solomon, "Since this is your heart's desire and you have not asked for wealth, possessions or honor, nor for the death of your enemies, and since you have not asked for a long life but for wisdom and knowledge to govern my people over whom I have made you king, therefore wisdom and knowledge will be given you. And I will also give you wealth, possessions and honor, such as no king who was before you ever had and none after you will have."

Then Solomon went to Jerusalem from the high place at Gibeon, from before the tent of meeting. And he reigned over Israel.

Solomon accumulated chariots and horses; he had fourteen hundred chariots and twelve thousand horses, which he kept in the chariot cities and also with him in Jerusalem. The king made silver and gold as common in Jerusalem as stones, and cedar as plentiful as sycamore-fig trees in the foothills. Solomon's horses were imported from Egypt and from Kue — the royal merchants purchased them from Kue at the current price. They imported a chariot from Egypt for six hundred shekels of silver, and a horse for a hundred and fifty. They also exported them to all the kings of the Hittites and of the Arameans.

Solomon gave orders to build a temple for the Name of the LORD and a royal palace for himself. He conscripted 70,000 men as carriers and 80,000 as stonecutters in the hills and 3,600 as foremen over them.

Solomon sent this message to Hiram king of Tyre:

"Send me cedar logs as you did for my father David when you sent him cedar to build a palace to live in. Now I am about to build a temple for the Name of the LORD my God and to dedicate it to him for burning fragrant incense before him, for setting out the consecrated bread regularly, and for making burnt offerings every morning and evening and on the Sabbaths, at the New Moons and at the appointed festivals of the LORD our God. This is a lasting ordinance for Israel.

"The temple I am going to build will be great, because our God is greater than all other gods. But who is able to build a temple for him, since the heavens, even the highest heavens, cannot contain him? Who then am I to build a temple for him, except as a place to burn sacrifices before him?

"Send me, therefore, a man skilled to work in gold and silver, bronze and iron, and in purple, crimson and blue yarn, and experienced in the art of engraving, to work in Judah and Jerusalem with my skilled workers, whom my father David provided.

"Send me also cedar, juniper and algum logs from Lebanon, for I know that your servants are skilled in cutting timber there. My servants will work with yours to provide me with plenty of lumber, because the temple I build must be large and magnificent. I will give your servants, the woodsmen who cut the timber, twenty thousand cors of ground wheat, twenty thousand cors of barley, twenty thousand baths of wine and twenty thousand baths of olive oil."

Hiram king of Tyre replied by letter to Solomon:

"Because the LORD loves his people, he has made you their king."

And Hiram added:

"Praise be to the LORD, the God of Israel, who made heaven and earth! He has given King David a wise son, endowed with intelligence and discernment, who will build a temple for the LORD and a palace for himself.

"I am sending you Huram-Abi, a man of great skill, whose mother was from Dan and whose father was from Tyre. He is trained to work in gold and silver, bronze and iron, stone and wood, and with purple and blue and crimson yarn and fine linen. He is experienced in all kinds of engraving and can execute any design given to him. He will work with your skilled workers and with those of my lord, David your father.

"Now let my lord send his servants the wheat and barley and the olive oil and wine he promised, and we will cut all the logs from Lebanon that you need and will float them as rafts by sea down to Joppa. You can then take them up to Jerusalem."

Solomon took a census of all the foreigners residing in Israel, after the census his father David had taken; and they were found to be 153,600. He assigned 70,000 of them to be carriers and 80,000 to be stonecutters in the hills, with 3,600 foremen over them to keep the people working.

Then Solomon began to build the temple of the Lord in Jerusalem on Mount Moriah, where the Lord had appeared to his father David. It was on the threshing floor of Araunah the Jebusite, the place provided by David. He began building on the second day of the second month in the fourth year of his reign.

The foundation Solomon laid for building the temple of God was sixty cubits long and twenty cubits wide (using the cubit of the old standard). The portico at the front of the temple was twenty cubits long across the width of the building and twenty cubits high.

He overlaid the inside with pure gold. He paneled the main hall with juniper and covered it with fine gold and decorated it with palm tree and chain designs. He adorned the temple with precious stones. And the gold he used was gold of Parvaim. He overlaid the ceiling beams, doorframes, walls and doors of the temple with gold, and he carved cherubim on the walls.

He built the Most Holy Place, its length corresponding to the width of the temple—twenty cubits long and twenty cubits wide. He overlaid the inside with six hundred talents of fine gold. The gold nails weighed fifty shekels. He also overlaid the upper parts with gold.

For the Most Holy Place he made a pair of sculptured cherubim and overlaid them with gold. The total wingspan of the cherubim was twenty cubits. One wing of the first cherub was five cubits long and touched the temple wall, while its other wing, also five cubits long, touched the wing of the other cherub. Similarly one wing of the second cherub was five cubits long and touched the other temple wall, and its other wing, also five cubits long, touched the wing of the first cherub. The wings of these cherubim extended twenty cubits. They stood on their feet, facing the main hall.

He made the curtain of blue, purple and crimson yarn and fine linen, with cherubim worked into it.

For the front of the temple he made two pillars, which together were thirty-five cubits long, each with a capital five cubits high. He made interwoven chains and put them on top of the pillars. He also made a hundred pomegranates and attached them to the chains. He erected the pillars in the front of the temple, one to the south and one to the north. The one to the south he named Jakin and the one to the north Boaz.

He made a bronze altar twenty cubits long, twenty cubits wide and ten cubits high. He made the Sea of cast metal, circular in shape, measuring ten cubits from rim to rim and five cubits high. It took a line of thirty cubits to measure around it. Below the rim, figures of bulls encircled it—ten to a cubit. The bulls were cast in two rows in one piece with the Sea.

The Sea stood on twelve bulls, three facing north, three facing west, three facing south and three facing east. The Sea rested on top of them, and their hindquarters were toward the center. It was a handbreadth in thickness, and its rim was like the rim of a cup, like a lily blossom. It held three thousand baths.

He then made ten basins for washing and placed five on the south side and five on the north. In them the things to be used for the burnt offerings were rinsed, but the Sea was to be used by the priests for washing.

He made ten gold lampstands according to the specifications for them and placed them in the temple, five on the south side and five on the north.

He made ten tables and placed them in the temple, five on the south side and five on the north. He also made a hundred gold sprinkling bowls.

He made the courtyard of the priests, and the large court and the doors for the court, and overlaid the doors with bronze. He placed the Sea on the south side, at the southeast corner.

And Huram also made the pots and shovels and sprinkling bowls.

So Huram finished the work he had undertaken for King Solomon in the temple of God:

the two pillars;

the two bowl-shaped capitals on top of the pillars;

the two sets of network decorating the two bowl-shaped capitals on top of the pillars;

the four hundred pomegranates for the two sets of network (two rows of pomegranates for each network, decorating the bowl-shaped capitals on top of the pillars);

the stands with their basins;

the Sea and the twelve bulls under it;

the pots, shovels, meat forks and all related articles.

All the objects that Huram-Abi made for King Solomon for the temple of the LORD were of polished bronze. The king had them cast in clay molds in the plain of the Jordan between Sukkoth and Zarethan. All these things that Solomon made amounted to so much that the weight of the bronze could not be calculated.

Solomon also made all the furnishings that were in God's temple:

the golden altar;
the tables on which was the bread of the Presence;
the lampstands of pure gold with their lamps, to burn in front
    of the inner sanctuary as prescribed;
the gold floral work and lamps and tongs (they were solid gold);
the pure gold wick trimmers, sprinkling bowls, dishes and cen-
    sers; and the gold doors of the temple: the inner doors to the
    Most Holy Place and the doors of the main hall.

When all the work Solomon had done for the temple of the
Lord was finished, he brought in the things his father David had
dedicated — the silver and gold and all the furnishings — and he
placed them in the treasuries of God's temple.

Then Solomon summoned to Jerusalem the elders of Israel, all the
heads of the tribes and the chiefs of the Israelite families, to bring
up the ark of the Lord's covenant from Zion, the City of David. And
all the Israelites came together to the king at the time of the festival
in the seventh month.

When all the elders of Israel had arrived, the Levites took up
the ark, and they brought up the ark and the tent of meeting and all
the sacred furnishings in it. The Levitical priests carried them up;
and King Solomon and the entire assembly of Israel that had gathered about him were before the ark, sacrificing so many sheep and
cattle that they could not be recorded or counted.

The priests then brought the ark of the Lord's covenant to its
place in the inner sanctuary of the temple, the Most Holy Place, and
put it beneath the wings of the cherubim. The cherubim spread
their wings over the place of the ark and covered the ark and its
carrying poles. These poles were so long that their ends, extending
from the ark, could be seen from in front of the inner sanctuary, but
not from outside the Holy Place; and they are still there today. There
was nothing in the ark except the two tablets that Moses had placed
in it at Horeb, where the Lord made a covenant with the Israelites
after they came out of Egypt.

The priests then withdrew from the Holy Place. All the priests
who were there had consecrated themselves, regardless of their
divisions. All the Levites who were musicians — Asaph, Heman,
Jeduthun and their sons and relatives — stood on the east side of
the altar, dressed in fine linen and playing cymbals, harps and
lyres. They were accompanied by 120 priests sounding trumpets.
The trumpeters and musicians joined in unison to give praise and
thanks to the Lord. Accompanied by trumpets, cymbals and other

instruments, the singers raised their voices in praise to the LORD and sang:

> "He is good;
> his love endures forever."

Then the temple of the LORD was filled with the cloud, and the priests could not perform their service because of the cloud, for the glory of the LORD filled the temple of God.

Then Solomon said, "The LORD has said that he would dwell in a dark cloud; I have built a magnificent temple for you, a place for you to dwell forever."

While the whole assembly of Israel was standing there, the king turned around and blessed them. Then he said:

"Praise be to the LORD, the God of Israel, who with his hands has fulfilled what he promised with his mouth to my father David. For he said, 'Since the day I brought my people out of Egypt, I have not chosen a city in any tribe of Israel to have a temple built so that my Name might be there, nor have I chosen anyone to be ruler over my people Israel. But now I have chosen Jerusalem for my Name to be there, and I have chosen David to rule my people Israel.'

"My father David had it in his heart to build a temple for the Name of the LORD, the God of Israel. But the LORD said to my father David, 'You did well to have it in your heart to build a temple for my Name. Nevertheless, you are not the one to build the temple, but your son, your own flesh and blood—he is the one who will build the temple for my Name.'

"The LORD has kept the promise he made. I have succeeded David my father and now I sit on the throne of Israel, just as the LORD promised, and I have built the temple for the Name of the LORD, the God of Israel. There I have placed the ark, in which is the covenant of the LORD that he made with the people of Israel."

Then Solomon stood before the altar of the LORD in front of the whole assembly of Israel and spread out his hands. Now he had made a bronze platform, five cubits long, five cubits wide and three cubits high, and had placed it in the center of the outer court. He stood on the platform and then knelt down before the whole assembly of Israel and spread out his hands toward heaven. He said:

"LORD, the God of Israel, there is no God like you in heaven or on earth—you who keep your covenant of love with your servants who continue wholeheartedly in your way. You have kept your promise to your servant David my father; with your

mouth you have promised and with your hand you have fulfilled it—as it is today.

"Now, Lord, the God of Israel, keep for your servant David my father the promises you made to him when you said,
'You shall never fail to have a successor to sit before me on the
throne of Israel, if only your descendants are careful in all they
do to walk before me according to my law, as you have done.'
And now, Lord, the God of Israel, let your word that you promised your servant David come true.

"But will God really dwell on earth with humans? The heavens, even the highest heavens, cannot contain you. How much
less this temple I have built! Yet, Lord my God, give attention
to your servant's prayer and his plea for mercy. Hear the cry
and the prayer that your servant is praying in your presence.
May your eyes be open toward this temple day and night, this
place of which you said you would put your Name there. May
you hear the prayer your servant prays toward this place. Hear
the supplications of your servant and of your people Israel when they pray toward this place. Hear from heaven, your
dwelling place; and when you hear, forgive.

"When anyone wrongs their neighbor and is required to take
an oath and they come and swear the oath before your altar
in t is temple, then hear from heaven and act. Judge between
y r servants, condemning the guilty and bringing down on
their heads what they have done, and vindicating the innocent
by treating them in accordance with their innocence.

"When your people Israel have been defeated by an enemy
because they have sinned against you and when they turn back
and give praise to your name, praying and making supplication
before you in this temple, then hear from heaven and forgive
the sin of your people Israel and bring them back to the land
you gave to them and their ancestors.

"When the heavens are shut up and there is no rain because
your people have sinned against you, and when they pray toward this place and give praise to your name and turn from
their sin because you have afflicted them, then hear from
heaven and forgive the sin of your servants, your people Israel. Teach them the right way to live, and send rain on the land
you gave your people for an inheritance.

"When famine or plague comes to the land, or blight or mil-
dew, locusts or grasshoppers, or when enemies besiege them in
any of their cities, whatever disaster or disease may come, and
when a prayer or plea is made by anyone among your people Israel—being aware of their afflictions and pains, and spreading out
their hands toward this temple—then hear from heaven, your

dwelling place. Forgive, and deal with everyone according to all they do, since you know their hearts (for you alone know the human heart), so that they will fear you and walk in obedience to you all the time they live in the land you gave our ancestors.

"As for the foreigner who does not belong to your people Israel but has come from a distant land because of your great name and your mighty hand and your outstretched arm— when they come and pray toward this temple, then hear from heaven, your dwelling place. Do whatever the foreigner asks of you, so that all the peoples of the earth may know your name and fear you, as do your own people Israel, and may know that this house I have built bears your Name.

"When your people go to war against their enemies, wherever you send them, and when they pray to you toward this city you have chosen and the temple I have built for your Name, then hear from heaven their prayer and their plea, and uphold their cause.

"When they sin against you—for there is no one who does not sin—and you become angry with them and give them over to the enemy, who takes them captive to a land far away or near; and if they have a change of heart in the land where they are held captive, and repent and plead with you in the land of their captivity and say, 'We have sinned, we have done wrong and acted wickedly'; and if they turn back to you with all their heart and soul in the land of their captivity where they were taken, and pray toward the land you gave their ancestors, toward the city you have chosen and toward the temple I have built for your Name; then from heaven, your dwelling place, hear their prayer and their pleas, and uphold their cause. And forgive your people, who have sinned against you.

"Now, my God, may your eyes be open and your ears attentive to the prayers offered in this place.

> "Now arise, Lord God, and come to your resting
>   place,
> you and the ark of your might.
>
> May your priests, Lord God, be clothed with
>   salvation,
> may your faithful people rejoice in your goodness.
>
> Lord God, do not reject your anointed one.
> Remember the great love promised to David your
>   servant."

When Solomon finished praying, fire came down from heaven and consumed the burnt offering and the sacrifices, and the glory of the Lord filled the temple. The priests could not enter the temple of the Lord because the glory of the Lord filled it. When all the Israelites saw the fire coming down and the glory of the Lord above the temple, they knelt on the pavement with their faces to the ground, and they worshiped and gave thanks to the Lord, saying,

> "He is good;
> his love endures forever."

Then the king and all the people offered sacrifices before the Lord. And King Solomon offered a sacrifice of twenty-two thousand head of cattle and a hundred and twenty thousand sheep and goats. So the king and all the people dedicated the temple of God. The priests took their positions, as did the Levites with the Lord's musical instruments, which King David had made for praising the Lord and which were used when he gave thanks, saying, "His love endures forever." Opposite the Levites, the priests blew their trumpets, and all the Israelites were standing.

Solomon consecrated the middle part of the courtyard in front of the temple of the Lord, and there he offered burnt offerings and the fat of the fellowship offerings, because the bronze altar he had made could not hold the burnt offerings, the grain offerings and the fat portions.

So Solomon observed the festival at that time for seven days, and all Israel with him — a vast assembly, people from Lebo Hamath to the Wadi of Egypt. On the eighth day they held an assembly, for they had celebrated the dedication of the altar for seven days and the festival for seven days more. On the twenty-third day of the seventh month he sent the people to their homes, joyful and glad in heart for the good things the Lord had done for David and Solomon and for his people Israel.

When Solomon had finished the temple of the Lord and the royal palace, and had succeeded in carrying out all he had in mind to do in the temple of the Lord and in his own palace, the Lord appeared to him at night and said:

"I have heard your prayer and have chosen this place for myself as a temple for sacrifices.

"When I shut up the heavens so that there is no rain, or command locusts to devour the land or send a plague among my people, if my people, who are called by my name, will humble themselves and pray and seek my face and turn from their wicked ways, then I will hear from heaven, and I will forgive their sin and will heal their land. Now my eyes will be open and my ears attentive to the prayers offered in this place. I have chosen and consecrated this temple so that my Name may be there forever. My eyes and my heart will always be there.

"As for you, if you walk before me faithfully as David your father did, and do all I command, and observe my decrees and laws, I will establish your royal throne, as I covenanted with David your father when I said, 'You shall never fail to have a successor to rule over Israel.'

"But if you turn away and forsake the decrees and commands I have given you and go off to serve other gods and worship them, then I will uproot Israel from my land, which I have given them, and will reject this temple I have consecrated for my Name. I will make it a byword and an object of ridicule among all peoples. This temple will become a heap of rubble. All who pass by will be appalled and say, 'Why has the LORD done such a thing to this land and to this temple?' People will answer, 'Because they have forsaken the LORD, the God of their ancestors, who brought them out of Egypt, and have embraced other gods, worshiping and serving them — that is why he brought all this disaster on them.'"

At the end of twenty years, during which Solomon built the temple of the LORD and his own palace, Solomon rebuilt the villages that Hiram had given him, and settled Israelites in them. Solomon then went to Hamath Zobah and captured it. He also built up Tadmor in the desert and all the store cities he had built in Hamath. He rebuilt Upper Beth Horon and Lower Beth Horon as fortified cities, with walls and with gates and bars, as well as Baalath and all his store cities, and all the cities for his chariots and for his horses — whatever he desired to build in Jerusalem, in Lebanon and throughout all the territory he ruled.

There were still people left from the Hittites, Amorites, Perizzites, Hivites and Jebusites (these people were not Israelites). Solomon conscripted the descendants of all these people remaining in the land — whom the Israelites had not destroyed — to serve as slave labor, as it is to this day. But Solomon did not make slaves of the Israelites for his work; they were his fighting men, commanders of his captains, and commanders of his chariots and charioteers. They were also King Solomon's chief officials — two hundred and fifty officials supervising the men.

Solomon brought Pharaoh's daughter up from the City of David to the palace he had built for her, for he said, "My wife must not live in the palace of David king of Israel, because the places the ark of the LORD has entered are holy."

On the altar of the LORD that he had built in front of the portico, Solomon sacrificed burnt offerings to the LORD, according to the daily requirement for offerings commanded by Moses for the Sabbaths, the New Moons and the three annual festivals — the Festival of Unleavened Bread, the Festival of Weeks and the Festival of Tabernacles. In keeping with the ordinance of his father David, he appointed the divisions of the priests for their duties, and the Levites to lead the praise and to assist the priests according to each day's requirement. He also appointed the gatekeepers by divisions for the various gates, because this was what David the man of God had ordered. They did not deviate from the king's commands to the priests or to the Levites in any matter, including that of the treasuries.

All Solomon's work was carried out, from the day the foundation of the temple of the Lord was laid until its completion. So the temple of the Lord was finished.

Then Solomon went to Ezion Geber and Elath on the coast of Edom. And Hiram sent him ships commanded by his own men, sailors who knew the sea. These, with Solomon's men, sailed to Ophir and brought back four hundred and fifty talents of gold, which they delivered to King Solomon.

When the queen of Sheba heard of Solomon's fame, she came to Jerusalem to test him with hard questions. Arriving with a very great caravan — with camels carrying spices, large quantities of gold, and precious stones — she came to Solomon and talked with him about all she had on her mind. Solomon answered all her questions; nothing was too hard for him to explain to her. When the queen of Sheba saw the wisdom of Solomon, as well as the palace he had built, the food on his table, the seating of his officials, the attending servants in their robes, the cupbearers in their robes and the burnt offerings he made at the temple of the Lord, she was overwhelmed.

She said to the king, "The report I heard in my own country about your achievements and your wisdom is true. But I did not believe what they said until I came and saw with my own eyes. Indeed, not even half the greatness of your wisdom was told me; you have far exceeded the report I heard. How happy your people must be! How happy your officials, who continually stand before you and hear your wisdom! Praise be to the Lord your God, who has delighted in you and placed you on his throne as king to rule for the Lord your God. Because of the love of your God for Israel and his desire to uphold them forever, he has made you king over them, to maintain justice and righteousness."

Then she gave the king 120 talents of gold, large quantities of spices, and precious stones. There had never been such spices as those the queen of Sheba gave to King Solomon.

(The servants of Hiram and the servants of Solomon brought gold from Ophir; they also brought algumwood and precious stones.

The king used the algumwood to make steps for the temple of the LORD and for the royal palace, and to make harps and lyres for the musicians. Nothing like them had ever been seen in Judah.)

King Solomon gave the queen of Sheba all she desired and asked for; he gave her more than she had brought to him. Then she left and returned with her retinue to her own country.

The weight of the gold that Solomon received yearly was 666 talents, not including the revenues brought in by merchants and traders. Also all the kings of Arabia and the governors of the territories brought gold and silver to Solomon.

King Solomon made two hundred large shields of hammered gold; six hundred shekels of hammered gold went into each shield. He also made three hundred small shields of hammered gold, with three hundred shekels of gold in each shield. The king put them in the Palace of the Forest of Lebanon.

Then the king made a great throne covered with ivory and overlaid with pure gold. The throne had six steps, and a footstool of gold was attached to it. On both sides of the seat were armrests, with a lion standing beside each of them. Twelve lions stood on the six steps, one at either end of each step. Nothing like it had ever been made for any other kingdom. All King Solomon's goblets were gold, and all the household articles in the Palace of the Forest of Lebanon were pure gold. Nothing was made of silver, because silver was considered of little value in Solomon's day. The king had a fleet of trading ships manned by Hiram's servants. Once every three years it returned, carrying gold, silver and ivory, and apes and baboons.

King Solomon was greater in riches and wisdom than all the other kings of the earth. All the kings of the earth sought audience with Solomon to hear the wisdom God had put in his heart. Year after year, everyone who came brought a gift—articles of silver and gold, and robes, weapons and spices, and horses and mules.

Solomon had four thousand stalls for horses and chariots, and twelve thousand horses, which he kept in the chariot cities and also with him in Jerusalem. He ruled over all the kings from the Euphrates River to the land of the Philistines, as far as the border of Egypt. The king made silver as common in Jerusalem as stones, and cedar as plentiful as sycamore-fig trees in the foothills. Solomon's horses were imported from Egypt and from all other countries.

As for the other events of Solomon's reign, from beginning to end, are they not written in the records of Nathan the prophet, in the prophecy of Ahijah the Shilonite and in the visions of Iddo the seer concerning Jeroboam son of Nebat? Solomon reigned in Jerusalem over all Israel forty years. Then he rested with his ancestors and was buried in the city of David his father. And Rehoboam his son succeeded him as king.

R ehoboam went to Shechem, for all Israel had gone there to make him king. When Jeroboam son of Nebat heard this (he was in Egypt, where he had fled from King Solomon), he returned from Egypt. So they sent for Jeroboam, and he and all Israel went to Rehoboam and said to him: "Your father put a heavy yoke on us, but now lighten the harsh labor and the heavy yoke he put on us, and we will serve you."

Rehoboam answered, "Come back to me in three days." So the people went away.

Then King Rehoboam consulted the elders who had served his father Solomon during his lifetime. "How would you advise me to answer these people?" he asked.

They replied, "If you will be kind to these people and please them and give them a favorable answer, they will always be your servants."

But Rehoboam rejected the advice the elders gave him and consulted the young men who had grown up with him and were serving him. He asked them, "What is your advice? How should we answer these people who say to me, 'Lighten the yoke your father put on us'?"

The young men who had grown up with him replied, "The people have said to you, 'Your father put a heavy yoke on us, but make our yoke lighter.' Now tell them, 'My little finger is thicker than my father's waist. My father laid on you a heavy yoke; I will make it even heavier. My father scourged you with whips; I will scourge you with scorpions.'"

Three days later Jeroboam and all the people returned to Rehoboam, as the king had said, "Come back to me in three days." The king answered them harshly. Rejecting the advice of the elders, he followed the advice of the young men and said, "My father made your yoke heavy; I will make it even heavier. My father scourged you with whips; I will scourge you with scorpions." So the king did not listen to the people, for this turn of events was from God, to fulfill the word the Lord had spoken to Jeroboam son of Nebat through Ahijah the Shilonite.

When all Israel saw that the king refused to listen to them, they answered the king:

> "What share do we have in David,
> what part in Jesse's son?

> To your tents, Israel!
> Look after your own house, David!"

So all the Israelites went home. But as for the Israelites who were living in the towns of Judah, Rehoboam still ruled over them.

King Rehoboam sent out Adoniram, who was in charge of forced labor, but the Israelites stoned him to death. King Rehoboam, however, managed to get into his chariot and escape to Jerusalem. So Israel has been in rebellion against the house of David to this day.

When Rehoboam arrived in Jerusalem, he mustered Judah and Benjamin — a hundred and eighty thousand able young men — to go to war against Israel and to regain the kingdom for Rehoboam.

But this word of the LORD came to Shemaiah the man of God: "Say to Rehoboam son of Solomon king of Judah and to all Israel in Judah and Benjamin, 'This is what the LORD says: Do not go up to fight against your fellow Israelites. Go home, every one of you, for this is my doing.'" So they obeyed the words of the LORD and turned back from marching against Jeroboam.

Rehoboam lived in Jerusalem and built up towns for defense in Judah: Bethlehem, Etam, Tekoa, Beth Zur, Soko, Adullam, Gath, Mareshah, Ziph, Adoraim, Lachish, Azekah, Zorah, Aijalon and Hebron. These were fortified cities in Judah and Benjamin. He strengthened their defenses and put commanders in them, with supplies of food, olive oil and wine. He put shields and spears in all the cities, and made them very strong. So Judah and Benjamin were his.

The priests and Levites from all their districts throughout Israel sided with him. The Levites even abandoned their pasturelands and property and came to Judah and Jerusalem, because Jeroboam and his sons had rejected them as priests of the LORD when he appointed his own priests for the high places and for the goat and calf idols he had made. Those from every tribe of Israel who set their hearts on seeking the LORD, the God of Israel, followed the Levites to Jerusalem to offer sacrifices to the LORD, the God of their ancestors. They strengthened the kingdom of Judah and supported Rehoboam son of Solomon three years, following the ways of David and Solomon during this time.

Rehoboam married Mahalath, who was the daughter of David's son Jerimoth and of Abihail, the daughter of Jesse's son Eliab. She bore him sons: Jeush, Shemariah and Zaham. Then he married Maakah daughter of Absalom, who bore him Abijah, Attai, Ziza and Shelomith. Rehoboam loved Maakah daughter of Absalom more than any of his other wives and concubines. In all, he had eighteen wives and sixty concubines, twenty-eight sons and sixty daughters.

Rehoboam appointed Abijah son of Maakah as crown prince among his brothers, in order to make him king. He acted wisely, dispersing some of his sons throughout the districts of Judah and Benjamin, and to all the fortified cities. He gave them abundant provisions and took many wives for them.

After Rehoboam's position as king was established and he had become strong, he and all Israel with him abandoned the law of the Lord. Because they had been unfaithful to the Lord, Shishak king of Egypt attacked Jerusalem in the fifth year of King Rehoboam. With twelve hundred chariots and sixty thousand horsemen and the innumerable troops of Libyans, Sukkites and Cushites that came with him from Egypt, he captured the fortified cities of Judah and came as far as Jerusalem.

Then the prophet Shemaiah came to Rehoboam and to the leaders of Judah who had assembled in Jerusalem for fear of Shishak, and he said to them, "This is what the Lord says, 'You have abandoned me; therefore, I now abandon you to Shishak.'"

The leaders of Israel and the king humbled themselves and said, "The Lord is just."

When the Lord saw that they humbled themselves, this word of the Lord came to Shemaiah: "Since they have humbled themselves, I will not destroy them but will soon give them deliverance. My wrath will not be poured out on Jerusalem through Shishak. They will, however, become subject to him, so that they may learn the difference between serving me and serving the kings of other lands."

When Shishak king of Egypt attacked Jerusalem, he carried off the treasures of the temple of the Lord and the treasures of the royal palace. He took everything, including the gold shields Solomon had made. So King Rehoboam made bronze shields to replace them and assigned these to the commanders of the guard on duty at the entrance to the royal palace. Whenever the king went to the Lord's temple, the guards went with him, bearing the shields, and afterward they returned them to the guardroom.

Because Rehoboam humbled himself, the Lord's anger turned from him, and he was not totally destroyed. Indeed, there was some good in Judah.

King Rehoboam established himself firmly in Jerusalem and continued as king. He was forty-one years old when he became king, and he reigned seventeen years in Jerusalem, the city the Lord had chosen out of all the tribes of Israel in which to put his Name. His mother's name was Naamah; she was an Ammonite. He did evil because he had not set his heart on seeking the Lord.

As for the events of Rehoboam's reign, from beginning to end, are they not written in the records of Shemaiah the prophet and of Iddo the seer that deal with genealogies? There was continual warfare between Rehoboam and Jeroboam. Rehoboam rested with his ancestors and was buried in the City of David. And Abijah his son succeeded him as king.

I n the eighteenth year of the reign of Jeroboam, Abijah became king of Judah, and he reigned in Jerusalem three years. His mother's name was Maakah, a daughter of Uriel of Gibeah.

There was war between Abijah and Jeroboam. Abijah went into battle with an army of four hundred thousand able fighting men, and Jeroboam drew up a battle line against him with eight hundred thousand able troops.

Abijah stood on Mount Zemaraim, in the hill country of Ephraim, and said, "Jeroboam and all Israel, listen to me! Don't you know that the Lord, the God of Israel, has given the kingship of Israel to David and his descendants forever by a covenant of salt? Yet Jeroboam son of Nebat, an official of Solomon son of David, rebelled against his master. Some worthless scoundrels gathered around him and opposed Rehoboam son of Solomon when he was young and indecisive and not strong enough to resist them.

"And now you plan to resist the kingdom of the Lord, which is in the hands of David's descendants. You are indeed a vast army and have with you the golden calves that Jeroboam made to be your gods. But didn't you drive out the priests of the Lord, the sons of Aaron, and the Levites, and make priests of your own as the peoples of other lands do? Whoever comes to consecrate himself with a young bull and seven rams may become a priest of what are not gods.

"As for us, the Lord is our God, and we have not forsaken him. The priests who serve the Lord are sons of Aaron, and the Levites assist them. Every morning and evening they present burnt offerings and fragrant incense to the Lord. They set out the bread on the ceremonially clean table and light the lamps on the gold lampstand every evening. We are observing the requirements of the Lord our God. But you have forsaken him. God is with us; he is our leader. His priests with their trumpets will sound the battle cry against you. People of Israel, do not fight against the Lord, the God of your ancestors, for you will not succeed."

Now Jeroboam had sent troops around to the rear, so that while he was in front of Judah the ambush was behind them. Judah turned and saw that they were being attacked at both front and rear. Then they cried out to the LORD. The priests blew their trumpets and the men of Judah raised the battle cry. At the sound of their battle cry, God routed Jeroboam and all Israel before Abijah and Judah. The Israelites fled before Judah, and God delivered them into their hands. Abijah and his troops inflicted heavy losses on them, so that there were five hundred thousand casualties among Israel's able men. The Israelites were subdued on that occasion, and the people of Judah were victorious because they relied on the LORD, the God of their ancestors.

Abijah pursued Jeroboam and took from him the towns of Bethel, Jeshanah and Ephron, with their surrounding villages. Jeroboam did not regain power during the time of Abijah. And the LORD struck him down and he died.

But Abijah grew in strength. He married fourteen wives and had twenty-two sons and sixteen daughters.

The other events of Abijah's reign, what he did and what he said, are written in the annotations of the prophet Iddo.

And Abijah rested with his ancestors and was buried in the City of David. Asa his son succeeded him as king, and in his days the country was at peace for ten years.

A sa did what was good and right in the eyes of the LORD his God. He removed the foreign altars and the high places, smashed the sacred stones and cut down the Asherah poles. He commanded Judah to seek the LORD, the God of their ancestors, and to obey his laws and commands. He removed the high places and incense altars in every town in Judah, and the kingdom was at peace under him. He built up the fortified cities of Judah, since the land was at peace. No one was at war with him during those years, for the LORD gave him rest.

"Let us build up these towns," he said to Judah, "and put walls around them, with towers, gates and bars. The land is still ours, because we have sought the LORD our God; we sought him and he has given us rest on every side." So they built and prospered.

Asa had an army of three hundred thousand men from Judah, equipped with large shields and with spears, and two hundred and eighty thousand from Benjamin, armed with small shields and with bows. All these were brave fighting men.

Zerah the Cushite marched out against them with an army of thousands upon thousands and three hundred chariots, and came as far as Mareshah. Asa went out to meet him, and they took up battle positions in the Valley of Zephathah near Mareshah.

Then Asa called to the Lord his God and said, "Lord, there is no one like you to help the powerless against the mighty. Help us, Lord our God, for we rely on you, and in your name we have come against this vast army. Lord, you are our God; do not let mere mortals prevail against you."

The Lord struck down the Cushites before Asa and Judah. The Cushites fled, and Asa and his army pursued them as far as Gerar. Such a great number of Cushites fell that they could not recover; they were crushed before the Lord and his forces. The men of Judah carried off a large amount of plunder. They destroyed all the villages around Gerar, for the terror of the Lord had fallen on them. They looted all these villages, since there was much plunder there. They also attacked the camps of the herders and carried off droves of sheep and goats and camels. Then they returned to Jerusalem.

The Spirit of God came on Azariah son of Oded. He went out to meet Asa and said to him, "Listen to me, Asa and all Judah and Benjamin. The Lord is with you when you are with him. If you seek him, he will be found by you, but if you forsake him, he will forsake you. For a long time Israel was without the true God, without a priest to teach and without the law. But in their distress they turned to the Lord, the God of Israel, and sought him, and he was found by them. In those days it was not safe to travel about, for all the inhabitants of the lands were in great turmoil. One nation was being crushed by another and one city by another, because God was troubling them with every kind of distress. But as for you, be strong and do not give up, for your work will be rewarded."

When Asa heard these words and the prophecy of Azariah son of Oded the prophet, he took courage. He removed the detestable idols from the whole land of Judah and Benjamin and from the towns he had captured in the hills of Ephraim. He repaired the altar of the Lord that was in front of the portico of the Lord's temple.

Then he assembled all Judah and Benjamin and the people from Ephraim, Manasseh and Simeon who had settled among them, for large numbers had come over to him from Israel when they saw that the Lord his God was with him.

They assembled at Jerusalem in the third month of the fifteenth year of Asa's reign. At that time they sacrificed to the Lord seven hundred head of cattle and seven thousand sheep and goats from the plunder they had brought back. They entered into a covenant to seek the Lord, the God of their ancestors, with all their heart and soul. All who would not seek the Lord, the God of Israel, were to be put to death, whether small or great, man or woman. They took an oath to the Lord with loud acclamation, with shouting and with trumpets and horns. All Judah rejoiced about the oath because they had sworn it wholeheartedly. They sought God eagerly, and he was found by them. So the LORD gave them rest on every side.

King Asa also deposed his grandmother Maakah from her position as queen mother, because she had made a repulsive image for the worship of Asherah. Asa cut it down, broke it up and burned it in the Kidron Valley. Although he did not remove the high places from Israel, Asa's heart was fully committed to the LORD all his life. He brought into the temple of God the silver and gold and the articles that he and his father had dedicated.

There was no more war until the thirty-fifth year of Asa's reign.

In the thirty-sixth year of Asa's reign Baasha king of Israel went up against Judah and fortified Ramah to prevent anyone from leaving or entering the territory of Asa king of Judah.

Asa then took the silver and gold out of the treasuries of the LORD's temple and of his own palace and sent it to Ben-Hadad king of Aram, who was ruling in Damascus. "Let there be a treaty between me and you," he said, "as there was between my father and your father. See, I am sending you silver and gold. Now break your treaty with Baasha king of Israel so he will withdraw from me."

Ben-Hadad agreed with King Asa and sent the commanders of his forces against the towns of Israel. They conquered Ijon, Dan, Abel Maim and all the store cities of Naphtali. When Baasha heard this, he stopped building Ramah and abandoned his work. Then King Asa brought all the men of Judah, and they carried away from Ramah the stones and timber Baasha had been using. With them he built up Geba and Mizpah.

At that time Hanani the seer came to Asa king of Judah and said to him: "Because you relied on the king of Aram and not on the LORD your God, the army of the king of Aram has escaped from your hand. Were not the Cushites and Libyans a mighty army with great numbers of chariots and horsemen? Yet when you relied on the LORD, he delivered them into your hand. For the eyes of the LORD range throughout the earth to strengthen those whose hearts are fully committed to him. You have done a foolish thing, and from now on you will be at war."

Asa was angry with the seer because of this; he was so enraged that he put him in prison. At the same time Asa brutally oppressed some of the people.

The events of Asa's reign, from beginning to end, are written in the book of the kings of Judah and Israel. In the thirty-ninth year of his reign Asa was afflicted with a disease in his feet. Though his disease was severe, even in his illness he did not seek help from the LORD, but only from the physicians. Then in the forty-first year of his reign Asa died and rested with his ancestors. They buried him in the tomb that he had cut out for himself in the City of David. They laid him on a bier covered with spices and various blended perfumes, and they made a huge fire in his honor.

Jehoshaphat his son succeeded him as king and strengthened himself against Israel. He stationed troops in all the fortified cities of Judah and put garrisons in Judah and in the towns of Ephraim that his father Asa had captured.

The Lord was with Jehoshaphat because he followed the ways of his father David before him. He did not consult the Baals but sought the God of his father and followed his commands rather than the practices of Israel. The Lord established the kingdom under his control; and all Judah brought gifts to Jehoshaphat, so that he had great wealth and honor. His heart was devoted to the ways of the Lord; furthermore, he removed the high places and the Asherah poles from Judah.

In the third year of his reign he sent his officials Ben-Hail, Obadiah, Zechariah, Nethanel and Micaiah to teach in the towns of Judah. With them were certain Levites—Shemaiah, Nethaniah, Zebadiah, Asahel, Shemiramoth, Jehonathan, Adonijah, Tobijah and Tob-Adonijah—and the priests Elishama and Jehoram. They taught throughout Judah, taking with them the Book of the Law of the Lord; they went around to all the towns of Judah and taught the people.

The fear of the Lord fell on all the kingdoms of the lands surrounding Judah, so that they did not go to war against Jehoshaphat. Some Philistines brought Jehoshaphat gifts and silver as tribute, and the Arabs brought him flocks: seven thousand seven hundred rams and seven thousand seven hundred goats.

Jehoshaphat became more and more powerful; he built forts and store cities in Judah and had large supplies in the towns of Judah. He also kept experienced fighting men in Jerusalem. Their enrollment by families was as follows:

> From Judah, commanders of units of 1,000:
>> Adnah the commander, with 300,000 fighting men;
>> next, Jehohanan the commander, with 280,000;
>> next, Amasiah son of Zikri, who volunteered himself for the service of the Lord, with 200,000.
> From Benjamin:
>> Eliada, a valiant soldier, with 200,000 men armed with bows and shields;
>> next, Jehozabad, with 180,000 men armed for battle.

These were the men who served the king, besides those he stationed in the fortified cities throughout Judah.

Now Jehoshaphat had great wealth and honor, and he allied himself with Ahab by marriage. Some years later he went down to see Ahab in Samaria. Ahab slaughtered many sheep and cattle for him and the people with him and urged him to attack Ramoth Gilead. Ahab king of Israel asked Jehoshaphat king of Judah, "Will you go with me against Ramoth Gilead?"

Jehoshaphat replied, "I am as you are, and my people as your people; we will join you in the war." But Jehoshaphat also said to the king of Israel, "First seek the counsel of the LORD."

So the king of Israel brought together the prophets — four hundred men — and asked them, "Shall we go to war against Ramoth Gilead, or shall I not?"

"Go," they answered, "for God will give it into the king's hand."

But Jehoshaphat asked, "Is there no longer a prophet of the LORD here whom we can inquire of?"

The king of Israel answered Jehoshaphat, "There is still one prophet through whom we can inquire of the LORD, but I hate him because he never prophesies anything good about me, but always bad. He is Micaiah son of Imlah."

"The king should not say such a thing," Jehoshaphat replied.

So the king of Israel called one of his officials and said, "Bring Micaiah son of Imlah at once."

Dressed in their royal robes, the king of Israel and Jehoshaphat king of Judah were sitting on their thrones at the threshing floor by the entrance of the gate of Samaria, with all the prophets prophesying before them. Now Zedekiah son of Kenaanah had made iron horns, and he declared, "This is what the LORD says: 'With these you will gore the Arameans until they are destroyed.'"

All the other prophets were prophesying the same thing. "Attack Ramoth Gilead and be victorious," they said, "for the LORD will give it into the king's hand."

The messenger who had gone to summon Micaiah said to him, "Look, the other prophets without exception are predicting success for the king. Let your word agree with theirs, and speak favorably."

But Micaiah said, "As surely as the LORD lives, I can tell him only what my God says."

When he arrived, the king asked him, "Micaiah, shall we go to war against Ramoth Gilead, or shall I not?"

"Attack and be victorious," he answered, "for they will be given into your hand."

The king said to him, "How many times must I make you swear to tell me nothing but the truth in the name of the LORD?"

Then Micaiah answered, "I saw all Israel scattered on the hills like sheep without a shepherd, and the LORD said, 'These people have no master. Let each one go home in peace.'"

The king of Israel said to Jehoshaphat, "Didn't I tell you that he never prophesies anything good about me, but only bad?"

Micaiah continued, "Therefore hear the word of the LORD: I saw the LORD sitting on his throne with all the multitudes of heaven standing on his right and on his left. And the LORD said, 'Who will entice Ahab king of Israel into attacking Ramoth Gilead and going to his death there?'

"One suggested this, and another that. Finally, a spirit came forward, stood before the LORD and said, 'I will entice him.'

"'By what means?' the LORD asked.

"'I will go and be a deceiving spirit in the mouths of all his prophets,' he said.

"'You will succeed in enticing him,' said the LORD. 'Go and do it.'

"So now the LORD has put a deceiving spirit in the mouths of these prophets of yours. The LORD has decreed disaster for you."

Then Zedekiah son of Kenaanah went up and slapped Micaiah in the face. "Which way did the spirit from the LORD go when he went from me to speak to you?" he asked.

Micaiah replied, "You will find out on the day you go to hide in an inner room."

The king of Israel then ordered, "Take Micaiah and send him back to Amon the ruler of the city and to Joash the king's son, and say, 'This is what the king says: Put this fellow in prison and give him nothing but bread and water until I return safely.'"

Micaiah declared, "If you ever return safely, the LORD has not spoken through me." Then he added, "Mark my words, all you people!"

So the king of Israel and Jehoshaphat king of Judah went up to Ramoth Gilead. The king of Israel said to Jehoshaphat, "I will enter the battle in disguise, but you wear your royal robes." So the king of Israel disguised himself and went into battle.

Now the king of Aram had ordered his chariot commanders, "Do not fight with anyone, small or great, except the king of Israel." When the chariot commanders saw Jehoshaphat, they thought, "This is the king of Israel." So they turned to attack him, but Jehoshaphat cried out, and the LORD helped him. God drew them away from him, for when the chariot commanders saw that he was not the king of Israel, they stopped pursuing him.

But someone drew his bow at random and hit the king of Israel between the breastplate and the scale armor. The king told the chariot driver, "Wheel around and get me out of the fighting. I've been wounded." All day long the battle raged, and the king of Israel propped himself up in his chariot facing the Arameans until evening. Then at sunset he died.

When Jehoshaphat king of Judah returned safely to his palace in Jerusalem, Jehu the seer, the son of Hanani, went out to meet him and said to the king, "Should you help the wicked and love those who hate the Lord? Because of this, the wrath of the Lord is on you. There is, however, some good in you, for you have rid the land of the Asherah poles and have set your heart on seeking God."

Jehoshaphat lived in Jerusalem, and he went out again among the people from Beersheba to the hill country of Ephraim and turned them back to the Lord, the God of their ancestors. He appointed judges in the land, in each of the fortified cities of Judah. He told them, "Consider carefully what you do, because you are not judging for mere mortals but for the Lord, who is with you whenever you give a verdict. Now let the fear of the Lord be on you. Judge carefully, for with the Lord our God there is no injustice or partiality or bribery."

In Jerusalem also, Jehoshaphat appointed some of the Levites, priests and heads of Israelite families to administer the law of the Lord and to settle disputes. And they lived in Jerusalem. He gave them these orders: "You must serve faithfully and wholeheartedly in the fear of the Lord. In every case that comes before you from your people who live in the cities — whether bloodshed or other concerns of the law, commands, decrees or regulations — you are to warn them not to sin against the Lord; otherwise his wrath will come on you and your people. Do this, and you will not sin.

"Amariah the chief priest will be over you in any matter concerning the Lord, and Zebadiah son of Ishmael, the leader of the tribe of Judah, will be over you in any matter concerning the king, and the Levites will serve as officials before you. Act with courage, and may the Lord be with those who do well."

After this, the Moabites and Ammonites with some of the Meunites came to wage war against Jehoshaphat.

Some people came and told Jehoshaphat, "A vast army is coming against you from Edom, from the other side of the Dead Sea. It is already in Hazezon Tamar" (that is, En Gedi). Alarmed, Jehoshaphat resolved to inquire of the Lord, and he proclaimed a fast for all Judah. The people of Judah came together to seek help from the Lord; indeed, they came from every town in Judah to seek him.

Then Jehoshaphat stood up in the assembly of Judah and Jerusalem at the temple of the Lord in the front of the new courtyard and said:

"Lord, the God of our ancestors, are you not the God who is in heaven? You rule over all the kingdoms of the nations. Power and might are in your hand, and no one can withstand you. Our God, did you not drive out the inhabitants of this land before your people Israel and give it forever to the descendants of Abraham your friend? They have lived in it and have built in it a sanctuary for your Name, saying, 'If calamity comes upon us, whether the sword of judgment, or plague or famine, we will stand in your presence before this temple that bears your Name and will cry out to you in our distress, and you will hear us and save us.'

"But now here are men from Ammon, Moab and Mount Seir, whose territory you would not allow Israel to invade when they came from Egypt; so they turned away from them and did not destroy them. See how they are repaying us by coming to drive us out of the possession you gave us as an inheritance. Our God, will you not judge them? For we have no power to face this vast army that is attacking us. We do not know what to do, but our eyes are on you."

All the men of Judah, with their wives and children and little ones, stood there before the Lord.

Then the Spirit of the Lord came on Jahaziel son of Zechariah, the son of Benaiah, the son of Jeiel, the son of Mattaniah, a Levite and descendant of Asaph, as he stood in the assembly.

He said: "Listen, King Jehoshaphat and all who live in Judah and Jerusalem! This is what the Lord says to you: 'Do not be afraid or discouraged because of this vast army. For the battle is not yours, but God's. Tomorrow march down against them. They will be climbing up by the Pass of Ziz, and you will find them at the end of the gorge in the Desert of Jeruel. You will not have to fight this battle. Take up your positions; stand firm and see the deliverance the Lord will give you, Judah and Jerusalem. Do not be afraid; do not be discouraged. Go out to face them tomorrow, and the Lord will be with you.'"

Jehoshaphat bowed down with his face to the ground, and all the people of Judah and Jerusalem fell down in worship before the Lord. Then some Levites from the Kohathites and Korahites stood up and praised the Lord, the God of Israel, with a very loud voice.

Early in the morning they left for the Desert of Tekoa. As they set out, Jehoshaphat stood and said, "Listen to me, Judah and people of Jerusalem! Have faith in the Lord your God and you will be upheld; have faith in his prophets and you will be successful." After consulting the people, Jehoshaphat appointed men to sing to the Lord and to praise him for the splendor of his holiness as they went out at the head of the army, saying:

"Give thanks to the LORD,
for his love endures forever."

As they began to sing and praise, the LORD set ambushes against the men of Ammon and Moab and Mount Seir who were invading Judah, and they were defeated. The Ammonites and Moabites rose up against the men from Mount Seir to destroy and annihilate them. After they finished slaughtering the men from Seir, they helped to destroy one another.

When the men of Judah came to the place that overlooks the desert and looked toward the vast army, they saw only dead bodies lying on the ground; no one had escaped. So Jehoshaphat and his men went to carry off their plunder, and they found among them a great amount of equipment and clothing and also articles of value—more than they could take away. There was so much plunder that it took three days to collect it. On the fourth day they assembled in the Valley of Berakah, where they praised the LORD. This is why it is called the Valley of Berakah to this day.

Then, led by Jehoshaphat, all the men of Judah and Jerusalem returned joyfully to Jerusalem, for the LORD had given them cause to rejoice over their enemies. They entered Jerusalem and went to the temple of the LORD with harps and lyres and trumpets.

The fear of God came on all the surrounding kingdoms when they heard how the LORD had fought against the enemies of Israel. And the kingdom of Jehoshaphat was at peace, for his God had given him rest on every side.

So Jehoshaphat reigned over Judah. He was thirty-five years old when he became king of Judah, and he reigned in Jerusalem twenty-five years. His mother's name was Azubah daughter of Shilhi. He followed the ways of his father Asa and did not stray from them; he did what was right in the eyes of the LORD. The high places, however, were not removed, and the people still had not set their hearts on the God of their ancestors.

The other events of Jehoshaphat's reign, from beginning to end, are written in the annals of Jehu son of Hanani, which are recorded in the book of the kings of Israel.

Later, Jehoshaphat king of Judah made an alliance with Ahaziah king of Israel, whose ways were wicked. He agreed with him to construct a fleet of trading ships. After these were built at Ezion Geber, Eliezer son of Dodavahu of Mareshah prophesied against Jehoshaphat, saying, "Because you have made an alliance with Ahaziah, the LORD will destroy what you have made." The ships were wrecked and were not able to set sail to trade.

Then Jehoshaphat rested with his ancestors and was buried with them in the City of David. And Jehoram his son succeeded him as king. Jehoram's brothers, the sons of Jehoshaphat, were Azariah, Jehiel, Zechariah, Azariahu, Michael and Shephatiah. All these were sons of Jehoshaphat king of Israel. Their father had given them many gifts of silver and gold and articles of value, as well as fortified cities in Judah, but he had given the kingdom to Jehoram because he was his firstborn son.

When Jehoram established himself firmly over his father's kingdom, he put all his brothers to the sword along with some of the officials of Israel. Jehoram was thirty-two years old when he became king, and he reigned in Jerusalem eight years. He followed the ways of the kings of Israel, as the house of Ahab had done, for he married a daughter of Ahab. He did evil in the eyes of the Lord. Nevertheless, because of the covenant the Lord had made with David, the Lord was not willing to destroy the house of David. He had promised to maintain a lamp for him and his descendants forever.

In the time of Jehoram, Edom rebelled against Judah and set up its own king. So Jehoram went there with his officers and all his chariots. The Edomites surrounded him and his chariot commanders, but he rose up and broke through by night. To this day Edom has been in rebellion against Judah.

Libnah revolted at the same time, because Jehoram had forsaken the Lord, the God of his ancestors. He had also built high places on the hills of Judah and had caused the people of Jerusalem to prostitute themselves and had led Judah astray.

Jehoram received a letter from Elijah the prophet, which said:

"This is what the Lord, the God of your father David, says: 'You have not followed the ways of your father Jehoshaphat or of Asa king of Judah. But you have followed the ways of the kings of Israel, and you have led Judah and the people of Jerusalem to prostitute themselves, just as the house of Ahab did. You have also murdered your own brothers, members of your own family, men who were better than you. So now the Lord is about to strike your people, your sons, your wives and everything that is yours, with a heavy blow. You yourself will be very ill with a lingering disease of the bowels, until the disease causes your bowels to come out.'"

The Lord aroused against Jehoram the hostility of the Philistines and of the Arabs who lived near the Cushites. They attacked

Judah, invaded it and carried off all the goods found in the king's palace, together with his sons and wives. Not a son was left to him except Ahaziah, the youngest.

After all this, the Lord afflicted Jehoram with an incurable disease of the bowels. In the course of time, at the end of the second year, his bowels came out because of the disease, and he died in great pain. His people made no funeral fire in his honor, as they had for his predecessors.

Jehoram was thirty-two years old when he became king, and he reigned in Jerusalem eight years. He passed away, to no one's regret, and was buried in the City of David, but not in the tombs of the kings.

The people of Jerusalem made Ahaziah, Jehoram's youngest son, king in his place, since the raiders, who came with the Arabs into the camp, had killed all the older sons. So Ahaziah son of Jehoram king of Judah began to reign.

Ahaziah was twenty-two years old when he became king, and he reigned in Jerusalem one year. His mother's name was Athaliah, a granddaughter of Omri.

He too followed the ways of the house of Ahab, for his mother encouraged him to act wickedly. He did evil in the eyes of the Lord, as the house of Ahab had done, for after his father's death they became his advisers, to his undoing. He also followed their counsel when he went with Joram son of Ahab king of Israel to wage war against Hazael king of Aram at Ramoth Gilead. The Arameans wounded Joram; so he returned to Jezreel to recover from the wounds they had inflicted on him at Ramoth in his battle with Hazael king of Aram.

Then Ahaziah son of Jehoram king of Judah went down to Jezreel to see Joram son of Ahab because he had been wounded.

Through Ahaziah's visit to Joram, God brought about Ahaziah's downfall. When Ahaziah arrived, he went out with Joram to meet Jehu son of Nimshi, whom the Lord had anointed to destroy the house of Ahab. While Jehu was executing judgment on the house of Ahab, he found the officials of Judah and the sons of Ahaziah's relatives, who had been attending Ahaziah, and he killed them. He then went in search of Ahaziah, and his men captured him while he was hiding in Samaria. He was brought to Jehu and put to death. They buried him, for they said, "He was a son of Jehoshaphat, who sought the Lord with all his heart." So there was no one in the house of Ahaziah powerful enough to retain the kingdom.

W hen Athaliah the mother of Ahaziah saw that her son was dead, she proceeded to destroy the whole royal family of the house of Judah. But Jehosheba, the daughter of King Jehoram, took Joash son of Ahaziah and stole him away from among the royal princes who were about to be murdered and put him and his nurse in a bedroom. Because Jehosheba, the daughter of King Jehoram and wife of the priest Jehoiada, was Ahaziah's sister, she hid the child from Athaliah so she could not kill him. He remained hidden with them at the temple of God for six years while Athaliah ruled the land.

In the seventh year Jehoiada showed his strength. He made a covenant with the commanders of units of a hundred: Azariah son of Jeroham, Ishmael son of Jehohanan, Azariah son of Obed, Maaseiah son of Adaiah, and Elishaphat son of Zikri. They went throughout Judah and gathered the Levites and the heads of Israelite families from all the towns. When they came to Jerusalem, the whole assembly made a covenant with the king at the temple of God.

Jehoiada said to them, "The king's son shall reign, as the Lord promised concerning the descendants of David. Now this is what you are to do: A third of you priests and Levites who are going on duty on the Sabbath are to keep watch at the doors, a third of you at the royal palace and a third at the Foundation Gate, and all the others are to be in the courtyards of the temple of the Lord. No one is to enter the temple of the Lord except the priests and Levites on duty; they may enter because they are consecrated, but all the others are to observe the Lord's command not to enter. The Levites are to station themselves around the king, each with weapon in hand. Anyone who enters the temple is to be put to death. Stay close to the king wherever he goes."

The Levites and all the men of Judah did just as Jehoiada the priest ordered. Each one took his men—those who were going on duty on the Sabbath and those who were going off duty—for Jehoiada the priest had not released any of the divisions. Then he gave the commanders of units of a hundred the spears and the large and small shields that had belonged to King David and that were in the temple of God. He stationed all the men, each with his weapon in his hand, around the king—near the altar and the temple, from the south side to the north side of the temple.

Jehoiada and his sons brought out the king's son and put the crown on him; they presented him with a copy of the covenant and proclaimed him king. They anointed him and shouted, "Long live the king!"

When Athaliah heard the noise of the people running and cheering the king, she went to them at the temple of the LORD. She looked, and there was the king, standing by his pillar at the entrance. The officers and the trumpeters were beside the king, and all the people of the land were rejoicing and blowing trumpets, and musicians with their instruments were leading the praises. Then Athaliah tore her robes and shouted, "Treason! Treason!"

Jehoiada the priest sent out the commanders of units of a hundred, who were in charge of the troops, and said to them: "Bring her out between the ranks and put to the sword anyone who follows her." For the priest had said, "Do not put her to death at the temple of the LORD." So they seized her as she reached the entrance of the Horse Gate on the palace grounds, and there they put her to death.

Jehoiada then made a covenant that he, the people and the king would be the LORD's people. All the people went to the temple of Baal and tore it down. They smashed the altars and idols and killed Mattan the priest of Baal in front of the altars.

Then Jehoiada placed the oversight of the temple of the LORD in the hands of the Levitical priests, to whom David had made assignments in the temple, to present the burnt offerings of the LORD as written in the Law of Moses, with rejoicing and singing, as David had ordered. He also stationed gatekeepers at the gates of the LORD's temple so that no one who was in any way unclean might enter.

He took with him the commanders of hundreds, the nobles, the rulers of the people and all the people of the land and brought the king down from the temple of the LORD. They went into the palace through the Upper Gate and seated the king on the royal throne. All the people of the land rejoiced, and the city was calm, because Athaliah had been slain with the sword.

Joash was seven years old when he became king, and he reigned in Jerusalem forty years. His mother's name was Zibiah; she was from Beersheba. Joash did what was right in the eyes of the LORD all the years of Jehoiada the priest. Jehoiada chose two wives for him, and he had sons and daughters.

Some time later Joash decided to restore the temple of the LORD. He called together the priests and Levites and said to them, "Go to the towns of Judah and collect the money due annually from all Israel, to repair the temple of your God. Do it now." But the Levites did not act at once.

Therefore the king summoned Jehoiada the chief priest and said to him, "Why haven't you required the Levites to bring in from Judah and Jerusalem the tax imposed by Moses the servant of the LORD and by the assembly of Israel for the tent of the covenant law?"

Now the sons of that wicked woman Athaliah had broken into the temple of God and had used even its sacred objects for the Baals.

At the king's command, a chest was made and placed outside, at the gate of the temple of the LORD. A proclamation was then issued in Judah and Jerusalem that they should bring to the LORD the tax that Moses the servant of God had required of Israel in the wilderness. All the officials and all the people brought their contributions gladly, dropping them into the chest until it was full. Whenever the chest was brought in by the Levites to the king's officials and they saw that there was a large amount of money, the royal secretary and the officer of the chief priest would come and empty the chest and carry it back to its place. They did this regularly and collected a great amount of money. The king and Jehoiada gave it to those who carried out the work required for the temple of the LORD. They hired masons and carpenters to restore the LORD's temple, and also workers in iron and bronze to repair the temple.

The men in charge of the work were diligent, and the repairs progressed under them. They rebuilt the temple of God according to its original design and reinforced it. When they had finished, they brought the rest of the money to the king and Jehoiada, and with it were made articles for the LORD's temple: articles for the service and for the burnt offerings, and also dishes and other objects of gold and silver. As long as Jehoiada lived, burnt offerings were presented continually in the temple of the LORD.

Now Jehoiada was old and full of years, and he died at the age of a hundred and thirty. He was buried with the kings in the City of David, because of the good he had done in Israel for God and his temple.

After the death of Jehoiada, the officials of Judah came and paid homage to the king, and he listened to them. They abandoned the temple of the LORD, the God of their ancestors, and worshiped Asherah poles and idols. Because of their guilt, God's anger came on Judah and Jerusalem. Although the LORD sent prophets to the people to bring them back to him, and though they testified against them, they would not listen.

Then the Spirit of God came on Zechariah son of Jehoiada the priest. He stood before the people and said, "This is what God says: 'Why do you disobey the LORD's commands? You will not prosper. Because you have forsaken the LORD, he has forsaken you.'"

But they plotted against him, and by order of the king they stoned him to death in the courtyard of the LORD's temple. King Joash did not remember the kindness Zechariah's father Jehoiada had shown him but killed his son, who said as he lay dying, "May the LORD see this and call you to account."

At the turn of the year, the army of Aram marched against Joash; it invaded Judah and Jerusalem and killed all the leaders of the people. They sent all the plunder to their king in Damascus. Although the Aramean army had come with only a few men, the Lord delivered into their hands a much larger army. Because Judah had forsaken the Lord, the God of their ancestors, judgment was executed on Joash. When the Arameans withdrew, they left Joash severely wounded. His officials conspired against him for murdering the son of Jehoiada the priest, and they killed him in his bed. So he died and was buried in the City of David, but not in the tombs of the kings.

Those who conspired against him were Zabad, son of Shimeath an Ammonite woman, and Jehozabad, son of Shimrith a Moabite woman. The account of his sons, the many prophecies about him, and the record of the restoration of the temple of God are written in the annotations on the book of the kings. And Amaziah his son succeeded him as king.

A maziah was twenty-five years old when he became king, and he reigned in Jerusalem twenty-nine years. His mother's name was Jehoaddan; she was from Jerusalem. He did what was right in the eyes of the Lord, but not wholeheartedly. After the kingdom was firmly in his control, he executed the officials who had murdered his father the king. Yet he did not put their children to death, but acted in accordance with what is written in the Law, in the Book of Moses, where the Lord commanded: "Parents shall not be put to death for their children, nor children be put to death for their parents; each will die for their own sin."

Amaziah called the people of Judah together and assigned them according to their families to commanders of thousands and commanders of hundreds for all Judah and Benjamin. He then mustered those twenty years old or more and found that there were three hundred thousand men fit for military service, able to handle the spear and shield. He also hired a hundred thousand fighting men from Israel for a hundred talents of silver.

But a man of God came to him and said, "Your Majesty, these troops from Israel must not march with you, for the Lord is not with Israel — not with any of the people of Ephraim. Even if you go and fight courageously in battle, God will overthrow you before the enemy, for God has the power to help or to overthrow."

Amaziah asked the man of God, "But what about the hundred talents I paid for these Israelite troops?"

The man of God replied, "The Lord can give you much more than that."

So Amaziah dismissed the troops who had come to him from Ephraim and sent them home. They were furious with Judah and left for home in a great rage.

Amaziah then marshaled his strength and led his army to the Valley of Salt, where he killed ten thousand men of Seir. The army of Judah also captured ten thousand men alive, took them to the top of a cliff and threw them down so that all were dashed to pieces.

Meanwhile the troops that Amaziah had sent back and had not allowed to take part in the war raided towns belonging to Judah from Samaria to Beth Horon. They killed three thousand people and carried off great quantities of plunder.

When Amaziah returned from slaughtering the Edomites, he brought back the gods of the people of Seir. He set them up as his own gods, bowed down to them and burned sacrifices to them. The anger of the LORD burned against Amaziah, and he sent a prophet to him, who said, "Why do you consult this people's gods, which could not save their own people from your hand?"

While he was still speaking, the king said to him, "Have we appointed you an adviser to the king? Stop! Why be struck down?"

So the prophet stopped but said, "I know that God has determined to destroy you, because you have done this and have not listened to my counsel."

After Amaziah king of Judah consulted his advisers, he sent this challenge to Jehoash son of Jehoahaz, the son of Jehu, king of Israel: "Come, let us face each other in battle."

But Jehoash king of Israel replied to Amaziah king of Judah: "A thistle in Lebanon sent a message to a cedar in Lebanon, 'Give your daughter to my son in marriage.' Then a wild beast in Lebanon came along and trampled the thistle underfoot. You say to yourself that you have defeated Edom, and now you are arrogant and proud. But stay at home! Why ask for trouble and cause your own downfall and that of Judah also?"

Amaziah, however, would not listen, for God so worked that he might deliver them into the hands of Jehoash, because they sought the gods of Edom. So Jehoash king of Israel attacked. He and Amaziah king of Judah faced each other at Beth Shemesh in Judah. Judah was routed by Israel, and every man fled to his home. Jehoash king of Israel captured Amaziah king of Judah, the son of Joash, the son of Ahaziah, at Beth Shemesh. Then Jehoash brought him to Jerusalem and broke down the wall of Jerusalem from the Ephraim Gate to the Corner Gate—a section about four hundred cubits long. He took all the gold and silver and all the articles found in the temple of God that had been in the care of Obed-Edom, together with the palace treasures and the hostages, and returned to Samaria.

Amaziah son of Joash king of Judah lived for fifteen years after the death of Jehoash son of Jehoahaz king of Israel. As for the other events of Amaziah's reign, from beginning to end, are they not written in the book of the kings of Judah and Israel? From the time that Amaziah turned away from following the LORD, they conspired against him in Jerusalem and he fled to Lachish, but they sent men after him to Lachish and killed him there. He was brought back by horse and was buried with his ancestors in the City of Judah.

T hen all the people of Judah took Uzziah, who was sixteen years old, and made him king in place of his father Amaziah. He was the one who rebuilt Elath and restored it to Judah after Amaziah rested with his ancestors.

Uzziah was sixteen years old when he became king, and he reigned in Jerusalem fifty-two years. His mother's name was Jekoliah; she was from Jerusalem. He did what was right in the eyes of the LORD, just as his father Amaziah had done. He sought God during the days of Zechariah, who instructed him in the fear of God. As long as he sought the LORD, God gave him success.

He went to war against the Philistines and broke down the walls of Gath, Jabneh and Ashdod. He then rebuilt towns near Ashdod and elsewhere among the Philistines. God helped him against the Philistines and against the Arabs who lived in Gur Baal and against the Meunites. The Ammonites brought tribute to Uzziah, and his fame spread as far as the border of Egypt, because he had become very powerful.

Uzziah built towers in Jerusalem at the Corner Gate, at the Valley Gate and at the angle of the wall, and he fortified them. He also built towers in the wilderness and dug many cisterns, because he had much livestock in the foothills and in the plain. He had people working his fields and vineyards in the hills and in the fertile lands, for he loved the soil.

Uzziah had a well-trained army, ready to go out by divisions according to their numbers as mustered by Jeiel the secretary and Maaseiah the officer under the direction of Hananiah, one of the royal officials. The total number of family leaders over the fighting men was 2,600. Under their command was an army of 307,500 men trained for war, a powerful force to support the king against his enemies. Uzziah provided shields, spears, helmets, coats of armor, bows and slingstones for the entire army. In Jerusalem he made devices invented for use on the towers and on the corner defenses so that soldiers could shoot arrows and hurl large stones from the walls. His fame spread far and wide, for he was greatly helped until he became powerful.

But after Uzziah became powerful, his pride led to his downfall. He was unfaithful to the LORD his God, and entered the temple of the LORD to burn incense on the altar of incense. Azariah the priest with eighty other courageous priests of the LORD followed him in. They confronted King Uzziah and said, "It is not right for you, Uzziah, to burn incense to the LORD. That is for the priests, the descendants of Aaron, who have been consecrated to burn incense. Leave the sanctuary, for you have been unfaithful; and you will not be honored by the LORD God."

Uzziah, who had a censer in his hand ready to burn incense, became angry. While he was raging at the priests in their presence before the incense altar in the LORD's temple, leprosy broke out on his forehead. When Azariah the chief priest and all the other priests looked at him, they saw that he had leprosy on his forehead, so they hurried him out. Indeed, he himself was eager to leave, because the LORD had afflicted him.

King Uzziah had leprosy until the day he died. He lived in a separate house—leprous, and banned from the temple of the LORD. Jotham his son had charge of the palace and governed the people of the land.

The other events of Uzziah's reign, from beginning to end, are recorded by the prophet Isaiah son of Amoz. Uzziah rested with his ancestors and was buried near them in a cemetery that belonged to the kings, for people said, "He had leprosy." And Jotham his son succeeded him as king.

Jotham was twenty-five years old when he became king, and he reigned in Jerusalem sixteen years. His mother's name was Jerusha daughter of Zadok. He did what was right in the eyes of the LORD, just as his father Uzziah had done, but unlike him he did not enter the temple of the LORD. The people, however, continued their corrupt practices. Jotham rebuilt the Upper Gate of the temple of the LORD and did extensive work on the wall at the hill of Ophel. He built towns in the hill country of Judah and forts and towers in the wooded areas.

Jotham waged war against the king of the Ammonites and conquered them. That year the Ammonites paid him a hundred talents of silver, ten thousand cors of wheat and ten thousand cors of barley. The Ammonites brought him the same amount also in the second and third years.

Jotham grew powerful because he walked steadfastly before the Lord his God.

The other events in Jotham's reign, including all his wars and the other things he did, are written in the book of the kings of Israel and Judah. He was twenty-five years old when he became king, and he reigned in Jerusalem sixteen years. Jotham rested with his ancestors and was buried in the City of David. And Ahaz his son succeeded him as king.

A haz was twenty years old when he became king, and he reigned in Jerusalem sixteen years. Unlike David his father, he did not do what was right in the eyes of the Lord. He followed the ways of the kings of Israel and also made idols for worshiping the Baals. He burned sacrifices in the Valley of Ben Hinnom and sacrificed his children in the fire, engaging in the detestable practices of the nations the Lord had driven out before the Israelites. He offered sacrifices and burned incense at the high places, on the hilltops and under every spreading tree.

Therefore the Lord his God delivered him into the hands of the king of Aram. The Arameans defeated him and took many of his people as prisoners and brought them to Damascus.

He was also given into the hands of the king of Israel, who inflicted heavy casualties on him. In one day Pekah son of Remaliah killed a hundred and twenty thousand soldiers in Judah — because Judah had forsaken the Lord, the God of their ancestors. Zikri, an Ephraimite warrior, killed Maaseiah the king's son, Azrikam the officer in charge of the palace, and Elkanah, second to the king. The men of Israel took captive from their fellow Israelites who were from Judah two hundred thousand wives, sons and daughters. They also took a great deal of plunder, which they carried back to Samaria.

But a prophet of the Lord named Oded was there, and he went out to meet the army when it returned to Samaria. He said to them, "Because the Lord, the God of your ancestors, was angry with Judah, he gave them into your hand. But you have slaughtered them in a rage that reaches to heaven. And now you intend to make the men and women of Judah and Jerusalem your slaves. But aren't you also guilty of sins against the Lord your God? Now listen to me! Send back your fellow Israelites you have taken as prisoners, for the Lord's fierce anger rests on you."

Then some of the leaders in Ephraim — Azariah son of Jehohanan, Berekiah son of Meshillemoth, Jehizkiah son of Shallum, and

Amasa son of Hadlai—confronted those who were arriving from the war. "You must not bring those prisoners here," they said, "or we will be guilty before the Lord. Do you intend to add to our sin and guilt? For our guilt is already great, and his fierce anger rests on Israel."

So the soldiers gave up the prisoners and plunder in the presence of the officials and all the assembly. The men designated by name took the prisoners, and from the plunder they clothed all who were naked. They provided them with clothes and sandals, food and drink, and healing balm. All those who were weak they put on donkeys. So they took them back to their fellow Israelites at Jericho, the City of Palms, and returned to Samaria.

At that time King Ahaz sent to the kings of Assyria for help. The Edomites had again come and attacked Judah and carried away prisoners, while the Philistines had raided towns in the foothills and in the Negev of Judah. They captured and occupied Beth Shemesh, Aijalon and Gederoth, as well as Soko, Timnah and Gimzo, with their surrounding villages. The Lord had humbled Judah because of Ahaz king of Israel, for he had promoted wickedness in Judah and had been most unfaithful to the Lord. Tiglath-Pileser king of Assyria came to him, but he gave him trouble instead of help. Ahaz took some of the things from the temple of the Lord and from the royal palace and from the officials and presented them to the king of Assyria, but that did not help him.

In his time of trouble King Ahaz became even more unfaithful to the Lord. He offered sacrifices to the gods of Damascus, who had defeated him; for he thought, "Since the gods of the kings of Aram have helped them, I will sacrifice to them so they will help me." But they were his downfall and the downfall of all Israel.

Ahaz gathered together the furnishings from the temple of God and cut them in pieces. He shut the doors of the Lord's temple and set up altars at every street corner in Jerusalem. In every town in Judah he built high places to burn sacrifices to other gods and aroused the anger of the Lord, the God of his ancestors.

The other events of his reign and all his ways, from beginning to end, are written in the book of the kings of Judah and Israel. Ahaz rested with his ancestors and was buried in the city of Jerusalem, but he was not placed in the tombs of the kings of Israel. And Hezekiah his son succeeded him as king.

Hezekiah was twenty-five years old when he became king, and he reigned in Jerusalem twenty-nine years. His mother's name

was Abijah daughter of Zechariah. He did what was right in the eyes
of the LORD, just as his father David had done.

In the first month of the first year of his reign, he opened the
doors of the temple of the LORD and repaired them. He brought in
the priests and the Levites, assembled them in the square on the
east side and said: "Listen to me, Levites! Consecrate yourselves
now and consecrate the temple of the LORD, the God of your ancestors. Remove all defilement from the sanctuary. Our parents were
unfaithful; they did evil in the eyes of the LORD our God and for-
sook him. They turned their faces away from the LORD's dwelling
place and turned their backs on him. They also shut the doors of
the portico and put out the lamps. They did not burn incense or
present any burnt offerings at the sanctuary to the God of Israel.
Therefore, the anger of the LORD has fallen on Judah and Jerusalem; he has made them an object of dread and horror and scorn,
as you can see with your own eyes. This is why our fathers have
fallen by the sword and why our sons and daughters and our wives
are in captivity. Now I intend to make a covenant with the LORD,
the God of Israel, so that his fierce anger will turn away from us.
My sons, do not be negligent now, for the LORD has chosen you to
stand before him and serve him, to minister before him and to burn
incense."

Then these Levites set to work:
  from the Kohathites,
    Mahath son of Amasai and Joel son of Azariah;
  from the Merarites,
    Kish son of Abdi and Azariah son of Jehallelel;
  from the Gershonites,
    Joah son of Zimmah and Eden son of Joah;
  from the descendants of Elizaphan,
    Shimri and Jeiel;
  from the descendants of Asaph,
    Zechariah and Mattaniah;
  from the descendants of Heman,
    Jehiel and Shimei;
  from the descendants of Jeduthun,
    Shemaiah and Uzziel.

When they had assembled their fellow Levites and consecrated
themselves, they went in to purify the temple of the LORD, as the
king had ordered, following the word of the LORD. The priests went
into the sanctuary of the LORD to purify it. They brought out to the
courtyard of the LORD's temple everything unclean that they found
in the temple of the LORD. The Levites took it and carried it out to
the Kidron Valley. They began the consecration on the first day of
the first month, and by the eighth day of the month they reached

the portico of the Lord. For eight more days they consecrated the temple of the Lord itself, finishing on the sixteenth day of the first month.

Then they went in to King Hezekiah and reported: "We have purified the entire temple of the Lord, the altar of burnt offering with all its utensils, and the table for setting out the consecrated bread, with all its articles. We have prepared and consecrated all the articles that King Ahaz removed in his unfaithfulness while he was king. They are now in front of the Lord's altar."

Early the next morning King Hezekiah gathered the city officials together and went up to the temple of the Lord. They brought seven bulls, seven rams, seven male lambs and seven male goats as a sin offering for the kingdom, for the sanctuary and for Judah. The king commanded the priests, the descendants of Aaron, to offer these on the altar of the Lord. So they slaughtered the bulls, and the priests took the blood and splashed it against the altar; next they slaughtered the rams and splashed their blood against the altar; then they slaughtered the lambs and splashed their blood against the altar. The goats for the sin offering were brought before the king and the assembly, and they laid their hands on them. The priests then slaughtered the goats and presented their blood on the altar for a sin offering to atone for all Israel, because the king had ordered the burnt offering and the sin offering for all Israel.

He stationed the Levites in the temple of the Lord with cymbals, harps and lyres in the way prescribed by David and Gad the king's seer and Nathan the prophet; this was commanded by the Lord through his prophets. So the Levites stood ready with David's instruments, and the priests with their trumpets.

Hezekiah gave the order to sacrifice the burnt offering on the altar. As the offering began, singing to the Lord began also, accompanied by trumpets and the instruments of David king of Israel. The whole assembly bowed in worship, while the musicians played and the trumpets sounded. All this continued until the sacrifice of the burnt offering was completed.

When the offerings were finished, the king and everyone present with him knelt down and worshiped. King Hezekiah and his officials ordered the Levites to praise the Lord with the words of David and of Asaph the seer. So they sang praises with gladness and bowed down and worshiped.

Then Hezekiah said, "You have now dedicated yourselves to the Lord. Come and bring sacrifices and thank offerings to the temple of the Lord." So the assembly brought sacrifices and thank offerings, and all whose hearts were willing brought burnt offerings.

The number of burnt offerings the assembly brought was seventy bulls, a hundred rams and two hundred male lambs — all of them for burnt offerings to the Lord. The animals consecrated as sacrifices amounted to six hundred bulls and three thousand sheep and goats. The priests, however, were too few to skin all the burnt offerings; so their relatives the Levites helped them until the task was finished and until other priests had been consecrated, for the Levites had been more conscientious in consecrating themselves than the priests had been. There were burnt offerings in abundance, together with the fat of the fellowship offerings and the drink offerings that accompanied the burnt offerings.

So the service of the temple of the Lord was reestablished. Hezekiah and all the people rejoiced at what God had brought about for his people, because it was done so quickly.

Hezekiah sent word to all Israel and Judah and also wrote letters to Ephraim and Manasseh, inviting them to come to the temple of the Lord in Jerusalem and celebrate the Passover to the Lord, the God of Israel. The king and his officials and the whole assembly in Jerusalem decided to celebrate the Passover in the second month. They had not been able to celebrate it at the regular time because not enough priests had consecrated themselves and the people had not assembled in Jerusalem. The plan seemed right both to the king and to the whole assembly. They decided to send a proclamation throughout Israel, from Beersheba to Dan, calling the people to come to Jerusalem and celebrate the Passover to the Lord, the God of Israel. It had not been celebrated in large numbers according to what was written.

At the king's command, couriers went throughout Israel and Judah with letters from the king and from his officials, which read:

"People of Israel, return to the Lord, the God of Abraham, Isaac and Israel, that he may return to you who are left, who have escaped from the hand of the kings of Assyria. Do not be like your parents and your fellow Israelites, who were unfaithful to the Lord, the God of their ancestors, so that he made them an object of horror, as you see. Do not be stiff-necked, as your ancestors were; submit to the Lord. Come to his sanctuary, which he has consecrated forever. Serve the Lord your God, so that his fierce anger will turn away from you. If you return to the Lord, then your fellow Israelites and your children will be shown compassion by their captors and will return to this land, for the Lord your God is gracious and compassionate. He will not turn his face from you if you return to him."

The couriers went from town to town in Ephraim and Manasseh, as far as Zebulun, but people scorned and ridiculed them.

Nevertheless, some from Asher, Manasseh and Zebulun humbled themselves and went to Jerusalem. Also in Judah the hand of God was on the people to give them unity of mind to carry out what the king and his officials had ordered, following the word of the LORD.

A very large crowd of people assembled in Jerusalem to celebrate the Festival of Unleavened Bread in the second month. They removed the altars in Jerusalem and cleared away the incense altars and threw them into the Kidron Valley.

They slaughtered the Passover lamb on the fourteenth day of the second month. The priests and the Levites were ashamed and consecrated themselves and brought burnt offerings to the temple of the LORD. Then they took up their regular positions as prescribed in the Law of Moses the man of God. The priests splashed against the altar the blood handed to them by the Levites. Since many in the crowd had not consecrated themselves, the Levites had to kill the Passover lambs for all those who were not ceremonially clean and could not consecrate their lambs to the LORD. Although most of the many people who came from Ephraim, Manasseh, Issachar and Zebulun had not purified themselves, yet they ate the Passover, contrary to what was written. But Hezekiah prayed for them, saying, "May the LORD, who is good, pardon everyone who sets their heart on seeking God—the LORD, the God of their ancestors—even if they are not clean according to the rules of the sanctuary." And the LORD heard Hezekiah and healed the people.

The Israelites who were present in Jerusalem celebrated the Festival of Unleavened Bread for seven days with great rejoicing, while the Levites and priests praised the LORD every day with resounding instruments dedicated to the LORD.

Hezekiah spoke encouragingly to all the Levites, who showed good understanding of the service of the LORD. For the seven days they ate their assigned portion and offered fellowship offerings and praised the LORD, the God of their ancestors.

The whole assembly then agreed to celebrate the festival seven more days; so for another seven days they celebrated joyfully. Hezekiah king of Judah provided a thousand bulls and seven thousand sheep and goats for the assembly, and the officials provided them with a thousand bulls and ten thousand sheep and goats. A great number of priests consecrated themselves. The entire assembly of Judah rejoiced, along with the priests and Levites and all who had assembled from Israel, including the foreigners who had come from Israel and also those who resided in Judah. There was great joy in Jerusalem, for since the days of Solomon son of David king of Israel there had been nothing like this in Jerusalem. The priests and the Levites stood to bless the people, and God heard them, for their prayer reached heaven, his holy dwelling place.

When all this had ended, the Israelites who were there went out to the towns of Judah, smashed the sacred stones and cut down the Asherah poles. They destroyed the high places and the altars throughout Judah and Benjamin and in Ephraim and Manasseh. After they had destroyed all of them, the Israelites returned to their own towns and to their own property.

Hezekiah assigned the priests and Levites to divisions — each of them according to their duties as priests or Levites — to offer burnt offerings and fellowship offerings, to minister, to give thanks and to sing praises at the gates of the Lord's dwelling. The king contributed from his own possessions for the morning and evening burnt offerings and for the burnt offerings on the Sabbaths, at the New Moons and at the appointed festivals as written in the Law of the Lord. He ordered the people living in Jerusalem to give the portion due the priests and Levites so they could devote themselves to the Law of the Lord. As soon as the order went out, the Israelites generously gave the firstfruits of their grain, new wine, olive oil and honey and all that the fields produced. They brought a great amount, a tithe of everything. The people of Israel and Judah who lived in the towns of Judah also brought a tithe of their herds and flocks and a tithe of the holy things dedicated to the Lord their God, and they piled them in heaps. They began doing this in the third month and finished in the seventh month. When Hezekiah and his officials came and saw the heaps, they praised the Lord and blessed his people Israel.

Hezekiah asked the priests and Levites about the heaps; and Azariah the chief priest, from the family of Zadok, answered, "Since the people began to bring their contributions to the temple of the Lord, we have had enough to eat and plenty to spare, because the Lord has blessed his people, and this great amount is left over."

Hezekiah gave orders to prepare storerooms in the temple of the Lord, and this was done. Then they faithfully brought in the contributions, tithes and dedicated gifts. Konaniah, a Levite, was the overseer in charge of these things, and his brother Shimei was next in rank. Jehiel, Azaziah, Nahath, Asahel, Jerimoth, Jozabad, Eliel, Ismakiah, Mahath and Benaiah were assistants of Konaniah and Shimei his brother. All these served by appointment of King Hezekiah and Azariah the official in charge of the temple of God.

Kore son of Imnah the Levite, keeper of the East Gate, was in charge of the freewill offerings given to God, distributing the contributions made to the Lord and also the consecrated gifts. Eden, Miniamin, Jeshua, Shemaiah, Amariah and Shekaniah assisted him faithfully in the towns of the priests, distributing to their fellow priests according to their divisions, old and young alike.

In addition, they distributed to the males three years old or more whose names were in the genealogical records — all who would enter the temple of the LORD to perform the daily duties of their various tasks, according to their responsibilities and their divisions. And they distributed to the priests enrolled by their families in the genealogical records and likewise to the Levites twenty years old or more, according to their responsibilities and their divisions. They included all the little ones, the wives, and the sons and daughters of the whole community listed in these genealogical records. For they were faithful in consecrating themselves.

As for the priests, the descendants of Aaron, who lived on the farmlands around their towns or in any other towns, men were designated by name to distribute portions to every male among them and to all who were recorded in the genealogies of the Levites.

This is what Hezekiah did throughout Judah, doing what was good and right and faithful before the LORD his God. In everything that he undertook in the service of God's temple and in obedience to the law and the commands, he sought his God and worked wholeheartedly. And so he prospered.

After all that Hezekiah had so faithfully done, Sennacherib king of Assyria came and invaded Judah. He laid siege to the fortified cities, thinking to conquer them for himself. When Hezekiah saw that Sennacherib had come and that he intended to wage war against Jerusalem, he consulted with his officials and military staff about blocking off the water from the springs outside the city, and they helped him. They gathered a large group of people who blocked all the springs and the stream that flowed through the land. "Why should the kings of Assyria come and find plenty of water?" they said. Then he worked hard repairing all the broken sections of the wall and building towers on it. He built another wall outside that one and reinforced the terraces of the City of David. He also made large numbers of weapons and shields.

He appointed military officers over the people and assembled them before him in the square at the city gate and encouraged them with these words: "Be strong and courageous. Do not be afraid or discouraged because of the king of Assyria and the vast army with him, for there is a greater power with us than with him. With him is only the arm of flesh, but with us is the LORD our God to help us and to fight our battles." And the people gained confidence from what Hezekiah the king of Judah said.

Later, when Sennacherib king of Assyria and all his forces were laying siege to Lachish, he sent his officers to Jerusalem with this message for Hezekiah king of Judah and for all the people of Judah who were there:

"This is what Sennacherib king of Assyria says: On what are you basing your confidence, that you remain in Jerusalem under siege? When Hezekiah says, 'The Lord our God will save us from the hand of the king of Assyria,' he is misleading you, to let you die of hunger and thirst. Did not Hezekiah himself remove this god's high places and altars, saying to Judah and Jerusalem, 'You must worship before one altar and burn sacrifices on it'?

"Do you not know what I and my predecessors have done to all the peoples of the other lands? Were the gods of those nations ever able to deliver their land from my hand? Who of all the gods of these nations that my predecessors destroyed has been able to save his people from me? How then can your god deliver you from my hand? Now do not let Hezekiah deceive you and mislead you like this. Do not believe him, for no god of any nation or kingdom has been able to deliver his people from my hand or the hand of my predecessors. How much less will your god deliver you from my hand!"

Sennacherib's officers spoke further against the Lord God and against his servant Hezekiah. The king also wrote letters ridiculing the Lord, the God of Israel, and saying this against him: "Just as the gods of the peoples of the other lands did not rescue their people from my hand, so the god of Hezekiah will not rescue his people from my hand." Then they called out in Hebrew to the people of Jerusalem who were on the wall, to terrify them and make them afraid in order to capture the city. They spoke about the God of Jerusalem as they did about the gods of the other peoples of the world—the work of human hands.

King Hezekiah and the prophet Isaiah son of Amoz cried out in prayer to heaven about this. And the Lord sent an angel, who annihilated all the fighting men and the commanders and officers in the camp of the Assyrian king. So he withdrew to his own land in disgrace. And when he went into the temple of his god, some of his sons, his own flesh and blood, cut him down with the sword.

So the Lord saved Hezekiah and the people of Jerusalem from the hand of Sennacherib king of Assyria and from the hand of all others. He took care of them on every side. Many brought offerings to Jerusalem for the Lord and valuable gifts for Hezekiah king of Judah. From then on he was highly regarded by all the nations.

In those days Hezekiah became ill and was at the point of death. He prayed to the Lord, who answered him and gave him a miraculous sign. But Hezekiah's heart was proud and he did not respond to the kindness shown him; therefore the Lord's wrath was on him and on Judah and Jerusalem. Then Hezekiah repented of the pride of his heart, as did the people of Jerusalem; therefore the Lord's wrath did not come on them during the days of Hezekiah.

Hezekiah had very great wealth and honor, and he made treasuries for his silver and gold and for his precious stones, spices, shields and all kinds of valuables. He also made buildings to store the harvest of grain, new wine and olive oil; and he made stalls for various kinds of cattle, and pens for the flocks. He built villages and acquired great numbers of flocks and herds, for God had given him very great riches.

It was Hezekiah who blocked the upper outlet of the Gihon spring and channeled the water down to the west side of the City of David. He succeeded in everything he undertook. But when envoys were sent by the rulers of Babylon to ask him about the miraculous sign that had occurred in the land, God left him to test him and to know everything that was in his heart.

The other events of Hezekiah's reign and his acts of devotion are written in the vision of the prophet Isaiah son of Amoz in the book of the kings of Judah and Israel. Hezekiah rested with his ancestors and was buried on the hill where the tombs of David's descendants are. All Judah and the people of Jerusalem honored him when he died. And Manasseh his son succeeded him as king.

Manasseh was twelve years old when he became king, and he reigned in Jerusalem fifty-five years. He did evil in the eyes of the Lord, following the detestable practices of the nations the Lord had driven out before the Israelites. He rebuilt the high places his father Hezekiah had demolished; he also erected altars to the Baals and made Asherah poles. He bowed down to all the starry hosts and worshiped them. He built altars in the temple of the Lord, of which the Lord had said, "My Name will remain in Jerusalem forever." In both courts of the temple of the Lord, he built altars to all the starry hosts. He sacrificed his children in the fire in the Valley of Ben Hinnom, practiced divination and witchcraft, sought omens, and consulted mediums and spiritists. He did much evil in the eyes of the Lord, arousing his anger.

He took the image he had made and put it in God's temple, of which God had said to David and to his son Solomon, "In this temple and in Jerusalem, which I have chosen out of all the tribes of Israel, I will put my Name forever. I will not again make the feet of the Israelites leave the land I assigned to your ancestors, if only they will be careful to do everything I commanded them concerning all the laws, decrees and regulations given through Moses." But Manasseh led Judah and the people of Jerusalem astray, so that they did more evil than the nations the LORD had destroyed before the Israelites.

The LORD spoke to Manasseh and his people, but they paid no attention. So the LORD brought against them the army commanders of the king of Assyria, who took Manasseh prisoner, put a hook in his nose, bound him with bronze shackles and took him to Babylon. In his distress he sought the favor of the LORD his God and humbled himself greatly before the God of his ancestors. And when he prayed to him, the LORD was moved by his entreaty and listened to his plea; so he brought him back to Jerusalem and to his kingdom. Then Manasseh knew that the LORD is God.

Afterward he rebuilt the outer wall of the City of David, west of the Gihon spring in the valley, as far as the entrance of the Fish Gate and encircling the hill of Ophel; he also made it much higher. He stationed military commanders in all the fortified cities in Judah.

He got rid of the foreign gods and removed the image from the temple of the LORD, as well as all the altars he had built on the temple hill and in Jerusalem; and he threw them out of the city. Then he restored the altar of the LORD and sacrificed fellowship offerings and thank offerings on it, and told Judah to serve the LORD, the God of Israel. The people, however, continued to sacrifice at the high places, but only to the LORD their God.

The other events of Manasseh's reign, including his prayer to his God and the words the seers spoke to him in the name of the LORD, the God of Israel, are written in the annals of the kings of Israel. His prayer and how God was moved by his entreaty, as well as all his sins and unfaithfulness, and the sites where he built high places and set up Asherah poles and idols before he humbled himself—all these are written in the records of the seers. Manasseh rested with his ancestors and was buried in his palace. And Amon his son succeeded him as king.

A mon was twenty-two years old when he became king, and he reigned in Jerusalem two years. He did evil in the eyes of the LORD, as his father Manasseh had done. Amon worshiped and offered sacrifices to all the idols Manasseh had made. But unlike his father Manasseh, he did not humble himself before the LORD; Amon increased his guilt.

Amon's officials conspired against him and assassinated him in his palace. Then the people of the land killed all who had plotted against King Amon, and they made Josiah his son king in his place.

J osiah was eight years old when he became king, and he reigned in Jerusalem thirty-one years. He did what was right in the eyes of the Lord and followed the ways of his father David, not turning aside to the right or to the left.

In the eighth year of his reign, while he was still young, he began to seek the God of his father David. In his twelfth year he began to purge Judah and Jerusalem of high places, Asherah poles and idols. Under his direction the altars of the Baals were torn down; he cut to pieces the incense altars that were above them, and smashed the Asherah poles and the idols. These he broke to pieces and scattered over the graves of those who had sacrificed to them. He burned the bones of the priests on their altars, and so he purged Judah and Jerusalem. In the towns of Manasseh, Ephraim and Simeon, as far as Naphtali, and in the ruins around them, he tore down the altars and the Asherah poles and crushed the idols to powder and cut to pieces all the incense altars throughout Israel. Then he went back to Jerusalem.

In the eighteenth year of Josiah's reign, to purify the land and the temple, he sent Shaphan son of Azaliah and Maaseiah the ruler of the city, with Joah son of Joahaz, the recorder, to repair the temple of the Lord his God.

They went to Hilkiah the high priest and gave him the money that had been brought into the temple of God, which the Levites who were the gatekeepers had collected from the people of Manasseh, Ephraim and the entire remnant of Israel and from all the people of Judah and Benjamin and the inhabitants of Jerusalem. Then they entrusted it to the men appointed to supervise the work on the Lord's temple. These men paid the workers who repaired and restored the temple. They also gave money to the carpenters and builders to purchase dressed stone, and timber for joists and beams for the buildings that the kings of Judah had allowed to fall into ruin.

The workers labored faithfully. Over them to direct them were Jahath and Obadiah, Levites descended from Merari, and Zechariah and Meshullam, descended from Kohath. The Levites — all who were skilled in playing musical instruments — had charge of the laborers and supervised all the workers from job to job. Some of the Levites were secretaries, scribes and gatekeepers.

While they were bringing out the money that had been taken into the temple of the Lord, Hilkiah the priest found the Book of the Law of the Lord that had been given through Moses. Hilkiah said to Shaphan the secretary, "I have found the Book of the Law in the temple of the Lord." He gave it to Shaphan.

Then Shaphan took the book to the king and reported to him: "Your officials are doing everything that has been committed to them. They have paid out the money that was in the temple of the Lord and have entrusted it to the supervisors and workers." Then Shaphan the secretary informed the king, "Hilkiah the priest has given me a book." And Shaphan read from it in the presence of the king.

When the king heard the words of the Law, he tore his robes. He gave these orders to Hilkiah, Ahikam son of Shaphan, Abdon son of Micah, Shaphan the secretary and Asaiah the king's attendant: "Go and inquire of the Lord for me and for the remnant in Israel and Judah about what is written in this book that has been found. Great is the Lord's anger that is poured out on us because those who have gone before us have not kept the word of the Lord; they have not acted in accordance with all that is written in this book."

Hilkiah and those the king had sent with him went to speak to the prophet Huldah, who was the wife of Shallum son of Tokhath, the son of Hasrah, keeper of the wardrobe. She lived in Jerusalem, in the New Quarter.

She said to them, "This is what the Lord, the God of Israel, says: Tell the man who sent you to me, 'This is what the Lord says: I am going to bring disaster on this place and its people—all the curses written in the book that has been read in the presence of the king of Judah. Because they have forsaken me and burned incense to other gods and aroused my anger by all that their hands have made, my anger will be poured out on this place and will not be quenched.' Tell the king of Judah, who sent you to inquire of the Lord, 'This is what the Lord, the God of Israel, says concerning the words you heard: Because your heart was responsive and you humbled yourself before God when you heard what he spoke against this place and its people, and because you humbled yourself before me and tore your robes and wept in my presence, I have heard you, declares the Lord. Now I will gather you to your ancestors, and you will be buried in peace. Your eyes will not see all the disaster I am going to bring on this place and on those who live here.'"

So they took her answer back to the king.

Then the king called together all the elders of Judah and Jerusalem. He went up to the temple of the Lord with the people of Judah, the inhabitants of Jerusalem, the priests and the Levites—all the people from the least to the greatest. He read in their hearing all the words of the Book of the Covenant, which had been found in the temple of the Lord. The king stood by his pillar and renewed the covenant in the presence of the LORD — to follow the LORD and keep his commands, statutes and decrees with all his heart and all his soul, and to obey the words of the covenant written in this book.

Then he had everyone in Jerusalem and Benjamin pledge themselves to it; the people of Jerusalem did this in accordance with the covenant of God, the God of their ancestors.

Josiah removed all the detestable idols from all the territory belonging to the Israelites, and he had all who were present in Israel serve the LORD their God. As long as he lived, they did not fail to follow the LORD, the God of their ancestors.

Josiah celebrated the Passover to the LORD in Jerusalem, and the Passover lamb was slaughtered on the fourteenth day of the first month. He appointed the priests to their duties and encouraged them in the service of the LORD's temple. He said to the Levites, who instructed all Israel and who had been consecrated to the LORD: "Put the sacred ark in the temple that Solomon son of David king of Israel built. It is not to be carried about on your shoulders. Now serve the LORD your God and his people Israel. Prepare yourselves by families in your divisions, according to the instructions written by David king of Israel and by his son Solomon.

"Stand in the holy place with a group of Levites for each subdivision of the families of your fellow Israelites, the lay people. Slaughter the Passover lambs, consecrate yourselves and prepare the lambs for your fellow Israelites, doing what the LORD commanded through Moses."

Josiah provided for all the lay people who were there a total of thirty thousand lambs and goats for the Passover offerings, and also three thousand cattle — all from the king's own possessions.

His officials also contributed voluntarily to the people and the priests and Levites. Hilkiah, Zechariah and Jehiel, the officials in charge of God's temple, gave the priests twenty-six hundred Passover offerings and three hundred cattle. Also Konaniah along with Shemaiah and Nethanel, his brothers, and Hashabiah, Jeiel and Jozabad, the leaders of the Levites, provided five thousand Passover offerings and five hundred head of cattle for the Levites.

The service was arranged and the priests stood in their places with the Levites in their divisions as the king had ordered. The Passover lambs were slaughtered, and the priests splashed against the altar the blood handed to them, while the Levites skinned the animals. They set aside the burnt offerings to give them to the subdivisions of the families of the people to offer to the LORD, as it is written in the Book of Moses. They did the same with the cattle. They roasted the Passover animals over the fire as prescribed, and boiled the holy offerings in pots, caldrons and pans and served them quickly to all the people. After this, they made preparations for themselves and for the priests, because the priests, the descendants of Aaron, were sacrificing the burnt offerings and the fat portions until nightfall. So the Levites made preparations for themselves and for the Aaronic priests.

The musicians, the descendants of Asaph, were in the places prescribed by David, Asaph, Heman and Jeduthun the king's seer. The gatekeepers at each gate did not need to leave their posts, because their fellow Levites made the preparations for them.

So at that time the entire service of the LORD was carried out for the celebration of the Passover and the offering of burnt offerings on the altar of the LORD, as King Josiah had ordered. The Israelites who were present celebrated the Passover at that time and observed the Festival of Unleavened Bread for seven days. The Passover had not been observed like this in Israel since the days of the prophet Samuel; and none of the kings of Israel had ever celebrated such a Passover as did Josiah, with the priests, the Levites and all Judah and Israel who were there with the people of Jerusalem. This Passover was celebrated in the eighteenth year of Josiah's reign.

After all this, when Josiah had set the temple in order, Necho king of Egypt went up to fight at Carchemish on the Euphrates, and Josiah marched out to meet him in battle. But Necho sent messengers to him, saying, "What quarrel is there, king of Judah, between you and me? It is not you I am attacking at this time, but the house with which I am at war. God has told me to hurry; so stop opposing God, who is with me, or he will destroy you."

Josiah, however, would not turn away from him, but disguised himself to engage him in battle. He would not listen to what Necho had said at God's command but went to fight him on the plain of Megiddo.

Archers shot King Josiah, and he told his officers, "Take me away; I am badly wounded." So they took him out of his chariot, put him in his other chariot and brought him to Jerusalem, where he died. He was buried in the tombs of his ancestors, and all Judah and Jerusalem mourned for him.

Jeremiah composed laments for Josiah, and to this day all the male and female singers commemorate Josiah in the laments. These became a tradition in Israel and are written in the Laments.

The other events of Josiah's reign and his acts of devotion in accordance with what is written in the Law of the LORD — all the events, from beginning to end, are written in the book of the kings of Israel and Judah. And the people of the land took Jehoahaz son of Josiah and made him king in Jerusalem in place of his father.

Jehoahaz was twenty-three years old when he became king, and he reigned in Jerusalem three months. The king of Egypt dethroned him in Jerusalem and imposed on Judah a levy of a hundred talents of silver and a talent of gold. The king of Egypt made Eliakim, a brother of Jehoahaz, king over Judah and Jerusalem and changed Eliakim's name to Jehoiakim. But Necho took Eliakim's brother Jehoahaz and carried him off to Egypt.

Jehoiakim was twenty-five years old when he became king, and he reigned in Jerusalem eleven years. He did evil in the eyes of the Lord his God. Nebuchadnezzar king of Babylon attacked him and bound him with bronze shackles to take him to Babylon. Nebuchadnezzar also took to Babylon articles from the temple of the Lord and put them in his temple there.

The other events of Jehoiakim's reign, the detestable things he did and all that was found against him, are written in the book of the kings of Israel and Judah. And Jehoiachin his son succeeded him as king.

Jehoiachin was eighteen years old when he became king, and he reigned in Jerusalem three months and ten days. He did evil in the eyes of the Lord. In the spring, King Nebuchadnezzar sent for him and brought him to Babylon, together with articles of value from the temple of the Lord, and he made Jehoiachin's uncle, Zedekiah, king over Judah and Jerusalem.

Zedekiah was twenty-one years old when he became king, and he reigned in Jerusalem eleven years. He did evil in the eyes of the Lord his God and did not humble himself before Jeremiah the prophet, who spoke the word of the Lord. He also rebelled against King Nebuchadnezzar, who had made him take an oath in God's name. He became stiff-necked and hardened his heart and would not turn to the Lord, the God of Israel. Furthermore, all the leaders of the priests and the people became more and more unfaithful, following all the detestable practices of the nations and defiling the temple of the Lord, which he had consecrated in Jerusalem.

The LORD, the God of their ancestors, sent word to them through his messengers again and again, because he had pity on his people and on his dwelling place. But they mocked God's messengers, despised his words and scoffed at his prophets until the wrath of the LORD was aroused against his people and there was no remedy. He brought up against them the king of the Babylonians, who killed their young men with the sword in the sanctuary, and did not spare young men or young women, the elderly or the infirm. God gave them all into the hands of Nebuchadnezzar. He carried to Babylon all the articles from the temple of God, both large and small, and the treasures of the LORD's temple and the treasures of the king and his officials. They set fire to God's temple and broke down the wall of Jerusalem; they burned all the palaces and destroyed everything of value there.

He carried into exile to Babylon the remnant, who escaped from the sword, and they became servants to him and his successors until the kingdom of Persia came to power. The land enjoyed its sabbath rests; all the time of its desolation it rested, until the seventy years were completed in fulfillment of the word of the LORD spoken by Jeremiah.

In the first year of Cyrus king of Persia, in order to fulfill the word of the LORD spoken by Jeremiah, the LORD moved the heart of Cyrus king of Persia to make a proclamation throughout his realm and also to put it in writing:

"This is what Cyrus king of Persia says:

" 'The LORD, the God of heaven, has given me all the kingdoms of the earth and he has appointed me to build a temple for him at Jerusalem in Judah. Any of his people among you may go up, and may the LORD their God be with them.' "

In the first year of Cyrus king of Persia, in order to fulfill the word of the LORD spoken by Jeremiah, the LORD moved the heart of Cyrus king of Persia to make a proclamation throughout his realm and also to put it in writing:

"This is what Cyrus king of Persia says:

" 'The LORD, the God of heaven, has given me all the kingdoms of the earth and he has appointed me to build a temple for him at Jerusalem in Judah. Any of his people among you may go up to Jerusalem in Judah and build the temple of the LORD, the God of Israel, the God who is in Jerusalem, and may their God be with them. And in any locality where survivors may now be living, the people are to provide them with silver and gold, with goods and livestock, and with freewill offerings for the temple of God in Jerusalem.' "

Then the family heads of Judah and Benjamin, and the priests and Levites — everyone whose heart God had moved — prepared to go up and build the house of the LORD in Jerusalem. All their neighbors assisted them with articles of silver and gold, with goods and livestock, and with valuable gifts, in addition to all the freewill offerings.

Moreover, King Cyrus brought out the articles belonging to the temple of the LORD, which Nebuchadnezzar had carried away from Jerusalem and had placed in the temple of his god. Cyrus king of Persia had them brought by Mithredath the treasurer, who counted them out to Sheshbazzar the prince of Judah.

This was the inventory:

gold dishes	30
silver dishes	1,000
silver pans	29
gold bowls	30
matching silver bowls	410
other articles	1,000

In all, there were 5,400 articles of gold and of silver. Sheshbazzar brought all these along with the exiles when they came up from Babylon to Jerusalem.

Now these are the people of the province who came up from the captivity of the exiles, whom Nebuchadnezzar king of Babylon had taken captive to Babylon (they returned to Jerusalem and Judah, each to their own town, in company with Zerubbabel, Joshua, Nehemiah, Seraiah, Reelaiah, Mordecai, Bilshan, Mispar, Bigvai, Rehum and Baanah):

The list of the men of the people of Israel:

the descendants of Parosh	2,172
of Shephatiah	372
of Arah	775
of Pahath-Moab (through the line of Jeshua and Joab)	2,812
of Elam	1,254
of Zattu	945
of Zakkai	760
of Bani	642
of Bebai	623
of Azgad	1,222

of Adonikam	666
of Bigvai	2,056
of Adin	454
of Ater (through Hezekiah)	98
of Bezai	323
of Jorah	112
of Hashum	223
of Gibbar	95
the men of Bethlehem	123
of Netophah	56
of Anathoth	128
of Azmaveth	42
of Kiriath Jearim, Kephirah and Beeroth	743
of Ramah and Geba	621
of Mikmash	122
of Bethel and Ai	223
of Nebo	52
of Magbish	156
of the other Elam	1,254
of Harim	320
of Lod, Hadid and Ono	725
of Jericho	345
of Senaah	3,630

The priests:

the descendants of Jedaiah (through the family of Jeshua)	973
of Immer	1,052
of Pashhur	1,247
of Harim	1,017

The Levites:

the descendants of Jeshua and Kadmiel (of the line of Hodaviah)	74

The musicians:

the descendants of Asaph	128

The gatekeepers of the temple:

the descendants of Shallum, Ater, Talmon, Akkub, Hatita and Shobai	139

The temple servants:

the descendants of
Ziha, Hasupha, Tabbaoth,
Keros, Siaha, Padon,
Lebanah, Hagabah, Akkub,
Hagab, Shalmai, Hanan,
Giddel, Gahar, Reaiah,
Rezin, Nekoda, Gazzam,
Uzza, Paseah, Besai,
Asnah, Meunim, Nephusim,
Bakbuk, Hakupha, Harhur,
Bazluth, Mehida, Harsha,
Barkos, Sisera, Temah,
Neziah and Hatipha

The descendants of the servants of Solomon:

the descendants of
Sotai, Hassophereth, Peruda,
Jaala, Darkon, Giddel,
Shephatiah, Hattil,
Pokereth-Hazzebaim and Ami

The temple servants and the descendants
of the servants
of Solomon   392

The following came up from the towns of Tel Melah, Tel
Harsha, Kerub, Addon and Immer, but they could not show
that their families were descended from Israel:

The descendants of
Delaiah, Tobiah and Nekoda   652

And from among the priests:

The descendants of
Hobaiah, Hakkoz and Barzillai (a man who had married
a daughter of Barzillai the Gileadite and was called by
that name).
These searched for their family records, but they could not
find them and so were excluded from the priesthood as unclean. The governor ordered them not to eat any of the most
sacred food until there was a priest ministering with the Urim
and Thummim.

The whole company numbered 42,360, besides their 7,337
male and female slaves; and they also had 200 male and fe-

male singers. They had 736 horses, 245 mules, 435 camels and 6,720 donkeys.

When they arrived at the house of the Lord in Jerusalem, some of the heads of the families gave freewill offerings toward the rebuilding of the house of God on its site. According to their ability they gave to the treasury for this work 61,000 darics of gold, 5,000 minas of silver and 100 priestly garments.

The priests, the Levites, the musicians, the gatekeepers and the temple servants settled in their own towns, along with some of the other people, and the rest of the Israelites settled in their towns.

When the seventh month came and the Israelites had settled in their towns, the people assembled together as one in Jerusalem. Then Joshua son of Jozadak and his fellow priests and Zerubbabel son of Shealtiel and his associates began to build the altar of the God of Israel to sacrifice burnt offerings on it, in accordance with what is written in the Law of Moses the man of God. Despite their fear of the peoples around them, they built the altar on its foundation and sacrificed burnt offerings on it to the Lord, both the morning and evening sacrifices. Then in accordance with what is written, they celebrated the Festival of Tabernacles with the required number of burnt offerings prescribed for each day. After that, they presented the regular burnt offerings, the New Moon sacrifices and the sacrifices for all the appointed sacred festivals of the Lord, as well as those brought as freewill offerings to the Lord. On the first day of the seventh month they began to offer burnt offerings to the Lord, though the foundation of the Lord's temple had not yet been laid.

Then they gave money to the masons and carpenters, and gave food and drink and olive oil to the people of Sidon and Tyre, so that they would bring cedar logs by sea from Lebanon to Joppa, as authorized by Cyrus king of Persia.

In the second month of the second year after their arrival at the house of God in Jerusalem, Zerubbabel son of Shealtiel, Joshua son of Jozadak and the rest of the people (the priests and the Levites and all who had returned from the captivity to Jerusalem) began the work. They appointed Levites twenty years old and older to supervise the building of the house of the Lord. Joshua and his sons and brothers and Kadmiel and his sons (descendants of Hodaviah) and the sons of Henadad and their sons and brothers — all Levites — joined together in supervising those working on the house of God.

When the builders laid the foundation of the temple of the LORD, the priests in their vestments and with trumpets, and the Levites (the sons of Asaph) with cymbals, took their places to praise the LORD, as prescribed by David king of Israel. With praise and thanksgiving they sang to the LORD:

"He is good;
  his love toward Israel endures forever."

And all the people gave a great shout of praise to the LORD, because the foundation of the house of the LORD was laid. But many of the older priests and Levites and family heads, who had seen the former temple, wept aloud when they saw the foundation of this temple being laid, while many others shouted for joy. No one could distinguish the sound of the shouts of joy from the sound of weeping, because the people made so much noise. And the sound was heard far away.

When the enemies of Judah and Benjamin heard that the exiles were building a temple for the LORD, the God of Israel, they came to Zerubbabel and to the heads of the families and said, "Let us help you build because, like you, we seek your God and have been sacrificing to him since the time of Esarhaddon king of Assyria, who brought us here."

But Zerubbabel, Joshua and the rest of the heads of the families of Israel answered, "You have no part with us in building a temple to our God. We alone will build it for the LORD, the God of Israel, as King Cyrus, the king of Persia, commanded us."

Then the peoples around them set out to discourage the people of Judah and make them afraid to go on building. They bribed officials to work against them and frustrate their plans during the entire reign of Cyrus king of Persia and down to the reign of Darius king of Persia.

At the beginning of the reign of Xerxes, they lodged an accusation against the people of Judah and Jerusalem.

And in the days of Artaxerxes king of Persia, Bishlam, Mithredath, Tabeel and the rest of his associates wrote a letter to Artaxerxes. The letter was written in Aramaic script and in the Aramaic language.

Rehum the commanding officer and Shimshai the secretary wrote a letter against Jerusalem to Artaxerxes the king as follows:

Rehum the commanding officer and Shimshai the secretary, together with the rest of their associates — the judges, officials and administrators over the people from Persia, Uruk and

Babylon, the Elamites of Susa, and the other people whom the great and honorable Ashurbanipal deported and settled in the city of Samaria and elsewhere in Trans-Euphrates.

(This is a copy of the letter they sent him.)

To King Artaxerxes,

From your servants in Trans-Euphrates:

The king should know that the people who came up to us from you have gone to Jerusalem and are rebuilding that rebellious and wicked city. They are restoring the walls and repairing the foundations.

Furthermore, the king should know that if this city is built and its walls are restored, no more taxes, tribute or duty will be paid, and eventually the royal revenues will suffer. Now since we are under obligation to the palace and it is not proper for us to see the king dishonored, we are sending this message to inform the king, so that a search may be made in the archives of your predecessors. In these records you will find that this city is a rebellious city, troublesome to kings and provinces, a place with a long history of sedition. That is why this city was destroyed. We inform the king that if this city is built and its walls are restored, you will be left with nothing in Trans-Euphrates.

The king sent this reply:

To Rehum the commanding officer, Shimshai the secretary and the rest of their associates living in Samaria and elsewhere in Trans-Euphrates:

Greetings.

The letter you sent us has been read and translated in my presence. I issued an order and a search was made, and it was found that this city has a long history of revolt against kings and has been a place of rebellion and sedition. Jerusalem has had powerful kings ruling over the whole of Trans-Euphrates, and taxes, tribute and duty were paid to them. Now issue an order to these men to stop work, so that this city will not be rebuilt until I so order. Be careful not to neglect this matter. Why let this threat grow, to the detriment of the royal interests?

As soon as the copy of the letter of King Artaxerxes was read to Rehum and Shimshai the secretary and their associates, they went immediately to the Jews in Jerusalem and compelled them by force to stop.

Thus the work on the house of God in Jerusalem came to a standstill until the second year of the reign of Darius king of Persia.

Now Haggai the prophet and Zechariah the prophet, a descendant of Iddo, prophesied to the Jews in Judah and Jerusalem in the name of the God of Israel, who was over them. Then Zerubbabel son of Shealtiel and Joshua son of Jozadak set to work to rebuild the house of God in Jerusalem. And the prophets of God were with them, supporting them.

At that time Tattenai, governor of Trans-Euphrates, and Shethar-Bozenai and their associates went to them and asked, "Who authorized you to rebuild this temple and to finish it?" They also asked, "What are the names of those who are constructing this building?" But the eye of their God was watching over the elders of the Jews, and they were not stopped until a report could go to Darius and his written reply be received.

This is a copy of the letter that Tattenai, governor of Trans-Euphrates, and Shethar-Bozenai and their associates, the officials of Trans-Euphrates, sent to King Darius. The report they sent him read as follows:

To King Darius:

Cordial greetings.

The king should know that we went to the district of Judah, to the temple of the great God. The people are building it with large stones and placing the timbers in the walls. The work is being carried on with diligence and is making rapid progress under their direction.

We questioned the elders and asked them, "Who authorized you to rebuild this temple and to finish it?" We also asked them their names, so that we could write down the names of their leaders for your information.

This is the answer they gave us:

"We are the servants of the God of heaven and earth, and we are rebuilding the temple that was built many years ago, one that a great king of Israel built and finished. But because our ancestors angered the God of heaven, he gave them into the hands of Nebuchadnezzar the Chaldean, king of Babylon, who destroyed this temple and deported the people to Babylon.

"However, in the first year of Cyrus king of Babylon, King Cyrus issued a decree to rebuild this house of God. He even removed from the temple of Babylon the gold and silver articles of the house of God, which Nebuchadnezzar had taken from the temple in Jerusalem and brought to the temple in Babylon. Then King Cyrus gave them to a man named Sheshbazzar, whom he had appointed governor, and he told him, 'Take these articles and go and deposit them in the temple in Jerusalem. And rebuild the house of God on its site.'

"So this Sheshbazzar came and laid the foundations of the house of God in Jerusalem. From that day to the present it has been under construction but is not yet finished."

Now if it pleases the king, let a search be made in the royal archives of Babylon to see if King Cyrus did in fact issue a decree to rebuild this house of God in Jerusalem. Then let the king send us his decision in this matter.

King Darius then issued an order, and they searched in the archives stored in the treasury at Babylon. A scroll was found in the citadel of Ecbatana in the province of Media, and this was written on it:

Memorandum:

In the first year of King Cyrus, the king issued a decree concerning the temple of God in Jerusalem:

Let the temple be rebuilt as a place to present sacrifices, and let its foundations be laid. It is to be sixty cubits high and sixty cubits wide, with three courses of large stones and one of timbers. The costs are to be paid by the royal treasury. Also, the gold and silver articles of the house of God, which Nebuchadnezzar took from the temple in Jerusalem and brought to Babylon, are to be returned to their places in the temple in Jerusalem; they are to be deposited in the house of God.

Now then, Tattenai, governor of Trans-Euphrates, and Shethar-Bozenai and you other officials of that province, stay away from there. Do not interfere with the work on this temple of God. Let the governor of the Jews and the Jewish elders rebuild this house of God on its site.

Moreover, I hereby decree what you are to do for these elders of the Jews in the construction of this house of God:

Their expenses are to be fully paid out of the royal treasury, from the revenues of Trans-Euphrates, so that the work will not stop. Whatever is needed—young bulls, rams, male lambs for burnt offerings to the God of heaven, and wheat, salt, wine and olive oil, as requested by the priests in Jerusalem—

must be given them daily without fail, so that they may offer sacrifices pleasing to the God of heaven and pray for the well-being of the king and his sons.

Furthermore, I decree that if anyone defies this edict, a beam is to be pulled from their house and they are to be impaled on it. And for this crime their house is to be made a pile of rubble. May God, who has caused his Name to dwell there, overthrow any king or people who lifts a hand to change this decree or to destroy this temple in Jerusalem.

I Darius have decreed it. Let it be carried out with diligence.

Then, because of the decree King Darius had sent, Tattenai, governor of Trans-Euphrates, and Shethar-Bozenai and their associates carried it out with diligence. So the elders of the Jews continued to build and prosper under the preaching of Haggai the prophet and Zechariah, a descendant of Iddo. They finished building the temple according to the command of the God of Israel and the decrees of Cyrus, Darius and Artaxerxes, kings of Persia. The temple was completed on the third day of the month Adar, in the sixth year of the reign of King Darius.

Then the people of Israel—the priests, the Levites and the rest of the exiles—celebrated the dedication of the house of God with joy. For the dedication of this house of God they offered a hundred bulls, two hundred rams, four hundred male lambs and, as a sin offering for all Israel, twelve male goats, one for each of the tribes of Israel. And they installed the priests in their divisions and the Levites in their groups for the service of God at Jerusalem, according to what is written in the Book of Moses.

On the fourteenth day of the first month, the exiles celebrated the Passover. The priests and Levites had purified themselves and were all ceremonially clean. The Levites slaughtered the Passover lamb for all the exiles, for their relatives the priests and for themselves. So the Israelites who had returned from the exile ate it, together with all who had separated themselves from the unclean practices of their Gentile neighbors in order to seek the Lord, the God of Israel. For seven days they celebrated with joy the Festival of Unleavened Bread, because the Lord had filled them with joy by changing the attitude of the king of Assyria so that he assisted them in the work on the house of God, the God of Israel.

After these things, during the reign of Artaxerxes king of Persia, Ezra son of Seraiah, the son of Azariah, the son of Hilkiah, the son of Shallum, the son of Zadok, the son of Ahitub, the son of

Amariah, the son of Azariah, the son of Meraioth, the son of Zerahiah, the son of Uzzi, the son of Bukki, the son of Abishua, the son of Phinehas, the son of Eleazar, the son of Aaron the chief priest— this Ezra came up from Babylon. He was a teacher well versed in the Law of Moses, which the LORD, the God of Israel, had given. The king had granted him everything he asked, for the hand of the LORD his God was on him. Some of the Israelites, including priests, Levites, musicians, gatekeepers and temple servants, also came up to Jerusalem in the seventh year of King Artaxerxes.

Ezra arrived in Jerusalem in the fifth month of the seventh year of the king. He had begun his journey from Babylon on the first day of the first month, and he arrived in Jerusalem on the first day of the fifth month, for the gracious hand of his God was on him. For Ezra had devoted himself to the study and observance of the Law of the LORD, and to teaching its decrees and laws in Israel.

This is a copy of the letter King Artaxerxes had given to Ezra the priest, a teacher of the Law, a man learned in matters concerning the commands and decrees of the LORD for Israel:

Artaxerxes, king of kings,

To Ezra the priest, teacher of the Law of the God of heaven:

Greetings.

Now I decree that any of the Israelites in my kingdom, including priests and Levites, who volunteer to go to Jerusalem with you, may go. You are sent by the king and his seven advisers to inquire about Judah and Jerusalem with regard to the Law of your God, which is in your hand. Moreover, you are to take with you the silver and gold that the king and his advisers have freely given to the God of Israel, whose dwelling is in Jerusalem, together with all the silver and gold you may obtain from the province of Babylon, as well as the freewill offerings of the people and priests for the temple of their God in Jerusalem. With this money be sure to buy bulls, rams and male lambs, together with their grain offerings and drink offerings, and sacrifice them on the altar of the temple of your God in Jerusalem.

You and your fellow Israelites may then do whatever seems best with the rest of the silver and gold, in accordance with the will of your God. Deliver to the God of Jerusalem all the articles entrusted to you for worship in the temple of your God. And anything else needed for the temple of your God that you are responsible to supply, you may provide from the royal treasury.

Now I, King Artaxerxes, decree that all the treasurers of Trans-Euphrates are to provide with diligence whatever Ezra the priest, the teacher of the Law of the God of heaven, may ask of you—up to a hundred talents of silver, a hundred cors of wheat, a hundred baths of wine, a hundred baths of olive oil, and salt without limit. Whatever the God of heaven has prescribed, let it be done with diligence for the temple of the God of heaven. Why should his wrath fall on the realm of the king and of his sons? You are also to know that you have no authority to impose taxes, tribute or duty on any of the priests, Levites, musicians, gatekeepers, temple servants or other workers at this house of God.

And you, Ezra, in accordance with the wisdom of your God, which you possess, appoint magistrates and judges to administer justice to all the people of Trans-Euphrates—all who know the laws of your God. And you are to teach any who do not know them. Whoever does not obey the law of your God and the law of the king must surely be punished by death, banishment, confiscation of property, or imprisonment.

Praise be to the LORD, the God of our ancestors, who has put it into the king's heart to bring honor to the house of the LORD in Jerusalem in this way and who has extended his good favor to me before the king and his advisers and all the king's powerful officials. Because the hand of the LORD my God was on me, I took courage and gathered leaders from Israel to go up with me.

These are the family heads and those registered with them who came up with me from Babylon during the reign of King Artaxerxes:

of the descendants of Phinehas, Gershom;

of the descendants of Ithamar, Daniel;

of the descendants of David, Hattush of the descendants of Shekaniah;

of the descendants of Parosh, Zechariah, and with him were registered 150 men;

of the descendants of Pahath-Moab, Eliehoenai son of Zerahiah, and with him 200 men;

of the descendants of Zattu, Shekaniah son of Jahaziel, and with him 300 men;

of the descendants of Adin, Ebed son of Jonathan, and with him 50 men;

of the descendants of Elam, Jeshaiah son of Athaliah, and with him 70 men;

of the descendants of Shephatiah, Zebadiah son of Michael, and with him 80 men;

of the descendants of Joab, Obadiah son of Jehiel, and with him 218 men;

of the descendants of Bani, Shelomith son of Josiphiah, and
with him 160 men;
of the descendants of Bebai, Zechariah son of Bebai, and with
him 28 men;
of the descendants of Azgad, Johanan son of Hakkatan, and
with him 110 men;
of the descendants of Adonikam, the last ones, whose names
were Eliphelet, Jeuel and Shemaiah, and with them 60 men;
of the descendants of Bigvai, Uthai and Zakkur, and with them
70 men.

I assembled them at the canal that flows toward Ahava, and
we camped there three days. When I checked among the people
and the priests, I found no Levites there. So I summoned Eliezer,
Ariel, Shemaiah, Elnathan, Jarib, Elnathan, Nathan, Zechariah and
Meshullam, who were leaders, and Joiarib and Elnathan, who were
men of learning, and I ordered them to go to Iddo, the leader in Kasiphia. I told them what to say to Iddo and his fellow Levites, the
temple servants in Kasiphia, so that they might bring attendants
to us for the house of our God. Because the gracious hand of our
God was on us, they brought us Sherebiah, a capable man, from the
descendants of Mahli son of Levi, the son of Israel, and Sherebiah's
sons and brothers, 18 in all; and Hashabiah, together with Jeshaiah from the descendants of Merari, and his brothers and nephews,
20 in all. They also brought 220 of the temple servants — a body
that David and the officials had established to assist the Levites. All
were registered by name.

There, by the Ahava Canal, I proclaimed a fast, so that we might
humble ourselves before our God and ask him for a safe journey for
us and our children, with all our possessions. I was ashamed to ask
the king for soldiers and horsemen to protect us from enemies on
the road, because we had told the king, "The gracious hand of our
God is on everyone who looks to him, but his great anger is against
all who forsake him." So we fasted and petitioned our God about
this, and he answered our prayer.

Then I set apart twelve of the leading priests, namely, Sherebiah, Hashabiah and ten of their brothers, and I weighed out to them
the offering of silver and gold and the articles that the king, his advisers, his officials and all Israel present there had donated for the
house of our God. I weighed out to them 650 talents of silver, silver
articles weighing 100 talents, 100 talents of gold, 20 bowls of gold
valued at 1,000 darics, and two fine articles of polished bronze, as
precious as gold.

I said to them, "You as well as these articles are consecrated to
the Lord. The silver and gold are a freewill offering to the Lord, the

God of your ancestors. Guard them carefully until you weigh them out in the chambers of the house of the Lord in Jerusalem before the leading priests and the Levites and the family heads of Israel." Then the priests and Levites received the silver and gold and sacred articles that had been weighed out to be taken to the house of our God in Jerusalem.

On the twelfth day of the first month we set out from the Ahava Canal to go to Jerusalem. The hand of our God was on us, and he protected us from enemies and bandits along the way. So we arrived in Jerusalem, where we rested three days.

On the fourth day, in the house of our God, we weighed out the silver and gold and the sacred articles into the hands of Meremoth son of Uriah, the priest. Eleazar son of Phinehas was with him, and so were the Levites Jozabad son of Jeshua and Noadiah son of Binnui. Everything was accounted for by number and weight, and the entire weight was recorded at that time.

Then the exiles who had returned from captivity sacrificed burnt offerings to the God of Israel: twelve bulls for all Israel, ninety-six rams, seventy-seven male lambs and, as a sin offering, twelve male goats. All this was a burnt offering to the Lord. They also delivered the king's orders to the royal satraps and to the governors of Trans-Euphrates, who then gave assistance to the people and to the house of God.

After these things had been done, the leaders came to me and said, "The people of Israel, including the priests and the Levites, have not kept themselves separate from the neighboring peoples with their detestable practices, like those of the Canaanites, Hittites, Perizzites, Jebusites, Ammonites, Moabites, Egyptians and Amorites. They have taken some of their daughters as wives for themselves and their sons, and have mingled the holy race with the peoples around them. And the leaders and officials have led the way in this unfaithfulness."

When I heard this, I tore my tunic and cloak, pulled hair from my head and beard and sat down appalled. Then everyone who trembled at the words of the God of Israel gathered around me because of this unfaithfulness of the exiles. And I sat there appalled until the evening sacrifice.

Then, at the evening sacrifice, I rose from my self-abasement, with my tunic and cloak torn, and fell on my knees with my hands spread out to the Lord my God and prayed:

"I am too ashamed and disgraced, my God, to lift up my face to you, because our sins are higher than our heads and our guilt has reached to the heavens. From the days of our ancestors until now, our guilt has been great. Because of our sins, we and our kings and our priests have been subjected to the sword and captivity, to pillage and humiliation at the hand of foreign kings, as it is today.

"But now, for a brief moment, the Lord our God has been gracious in leaving us a remnant and giving us a firm place in his sanctuary, and so our God gives light to our eyes and a little relief in our bondage. Though we are slaves, our God has not forsaken us in our bondage. He has shown us kindness in the sight of the kings of Persia: He has granted us new life to rebuild the house of our God and repair its ruins, and he has given us a wall of protection in Judah and Jerusalem.

"But now, our God, what can we say after this? For we have forsaken the commands you gave through your servants the prophets when you said: 'The land you are entering to possess is a land polluted by the corruption of its peoples. By their detestable practices they have filled it with their impurity from one end to the other. Therefore, do not give your daughters in marriage to their sons or take their daughters for your sons. Do not seek a treaty of friendship with them at any time, that you may be strong and eat the good things of the land and leave it to your children as an everlasting inheritance.'

"What has happened to us is a result of our evil deeds and our great guilt, and yet, our God, you have punished us less than our sins deserved and have given us a remnant like this. Shall we then break your commands again and intermarry with the peoples who commit such detestable practices? Would you not be angry enough with us to destroy us, leaving us no remnant or survivor? Lord, the God of Israel, you are righteous! We are left this day as a remnant. Here we are before you in our guilt, though because of it not one of us can stand in your presence."

While Ezra was praying and confessing, weeping and throwing himself down before the house of God, a large crowd of Israelites — men, women and children — gathered around him. They too wept bitterly. Then Shekaniah son of Jehiel, one of the descendants of Elam, said to Ezra, "We have been unfaithful to our God by marrying foreign women from the peoples around us. But in spite of this, there is still hope for Israel. Now let us make a covenant before our God to send away all these women and their children, in accordance with the counsel of my lord and of those who fear the commands of our God. Let it be done according to the Law. Rise up;

this matter is in your hands. We will support you, so take courage and do it."

So Ezra rose up and put the leading priests and Levites and all Israel under oath to do what had been suggested. And they took the oath. Then Ezra withdrew from before the house of God and went to the room of Jehohanan son of Eliashib. While he was there, he ate no food and drank no water, because he continued to mourn over the unfaithfulness of the exiles.

A proclamation was then issued throughout Judah and Jerusalem for all the exiles to assemble in Jerusalem. Anyone who failed to appear within three days would forfeit all his property, in accordance with the decision of the officials and elders, and would himself be expelled from the assembly of the exiles.

Within the three days, all the men of Judah and Benjamin had gathered in Jerusalem. And on the twentieth day of the ninth month, all the people were sitting in the square before the house of God, greatly distressed by the occasion and because of the rain. Then Ezra the priest stood up and said to them, "You have been unfaithful; you have married foreign women, adding to Israel's guilt. Now honor the Lord, the God of your ancestors, and do his will. Separate yourselves from the peoples around you and from your foreign wives."

The whole assembly responded with a loud voice: "You are right! We must do as you say. But there are many people here and it is the rainy season; so we cannot stand outside. Besides, this matter cannot be taken care of in a day or two, because we have sinned greatly in this thing. Let our officials act for the whole assembly. Then let everyone in our towns who has married a foreign woman come at a set time, along with the elders and judges of each town, until the fierce anger of our God in this matter is turned away from us." Only Jonathan son of Asahel and Jahzeiah son of Tikvah, supported by Meshullam and Shabbethai the Levite, opposed this.

So the exiles did as was proposed. Ezra the priest selected men who were family heads, one from each family division, and all of them designated by name. On the first day of the tenth month they sat down to investigate the cases, and by the first day of the first month they finished dealing with all the men who had married foreign women.

Among the descendants of the priests, the following had married foreign women:

From the descendants of Joshua son of Jozadak, and his brothers: Maaseiah, Eliezer, Jarib and Gedaliah. (They all gave

their hands in pledge to put away their wives, and for their guilt they each presented a ram from the flock as a guilt offering.)
From the descendants of Immer:
Hanani and Zebadiah.
From the descendants of Harim:
Maaseiah, Elijah, Shemaiah, Jehiel and Uzziah.
From the descendants of Pashhur:
Elioenai, Maaseiah, Ishmael, Nethanel, Jozabad and Elasah.

Among the Levites:

Jozabad, Shimei, Kelaiah (that is, Kelita), Pethahiah, Judah and Eliezer.
From the musicians:
Eliashib.
From the gatekeepers:
Shallum, Telem and Uri.

And among the other Israelites:

From the descendants of Parosh:
Ramiah, Izziah, Malkijah, Mijamin, Eleazar, Malkijah and Benaiah.
From the descendants of Elam:
Mattaniah, Zechariah, Jehiel, Abdi, Jeremoth and Elijah.
From the descendants of Zattu:
Elioenai, Eliashib, Mattaniah, Jeremoth, Zabad and Aziza.
From the descendants of Bebai:
Jehohanan, Hananiah, Zabbai and Athlai.
From the descendants of Bani:
Meshullam, Malluk, Adaiah, Jashub, Sheal and Jeremoth.
From the descendants of Pahath-Moab:
Adna, Kelal, Benaiah, Maaseiah, Mattaniah, Bezalel, Binnui and Manasseh.
From the descendants of Harim:
Eliezer, Ishijah, Malkijah, Shemaiah, Shimeon, Benjamin, Malluk and Shemariah.
From the descendants of Hashum:
Mattenai, Mattattah, Zabad, Eliphelet, Jeremai, Manasseh and Shimei.
From the descendants of Bani:
Maadai, Amram, Uel, Benaiah, Bedeiah, Keluhi, Vaniah, Meremoth, Eliashib, Mattaniah, Mattenai and Jaasu.
From the descendants of Binnui:
Shimei, Shelemiah, Nathan, Adaiah, Maknadebai, Shashai,

Sharai, Azarel, Shelemiah, Shemariah, Shallum, Amariah and Joseph.

From the descendants of Nebo:

Jeiel, Mattithiah, Zabad, Zebina, Jaddai, Joel and Benaiah.

All these had married foreign women, and some of them had children by these wives.

T he words of Nehemiah son of Hakaliah:

In the month of Kislev in the twentieth year, while I was in the citadel of Susa, Hanani, one of my brothers, came from Judah with some other men, and I questioned them about the Jewish remnant that had survived the exile, and also about Jerusalem.

They said to me, "Those who survived the exile and are back in the province are in great trouble and disgrace. The wall of Jerusalem is broken down, and its gates have been burned with fire."

When I heard these things, I sat down and wept. For some days I mourned and fasted and prayed before the God of heaven. Then I said:

"Lord, the God of heaven, the great and awesome God, who keeps his covenant of love with those who love him and keep his commandments, let your ear be attentive and your eyes open to hear the prayer your servant is praying before you day and night for your servants, the people of Israel. I confess the sins we Israelites, including myself and my father's family, have committed against you. We have acted very wickedly toward you. We have not obeyed the commands, decrees and laws you gave your servant Moses.

"Remember the instruction you gave your servant Moses, saying, 'If you are unfaithful, I will scatter you among the nations, but if you return to me and obey my commands, then even if your exiled people are at the farthest horizon, I will gather them from there and bring them to the place I have chosen as a dwelling for my Name.'

"They are your servants and your people, whom you redeemed by your great strength and your mighty hand. Lord, let your ear be attentive to the prayer of this your servant and to the prayer of your servants who delight in revering your name. Give your servant success today by granting him favor in the presence of this man."

I was cupbearer to the king.

In the month of Nisan in the twentieth year of King Artaxerxes, when wine was brought for him, I took the wine and gave it to the king. I had not been sad in his presence before, so the king asked me, "Why does your face look so sad when you are not ill? This can be nothing but sadness of heart."

I was very much afraid, but I said to the king, "May the king live forever! Why should my face not look sad when the city where my ancestors are buried lies in ruins, and its gates have been destroyed by fire?"

The king said to me, "What is it you want?"

Then I prayed to the God of heaven, and I answered the king, "If it pleases the king and if your servant has found favor in his sight, let him send me to the city in Judah where my ancestors are buried so that I can rebuild it."

Then the king, with the queen sitting beside him, asked me, "How long will your journey take, and when will you get back?" It pleased the king to send me; so I set a time.

I also said to him, "If it pleases the king, may I have letters to the governors of Trans-Euphrates, so that they will provide me safe-conduct until I arrive in Judah? And may I have a letter to Asaph, keeper of the royal park, so he will give me timber to make beams for the gates of the citadel by the temple and for the city wall and for the residence I will occupy?" And because the gracious hand of my God was on me, the king granted my requests. So I went to the governors of Trans-Euphrates and gave them the king's letters. The king had also sent army officers and cavalry with me.

When Sanballat the Horonite and Tobiah the Ammonite official heard about this, they were very much disturbed that someone had come to promote the welfare of the Israelites.

I went to Jerusalem, and after staying there three days I set out during the night with a few others. I had not told anyone what my God had put in my heart to do for Jerusalem. There were no mounts with me except the one I was riding on.

By night I went out through the Valley Gate toward the Jackal Well and the Dung Gate, examining the walls of Jerusalem, which had been broken down, and its gates, which had been destroyed by fire. Then I moved on toward the Fountain Gate and the King's Pool, but there was not enough room for my mount to get through; so I went up the valley by night, examining the wall. Finally, I turned back and reentered through the Valley Gate. The officials did not know where I had gone or what I was doing, because as yet I had said nothing to the Jews or the priests or nobles or officials or any others who would be doing the work.

Then I said to them, "You see the trouble we are in: Jerusalem lies in ruins, and its gates have been burned with fire. Come, let us rebuild the wall of Jerusalem, and we will no longer be in disgrace." I also told them about the gracious hand of my God on me and what the king had said to me.

They replied, "Let us start rebuilding." So they began this good work.

But when Sanballat the Horonite, Tobiah the Ammonite official and Geshem the Arab heard about it, they mocked and ridiculed us. "What is this you are doing?" they asked. "Are you rebelling against the king?"

I answered them by saying, "The God of heaven will give us success. We his servants will start rebuilding, but as for you, you have no share in Jerusalem or any claim or historic right to it."

Eliashib the high priest and his fellow priests went to work and rebuilt the Sheep Gate. They dedicated it and set its doors in place, building as far as the Tower of the Hundred, which they dedicated, and as far as the Tower of Hananel. The men of Jericho built the adjoining section, and Zakkur son of Imri built next to them.

The Fish Gate was rebuilt by the sons of Hassenaah. They laid its beams and put its doors and bolts and bars in place. Meremoth son of Uriah, the son of Hakkoz, repaired the next section. Next to him Meshullam son of Berekiah, the son of Meshezabel, made repairs, and next to him Zadok son of Baana also made repairs. The next section was repaired by the men of Tekoa, but their nobles would not put their shoulders to the work under their supervisors.

The Jeshanah Gate was repaired by Joiada son of Paseah and Meshullam son of Besodeiah. They laid its beams and put its doors with their bolts and bars in place. Next to them, repairs were made by men from Gibeon and Mizpah — Melatiah of Gibeon and Jadon of Meronoth — places under the authority of the governor of Trans-Euphrates. Uzziel son of Harhaiah, one of the goldsmiths, repaired the next section; and Hananiah, one of the perfume-makers, made repairs next to that. They restored Jerusalem as far as the Broad Wall. Rephaiah son of Hur, ruler of a half-district of Jerusalem, repaired the next section. Adjoining this, Jedaiah son of Harumaph made repairs opposite his house, and Hattush son of Hashabneiah made repairs next to him. Malkijah son of Harim and Hasshub son of Pahath-Moab repaired another section and the Tower of the Ovens. Shallum son of Hallohesh, ruler of a half-district of Jerusalem, repaired the next section with the help of his daughters.

The Valley Gate was repaired by Hanun and the residents of Zanoah. They rebuilt it and put its doors with their bolts and bars in place. They also repaired a thousand cubits of the wall as far as the Dung Gate.

The Dung Gate was repaired by Malkijah son of Rekab, ruler of the district of Beth Hakkerem. He rebuilt it and put its doors with their bolts and bars in place.

The Fountain Gate was repaired by Shallun son of Kol-Hozeh, ruler of the district of Mizpah. He rebuilt it, roofing it over and putting its doors and bolts and bars in place. He also repaired the wall of the Pool of Siloam, by the King's Garden, as far as the steps going down from the City of David. Beyond him, Nehemiah son of Azbuk, ruler of a half-district of Beth Zur, made repairs up to a point opposite the tombs of David, as far as the artificial pool and the House of the Heroes.

Next to him, the repairs were made by the Levites under Rehum son of Bani. Beside him, Hashabiah, ruler of half the district of Keilah, carried out repairs for his district. Next to him, the repairs were made by their fellow Levites under Binnui son of Henadad, ruler of the other half-district of Keilah. Next to him, Ezer son of Jeshua, ruler of Mizpah, repaired another section, from a point facing the ascent to the armory as far as the angle of the wall. Next to him, Baruch son of Zabbai zealously repaired another section, from the ar 'e to the entrance of the house of Eliashib the high priest. Nex o him, Meremoth son of Uriah, the son of Hakkoz, repaired another section, from the entrance of Eliashib's house to the end of it.

The repairs next to him were made by the priests from the surrounding region. Beyond them, Benjamin and Hasshub made repairs in front of their house; and next to them, Azariah son of Maaseiah, the son of Ananiah, made repairs beside his house. Next to him, Binnui son of Henadad repaired another section, from Azariah's house to the angle and the corner, and Palal son of Uzai worked opposite the angle and the tower projecting from the upper palace near the court of the guard. Next to him, Pedaiah son of Parosh and the temple servants living on the hill of Ophel made repairs up to a point opposite the Water Gate toward the east and the projecting tower. Next to them, the men of Tekoa repaired another section, from the great projecting tower to the wall of Ophel.

Above the Horse Gate, the priests made repairs, each in front of his own house. Next to them, Zadok son of Immer made repairs opposite his house. Next to him, Shemaiah son of Shekaniah, the guard at the East Gate, made repairs. Next to him, Hananiah son of Shelemiah, and Hanun, the sixth son of Zalaph, repaired another section. Next to them, Meshullam son of Berekiah made repairs opposite his living quarters. Next to him, Malkijah, one of the gold-smiths, made repairs as far as the house of the temple servants and the merchants, opposite the Inspection Gate, and as far as the room above the corner; and between the room above the corner and the Sheep Gate the goldsmiths and merchants made repairs.

When Sanballat heard that we were rebuilding the wall, he be-came angry and was greatly incensed. He ridiculed the Jews, and in the presence of his associates and the army of Samaria, he said, "What are those feeble Jews doing? Will they restore their wall? Will they offer sacrifices? Will they finish in a day? Can they bring the stones back to life from those heaps of rubble—burned as they are?"

Tobiah the Ammonite, who was at his side, said, "What they are building—even a fox climbing up on it would break down their wall of stones!"

Hear us, our God, for we are despised. Turn their insults back on their own heads. Give them over as plunder in a land of captivity. Do not cover up their guilt or blot out their sins from your sight, for they have thrown insults in the face of the builders.

So we rebuilt the wall till all of it reached half its height, for the people worked with all their heart.

But when Sanballat, Tobiah, the Arabs, the Ammonites and the people of Ashdod heard that the repairs to Jerusalem's walls had gone ahead and that the gaps were being closed, they were very an-gry. They all plotted together to come and fight against Jerusalem and stir up trouble against it. But we prayed to our God and posted a guard day and night to meet this threat.

Meanwhile, the people in Judah said, "The strength of the la-borers is giving out, and there is so much rubble that we cannot rebuild the wall."

Also our enemies said, "Before they know it or see us, we will be right there among them and will kill them and put an end to the work."

Then the Jews who lived near them came and told us ten times over, "Wherever you turn, they will attack us."

Therefore I stationed some of the people behind the lowest points of the wall at the exposed places, posting them by families, with their swords, spears and bows. After I looked things over, I stood up and said to the nobles, the officials and the rest of the peo-ple, "Don't be afraid of them. Remember the Lord, who is great and awesome, and fight for your families, your sons and your daughters, your wives and your homes."

When our enemies heard that we were aware of their plot and

that God had frustrated it, we all returned to the wall, each to our own work.

From that day on, half of my men did the work, while the other half were equipped with spears, shields, bows and armor. The officers posted themselves behind all the people of Judah who were building the wall. Those who carried materials did their work with one hand and held a weapon in the other, and each of the builders wore his sword at his side as he worked. But the man who sounded the trumpet stayed with me.

Then I said to the nobles, the officials and the rest of the people, "The work is extensive and spread out, and we are widely separated from each other along the wall. Wherever you hear the sound of the trumpet, join us there. Our God will fight for us!"

So we continued the work with half the men holding spears, from the first light of dawn till the stars came out. At that time I also said to the people, "Have every man and his helper stay inside Jerusalem at night, so they can serve us as guards by night and as workers by day." Neither I nor my brothers nor my men nor the guards with me took off our clothes; each had his weapon, even when he went for water.

Now the men and their wives raised a great outcry against their fellow Jews. Some were saying, "We and our sons and daughters are numerous; in order for us to eat and stay alive, we must get grain."

Others were saying, "We are mortgaging our fields, our vineyards and our homes to get grain during the famine."

Still others were saying, "We have had to borrow money to pay the king's tax on our fields and vineyards. Although we are of the same flesh and blood as our fellow Jews and though our children are as good as theirs, yet we have to subject our sons and daughters to slavery. Some of our daughters have already been enslaved, but we are powerless, because our fields and our vineyards belong to others."

When I heard their outcry and these charges, I was very angry. I pondered them in my mind and then accused the nobles and officials. I told them, "You are charging your own people interest!" So I called together a large meeting to deal with them and said: "As far as possible, we have bought back our fellow Jews who were sold to the Gentiles. Now you are selling your own people, only for them to be sold back to us!" They kept quiet, because they could find nothing to say.

So I continued, "What you are doing is not right. Shouldn't you walk in the fear of our God to avoid the reproach of our Gentile enemies? I and my brothers and my men are also lending the people money and grain. But let us stop charging interest! Give back to them immediately their fields, vineyards, olive groves and houses, and also the interest you are charging them — one percent of the money, grain, new wine and olive oil."

"We will give it back," they said. "And we will not demand anything more from them. We will do as you say."

Then I summoned the priests and made the nobles and officials take an oath to do what they had promised. I also shook out the folds of my robe and said, "In this way may God shake out of their house and possessions anyone who does not keep this promise. So may such a person be shaken out and emptied!"

At this the whole assembly said, "Amen," and praised the LORD. And the people did as they had promised.

Moreover, from the twentieth year of King Artaxerxes, when I was appointed to be their governor in the land of Judah, until his thirty-second year — twelve years — neither I nor my brothers ate the food allotted to the governor. But the earlier governors — those preceding me — placed a heavy burden on the people and took forty shekels of silver from them in addition to food and wine. Their assistants also lorded it over the people. But out of reverence for God I did not act like that. Instead, I devoted myself to the work on this wall. All my men were assembled there for the work; we did not acquire any land.

Furthermore, a hundred and fifty Jews and officials ate at my table, as well as those who came to us from the surrounding nations. Each day one ox, six choice sheep and some poultry were prepared for me, and every ten days an abundant supply of wine of all kinds. In spite of all this, I never demanded the food allotted to the governor, because the demands were heavy on these people.

Remember me with favor, my God, for all I have done for these people.

When word came to Sanballat, Tobiah, Geshem the Arab and the rest of our enemies that I had rebuilt the wall and not a gap was left in it — though up to that time I had not set the doors in the gates — Sanballat and Geshem sent me this message: "Come, let us meet together in one of the villages on the plain of Ono."

But they were scheming to harm me; so I sent messengers to them with this reply: "I am carrying on a great project and cannot go down. Why should the work stop while I leave it and go down to you?" Four times they sent me the same message, and each time I gave them the same answer.

Then, the fifth time, Sanballat sent his aide to me with the same message, and in his hand was an unsealed letter in which was written:

"It is reported among the nations — and Geshem says it is true — that you and the Jews are plotting to revolt, and therefore you are building the wall. Moreover, according to these reports you are about to become their king and have even appointed prophets to make this proclamation about you in Jerusalem: 'There is a king in Judah!' Now this report will get back to the king; so come, let us meet together."

I sent him this reply: "Nothing like what you are saying is happening; you are just making it up out of your head."

They were all trying to frighten us, thinking, "Their hands will get too weak for the work, and it will not be completed."

But I prayed, "Now strengthen my hands."

One day I went to the house of Shemaiah son of Delaiah, the son of Mehetabel, who was shut in at his home. He said, "Let us meet in the house of God, inside the temple, and let us close the temple doors, because men are coming to kill you — by night they are coming to kill you."

But I said, "Should a man like me run away? Or should someone like me go into the temple to save his life? I will not go!" I realized that God had not sent him, but that he had prophesied against me because Tobiah and Sanballat had hired him. He had been hired to intimidate me so that I would commit a sin by doing this, and then they would give me a bad name to discredit me.

Remember Tobiah and Sanballat, my God, because of what they have done; remember also the prophet Noadiah and how she and the rest of the prophets have been trying to intimidate me. So the wall was completed on the twenty-fifth of Elul, in fifty-two days.

When all our enemies heard about this, all the surrounding nations were afraid and lost their self-confidence, because they realized that this work had been done with the help of our God.

Also, in those days the nobles of Judah were sending many letters to Tobiah, and replies from Tobiah kept coming to them. For many in Judah were under oath to him, since he was son-in-law to Shekaniah son of Arah, and his son Jehohanan had married the daughter of Meshullam son of Berekiah. Moreover, they kept reporting to me his good deeds and then telling him what I said. And Tobiah sent letters to intimidate me.

After the wall had been rebuilt and I had set the doors in place, the gatekeepers, the musicians and the Levites were appointed. I put in charge of Jerusalem my brother Hanani, along with Hananiah the commander of the citadel, because he was a man of integrity and feared God more than most people do. I said to them, "The gates of Jerusalem are not to be opened until the sun is hot. While the gatekeepers are still on duty, have them shut the doors and bar them. Also appoint residents of Jerusalem as guards, some at their posts and some near their own houses."

Now the city was large and spacious, but there were few people in it, and the houses had not yet been rebuilt. So my God put it into my heart to assemble the nobles, the officials and the common people for registration by families. I found the genealogical record of those who had been the first to return. This is what I found written there:

These are the people of the province who came up from the captivity of the exiles whom Nebuchadnezzar king of Babylon had taken captive (they returned to Jerusalem and Judah, each to his own town, in company with Zerubbabel, Joshua, Nehemiah, Azariah, Raamiah, Nahamani, Mordecai, Bilshan, Mispereth, Bigvai, Nehum and Baanah):

The list of the men of Israel:

the descendants of Parosh	2,172
of Shephatiah	372
of Arah	652
of Pahath-Moab (through the line of Jeshua and Joab)	2,818
of Elam	1,254
of Zattu	845
of Zakkai	760
of Binnui	648
of Bebai	628
of Azgad	2,322
of Adonikam	667
of Bigvai	2,067
of Adin	655
of Ater (through Hezekiah)	98
of Hashum	328
of Bezai	324
of Hariph	112
of Gibeon	95
the men of Bethlehem and Netophah	188
of Anathoth	128
of Beth Azmaveth	42
of Kiriath Jearim, Kephirah and Beeroth	743
of Ramah and Geba	621
of Mikmash	122

of Bethel and Ai	123
of the other Nebo	52
of the other Elam	1,254
of Harim	320
of Jericho	345
of Lod, Hadid and Ono	721
of Senaah	3,930

The priests:

the descendants of Jedaiah (through the family of Jeshua)	973
of Immer	1,052
of Pashhur	1,247
of Harim	1,017

The Levites:

the descendants of Jeshua (through Kadmiel through the line of Hodaviah)	74

The musicians:

the descendants of Asaph	148

The gatekeepers:

the descendants of Shallum, Ater, Talmon, Akkub, Hatita and Shobai	138

The temple servants:

the descendants of
Ziha, Hasupha, Tabbaoth,
Keros, Sia, Padon,
Lebana, Hagaba, Shalmai,
Hanan, Giddel, Gahar,
Reaiah, Rezin, Nekoda,
Gazzam, Uzza, Paseah,
Besai, Meunim, Nephusim,
Bakbuk, Hakupha, Harhur,
Bazluth, Mehida, Harsha,
Barkos, Sisera, Temah,
Neziah and Hatipha

The descendants of the servants of Solomon:

the descendants of
Sotai, Sophereth, Perida,
Jaala, Darkon, Giddel,

Shephatiah, Hattil,
Pokereth-Hazzebaim and Amon

The temple servants and the descendants
of the servants of Solomon   392

The following came up from the towns of Tel Melah, Tel Harsha, Kerub, Addon and Immer, but they could not show that their families were descended from Israel:

the descendants of
Delaiah, Tobiah and Nekoda   642

And from among the priests:

the descendants of
Hobaiah, Hakkoz and Barzillai (a man who had married
a daughter of Barzillai the Gileadite and was called by
that name).

These searched for their family records, but they could not find them and so were excluded from the priesthood as unclean. The governor, therefore, ordered them not to eat any of the most sacred food until there should be a priest ministering with the Urim and Thummim.

The whole company numbered 42,360, besides their 7,337 male and female slaves; and they also had 245 male and female singers. There were 736 horses, 245 mules, 435 camels and 6,720 donkeys.

Some of the heads of the families contributed to the work. The governor gave to the treasury 1,000 darics of gold, 50 bowls and 530 garments for priests. Some of the heads of the families gave to the treasury for the work 20,000 darics of gold and 2,200 minas of silver. The total given by the rest of the people was 20,000 darics of gold, 2,000 minas of silver and 67 garments for priests.

The priests, the Levites, the gatekeepers, the musicians and the temple servants, along with certain of the people and the rest of the Israelites, settled in their own towns.

W hen the seventh month came and the Israelites had settled in their towns, all the people came together as one in the square before the Water Gate. They told Ezra the teacher of the Law to bring out the Book of the Law of Moses, which the LORD had commanded for Israel.

So on the first day of the seventh month Ezra the priest brought the Law before the assembly, which was made up of men and women and all who were able to understand. He read it aloud from daybreak till noon as he faced the square before the Water Gate in the presence of the men, women and others who could understand. And all the people listened attentively to the Book of the Law.

Ezra the teacher of the Law stood on a high wooden platform built for the occasion. Beside him on his right stood Mattithiah, Shema, Anaiah, Uriah, Hilkiah and Maaseiah; and on his left were Pedaiah, Mishael, Malkijah, Hashum, Hashbaddanah, Zechariah and Meshullam.

Ezra opened the book. All the people could see him because he was standing above them; and as he opened it, the people all stood up. Ezra praised the Lord, the great God; and all the people lifted their hands and responded, "Amen! Amen!" Then they bowed down and worshiped the Lord with their faces to the ground.

The Levites — Jeshua, Bani, Sherebiah, Jamin, Akkub, Shabbethai, Hodiah, Maaseiah, Kelita, Azariah, Jozabad, Hanan and Pelaiah — instructed the people in the Law while the people were standing there. They read from the Book of the Law of God, making it clear and giving the meaning so that the people understood what was being read.

Then Nehemiah the governor, Ezra the priest and teacher of the Law, and the Levites who were instructing the people said to them all, "This day is holy to the Lord your God. Do not mourn or weep." For all the people had been weeping as they listened to the words of the Law.

Nehemiah said, "Go and enjoy choice food and sweet drinks, and send some to those who have nothing prepared. This day is holy to our Lord. Do not grieve, for the joy of the Lord is your strength."

The Levites calmed all the people, saying, "Be still, for this is a holy day. Do not grieve."

Then all the people went away to eat and drink, to send portions of food and to celebrate with great joy, because they now understood the words that had been made known to them.

On the second day of the month, the heads of all the families, along with the priests and the Levites, gathered around Ezra the teacher to give attention to the words of the Law. They found written in the Law, which the Lord had commanded through Moses, that the Israelites were to live in temporary shelters during the festival of the seventh month and that they should proclaim this word and spread it throughout their towns and in Jerusalem: "Go out into the hill country and bring back branches from olive and wild olive trees, and from myrtles, palms and shade trees, to make temporary shelters" — as it is written.

So the people went out and brought back branches and built

themselves temporary shelters on their own roofs, in their courtyards, in the courts of the house of God and in the square by the
Water Gate and the one by the Gate of Ephraim. The whole company that had returned from exile built temporary shelters and
lived in them. From the days of Joshua son of Nun until that day,
the Israelites had not celebrated it like this. And their joy was very
great.

Day after day, from the first day to the last, Ezra read from the
Book of the Law of God. They celebrated the festival for seven days,
and on the eighth day, in accordance with the regulation, there was
an assembly.

On the twenty-fourth day of the same month, the Israelites gathered together, fasting and wearing sackcloth and putting dust on
their heads. Those of Israelite descent had separated themselves
from all foreigners. They stood in their places and confessed their
sins and the sins of their ancestors. They stood where they were
and read from the Book of the Law of the LORD their God for a quarter of the day, and spent another quarter in confession and in worshiping the LORD their God. Standing on the stairs of the Levites
were Jeshua, Bani, Kadmiel, Shebaniah, Bunni, Sherebiah, Bani and
Kenani. They cried out with loud voices to the LORD their God. And
the Levites — Jeshua, Kadmiel, Bani, Hashabneiah, Sherebiah, Hodiah, Shebaniah and Pethahiah — said: "Stand up and praise the
LORD your God, who is from everlasting to everlasting."

"Blessed be your glorious name, and may it be exalted above
all blessing and praise. You alone are the LORD. You made the
heavens, even the highest heavens, and all their starry host,
the earth and all that is on it, the seas and all that is in them.
You give life to everything, and the multitudes of heaven worship you.

"You are the LORD God, who chose Abram and brought him
out of Ur of the Chaldeans and named him Abraham. You
found his heart faithful to you, and you made a covenant with
him to give to his descendants the land of the Canaanites, Hittites, Amorites, Perizzites, Jebusites and Girgashites. You have
kept your promise because you are righteous.

"You saw the suffering of our ancestors in Egypt; you heard
their cry at the Red Sea. You sent signs and wonders against
Pharaoh, against all his officials and all the people of his land,
for you knew how arrogantly the Egyptians treated them. You
made a name for yourself, which remains to this day. You divided the sea before them, so that they passed through it on
dry ground, but you hurled their pursuers into the depths, like

a stone into mighty waters. By day you led them with a pillar of cloud, and by night with a pillar of fire to give them light on the way they were to take.

"You came down on Mount Sinai; you spoke to them from heaven. You gave them regulations and laws that are just and right, and decrees and commands that are good. You made known to them your holy Sabbath and gave them commands, decrees and laws through your servant Moses. In their hunger you gave them bread from heaven and in their thirst you brought them water from the rock; you told them to go in and take possession of the land you had sworn with uplifted hand to give them.

"But they, our ancestors, became arrogant and stiff-necked, and they did not obey your commands. They refused to listen and failed to remember the miracles you performed among them. They became stiff-necked and in their rebellion appointed a leader in order to return to their slavery. But you are a forgiving God, gracious and compassionate, slow to anger and abounding in love. Therefore you did not desert them, even when they cast for themselves an image of a calf and said, 'This is your god, who brought you up out of Egypt,' or when they committed awful blasphemies.

"Because of your great compassion you did not abandon them in the wilderness. By day the pillar of cloud did not fail to guide them on their path, nor the pillar of fire by night to shine on the way they were to take. You gave your good Spirit to instruct them. You did not withhold your manna from their mouths, and you gave them water for their thirst. For forty years you sustained them in the wilderness; they lacked nothing, their clothes did not wear out nor did their feet become swollen.

"You gave them kingdoms and nations, allotting to them even the remotest frontiers. They took over the country of Sihon king of Heshbon and the country of Og king of Bashan. You made their children as numerous as the stars in the sky, and you brought them into the land that you told their parents to enter and possess. Their children went in and took possession of the land. You subdued before them the Canaanites, who lived in the land; you gave the Canaanites into their hands, along with their kings and the peoples of the land, to deal with them as they pleased. They captured fortified cities and fertile land; they took possession of houses filled with all kinds of good things, wells already dug, vineyards, olive groves and fruit trees in abundance. They ate to the full and were well-nourished; they reveled in your great goodness.

"But they were disobedient and rebelled against you; they

turned their backs on your law. They killed your prophets, who had warned them in order to turn them back to you; they committed awful blasphemies. So you delivered them into the hands of their enemies, who oppressed them. But when they were oppressed they cried out to you. From heaven you heard them, and in your great compassion you gave them deliverers, who rescued them from the hand of their enemies.

"But as soon as they were at rest, they again did what was evil in your sight. Then you abandoned them to the hand of their enemies so that they ruled over them. And when they cried out to you again, you heard from heaven, and in your compassion you delivered them time after time.

"You warned them in order to turn them back to your law, but they became arrogant and disobeyed your commands. They sinned against your ordinances, of which you said, 'The person who obeys them will live by them.' Stubbornly they turned their backs on you, became stiff-necked and refused to listen. For many years you were patient with them. By your Spirit you warned them through your prophets. Yet they paid no attention, so you gave them into the hands of the neighboring peoples. But in your great mercy you did not put an end to them or abandon them, for you are a gracious and merciful God.

"Now therefore, our God, the great God, mighty and awesome, who keeps his covenant of love, do not let all this hardship seem trifling in your eyes — the hardship that has come on us, on our kings and leaders, on our priests and prophets, on our ancestors and all your people, from the days of the kings of Assyria until today. In all that has happened to us, you have remained righteous; you have acted faithfully, while we acted wickedly. Our kings, our leaders, our priests and our ancestors did not follow your law; they did not pay attention to your commands or the statutes you warned them to keep. Even while they were in their kingdom, enjoying your great goodness to them in the spacious and fertile land you gave them, they did not serve you or turn from their evil ways.

"But see, we are slaves today, slaves in the land you gave our ancestors so they could eat its fruit and the other good things it produces. Because of our sins, its abundant harvest goes to the kings you have placed over us. They rule over our bodies and our cattle as they please. We are in great distress.

"In view of all this, we are making a binding agreement, putting it in writing, and our leaders, our Levites and our priests are affixing their seals to it."

Those who sealed it were:

Nehemiah the governor, the son of Hakaliah.

Zedekiah, Seraiah, Azariah, Jeremiah,
Pashhur, Amariah, Malkijah,
Hattush, Shebaniah, Malluk,
Harim, Meremoth, Obadiah,
Daniel, Ginnethon, Baruch,
Meshullam, Abijah, Mijamin,
Maaziah, Bilgai and Shemaiah.
These were the priests.

The Levites:

Jeshua son of Azaniah, Binnui of the sons of Henadad, Kadmiel,
and their associates: Shebaniah,
Hodiah, Kelita, Pelaiah, Hanan,
Mika, Rehob, Hashabiah,
Zakkur, Sherebiah, Shebaniah,
Hodiah, Bani and Beninu.

The leaders of the people:

Parosh, Pahath-Moab, Elam, Zattu, Bani,
Bunni, Azgad, Bebai,
Adonijah, Bigvai, Adin,
Ater, Hezekiah, Azzur,
Hodiah, Hashum, Bezai,
Hariph, Anathoth, Nebai,
Magpiash, Meshullam, Hezir,
Meshezabel, Zadok, Jaddua,
Pelatiah, Hanan, Anaiah,
Hoshea, Hananiah, Hasshub,
Hallohesh, Pilha, Shobek,
Rehum, Hashabnah, Maaseiah,
Ahiah, Hanan, Anan,
Malluk, Harim and Baanah.

"The rest of the people — priests, Levites, gatekeepers, musicians, temple servants and all who separated themselves from the neighboring peoples for the sake of the Law of God, together with their wives and all their sons and daughters who are able to understand — all these now join their fellow Israelites the nobles, and bind themselves with a curse and an oath to follow the Law of God given through Moses the servant of God and to obey carefully all the commands, regulations and decrees of the LORD our Lord.

"We promise not to give our daughters in marriage to the peoples around us or take their daughters for our sons.

"When the neighboring peoples bring merchandise or grain to sell on the Sabbath, we will not buy from them on the Sabbath or on any holy day. Every seventh year we will forgo working the land and will cancel all debts.

"We assume the responsibility for carrying out the commands to give a third of a shekel each year for the service of the house of our God: for the bread set out on the table; for the regular grain offerings and burnt offerings; for the offerings on the Sabbaths, at the New Moon feasts and at the appointed festivals; for the holy offerings; for sin offerings to make atonement for Israel; and for all the duties of the house of our God.

"We—the priests, the Levites and the people—have cast lots to determine when each of our families is to bring to the house of our God at set times each year a contribution of wood to burn on the altar of the Lord our God, as it is written in the Law.

"We also assume responsibility for bringing to the house of the Lord each year the firstfruits of our crops and of every fruit tree.

"As it is also written in the Law, we will bring the firstborn of our sons and of our cattle, of our herds and of our flocks to the house of our God, to the priests ministering there.

"Moreover, we will bring to the storerooms of the house of our God, to the priests, the first of our ground meal, of our grain offerings, of the fruit of all our trees and of our new wine and olive oil. And we will bring a tithe of our crops to the Levites, for it is the Levites who collect the tithes in all the towns where we work. A priest descended from Aaron is to accompany the Levites when they receive the tithes, and the Levites are to bring a tenth of the tithes up to the house of our God, to the storerooms of the treasury. The people of Israel, including the Levites, are to bring their contributions of grain, new wine and olive oil to the storerooms, where the articles for the sanctuary and for the ministering priests, the gatekeepers and the musicians are also kept.

"We will not neglect the house of our God."

Now the leaders of the people settled in Jerusalem. The rest of the people cast lots to bring one out of every ten of them to live in Jerusalem, the holy city, while the remaining nine were to stay in their own towns. The people commended all who volunteered to live in Jerusalem.

These are the provincial leaders who settled in Jerusalem (now some Israelites, priests, Levites, temple servants and descendants of Solomon's servants lived in the towns of Judah, each on their own property in the various towns, while other people from both Judah and Benjamin lived in Jerusalem):

From the descendants of Judah:

Athaiah son of Uzziah, the son of Zechariah, the son of Amariah, the son of Shephatiah, the son of Mahalalel, a descendant of Perez; and Maaseiah son of Baruch, the son of Kol-Hozeh, the son of Hazaiah, the son of Adaiah, the son of Joiarib, the son of Zechariah, a descendant of Shelah. The descendants of Perez who lived in Jerusalem totaled 468 men of standing.

From the descendants of Benjamin:

Sallu son of Meshullam, the son of Joed, the son of Pedaiah, the son of Kolaiah, the son of Maaseiah, the son of Ithiel, the son of Jeshaiah, and his followers, Gabbai and Sallai — 928 men. Joel son of Zikri was their chief officer, and Judah son of Hassenuah was over the New Quarter of the city.

From the priests:

Jedaiah; the son of Joiarib; Jakin; Seraiah son of Hilkiah, the son of Meshullam, the son of Zadok, the son of Meraioth, the son of Ahitub, the official in charge of the house of God, and their associates, who carried on work for the temple — 822 men; Adaiah son of Jeroham, the son of Pelaliah, the son of Amzi, the son of Zechariah, the son of Pashhur, the son of Malkijah, and his associates, who were heads of families — 242 men; Amashsai son of Azarel, the son of Ahzai, the son of Meshillemoth, the son of Immer, and his associates, who were men of standing — 128. Their chief officer was Zabdiel son of Haggedolim.

From the Levites:

Shemaiah son of Hasshub, the son of Azrikam, the son of Hashabiah, the son of Bunni; Shabbethai and Jozabad, two of the heads of the Levites, who had charge of the outside work of the house of God; Mattaniah son of Mika, the son of Zabdi, the son of Asaph, the director who led in thanksgiving and prayer; Bakbukiah, second among his associates; and Abda son of Shammua, the son of Galal, the son of Jeduthun. The Levites in the holy city totaled 284.

The gatekeepers:

Akkub, Talmon and their associates, who kept watch at the gates — 172 men.

The rest of the Israelites, with the priests and Levites, were in all the towns of Judah, each on their ancestral property.

The temple servants lived on the hill of Ophel, and Ziha and Gishpa were in charge of them.

The chief officer of the Levites in Jerusalem was Uzzi son of Bani, the son of Hashabiah, the son of Mattaniah, the son of Mika. Uzzi was one of Asaph's descendants, who were the musicians responsible for the service of the house of God. The musicians were under the king's orders, which regulated their daily activity.

Pethahiah son of Meshezabel, one of the descendants of Zerah son of Judah, was the king's agent in all affairs relating to the people.

As for the villages with their fields, some of the people of Judah lived in Kiriath Arba and its surrounding settlements, in Dibon and its settlements, in Jekabzeel and its villages, in Jeshua, in Moladah, in Beth Pelet, in Hazar Shual, in Beersheba and its settlements, in Ziklag, in Mekonah and its settlements, in En Rimmon, in Zorah, in Jarmuth, Zanoah, Adullam and their villages, in Lachish and its fields, and in Azekah and its settlements. So they were living all the way from Beersheba to the Valley of Hinnom.

The descendants of the Benjamites from Geba lived in Mikmash, Aija, Bethel and its settlements, in Anathoth, Nob and Ananiah, in Hazor, Ramah and Gittaim, in Hadid, Zeboim and Neballat, in Lod and Ono, and in Ge Harashim.

Some of the divisions of the Levites of Judah settled in Benjamin.

These were the priests and Levites who returned with Zerubbabel son of Shealtiel and with Joshua:
Seraiah, Jeremiah, Ezra,
Amariah, Malluk, Hattush,
Shekaniah, Rehum, Meremoth,
Iddo, Ginnethon, Abijah,
Mijamin, Moadiah, Bilgah,
Shemaiah, Joiarib, Jedaiah,
Sallu, Amok, Hilkiah and Jedaiah.
These were the leaders of the priests and their associates in the days of Joshua.

The Levites were Jeshua, Binnui, Kadmiel, Sherebiah, Judah, and also Mattaniah, who, together with his associates, was in charge of the songs of thanksgiving. Bakbukiah and Unni, their associates, stood opposite them in the services.

Joshua was the father of Joiakim, Joiakim the father of Eliashib, Eliashib the father of Joiada, Joiada the father of Jonathan, and Jonathan the father of Jaddua.

In the days of Joiakim, these were the heads of the priestly families:

of Seraiah's family, Meraiah;

of Jeremiah's, Hananiah;

of Ezra's, Meshullam;

of Amariah's, Jehohanan;

of Malluk's, Jonathan;

of Shekaniah's, Joseph;

of Harim's, Adna;

of Meremoth's, Helkai;

of Iddo's, Zechariah;

of Ginnethon's, Meshullam;

of Abijah's, Zikri;

of Miniamin's and of Moadiah's, Piltai;

of Bilgah's, Shammua;

of Shemaiah's, Jehonathan;

of Joiarib's, Mattenai;

of Jedaiah's, Uzzi;

of Sallu's, Kallai;

of Amok's, Eber;

of Hilkiah's, Hashabiah;

of Jedaiah's, Nethanel.

The family heads of the Levites in the days of Eliashib, Joiada, Johanan and Jaddua, as well as those of the priests, were recorded in the reign of Darius the Persian. The family heads among the descendants of Levi up to the time of Johanan son of Eliashib were recorded in the book of the annals. And the leaders of the Levites were Hashabiah, Sherebiah, Jeshua son of Kadmiel, and their associates, who stood opposite them to give praise and thanksgiving, one section responding to the other, as prescribed by David the man of God.

Mattaniah, Bakbukiah, Obadiah, Meshullam, Talmon and Akkub were gatekeepers who guarded the storerooms at the gates. They served in the days of Joiakim son of Joshua, the son of Jozadak, and in the days of Nehemiah the governor and of Ezra the priest, the teacher of the Law.

A t the dedication of the wall of Jerusalem, the Levites were sought out from where they lived and were brought to Jerusalem to celebrate joyfully the dedication with songs of thanksgiving and with the music of cymbals, harps and lyres. The musicians also were brought together from the region around Jerusalem — from the villages of the Netophathites, from Beth Gilgal, and from the area of Geba and Azmaveth, for the musicians had built villages for themselves around Jerusalem. When the priests and Levites had purified themselves ceremonially, they purified the people, the gates and the wall.

I had the leaders of Judah go up on top of the wall. I also assigned two large choirs to give thanks. One was to proceed on top of the wall to the right, toward the Dung Gate. Hoshaiah and half the leaders of Judah followed them, along with Azariah, Ezra, Meshullam, Judah, Benjamin, Shemaiah, Jeremiah, as well as some priests with trumpets, and also Zechariah son of Jonathan, the son of Shemaiah, the son of Mattaniah, the son of Micaiah, the son of Zakkur, the son of Asaph, and his associates — Shemaiah, Azarel, Milalai, Gilalai, Maai, Nethanel, Judah and Hanani — with musical instruments prescribed by David the man of God. Ezra the teacher of the Law led the procession. At the Fountain Gate they continued directly up the steps of the City of David on the ascent to the wall and passed above the site of David's palace to the Water Gate on the east.

The second choir proceeded in the opposite direction. I followed them on top of the wall, together with half the people — past the Tower of the Ovens to the Broad Wall, over the Gate of Ephraim, the Jeshanah Gate, the Fish Gate, the Tower of Hananel and the Tower of the Hundred, as far as the Sheep Gate. At the Gate of the Guard they stopped.

The two choirs that gave thanks then took their places in the house of God; so did I, together with half the officials, as well as the priests — Eliakim, Maaseiah, Miniamin, Micaiah, Elioenai, Zechariah and Hananiah with their trumpets — and also Maaseiah, Shemaiah, Eleazar, Uzzi, Jehohanan, Malkijah, Elam and Ezer. The choirs sang under the direction of Jezrahiah. And on that day they offered great sacrifices, rejoicing because God had given them great joy. The women and children also rejoiced. The sound of rejoicing in Jerusalem could be heard far away.

At that time men were appointed to be in charge of the storerooms for the contributions, firstfruits and tithes. From the fields around the towns they were to bring into the storerooms the portions required by the Law for the priests and the Levites, for Judah was pleased with the ministering priests and Levites. They performed the service of their God and the service of purification, as did also the musicians and gatekeepers, according to the commands of David and his son Solomon. For long ago, in the days of David and Asaph, there had been directors for the musicians and for the songs of praise and thanksgiving to God. So in the days of Zerubbabel and of Nehemiah, all Israel contributed the daily portions for the musicians and the gatekeepers. They also set aside the portion for the other Levites, and the Levites set aside the portion for the descendants of Aaron.

On that day the Book of Moses was read aloud in the hearing of the people and there it was found written that no Ammonite or Moabite should ever be admitted into the assembly of God, because they had not met the Israelites with food and water but had hired Balaam to call a curse down on them. (Our God, however, turned the curse into a blessing.) When the people heard this law, they excluded from Israel all who were of foreign descent.

Before this, Eliashib the priest had been put in charge of the storerooms of the house of our God. He was closely associated with Tobiah, and he had provided him with a large room formerly used to store the grain offerings and incense and temple articles, and also the tithes of grain, new wine and olive oil prescribed for the Levites, musicians and gatekeepers, as well as the contributions for the priests.

But while all this was going on, I was not in Jerusalem, for in the thirty-second year of Artaxerxes king of Babylon I had returned to the king. Some time later I asked his permission and came back to Jerusalem. Here I learned about the evil thing Eliashib had done in providing Tobiah a room in the courts of the house of God. I was greatly displeased and threw all Tobiah's household goods out of the room. I gave orders to purify the rooms, and then I put back into them the equipment of the house of God, with the grain offerings and the incense.

I also learned that the portions assigned to the Levites had not been given to them, and that all the Levites and musicians responsible for the service had gone back to their own fields. So I rebuked the officials and asked them, "Why is the house of God neglected?" Then I called them together and stationed them at their posts.

All Judah brought the tithes of grain, new wine and olive oil into the storerooms. I put Shelemiah the priest, Zadok the scribe, and a Levite named Pedaiah in charge of the storerooms and made Hanan son of Zakkur, the son of Mattaniah, their assistant, because they were considered trustworthy. They were made responsible for distributing the supplies to their fellow Levites.

Remember me for this, my God, and do not blot out what I have so faithfully done for the house of my God and its services.

In those days I saw people in Judah treading winepresses on the Sabbath and bringing in grain and loading it on donkeys, together with wine, grapes, figs and all other kinds of loads. And they were bringing all this into Jerusalem on the Sabbath. Therefore I warned them against selling food on that day. People from Tyre who lived in Jerusalem were bringing in fish and all kinds of merchandise and selling them in Jerusalem on the Sabbath to the people of Judah. I rebuked the nobles of Judah and said to them, "What is this wicked thing you are doing — desecrating the Sabbath day? Didn't your ancestors do the same things, so that our God brought all this calamity on us and on this city? Now you are stirring up more wrath against Israel by desecrating the Sabbath."

When evening shadows fell on the gates of Jerusalem before the Sabbath, I ordered the doors to be shut and not opened until the Sabbath was over. I stationed some of my own men at the gates so that no load could be brought in on the Sabbath day. Once or twice the merchants and sellers of all kinds of goods spent the night outside Jerusalem. But I warned them and said, "Why do you spend the night by the wall? If you do this again, I will arrest you." From that time on they no longer came on the Sabbath. Then I commanded the Levites to purify themselves and go and guard the gates in order to keep the Sabbath day holy.

Remember me for this also, my God, and show mercy to me according to your great love.

Moreover, in those days I saw men of Judah who had married women from Ashdod, Ammon and Moab. Half of their children spoke the language of Ashdod or the language of one of the other peoples, and did not know how to speak the language of Judah. I rebuked them and called curses down on them. I beat some of the men and pulled out their hair. I made them take an oath in God's name and said: "You are not to give your daughters in marriage to their sons, nor are you to take their daughters in marriage for your sons or for yourselves. Was it not because of marriages like these that Solomon king of Israel sinned? Among the many nations there was no king like him. He was loved by his God, and God made him king over all Israel, but even he was led into sin by foreign women. Must we hear now that you too are doing all this terrible wickedness and are being unfaithful to our God by marrying foreign women?"

One of the sons of Joiada son of Eliashib the high priest was son-in-law to Sanballat the Horonite. And I drove him away from me.

Remember them, my God, because they defiled the priestly office and the covenant of the priesthood and of the Levites.

So I purified the priests and the Levites of everything foreign, and assigned them duties, each to his own task. I also made provision for contributions of wood at designated times, and for the firstfruits.

Remember me with favor, my God.

INVITATION TO
ESTHER

Chronicles–Ezra–Nehemiah insisted that it was vital for the Jews, as a people subject to other nations, to preserve their distinctness by maintaining the purity of their worship. This included observing their annual religious festivals at precisely those times and in precisely those ways commanded by the law of Moses. But in the Persian period, the Jews began celebrating an extra festival. This new holiday, Purim, didn't even have a Hebrew name. And it was observed on one day in the countryside, and on the following day in the cities. Could such a festival really be added safely to the sacred calendar? The book of Esther explains why it could be, and indeed should be. The law of Moses described God's mighty acts of deliverance that lay behind holidays such as Passover and Tabernacles. The book of Esther details how God intervened in the Persian period to save all the Jews in the empire. This great rescue was commemorated in the feast of Purim.

The book of Esther is a fast-moving narrative of events that occurred during the reign of a Persian king, Xerxes (most likely Xerxes I, 486–465 BC). It relates the intrigues and adventures that took place in his court when a Jewish exile named Esther and her cousin and guardian Mordecai worked to rescue their people from a plot to destroy them. (The book may be based in large part on an account by Mordecai, who *recorded these events*.) As it tells its story, the book also explains why the festival took its name from a Persian word, *pur*, meaning a lot that's cast in decision-making. While the story never mentions God by name, God's providential hand can constantly be detected just beneath the surface, in the timing and combination of events as they unfold.

The book features numerous banquets, including two hosted by Xerxes at the beginning, two given by Esther in the middle, and two celebrated on successive days by the grateful Jews at the end. Since its story was likely to be told to subsequent generations during the feasting of Purim itself, these banquets actually place the audience right in the middle of the action. And so those who read or hear it can not only join in celebrating God's deliverance, they can ask themselves, as Mordecai asked Esther, for what momentous purpose God may have brought them to their own position in life.

ESTHER

This is what happened during the time of Xerxes, the Xerxes who ruled over 127 provinces stretching from India to Cush: At that time King Xerxes reigned from his royal throne in the citadel of Susa, and in the third year of his reign he gave a banquet for all his nobles and officials. The military leaders of Persia and Media, the princes, and the nobles of the provinces were present.

For a full 180 days he displayed the vast wealth of his kingdom and the splendor and glory of his majesty. When these days were over, the king gave a banquet, lasting seven days, in the enclosed garden of the king's palace, for all the people from the least to the greatest who were in the citadel of Susa. The garden had hangings of white and blue linen, fastened with cords of white linen and purple material to silver rings on marble pillars. There were couches of gold and silver on a mosaic pavement of porphyry, marble, mother-of-pearl and other costly stones. Wine was served in goblets of gold, each one different from the other, and the royal wine was abundant, in keeping with the king's liberality. By the king's command each guest was allowed to drink with no restrictions, for the king instructed all the wine stewards to serve each man what he wished.

Queen Vashti also gave a banquet for the women in the royal palace of King Xerxes.

On the seventh day, when King Xerxes was in high spirits from wine, he commanded the seven eunuchs who served him — Mehuman, Biztha, Harbona, Bigtha, Abagtha, Zethar and Karkas — to bring before him Queen Vashti, wearing her royal crown, in order to display her beauty to the people and nobles, for she was lovely to look at. But when the attendants delivered the king's command, Queen Vashti refused to come. Then the king became furious and burned with anger.

Since it was customary for the king to consult experts in matters of law and justice, he spoke with the wise men who understood the times and were closest to the king — Karshena, Shethar, Admatha, Tarshish, Meres, Marsena and Memukan, the seven nobles of Persia and Media who had special access to the king and were highest in the kingdom.

"According to law, what must be done to Queen Vashti?" he asked. "She has not obeyed the command of King Xerxes that the eunuchs have taken to her."

Then Memukan replied in the presence of the king and the nobles, "Queen Vashti has done wrong, not only against the king but also against all the nobles and the peoples of all the provinces of King Xerxes. For the queen's conduct will become known to all the women, and so they will despise their husbands and say, 'King Xerxes commanded Queen Vashti to be brought before him, but she would not come.' This very day the Persian and Median women of the nobility who have heard about the queen's conduct will respond to all the king's nobles in the same way. There will be no end of disrespect and discord.

"Therefore, if it pleases the king, let him issue a royal decree and let it be written in the laws of Persia and Media, which cannot be repealed, that Vashti is never again to enter the presence of King Xerxes. Also let the king give her royal position to someone else who is better than she. Then when the king's edict is proclaimed throughout all his vast realm, all the women will respect their husbands, from the least to the greatest."

The king and his nobles were pleased with this advice, so the king did as Memukan proposed. He sent dispatches to all parts of the kingdom, to each province in its own script and to each people in their own language, proclaiming that every man should be ruler over his own household, using his native tongue.

Later when King Xerxes' fury had subsided, he remembered Vashti and what she had done and what he had decreed about her. Then the king's personal attendants proposed, "Let a search be made for beautiful young virgins for the king. Let the king appoint commissioners in every province of his realm to bring all these beautiful young women into the harem at the citadel of Susa. Let them be placed under the care of Hegai, the king's eunuch, who is in charge of the women; and let beauty treatments be given to them. Then let the young woman who pleases the king be queen instead of Vashti." This advice appealed to the king, and he followed it.

Now there was in the citadel of Susa a Jew of the tribe of Benjamin, named Mordecai son of Jair, the son of Shimei, the son of Kish, who had been carried into exile from Jerusalem by Nebuchadnezzar king of Babylon, among those taken captive with Jehoiachin king of Judah. Mordecai had a cousin named Hadassah, whom he had brought up because she had neither father nor mother. This young woman, who was also known as Esther, had a lovely figure and was beautiful. Mordecai had taken her as his own daughter when her father and mother died.

When the king's order and edict had been proclaimed, many young women were brought to the citadel of Susa and put under the care of Hegai. Esther also was taken to the king's palace and entrusted to Hegai, who had charge of the harem. She pleased him and won his favor. Immediately he provided her with her beauty treatments and special food. He assigned to her seven female attendants selected from the king's palace and moved her and her attendants into the best place in the harem.

Esther had not revealed her nationality and family background, because Mordecai had forbidden her to do so. Every day he walked back and forth near the courtyard of the harem to find out how Esther was and what was happening to her.

Before a young woman's turn came to go in to King Xerxes, she had to complete twelve months of beauty treatments prescribed for the women, six months with oil of myrrh and six with perfumes and cosmetics. And this is how she would go to the king: Anything she wanted was given her to take with her from the harem to the king's palace. In the evening she would go there and in the morning return to another part of the harem to the care of Shaashgaz, the king's eunuch who was in charge of the concubines. She would not return to the king unless he was pleased with her and summoned her by name.

When the turn came for Esther (the young woman Mordecai had adopted, the daughter of his uncle Abihail) to go to the king, she asked for nothing other than what Hegai, the king's eunuch who was in charge of the harem, suggested. And Esther won the favor of everyone who saw her. She was taken to King Xerxes in the royal residence in the tenth month, the month of Tebeth, in the seventh year of his reign.

Now the king was attracted to Esther more than to any of the other women, and she won his favor and approval more than any of the other virgins. So he set a royal crown on her head and made her queen instead of Vashti. And the king gave a great banquet, Esther's banquet, for all his nobles and officials. He proclaimed a holiday throughout the provinces and distributed gifts with royal liberality.

When the virgins were assembled a second time, Mordecai was sitting at the king's gate. But Esther had kept secret her family background and nationality just as Mordecai had told her to do, for she continued to follow Mordecai's instructions as she had done when he was bringing her up.

During the time Mordecai was sitting at the king's gate, Bigthana and Teresh, two of the king's officers who guarded the doorway, became angry and conspired to assassinate King Xerxes. But Mordecai found out about the plot and told Queen Esther, who in turn reported it to the king, giving credit to Mordecai. And when the report was investigated and found to be true, the two officials were impaled on poles. All this was recorded in the book of the annals in the presence of the king.

A fter these events, King Xerxes honored Haman son of Hammedatha, the Agagite, elevating him and giving him a seat of honor higher than that of all the other nobles. All the royal officials at the king's gate knelt down and paid honor to Haman, for the king had commanded this concerning him. But Mordecai would not kneel down or pay him honor.

Then the royal officials at the king's gate asked Mordecai, "Why do you disobey the king's command?" Day after day they spoke to him but he refused to comply. Therefore they told Haman about it to see whether Mordecai's behavior would be tolerated, for he had told them he was a Jew.

When Haman saw that Mordecai would not kneel down or pay him honor, he was enraged. Yet having learned who Mordecai's people were, he scorned the idea of killing only Mordecai. Instead Haman looked for a way to destroy all Mordecai's people, the Jews, throughout the whole kingdom of Xerxes.

In the twelfth year of King Xerxes, in the first month, the month of Nisan, the *pur* (that is, the lot) was cast in the presence of Haman to select a day and month. And the lot fell on the twelfth month, the month of Adar.

Then Haman said to King Xerxes, "There is a certain people dispersed among the peoples in all the provinces of your kingdom who keep themselves separate. Their customs are different from those of all other people, and they do not obey the king's laws; it is not in the king's best interest to tolerate them. If it pleases the king, let a decree be issued to destroy them, and I will give ten thousand talents of silver to the king's administrators for the royal treasury."

So the king took his signet ring from his finger and gave it to Haman son of Hammedatha, the Agagite, the enemy of the Jews. "Keep the money," the king said to Haman, "and do with the people as you please."

Then on the thirteenth day of the first month the royal secretaries were summoned. They wrote out in the script of each province and in the language of each people all Haman's orders to the king's satraps, the governors of the various provinces and the nobles of the various peoples. These were written in the name of King Xerxes himself and sealed with his own ring. Dispatches were sent by couriers to all the king's provinces with the order to destroy, kill and annihilate all the Jews — young and old, women and children—on a single day, the thirteenth day of the twelfth month, the month of Adar, and to plunder their goods. A copy of the text of the edict was to be issued as law in every province and made known to the people of every nationality so they would be ready for that day.

The couriers went out, spurred on by the king's command, and the edict was issued in the citadel of Susa. The king and Haman sat down to drink, but the city of Susa was bewildered.

When Mordecai learned of all that had been done, he tore his clothes, put on sackcloth and ashes, and went out into the city, wailing loudly and bitterly. But he went only as far as the king's gate, because no one clothed in sackcloth was allowed to enter it. In every province to which the edict and order of the king came, there was great mourning among the Jews, with fasting, weeping and wailing. Many lay in sackcloth and ashes.

When Esther's eunuchs and female attendants came and told her about Mordecai, she was in great distress. She sent clothes for him to put on instead of his sackcloth, but he would not accept them. Then Esther summoned Hathak, one of the king's eunuchs assigned to attend her, and ordered him to find out what was troubling Mordecai and why.

So Hathak went out to Mordecai in the open square of the city in front of the king's gate. Mordecai told him everything that had happened to him, including the exact amount of money Haman had promised to pay into the royal treasury for the destruction of the Jews. He also gave him a copy of the text of the edict for their annihilation, which had been published in Susa, to show to Esther and explain it to her, and he told him to instruct her to go into the king's presence to beg for mercy and plead with him for her people.

Hathak went back and reported to Esther what Mordecai had said. Then she instructed him to say to Mordecai, "All the king's officials and the people of the royal provinces know that for any man or woman who approaches the king in the inner court without being summoned the king has but one law: that they be put to death unless the king extends the gold scepter to them and spares their lives. But thirty days have passed since I was called to go to the king."

When Esther's words were reported to Mordecai, he sent back this answer: "Do not think that because you are in the king's house you alone of all the Jews will escape. For if you remain silent at this time, relief and deliverance for the Jews will arise from another place, but you and your father's family will perish. And who knows but that you have come to your royal position for such a time as this?"

Then Esther sent this reply to Mordecai: "Go, gather together all the Jews who are in Susa, and fast for me. Do not eat or drink for three days, night or day. I and my attendants will fast as you do. When this is done, I will go to the king, even though it is against the law. And if I perish, I perish."

So Mordecai went away and carried out all of Esther's instructions.

On the third day Esther put on her royal robes and stood in the inner court of the palace, in front of the king's hall. The king was sitting on his royal throne in the hall, facing the entrance. When he saw Queen Esther standing in the court, he was pleased with her and held out to her the gold scepter that was in his hand. So Esther approached and touched the tip of the scepter.

Then the king asked, "What is it, Queen Esther? What is your request? Even up to half the kingdom, it will be given you."

"If it pleases the king," replied Esther, "let the king, together with Haman, come today to a banquet I have prepared for him."

"Bring Haman at once," the king said, "so that we may do what Esther asks."

So the king and Haman went to the banquet Esther had prepared. As they were drinking wine, the king again asked Esther, "Now what is your petition? It will be given you. And what is your request? Even up to half the kingdom, it will be granted."

Esther replied, "My petition and my request is this: If the king regards me with favor and if it pleases the king to grant my petition and fulfill my request, let the king and Haman come tomorrow to the banquet I will prepare for them. Then I will answer the king's question."

Haman went out that day happy and in high spirits. But when he saw Mordecai at the king's gate and observed that he neither rose nor showed fear in his presence, he was filled with rage against Mordecai. Nevertheless, Haman restrained himself and went home.

Calling together his friends and Zeresh, his wife, Haman boasted to them about his vast wealth, his many sons, and all the ways the king had honored him and how he had elevated him above the other nobles and officials. "And that's not all," Haman added. "I'm the only person Queen Esther invited to accompany the king to the banquet she gave. And she has invited me along with the king tomorrow. But all this gives me no satisfaction as long as I see that Jew Mordecai sitting at the king's gate."

His wife Zeresh and all his friends said to him, "Have a pole set up, reaching to a height of fifty cubits, and ask the king in the morning to have Mordecai impaled on it. Then go with the king to the banquet and enjoy yourself." This suggestion delighted Haman, and he had the pole set up.

That night the king could not sleep; so he ordered the book of the chronicles, the record of his reign, to be brought in and read to him. It was found recorded there that Mordecai had exposed Bigthana and Teresh, two of the king's officers who guarded the doorway, who had conspired to assassinate King Xerxes.

"What honor and recognition has Mordecai received for this?" the king asked.

"Nothing has been done for him," his attendants answered.

The king said, "Who is in the court?" Now Haman had just entered the outer court of the palace to speak to the king about impaling Mordecai on the pole he had set up for him.

His attendants answered, "Haman is standing in the court."

"Bring him in," the king ordered.

When Haman entered, the king asked him, "What should be done for the man the king delights to honor?"

Now Haman thought to himself, "Who is there that the king would rather honor than me?" So he answered the king, "For the man the king delights to honor, have them bring a royal robe the king has worn and a horse the king has ridden, one with a royal crest placed on its head. Then let the robe and horse be entrusted to one of the king's most noble princes. Let them robe the man the king delights to honor, and lead him on the horse through the city streets, proclaiming before him, 'This is what is done for the man the king delights to honor!' "

"Go at once," the king commanded Haman. "Get the robe and the horse and do just as you have suggested for Mordecai the Jew, who sits at the king's gate. Do not neglect anything you have recommended."

So Haman got the robe and the horse. He robed Mordecai, and led him on horseback through the city streets, proclaiming before him, "This is what is done for the man the king delights to honor!"

Afterward Mordecai returned to the king's gate. But Haman rushed home, with his head covered in grief, and told Zeresh his wife and all his friends everything that had happened to him.

His advisers and his wife Zeresh said to him, "Since Mordecai, before whom your downfall has started, is of Jewish origin, you cannot stand against him—you will surely come to ruin!" While they were still talking with him, the king's eunuchs arrived and hurried Haman away to the banquet Esther had prepared.

So the king and Haman went to Queen Esther's banquet, and as they were drinking wine on the second day, the king again asked,

"Queen Esther, what is your petition? It will be given you. What is your request? Even up to half the kingdom, it will be granted."

Then Queen Esther answered, "If I have found favor with you, Your Majesty, and if it pleases you, grant me my life — this is my petition. And spare my people — this is my request. For I and my people have been sold to be destroyed, killed and annihilated. If we had merely been sold as male and female slaves, I would have kept quiet, because no such distress would justify disturbing the king."

King Xerxes asked Queen Esther, "Who is he? Where is he — the man who has dared to do such a thing?"

Esther said, "An adversary and enemy! This vile Haman!"

Then Haman was terrified before the king and queen. The king got up in a rage, left his wine and went out into the palace garden. But Haman, realizing that the king had already decided his fate, stayed behind to beg Queen Esther for his life.

Just as the king returned from the palace garden to the banquet hall, Haman was falling on the couch where Esther was reclining.

The king exclaimed, "Will he even molest the queen while she is with me in the house?"

As soon as the word left the king's mouth, they covered Haman's face. Then Harbona, one of the eunuchs attending the king, said, "A pole reaching to a height of fifty cubits stands by Haman's house. He had it set up for Mordecai, who spoke up to help the king."

The king said, "Impale him on it!" So they impaled Haman on the pole he had set up for Mordecai. Then the king's fury subsided.

That same day King Xerxes gave Queen Esther the estate of Haman, the enemy of the Jews. And Mordecai came into the presence of the king, for Esther had told how he was related to her. The king took off his signet ring, which he had reclaimed from Haman, and presented it to Mordecai. And Esther appointed him over Haman's estate.

Esther again pleaded with the king, falling at his feet and weeping. She begged him to put an end to the evil plan of Haman the Agagite, which he had devised against the Jews. Then the king extended the gold scepter to Esther and she arose and stood before him.

"If it pleases the king," she said, "and if he regards me with favor and thinks it the right thing to do, and if he is pleased with me, let an order be written overruling the dispatches that Haman son of Hammedatha, the Agagite, devised and wrote to destroy the Jews in all the king's provinces. For how can I bear to see disaster fall on my people? How can I bear to see the destruction of my family?"

King Xerxes replied to Queen Esther and to Mordecai the Jew, "Because Haman attacked the Jews, I have given his estate to Esther, and they have impaled him on the pole he set up. Now write another decree in the king's name in behalf of the Jews as seems best to you, and seal it with the king's signet ring—for no document written in the king's name and sealed with his ring can be revoked."

At once the royal secretaries were summoned—on the twenty-third day of the third month, the month of Sivan. They wrote out all Mordecai's orders to the Jews, and to the satraps, governors and nobles of the 127 provinces stretching from India to Cush. These orders were written in the script of each province and the language of each people and also to the Jews in their own script and language. Mordecai wrote in the name of King Xerxes, sealed the dispatches with the king's signet ring, and sent them by mounted couriers, who rode fast horses especially bred for the king.

The king's edict granted the Jews in every city the right to assemble and protect themselves; to destroy, kill and annihilate the armed men of any nationality or province who might attack them and their women and children, and to plunder the property of their enemies. The day appointed for the Jews to do this in all the provinces of King Xerxes was the thirteenth day of the twelfth month, the month of Adar. A copy of the text of the edict was to be issued as law in every province and made known to the people of every nationality so that the Jews would be ready on that day to avenge themselves on their enemies.

The couriers, riding the royal horses, went out, spurred on by the king's command, and the edict was issued in the citadel of Susa.

When Mordecai left the king's presence, he was wearing royal garments of blue and white, a large crown of gold and a purple robe of fine linen. And the city of Susa held a joyous celebration. For the Jews it was a time of happiness and joy, gladness and honor. In every province and in every city to which the edict of the king came, there was joy and gladness among the Jews, with feasting and celebrating. And many people of other nationalities became Jews because fear of the Jews had seized them.

On the thirteenth day of the twelfth month, the month of Adar, the edict commanded by the king was to be carried out. On this day the enemies of the Jews had hoped to overpower them, but now the tables were turned and the Jews got the upper hand over those who hated them. The Jews assembled in their cities in all the provinces of King Xerxes to attack those determined to destroy them. No one could stand against them, because the people of all the other nationalities were afraid of them. And all the nobles of the provinces, the satraps, the governors and the king's administrators helped the Jews, because fear of Mordecai had seized them. Mordecai was prominent in the palace; his reputation spread throughout the provinces, and he became more and more powerful.

The Jews struck down all their enemies with the sword, killing and destroying them, and they did what they pleased to those who hated them. In the citadel of Susa, the Jews killed and destroyed five hundred men. They also killed Parshandatha, Dalphon, Aspatha, Poratha, Adalia, Aridatha, Parmashta, Arisai, Aridai and Vaizatha, the ten sons of Haman son of Hammedatha, the enemy of the Jews. But they did not lay their hands on the plunder.

The number of those killed in the citadel of Susa was reported to the king that same day. The king said to Queen Esther, "The Jews have killed and destroyed five hundred men and the ten sons of Haman in the citadel of Susa. What have they done in the rest of the king's provinces? Now what is your petition? It will be given you. What is your request? It will also be granted."

"If it pleases the king," Esther answered, "give the Jews in Susa permission to carry out this day's edict tomorrow also, and let Haman's ten sons be impaled on poles."

So the king commanded that this be done. An edict was issued in Susa, and they impaled the ten sons of Haman. The Jews in Susa came together on the fourteenth day of the month of Adar, and they put to death in Susa three hundred men, but they did not lay their hands on the plunder.

Meanwhile, the remainder of the Jews who were in the king's provinces also assembled to protect themselves and get relief from their enemies. They killed seventy-five thousand of them but did not lay their hands on the plunder. This happened on the thirteenth day of the month of Adar, and on the fourteenth they rested and made it a day of feasting and joy.

The Jews in Susa, however, had assembled on the thirteenth and fourteenth, and then on the fifteenth they rested and made it a day of feasting and joy.

That is why rural Jews—those living in villages—observe the fourteenth of the month of Adar as a day of joy and feasting, a day for giving presents to each other.

Mordecai recorded these events, and he sent letters to all the Jews throughout the provinces of King Xerxes, near and far, to have them celebrate annually the fourteenth and fifteenth days of the month of Adar as the time when the Jews got relief from their enemies, and as the month when their sorrow was turned into joy and their mourning into a day of celebration. He wrote them to observe the days as days of feasting and joy and giving presents of food to one another and gifts to the poor.

So the Jews agreed to continue the celebration they had begun, doing what Mordecai had written to them. For Haman son of Hammedatha, the Agagite, the enemy of all the Jews, had plotted against the Jews to destroy them and had cast the *pur* (that is, the lot) for their ruin and destruction. But when the plot came to the king's attention, he issued written orders that the evil scheme Haman had devised against the Jews should come back onto his own head, and that he and his sons should be impaled on poles. (Therefore these days were called Purim, from the word *pur*.) Because of everything written in this letter and because of what they had seen and what had happened to them, the Jews took it on themselves to establish the custom that they and their descendants and all who join them should without fail observe these two days every year, in the way prescribed and at the time appointed. These days should be remembered and observed in every generation by every family, and in every province and in every city. And these days of Purim should never fail to be celebrated by the Jews — nor should the memory of these days die out among their descendants.

So Queen Esther, daughter of Abihail, along with Mordecai the Jew, wrote with full authority to confirm this second letter concerning Purim. And Mordecai sent letters to all the Jews in the 127 provinces of Xerxes' kingdom — words of goodwill and assurance — to establish these days of Purim at their designated times, as Mordecai the Jew and Queen Esther had decreed for them, and as they had established for themselves and their descendants in regard to their times of fasting and lamentation. Esther's decree confirmed these regulations about Purim, and it was written down in the records.

K ing Xerxes imposed tribute throughout the empire, to its distant shores. And all his acts of power and might, together with a full account of the greatness of Mordecai, whom the king had promoted, are they not written in the book of the annals of the kings of Media and Persia? Mordecai the Jew was second in rank to King Xerxes, preeminent among the Jews, and held in high esteem by his many fellow Jews, because he worked for the good of his people and spoke up for the welfare of all the Jews.

INVITATION TO
DANIEL

The book of Daniel combines two types of literature: narrative and apocalypse. The first part of the book presents six stories of how God preserved, protected and promoted four Judeans who were exiled to Babylon as young men. These Judeans were Daniel, the book's main character, and his friends Shadrach, Meshach and Abednego. Because they were faithful to God and refused to worship idols, God miraculously delivered them from deadly perils and gave them special abilities. God enabled Daniel to interpret dreams, and this earned him a valued place in the royal court of Babylon. The stories tell how he later served in the court of Persia as well.

The second part of the book describes four communications that Daniel received from God through angels in the later years of his life. Three of these were explanations of visions Daniel had just seen. The other communication came in response to Daniel's fervent prayer for the return of his people to their land. The visions, just like a dream Daniel interprets in one of the earlier stories, trace the succession of empires after Babylon and Persia. Their particular concern is the eventual emergence of an arrogant and ruthless ruler who will seek to end the worship of the true God in Israel. The angels promise Daniel that while this will be a time of great suffering, God ultimately will deliver all those who remain faithful. The *Most High* remains the true Ruler over all the earth. So the purpose of the visions and their explanations is to encourage God's people to persevere in their loyalty to the covenant.

These visions are presented in the cryptic language and symbolic terms typical of apocalyptic literature. Yet the outlines of Near Eastern history from the time of the exile forward are discernible within them: the empires of Babylon and Persia; the conquests of Alexander the Great; and the recurring strife between two successor dynasties of Alexander's empire, the Ptolemys in Egypt and the Seleucids in Syria. From this perspective, the evil ruler described in the visions would be the Seleucid emperor Antiochus IV Epiphanes, who, in one of the great crises of Jewish history, desecrated the Jerusalem temple in 167 BC. This led to the Maccabean revolt, which eventually restored the nation's independence and preserved the worship of the true God.

The visions in Daniel can also be understood to anticipate later times when God's people will experience extreme suffering and oppression. Both the visions and the stories in the book of Daniel therefore offer a message of challenge and consolation to those who are struggling through such times. The people of God can be sustained through their persecutions knowing that *the sovereignty, power and greatness of all the kingdoms under heaven will be handed over to the holy people of the Most High. His kingdom will be an everlasting kingdom, and all rulers will worship and obey him.*

DANIEL

In the third year of the reign of Jehoiakim king of Judah, Nebuchadnezzar king of Babylon came to Jerusalem and besieged it. And the Lord delivered Jehoiakim king of Judah into his hand, along with some of the articles from the temple of God. These he carried off to the temple of his god in Babylonia and put in the treasure house of his god.

Then the king ordered Ashpenaz, chief of his court officials, to bring into the king's service some of the Israelites from the royal family and the nobility — young men without any physical defect, handsome, showing aptitude for every kind of learning, well informed, quick to understand, and qualified to serve in the king's palace. He was to teach them the language and literature of the Babylonians. The king assigned them a daily amount of food and wine from the king's table. They were to be trained for three years, and after that they were to enter the king's service.

Among those who were chosen were some from Judah: Daniel, Hananiah, Mishael and Azariah. The chief official gave them new names: to Daniel, the name Belteshazzar; to Hananiah, Shadrach; to Mishael, Meshach; and to Azariah, Abednego.

But Daniel resolved not to defile himself with the royal food and wine, and he asked the chief official for permission not to defile himself this way. Now God had caused the official to show favor and compassion to Daniel, but the official told Daniel, "I am afraid of my lord the king, who has assigned your food and drink. Why should he see you looking worse than the other young men your age? The king would then have my head because of you."

Daniel then said to the guard whom the chief official had appointed over Daniel, Hananiah, Mishael and Azariah, "Please test your servants for ten days: Give us nothing but vegetables to eat and water to drink. Then compare our appearance with that of the young men who eat the royal food, and treat your servants in accordance with what you see." So he agreed to this and tested them for ten days.

At the end of the ten days they looked healthier and better nourished than any of the young men who ate the royal food. So the guard took away their choice food and the wine they were to drink and gave them vegetables instead.

To these four young men God gave knowledge and understanding of all kinds of literature and learning. And Daniel could understand visions and dreams of all kinds.

At the end of the time set by the king to bring them into his service, the chief official presented them to Nebuchadnezzar. The king talked with them, and he found none equal to Daniel, Hananiah, Mishael and Azariah; so they entered the king's service. In every matter of wisdom and understanding about which the king questioned them, he found them ten times better than all the magicians and enchanters in his whole kingdom.

And Daniel remained there until the first year of King Cyrus.

In the second year of his reign, Nebuchadnezzar had dreams; his mind was troubled and he could not sleep. So the king summoned the magicians, enchanters, sorcerers and astrologers to tell him what he had dreamed. When they came in and stood before the king, he said to them, "I have had a dream that troubles me and I want to know what it means."

Then the astrologers answered the king, "May the king live forever! Tell your servants the dream, and we will interpret it."

The king replied to the astrologers, "This is what I have firmly decided: If you do not tell me what my dream was and interpret it, I will have you cut into pieces and your houses turned into piles of rubble. But if you tell me the dream and explain it, you will receive from me gifts and rewards and great honor. So tell me the dream and interpret it for me."

Once more they replied, "Let the king tell his servants the dream, and we will interpret it."

Then the king answered, "I am certain that you are trying to gain time, because you realize that this is what I have firmly decided: If you do not tell me the dream, there is only one penalty for you. You have conspired to tell me misleading and wicked things, hoping the situation will change. So then, tell me the dream, and I will know that you can interpret it for me."

The astrologers answered the king, "There is no one on earth who can do what the king asks! No king, however great and mighty, has ever asked such a thing of any magician or enchanter or astrologer. What the king asks is too difficult. No one can reveal it to the king except the gods, and they do not live among humans."

This made the king so angry and furious that he ordered the execution of all the wise men of Babylon. So the decree was issued to put the wise men to death, and men were sent to look for Daniel and his friends to put them to death.

When Arioch, the commander of the king's guard, had gone out to put to death the wise men of Babylon, Daniel spoke to him with wisdom and tact. He asked the king's officer, "Why did the king issue such a harsh decree?" Arioch then explained the matter to Daniel. At this, Daniel went in to the king and asked for time, so that he might interpret the dream for him.

Then Daniel returned to his house and explained the matter to his friends Hananiah, Mishael and Azariah. He urged them to plead for mercy from the God of heaven concerning this mystery, so that he and his friends might not be executed with the rest of the wise men of Babylon. During the night the mystery was revealed to Daniel in a vision. Then Daniel praised the God of heaven and said:

> "Praise be to the name of God for ever and ever;
> wisdom and power are his.
>
> He changes times and seasons;
> he deposes kings and raises up others.
>
> He gives wisdom to the wise
> and knowledge to the discerning.
>
> He reveals deep and hidden things;
> he knows what lies in darkness,
> and light dwells with him.
>
> I thank and praise you, God of my ancestors:
> You have given me wisdom and power,
>
> you have made known to me what we asked of you,
> you have made known to us the dream of the king."

Then Daniel went to Arioch, whom the king had appointed to execute the wise men of Babylon, and said to him, "Do not execute the wise men of Babylon. Take me to the king, and I will interpret his dream for him."

Arioch took Daniel to the king at once and said, "I have found a man among the exiles from Judah who can tell the king what his dream means."

The king asked Daniel (also called Belteshazzar), "Are you able to tell me what I saw in my dream and interpret it?"

Daniel replied, "No wise man, enchanter, magician or diviner can explain to the king the mystery he has asked about, but there is a God in heaven who reveals mysteries. He has shown King Nebuchadnezzar what will happen in days to come. Your dream and the visions that passed through your mind as you were lying in bed are these:

"As Your Majesty was lying there, your mind turned to things to come, and the revealer of mysteries showed you what is going to happen. As for me, this mystery has been revealed to me, not because I have greater wisdom than anyone else alive, but so that Your Majesty may know the interpretation and that you may understand what went through your mind.

"Your Majesty looked, and there before you stood a large statue — an enormous, dazzling statue, awesome in appearance. The head of the statue was made of pure gold, its chest and arms of silver, its belly and thighs of bronze, its legs of iron, its feet partly of iron and partly of baked clay. While you were watching, a rock was cut out, but not by human hands. It struck the statue on its feet of iron and clay and smashed them. Then the iron, the clay, the bronze, the silver and the gold were all broken to pieces and became like chaff on a threshing floor in the summer. The wind swept them away without leaving a trace. But the rock that struck the statue became a huge mountain and filled the whole earth.

"This was the dream, and now we will interpret it to the king. Your Majesty, you are the king of kings. The God of heaven has given you dominion and power and might and glory; in your hands he has placed all mankind and the beasts of the field and the birds in the sky. Wherever they live, he has made you ruler over them all. You are that head of gold.

"After you, another kingdom will arise, inferior to yours. Next, a third kingdom, one of bronze, will rule over the whole earth. Finally, there will be a fourth kingdom, strong as iron — for iron breaks and smashes everything — and as iron breaks things to pieces, so it will crush and break all the others. Just as you saw that the feet and toes were partly of baked clay and partly of iron, so this will be a divided kingdom; yet it will have some of the strength of iron in it, even as you saw iron mixed with clay. As the toes were partly iron and partly clay, so this kingdom will be partly strong and partly brittle. And just as you saw the iron mixed with baked clay, so the people will be a mixture and will not remain united, any more than iron mixes with clay.

"In the time of those kings, the God of heaven will set up a kingdom that will never be destroyed, nor will it be left to another people. It will crush all those kingdoms and bring them to an end, but it will itself endure forever. This is the meaning of the vision of the rock cut out of a mountain, but not by human hands — a rock that broke the iron, the bronze, the clay, the silver and the gold to pieces.

"The great God has shown the king what will take place in the future. The dream is true and its interpretation is trustworthy."

Then King Nebuchadnezzar fell prostrate before Daniel and

paid him honor and ordered that an offering and incense be presented to him. The king said to Daniel, "Surely your God is the God of gods and the Lord of kings and a revealer of mysteries, for you were able to reveal this mystery."

Then the king placed Daniel in a high position and lavished many gifts on him. He made him ruler over the entire province of Babylon and placed him in charge of all its wise men. Moreover, at Daniel's request the king appointed Shadrach, Meshach and Abednego administrators over the province of Babylon, while Daniel himself remained at the royal court.

King Nebuchadnezzar made an image of gold, sixty cubits high and six cubits wide, and set it up on the plain of Dura in the province of Babylon. He then summoned the satraps, prefects, governors, advisers, treasurers, judges, magistrates and all the other provincial officials to come to the dedication of the image he had set up. So the satraps, prefects, governors, advisers, treasurers, judges, magistrates and all the other provincial officials assembled for the dedication of the image that King Nebuchadnezzar had set up, and they stood before it.

Then the herald loudly proclaimed, "Nations and peoples of every language, this is what you are commanded to do: As soon as you hear the sound of the horn, flute, zither, lyre, harp, pipe and all kinds of music, you must fall down and worship the image of gold that King Nebuchadnezzar has set up. Whoever does not fall down and worship will immediately be thrown into a blazing furnace."

Therefore, as soon as they heard the sound of the horn, flute, zither, lyre, harp and all kinds of music, all the nations and peoples of every language fell down and worshiped the image of gold that King Nebuchadnezzar had set up.

At this time some astrologers came forward and denounced the Jews. They said to King Nebuchadnezzar, "May the king live forever! Your Majesty has issued a decree that everyone who hears the sound of the horn, flute, zither, lyre, harp, pipe and all kinds of music must fall down and worship the image of gold, and that whoever does not fall down and worship will be thrown into a blazing furnace. But there are some Jews whom you have set over the affairs of the province of Babylon — Shadrach, Meshach and Abednego — who pay no attention to you, Your Majesty. They neither serve your gods nor worship the image of gold you have set up."

Furious with rage, Nebuchadnezzar summoned Shadrach, Meshach and Abednego. So these men were brought before the king, and Nebuchadnezzar said to them, "Is it true, Shadrach, Meshach and Abednego, that you do not serve my gods or worship the image of gold I have set up? Now when you hear the sound of the horn, flute, zither, lyre, harp, pipe and all kinds of music, if you are ready to fall down and worship the image I made, very good. But if you do not worship it, you will be thrown immediately into a blazing furnace. Then what god will be able to rescue you from my hand?"

Shadrach, Meshach and Abednego replied to him, "King Nebuchadnezzar, we do not need to defend ourselves before you in this matter. If we are thrown into the blazing furnace, the God we serve is able to deliver us from it, and he will deliver us from Your Majesty's hand. But even if he does not, we want you to know, Your Majesty, that we will not serve your gods or worship the image of gold you have set up."

Then Nebuchadnezzar was furious with Shadrach, Meshach and Abednego, and his attitude toward them changed. He ordered the furnace heated seven times hotter than usual and commanded some of the strongest soldiers in his army to tie up Shadrach, Meshach and Abednego and throw them into the blazing furnace. So these men, wearing their robes, trousers, turbans and other clothes, were bound and thrown into the blazing furnace. The king's command was so urgent and the furnace so hot that the flames of the fire killed the soldiers who took up Shadrach, Meshach and Abednego, and these three men, firmly tied, fell into the blazing furnace.

Then King Nebuchadnezzar leaped to his feet in amazement and asked his advisers, "Weren't there three men that we tied up and threw into the fire?"

They replied, "Certainly, Your Majesty."

He said, "Look! I see four men walking around in the fire, unbound and unharmed, and the fourth looks like a son of the gods."

Nebuchadnezzar then approached the opening of the blazing furnace and shouted, "Shadrach, Meshach and Abednego, servants of the Most High God, come out! Come here!"

So Shadrach, Meshach and Abednego came out of the fire, and the satraps, prefects, governors and royal advisers crowded around them. They saw that the fire had not harmed their bodies, nor was a hair of their heads singed; their robes were not scorched, and there was no smell of fire on them.

Then Nebuchadnezzar said, "Praise be to the God of Shadrach, Meshach and Abednego, who has sent his angel and rescued his servants! They trusted in him and defied the king's command and were willing to give up their lives rather than serve or worship any god except their own God. Therefore I decree that the people of any nation or language who say anything against the God of Shadrach, Meshach and Abednego be cut into pieces and their houses be turned into piles of rubble, for no other god can save in this way."

Then the king promoted Shadrach, Meshach and Abednego in the province of Babylon.

King Nebuchadnezzar,

To the nations and peoples of every language, who live in all the earth:

May you prosper greatly!

It is my pleasure to tell you about the miraculous signs and wonders that the Most High God has performed for me.

> How great are his signs,
> how mighty his wonders!
> His kingdom is an eternal kingdom;
> his dominion endures from generation to
> generation.

I, Nebuchadnezzar, was at home in my palace, contented and prosperous. I had a dream that made me afraid. As I was lying in bed, the images and visions that passed through my mind terrified me. So I commanded that all the wise men of Babylon be brought before me to interpret the dream for me. When the magicians, enchanters, astrologers and diviners came, I told them the dream, but they could not interpret it for me. Finally, Daniel came into my presence and I told him the dream. (He is called Belteshazzar, after the name of my god, and the spirit of the holy gods is in him.)

I said, "Belteshazzar, chief of the magicians, I know that the spirit of the holy gods is in you, and no mystery is too difficult for you. Here is my dream; interpret it for me. These are the visions I saw while lying in bed: I looked, and there before me stood a tree in the middle of the land. Its height was enormous. The tree grew large and strong and its top touched the sky; it was visible to the ends of the earth. Its leaves were beautiful, its fruit abundant, and on it was food for all. Under it the wild animals found shelter, and the birds lived in its branches; from it every creature was fed.

"In the visions I saw while lying in bed, I looked, and there before me was a holy one, a messenger, coming down from heaven. He called in a loud voice: 'Cut down the tree and trim off its branches; strip off its leaves and scatter its fruit. Let the animals flee from under it and the birds from its branches. But let the stump and its roots, bound with iron and bronze, remain in the ground, in the grass of the field.

" 'Let him be drenched with the dew of heaven, and let him live with the animals among the plants of the earth. Let his mind be changed from that of a man and let him be given the mind of an animal, till seven times pass by for him.

" 'The decision is announced by messengers, the holy ones declare the verdict, so that the living may know that the Most High is sovereign over all kingdoms on earth and gives them to anyone he wishes and sets over them the lowliest of people.'

"This is the dream that I, King Nebuchadnezzar, had. Now, Belteshazzar, tell me what it means, for none of the wise men in my kingdom can interpret it for me. But you can, because the spirit of the holy gods is in you."

Then Daniel (also called Belteshazzar) was greatly perplexed for a time, and his thoughts terrified him. So the king said, "Belteshazzar, do not let the dream or its meaning alarm you."

Belteshazzar answered, "My lord, if only the dream applied to your enemies and its meaning to your adversaries! The tree you saw, which grew large and strong, with its top touching the sky, visible to the whole earth, with beautiful leaves and abundant fruit, providing food for all, giving shelter to the wild animals, and having nesting places in its branches for the birds — Your Majesty, you are that tree! You have become great and strong; your greatness has grown until it reaches the sky, and your dominion extends to distant parts of the earth.

"Your Majesty saw a holy one, a messenger, coming down from heaven and saying, 'Cut down the tree and destroy it, but leave the stump, bound with iron and bronze, in the grass of the field, while its roots remain in the ground. Let him be drenched with the dew of heaven; let him live with the wild animals, until seven times pass by for him.'

"This is the interpretation, Your Majesty, and this is the decree the Most High has issued against my lord the king: You will be driven away from people and will live with the wild animals; you will eat grass like the ox and be drenched with the dew of heaven. Seven times will pass by for you until you acknowledge that the Most High is sovereign over all kingdoms on earth and gives them to anyone he wishes. The command to leave the stump of the tree with its roots means that your kingdom will be restored to you when you acknowledge that Heaven rules. Therefore, Your Majesty, be pleased to accept my advice: Renounce your sins by doing what is right, and your wickedness by being kind to the oppressed. It may be that then your prosperity will continue."

All this happened to King Nebuchadnezzar. Twelve months later, as the king was walking on the roof of the royal palace of Babylon, he said, "Is not this the great Babylon I have built as the royal residence, by my mighty power and for the glory of my majesty?"

Even as the words were on his lips, a voice came from heaven, "This is what is decreed for you, King Nebuchadnezzar: Your royal authority has been taken from you. You will be driven away from people and will live with the wild animals; you will eat grass like the ox. Seven times will pass by for you until you acknowledge that the Most High is sovereign over all kingdoms on earth and gives them to anyone he wishes."

Immediately what had been said about Nebuchadnezzar was fulfilled. He was driven away from people and ate grass like the ox. His body was drenched with the dew of heaven until his hair grew like the feathers of an eagle and his nails like the claws of a bird.

At the end of that time, I, Nebuchadnezzar, raised my eyes toward heaven, and my sanity was restored. Then I praised the Most High; I honored and glorified him who lives forever.

> His dominion is an eternal dominion;
> his kingdom endures from generation to generation.
>
> All the peoples of the earth
> are regarded as nothing.
>
> He does as he pleases
> with the powers of heaven
> and the peoples of the earth.
>
> No one can hold back his hand
> or say to him: "What have you done?"

At the same time that my sanity was restored, my honor and splendor were returned to me for the glory of my kingdom. My advisers and nobles sought me out, and I was restored to my throne and became even greater than before. Now I, Nebuchadnezzar, praise and exalt and glorify the King of heaven, because everything he does is right and all his ways are just. And those who walk in pride he is able to humble.

King Belshazzar gave a great banquet for a thousand of his nobles and drank wine with them. While Belshazzar was drinking his wine, he gave orders to bring in the gold and silver goblets that Nebuchadnezzar his father had taken from the temple in Jerusalem, so that the king and his nobles, his wives and his concubines might drink from them. So they brought in the gold goblets that had been taken from the temple of God in Jerusalem, and the king and his nobles, his wives and his concubines drank from them. As they drank the wine, they praised the gods of gold and silver, of bronze, iron, wood and stone.

Suddenly the fingers of a human hand appeared and wrote on the plaster of the wall, near the lampstand in the royal palace. The king watched the hand as it wrote. His face turned pale and he was so frightened that his legs became weak and his knees were knocking.

The king summoned the enchanters, astrologers and diviners. Then he said to these wise men of Babylon, "Whoever reads this writing and tells me what it means will be clothed in purple and have a gold chain placed around his neck, and he will be made the third highest ruler in the kingdom."

Then all the king's wise men came in, but they could not read the writing or tell the king what it meant. So King Belshazzar became even more terrified and his face grew more pale. His nobles were baffled.

The queen, hearing the voices of the king and his nobles, came into the banquet hall. "May the king live forever!" she said. "Don't be alarmed! Don't look so pale! There is a man in your kingdom who has the spirit of the holy gods in him. In the time of your father he was found to have insight and intelligence and wisdom like that of the gods. Your father, King Nebuchadnezzar, appointed him chief of the magicians, enchanters, astrologers and diviners. He did this because Daniel, whom the king called Belteshazzar, was found to have a keen mind and knowledge and understanding, and also the ability to interpret dreams, explain riddles and solve difficult problems. Call for Daniel, and he will tell you what the writing means."

So Daniel was brought before the king, and the king said to him, "Are you Daniel, one of the exiles my father the king brought from Judah? I have heard that the spirit of the gods is in you and that you have insight, intelligence and outstanding wisdom. The wise men and enchanters were brought before me to read this writing and tell me what it means, but they could not explain it. Now I have heard that you are able to give interpretations and to solve difficult problems. If you can read this writing and tell me what it means, you will be clothed in purple and have a gold chain placed around your neck, and you will be made the third highest ruler in the kingdom."

Then Daniel answered the king, "You may keep your gifts for yourself and give your rewards to someone else. Nevertheless, I will read the writing for the king and tell him what it means.

"Your Majesty, the Most High God gave your father Nebuchadnezzar sovereignty and greatness and glory and splendor. Because of the high position he gave him, all the nations and peoples of every language dreaded and feared him. Those the king wanted to put to death, he put to death; those he wanted to spare, he spared; those he wanted to promote, he promoted; and those he wanted to humble, he humbled. But when his heart became arrogant and hardened with pride, he was deposed from his royal throne and stripped of his glory. He was driven away from people and given the mind of an animal; he lived with the wild donkeys and ate grass like the ox; and his body was drenched with the dew of heaven, until he acknowledged that the Most High God is sovereign over all kingdoms on earth and sets over them anyone he wishes.

"But you, Belshazzar, his son, have not humbled yourself, though you knew all this. Instead, you have set yourself up against the Lord of heaven. You had the goblets from his temple brought to you, and you and your nobles, your wives and your concubines drank wine from them. You praised the gods of silver and gold, of bronze, iron, wood and stone, which cannot see or hear or understand. But you did not honor the God who holds in his hand your life and all your ways. Therefore he sent the hand that wrote the inscription.

"This is the inscription that was written:

MENE, MENE, TEKEL, PARSIN

"Here is what these words mean:

Mene: God has numbered the days of your reign and brought it to an end.
Tekel: You have been weighed on the scales and found wanting.
Peres: Your kingdom is divided and given to the Medes and Persians."

Then at Belshazzar's command, Daniel was clothed in purple, a gold chain was placed around his neck, and he was proclaimed the third highest ruler in the kingdom.

That very night Belshazzar, king of the Babylonians, was slain, and Darius the Mede took over the kingdom, at the age of sixty-two.

It pleased Darius to appoint 120 satraps to rule throughout the kingdom, with three administrators over them, one of whom was Daniel. The satraps were made accountable to them so that the king might not suffer loss. Now Daniel so distinguished himself among the administrators and the satraps by his exceptional qualities that the king planned to set him over the whole kingdom. At this, the administrators and the satraps tried to find grounds for charges against Daniel in his conduct of government affairs, but they were unable to do so. They could find no corruption in him, because he was trustworthy and neither corrupt nor negligent. Finally these men said, "We will never find any basis for charges against this man Daniel unless it has something to do with the law of his God."

So these administrators and satraps went as a group to the king and said: "May King Darius live forever! The royal administrators, prefects, satraps, advisers and governors have all agreed that the king should issue an edict and enforce the decree that anyone who prays to any god or human being during the next thirty days, except to you, Your Majesty, shall be thrown into the lions' den. Now, Your Majesty, issue the decree and put it in writing so that it cannot be altered—in accordance with the law of the Medes and Persians, which cannot be repealed." So King Darius put the decree in writing.

Now when Daniel learned that the decree had been published, he went home to his upstairs room where the windows opened toward Jerusalem. Three times a day he got down on his knees and prayed, giving thanks to his God, just as he had done before. Then these men went as a group and found Daniel praying and asking God for help. So they went to the king and spoke to him about his royal decree: "Did you not publish a decree that during the next thirty days anyone who prays to any god or human being except to you, Your Majesty, would be thrown into the lions' den?"

The king answered, "The decree stands—in accordance with the law of the Medes and Persians, which cannot be repealed."

Then they said to the king, "Daniel, who is one of the exiles from Judah, pays no attention to you, Your Majesty, or to the decree you put in writing. He still prays three times a day." When the king heard this, he was greatly distressed; he was determined to rescue Daniel and made every effort until sundown to save him.

Then the men went as a group to King Darius and said to him, "Remember, Your Majesty, that according to the law of the Medes and Persians no decree or edict that the king issues can be changed."

So the king gave the order, and they brought Daniel and threw him into the lions' den. The king said to Daniel, "May your God, whom you serve continually, rescue you!"

A stone was brought and placed over the mouth of the den, and the king sealed it with his own signet ring and with the rings of his nobles, so that Daniel's situation might not be changed. Then the king returned to his palace and spent the night without eating and without any entertainment being brought to him. And he could not sleep.

At the first light of dawn, the king got up and hurried to the lions' den. When he came near the den, he called to Daniel in an anguished voice, "Daniel, servant of the living God, has your God, whom you serve continually, been able to rescue you from the lions?"

Daniel answered, "May the king live forever! My God sent his angel, and he shut the mouths of the lions. They have not hurt me, because I was found innocent in his sight. Nor have I ever done any wrong before you, Your Majesty."

The king was overjoyed and gave orders to lift Daniel out of the den. And when Daniel was lifted from the den, no wound was found on him, because he had trusted in his God.

At the king's command, the men who had falsely accused Daniel were brought in and thrown into the lions' den, along with their wives and children. And before they reached the floor of the den, the lions overpowered them and crushed all their bones.

Then King Darius wrote to all the nations and peoples of every language in all the earth:

"May you prosper greatly!

"I issue a decree that in every part of my kingdom people must fear and reverence the God of Daniel.

> "For he is the living God
> and he endures forever;
> his kingdom will not be destroyed,
> his dominion will never end.
>
> He rescues and he saves;
> he performs signs and wonders
> in the heavens and on the earth.
>
> He has rescued Daniel
> from the power of the lions."

So Daniel prospered during the reign of Darius and the reign of Cyrus the Persian.

I n the first year of Belshazzar king of Babylon, Daniel had a dream, and visions passed through his mind as he was lying in bed. He wrote down the substance of his dream.

Daniel said: "In my vision at night I looked, and there before me were the four winds of heaven churning up the great sea. Four great beasts, each different from the others, came up out of the sea.

"The first was like a lion, and it had the wings of an eagle. I watched until its wings were torn off and it was lifted from the ground so that it stood on two feet like a human being, and the mind of a human was given to it.

"And there before me was a second beast, which looked like a bear. It was raised up on one of its sides, and it had three ribs in its mouth between its teeth. It was told, 'Get up and eat your fill of flesh!'

"After that, I looked, and there before me was another beast, one that looked like a leopard. And on its back it had four wings like those of a bird. This beast had four heads, and it was given authority to rule.

"After that, in my vision at night I looked, and there before me was a fourth beast—terrifying and frightening and very powerful. It had large iron teeth; it crushed and devoured its victims and trampled underfoot whatever was left. It was different from all the former beasts, and it had ten horns.

"While I was thinking about the horns, there before me was another horn, a little one, which came up among them; and three of the first horns were uprooted before it. This horn had eyes like the eyes of a human being and a mouth that spoke boastfully.

"As I looked,

"thrones were set in place,
and the Ancient of Days took his seat.

His clothing was as white as snow;
the hair of his head was white like wool.

His throne was flaming with fire,
and its wheels were all ablaze.

A river of fire was flowing,
coming out from before him.

Thousands upon thousands attended him;
ten thousand times ten thousand stood before him.

The court was seated,
and the books were opened.

"Then I continued to watch because of the boastful words the horn was speaking. I kept looking until the beast was slain and its body destroyed and thrown into the blazing fire. (The other beasts had been stripped of their authority, but were allowed to live for a period of time.)

"In my vision at night I looked, and there before me was one like a son of man, coming with the clouds of heaven. He approached the Ancient of Days and was led into his presence. He was given authority, glory and sovereign power; all nations and peoples of every language worshiped him. His dominion is an everlasting dominion that will not pass away, and his kingdom is one that will never be destroyed.

"I, Daniel, was troubled in spirit, and the visions that passed through my mind disturbed me. I approached one of those standing there and asked him the meaning of all this.

"So he told me and gave me the interpretation of these things: 'The four great beasts are four kings that will rise from the earth. But the holy people of the Most High will receive the kingdom and will possess it forever—yes, for ever and ever.'

"Then I wanted to know the meaning of the fourth beast, which was different from all the others and most terrifying, with its iron teeth and bronze claws—the beast that crushed and devoured its victims and trampled underfoot whatever was left. I also wanted to know about the ten horns on its head and about the other horn that came up, before which three of them fell—the horn that looked more imposing than the others and that had eyes and a mouth that spoke boastfully. As I watched, this horn was waging war against the holy people and defeating them, until the Ancient of Days came and pronounced judgment in favor of the holy people of the Most High, and the time came when they possessed the kingdom.

"He gave me this explanation: 'The fourth beast is a fourth kingdom that will appear on earth. It will be different from all the other kingdoms and will devour the whole earth, trampling it down and crushing it. The ten horns are ten kings who will come from this kingdom. After them another king will arise, different from the earlier ones; he will subdue three kings. He will speak against the Most High and oppress his holy people and try to change the set times and the laws. The holy people will be delivered into his hands for a time, times and half a time.

"'But the court will sit, and his power will be taken away and completely destroyed forever. Then the sovereignty, power and greatness of all the kingdoms under heaven will be handed over to the holy people of the Most High. His kingdom will be an everlasting kingdom, and all rulers will worship and obey him.'

"This is the end of the matter. I, Daniel, was deeply troubled by my thoughts, and my face turned pale, but I kept the matter to myself."

In the third year of King Belshazzar's reign, I, Daniel, had a vision, after the one that had already appeared to me. In my vision I saw myself in the citadel of Susa in the province of Elam; in the vision I was beside the Ulai Canal. I looked up, and there before me was a ram with two horns, standing beside the canal, and the horns were long. One of the horns was longer than the other but grew up later. I watched the ram as it charged toward the west and the north and the south. No animal could stand against it, and none could rescue from its power. It did as it pleased and became great.

As I was thinking about this, suddenly a goat with a prominent horn between its eyes came from the west, crossing the whole earth without touching the ground. It came toward the two-horned ram I had seen standing beside the canal and charged at it in great rage. I saw it attack the ram furiously, striking the ram and shattering its two horns. The ram was powerless to stand against it; the goat knocked it to the ground and trampled on it, and none could rescue the ram from its power. The goat became very great, but at the height of its power the large horn was broken off, and in its place four prominent horns grew up toward the four winds of heaven.

Out of one of them came another horn, which started small but grew in power to the south and to the east and toward the Beautiful Land. It grew until it reached the host of the heavens, and it threw some of the starry host down to the earth and trampled on them. It set itself up to be as great as the commander of the army of the LORD; it took away the daily sacrifice from the LORD, and his sanctuary was thrown down. Because of rebellion, the LORD's people and the daily sacrifice were given over to it. It prospered in everything it did, and truth was thrown to the ground.

Then I heard a holy one speaking, and another holy one said to him, "How long will it take for the vision to be fulfilled—the vision concerning the daily sacrifice, the rebellion that causes desolation, the surrender of the sanctuary and the trampling underfoot of the LORD's people?"

He said to me, "It will take 2,300 evenings and mornings; then the sanctuary will be reconsecrated."

While I, Daniel, was watching the vision and trying to understand it, there before me stood one who looked like a man. And I heard a man's voice from the Ulai calling, "Gabriel, tell this man the meaning of the vision."

As he came near the place where I was standing, I was terrified and fell prostrate. "Son of man," he said to me, "understand that the vision concerns the time of the end."

While he was speaking to me, I was in a deep sleep, with my face to the ground. Then he touched me and raised me to my feet.

He said: "I am going to tell you what will happen later in the time of wrath, because the vision concerns the appointed time of the end. The two-horned ram that you saw represents the kings of Media and Persia. The shaggy goat is the king of Greece, and the large horn between its eyes is the first king. The four horns that replaced the one that was broken off represent four kingdoms that will emerge from his nation but will not have the same power.

"In the latter part of their reign, when rebels have become completely wicked, a fierce-looking king, a master of intrigue, will arise. He will become very strong, but not by his own power. He will cause astounding devastation and will succeed in whatever he does. He will destroy those who are mighty, the holy people. He will cause deceit to prosper, and he will consider himself superior. When they feel secure, he will destroy many and take his stand against the Prince of princes. Yet he will be destroyed, but not by human power.

"The vision of the evenings and mornings that has been given you is true, but seal up the vision, for it concerns the distant future."

I, Daniel, was worn out. I lay exhausted for several days. Then I got up and went about the king's business. I was appalled by the vision; it was beyond understanding.

In the first year of Darius son of Xerxes (a Mede by descent), who was made ruler over the Babylonian kingdom — in the first year of his reign, I, Daniel, understood from the Scriptures, according to the word of the LORD given to Jeremiah the prophet, that the desolation of Jerusalem would last seventy years. So I turned to the Lord God and pleaded with him in prayer and petition, in fasting, and in sackcloth and ashes.

I prayed to the LORD my God and confessed:

"Lord, the great and awesome God, who keeps his covenant of love with those who love him and keep his commandments, we have sinned and done wrong. We have been wicked and have rebelled; we have turned away from your commands and laws. We have not listened to your servants the prophets, who spoke in your name to our kings, our princes and our ancestors, and to all the people of the land.

"Lord, you are righteous, but this day we are covered with shame — the people of Judah and the inhabitants of Jerusalem and all Israel, both near and far, in all the countries where you have scattered us because of our unfaithfulness to you. We and our kings, our princes and our ancestors are covered with shame, LORD, because we have sinned against you. The Lord our God is merciful and forgiving, even though we have rebelled against him; we have not obeyed the LORD our God or kept the laws he gave us through his servants the prophets. All Israel has transgressed your law and turned away, refusing to obey you.

"Therefore the curses and sworn judgments written in the Law of Moses, the servant of God, have been poured out on us, because we have sinned against you. You have fulfilled the words spoken against us and against our rulers by bringing on us great disaster. Under the whole heaven nothing has ever been done like what has been done to Jerusalem. Just as it is written in the Law of Moses, all this disaster has come on us, yet we have not sought the favor of the Lord our God by turning from our sins and giving attention to your truth. The Lord did not hesitate to bring the disaster on us, for the Lord our God is righteous in everything he does; yet we have not obeyed him.

"Now, Lord our God, who brought your people out of Egypt with a mighty hand and who made for yourself a name that endures to this day, we have sinned, we have done wrong. Lord, in keeping with all your righteous acts, turn away your anger and your wrath from Jerusalem, your city, your holy hill. Our sins and the iniquities of our ancestors have made Jerusalem and your people an object of scorn to all those around us.

"Now, our God, hear the prayers and petitions of your servant. For your sake, Lord, look with favor on your desolate sanctuary. Give ear, our God, and hear; open your eyes and see the desolation of the city that bears your Name. We do not make requests of you because we are righteous, but because of your great mercy. Lord, listen! Lord, forgive! Lord, hear and act! For your sake, my God, do not delay, because your city and your people bear your Name."

While I was speaking and praying, confessing my sin and the sin of my people Israel and making my request to the Lord my God for his holy hill — while I was still in prayer, Gabriel, the man I had seen in the earlier vision, came to me in swift flight about the time of the evening sacrifice. He instructed me and said to me, "Daniel, I have now come to give you insight and understanding. As soon as you began to pray, a word went out, which I have come to tell you, for you are highly esteemed. Therefore, consider the word and understand the vision:

"Seventy 'sevens' are decreed for your people and your holy city to finish transgression, to put an end to sin, to atone for wickedness, to bring in everlasting righteousness, to seal up vision and prophecy and to anoint the Most Holy Place.

"Know and understand this: From the time the word goes out to restore and rebuild Jerusalem until the Anointed One, the ruler, comes, there will be seven 'sevens,' and sixty-two 'sevens.' It will be rebuilt with streets and a trench, but in times of trouble. After the sixty-two 'sevens,' the Anointed One will be put to death and will have nothing. The people of the ruler who will come will destroy the city and the sanctuary. The end will come like a flood: War will continue until the end, and desolations have been decreed. He will confirm a covenant with many for one 'seven.' In the middle of the 'seven' he will put an end to sacrifice and offering. And at the temple he will set up an abomination that causes desolation, until the end that is decreed is poured out on him."

In the third year of Cyrus king of Persia, a revelation was given to Daniel (who was called Belteshazzar). Its message was true and it concerned a great war. The understanding of the message came to him in a vision.

At that time I, Daniel, mourned for three weeks. I ate no choice food; no meat or wine touched my lips; and I used no lotions at all until the three weeks were over.

On the twenty-fourth day of the first month, as I was standing on the bank of the great river, the Tigris, I looked up and there before me was a man dressed in linen, with a belt of fine gold from Uphaz around his waist. His body was like topaz, his face like lightning, his eyes like flaming torches, his arms and legs like the gleam of burnished bronze, and his voice like the sound of a multitude.

I, Daniel, was the only one who saw the vision; those who were with me did not see it, but such terror overwhelmed them that they fled and hid themselves. So I was left alone, gazing at this great vision; I had no strength left, my face turned deathly pale and I was helpless. Then I heard him speaking, and as I listened to him, I fell into a deep sleep, my face to the ground.

A hand touched me and set me trembling on my hands and knees. He said, "Daniel, you who are highly esteemed, consider carefully the words I am about to speak to you, and stand up, for I have now been sent to you." And when he said this to me, I stood up trembling.

Then he continued, "Do not be afraid, Daniel. Since the first day that you set your mind to gain understanding and to humble yourself before your God, your words were heard, and I have come in response to them. But the prince of the Persian kingdom resisted me twenty-one days. Then Michael, one of the chief princes, came to help me, because I was detained there with the king of Persia. Now I have come to explain to you what will happen to your people in the future, for the vision concerns a time yet to come."

While he was saying this to me, I bowed with my face toward the ground and was speechless. Then one who looked like a man touched my lips, and I opened my mouth and began to speak. I said the one standing before me, "I am overcome with anguish because of the vision, my lord, and I feel very weak. How can I, your servant, talk with you, my lord? My strength is gone and I can hardly breathe."

Again the one who looked like a man touched me and gave me strength. "Do not be afraid, you who are highly esteemed," he said. "Peace! Be strong now; be strong."

When he spoke to me, I was strengthened and said, "Speak, my lord, since you have given me strength."

So he said, "Do you know why I have come to you? Soon I will return to fight against the prince of Persia, and when I go, the prince of Greece will come; but first I will tell you what is written in the Book of Truth. (No one supports me against them except Michael, your prince. And in the first year of Darius the Mede, I took my stand to support and protect him.)

"Now then, I tell you the truth: Three more kings will arise in Persia, and then a fourth, who will be far richer than all the others. When he has gained power by his wealth, he will stir up everyone against the kingdom of Greece. Then a mighty king will arise, who will rule with great power and do as he pleases. After he has arisen, his empire will be broken up and parceled out toward the four winds of heaven. It will not go to his descendants, nor will it have the power he exercised, because his empire will be uprooted and given to others.

"The king of the South will become strong, but one of his commanders will become even stronger than he and will rule his own kingdom with great power. After some years, they will become allies. The daughter of the king of the South will go to the king of the North to make an alliance, but she will not retain her power, and he and his power will not last. In those days she will be betrayed, together with her royal escort and her father and the one who supported her.

"One from her family line will arise to take her place. He will attack the forces of the king of the North and enter his fortress; he will fight against them and be victorious. He will also seize their gods, their metal images and their valuable articles of silver and gold and carry them off to Egypt. For some years he will leave the king of the North alone. Then the king of the North will invade the realm of the king of the South but will retreat to his own country. His sons will prepare for war and assemble a great army, which will sweep on like an irresistible flood and carry the battle as far as his fortress.

"Then the king of the South will march out in a rage and fight against the king of the North, who will raise a large army, but it will be defeated. When the army is carried off, the king of the South will be filled with pride and will slaughter many thousands, yet he will not remain triumphant. For the king of the North will muster another army, larger than the first; and after several years, he will advance with a huge army fully equipped.

"In those times many will rise against the king of the South. Those who are violent among your own people will rebel in fulfillment of the vision, but without success. Then the king of the North will come and build up siege ramps and will capture a fortified city. The forces of the South will be powerless to resist; even their best troops will not have the strength to stand. The invader will do as he pleases; no one will be able to stand against him. He will establish himself in the Beautiful Land and will have the power to destroy it. He will determine to come with the might of his entire kingdom and will make an alliance with the king of the South. And he will give him a daughter in marriage in order to overthrow the kingdom, but his plans will not succeed or help him. Then he will turn his attention to the coastlands and will take many of them, but a commander will put an end to his insolence and will turn his insolence back on him. After this, he will turn back toward the fortresses of his own country but will stumble and fall, to be seen no more.

"His successor will send out a tax collector to maintain the royal splendor. In a few years, however, he will be destroyed, yet not in anger or in battle.

"He will be succeeded by a contemptible person who has not been given the honor of royalty. He will invade the kingdom when its people feel secure, and he will seize it through intrigue. Then an overwhelming army will be swept away before him; both it and a prince of the covenant will be destroyed. After coming to an agreement with him, he will act deceitfully, and with only a few people he will rise to power. When the richest provinces feel secure, he will invade them and will achieve what neither his fathers nor his forefathers did. He will distribute plunder, loot and wealth among his followers. He will plot the overthrow of fortresses — but only for a time.

"With a large army he will stir up his strength and courage against the king of the South. The king of the South will wage war with a large and very powerful army, but he will not be able to stand because of the plots devised against him. Those who eat from the king's provisions will try to destroy him; his army will be swept away, and many will fall in battle. The two kings, with their hearts bent on evil, will sit at the same table and lie to each other, but to no avail, because an end will still come at the appointed time. The king of the North will return to his own country with great wealth, but his heart will be set against the holy covenant. He will take action against it and then return to his own country.

"At the appointed time he will invade the South again, but this time the outcome will be different from what it was before. Ships of the western coastlands will oppose him, and he will lose heart. Then he will turn back and vent his fury against the holy covenant. He will return and show favor to those who forsake the holy covenant.

"His armed forces will rise up to desecrate the temple fortress and will abolish the daily sacrifice. Then they will set up the abomination that causes desolation. With flattery he will corrupt those who have violated the covenant, but the people who know their God will firmly resist him.

"Those who are wise will instruct many, though for a time they will fall by the sword or be burned or captured or plundered. When they fall, they will receive a little help, and many who are not sincere will join them. Some of the wise will stumble, so that they may be refined, purified and made spotless until the time of the end, for it will still come at the appointed time.

"The king will do as he pleases. He will exalt and magnify himself above every god and will say unheard-of things against the God of gods. He will be successful until the time of wrath is completed, for what has been determined must take place. He will show no regard for the gods of his ancestors or for the one desired by women, nor will he regard any god, but will exalt himself above them all. Instead of them, he will honor a god of fortresses; a god unknown to his ancestors he will honor with gold and silver, with precious stones and costly gifts. He will attack the mightiest fortresses with the help of a foreign god and will greatly honor those who acknowledge him. He will make them rulers over many people and will distribute the land at a price.

"At the time of the end the king of the South will engage him in battle, and the king of the North will storm out against him with chariots and cavalry and a great fleet of ships. He will invade many countries and sweep through them like a flood. He will also invade the Beautiful Land. Many countries will fall, but Edom, Moab and the leaders of Ammon will be delivered from his hand. He will extend his power over many countries; Egypt will not escape. He will gain control of the treasures of gold and silver and all the riches of Egypt, with the Libyans and Cushites in submission. But reports from the east and the north will alarm him, and he will set out in a great rage to destroy and annihilate many. He will pitch his royal tents between the seas at the beautiful holy mountain. Yet he will come to his end, and no one will help him.

"At that time Michael, the great prince who protects your people, will arise. There will be a time of distress such as has not happened from the beginning of nations until then. But at that time your people — everyone whose name is found written in the book — will be delivered. Multitudes who sleep in the dust of the earth will awake: some to everlasting life, others to shame and everlasting contempt. Those who are wise will shine like the brightness of the heavens, and those who lead many to righteousness, like the stars for ever and ever. But you, Daniel, roll up and seal the words of the scroll until the time of the end. Many will go here and there to increase knowledge."

Then I, Daniel, looked, and there before me stood two others, one on this bank of the river and one on the opposite bank. One of them said to the man clothed in linen, who was above the waters of the river, "How long will it be before these astonishing things are fulfilled?"

The man clothed in linen, who was above the waters of the river, lifted his right hand and his left hand toward heaven, and I heard him swear by him who lives forever, saying, "It will be for a time, times and half a time. When the power of the holy people has been finally broken, all these things will be completed."

I heard, but I did not understand. So I asked, "My lord, what will the outcome of all this be?"

He replied, "Go your way, Daniel, because the words are rolled up and sealed until the time of the end. Many will be purified, made spotless and refined, but the wicked will continue to be wicked. None of the wicked will understand, but those who are wise will understand.

"From the time that the daily sacrifice is abolished and the abomination that causes desolation is set up, there will be 1,290 days. Blessed is the one who waits for and reaches the end of the 1,335 days.

"As for you, go your way till the end. You will rest, and then at the end of the days you will rise to receive your allotted inheritance."

A WORD ABOUT
THE NIV

The goal of the New International Version (NIV) is to enable English-speaking people from around the world to read and hear God's eternal Word in their own language. Our work as translators is motivated by our conviction that the Bible is God's Word in written form. We believe that the Bible contains the divine answer to the deepest needs of humanity, sheds unique light on our path in a dark world and sets forth the way to our eternal well-being. Out of these deep convictions, we have sought to recreate as far as possible the experience of the original audience — blending transparency to the original text with accessibility for the millions of English speakers around the world. We have prioritized accuracy, clarity and literary quality with the goal of creating a translation suitable for public and private reading, evangelism, teaching, preaching, memorizing and liturgical use. We have also sought to preserve a measure of continuity with the long tradition of translating the Scriptures into English.

The complete NIV Bible was first published in 1978. It was a completely new translation made by over a hundred scholars working directly from the best available Hebrew, Aramaic and Greek texts. The translators came from the United States, Great Britain, Canada, Australia and New Zealand, giving the translation an international scope. They were from many denominations and churches — including Anglican, Assemblies of God, Baptist, Brethren, Christian Reformed, Church of Christ, Evangelical Covenant, Evangelical Free, Lutheran, Mennonite, Methodist, Nazarene, Presbyterian, Wesleyan and others. This breadth of denominational and theological perspective helped to safeguard the translation from sectarian bias. For these reasons, and by the grace of God, the NIV has gained a wide readership in all parts of the English-speaking world.

The work of translating the Bible is never finished. As good as they are, English translations must be regularly updated so that they will continue to communicate accurately the meaning of God's Word. Updates are needed in order to reflect the latest developments in our understanding of the biblical world and its languages and to keep pace with changes in English usage. Recognizing, then, that the NIV would retain its ability to communicate God's Word accurately only if it were regularly updated, the original translators established the Committee on Bible Translation (CBT). The Committee is a self-perpetuating group of biblical scholars charged with keeping abreast of advances in biblical scholarship and changes in English and issuing periodic updates to the NIV. The CBT is an independent, self-governing body and has sole responsibility for the NIV text. The Committee mirrors the original group of translators in its diverse international and denominational makeup and in its unifying commitment to the Bible as God's inspired Word.

In obedience to its mandate, the Committee has issued periodic updates to the NIV. An initial revision was released in 1984. A more thorough revision process was completed in 2005, resulting in the separately published TNIV. The updated NIV you now have in your hands builds on both the original NIV and the TNIV and represents the latest effort of the Committee to articulate God's unchanging Word in the way the original authors might have said it had they been speaking in English to the global English-speaking audience today.

Translation Philosophy

The Committee's translating work has been governed by three widely accepted principles about the way people use words and about the way we understand them.

First, the meaning of words is determined by the way that users of the language actually use them at any given time. For the biblical languages, therefore, the Committee utilizes the best and most recent scholarship on the way Hebrew, Aramaic and Greek words were being used in biblical times. At the same time, the Committee carefully studies the state of modern English. Good translation is like good communication: one must know the target audience so that the appropriate choices can be made about which English words to use to represent the original words of Scripture. From its inception, the NIV has had as its target the general English-speaking population all over the world, the "International" in its title reflecting this concern. The aim of the Committee is to put the Scriptures into natural English that will communicate effectively with the broadest possible audience of English speakers.

Modern technology has enhanced the Committee's ability to choose the right English words to convey the meaning of the original text. The field of computational linguistics harnesses the power of computers to provide broadly applicable and current data about the state of the language. Translators can now access huge databases of modern English to better understand the current meaning and usage of key words. The Committee utilized this resource in preparing the 2011 edition of the NIV. An area of especially rapid and significant change in English is the way certain nouns and pronouns are used to refer to human beings. The Committee therefore requested experts in computational linguistics at Collins Dictionaries to pose some key questions about this usage to its database of English—the largest in the world, with over 4.4 billion words, gathered from several English-speaking countries and including both spoken and written English. (The Collins Study, called "The Development and Use of Gender Language in Contemporary English," can be accessed at *http://www.thenivbible. com/about-the-niv/about-the-2011-edition/*.) The study revealed that the most popular words to describe the human race in modern U.S. English were "humanity," "man" and "mankind." The Committee then used this data in the updated NIV, choosing from among these three words (and occasionally others also) depending on the context.

A related issue creates a larger problem for modern translations: the move away from using the third-person masculine singular pronouns—"he/him/his"—to refer to men and women equally. This usage does persist in some forms of English, and this revision therefore occasionally uses these pronouns in a generic sense. But the tendency, recognized in day-to-day usage and confirmed by the Collins study, is away from the generic use of "he," "him" and "his." In recognition of this shift in language and in an effort to translate into the natural English that people are actually using, this revision of the NIV generally uses other constructions when the biblical text is plainly addressed to men and women equally. The reader will encounter especially frequently a "they," "their" or "them" to express a generic singular idea. Thus, for instance, Mark 8:36 reads: "What good is it for someone to gain the whole world, yet forfeit their soul?" This generic use of the "distributive" or "singular" "they/them/their" has been used for many centuries by respected writers of English and has now become established as standard English, spoken and written, all over the world.

A second linguistic principle that feeds into the Committee's translation work is that meaning is found not in individual words, as vital as they are, but in larger clusters: phrases, clauses, sentences, discourses. Translation is not, as many people think, a matter of word substitution: English word *x* in place of Hebrew word *y*. Translators must first determine the meaning of the words of the biblical languages in the context of the passage and then select English words that accurately communicate that meaning to modern listeners and readers. This means that accurate translation will not always reflect the exact structure of the original language. To be sure, there is debate over the degree to which translators should try to preserve the "form" of the original text in English. From the beginning, the NIV has taken a mediating position on this issue. The manual produced when the translation that became the NIV was first being planned states: "If the Greek or Hebrew syntax has a good parallel in modern English, it should be used. But if there is no good parallel, the English syntax appropriate to the meaning of the original is to be chosen." It is fine, in other words, to carry over the form of the biblical languages into English — but not at the expense of natural expression. The principle that meaning resides in larger clusters of words means that the Committee has not insisted on a "word-for-word" approach to translation. We certainly believe that every word of Scripture is inspired by God and therefore to be carefully studied to determine what God is saying to us. It is for this reason that the Committee labors over every single word of the original texts, working hard to determine how each of those words contributes to what the text is saying. Ultimately, however, it is how these individual words function in combination with other words that determines meaning.

A third linguistic principle guiding the Committee in its translation work is the recognition that words have a spectrum of meaning. It is popular to define a word by using another word, or "gloss," to substitute for it. This substitute word is then sometimes called the "literal" meaning of a word. In fact, however, words have a range of possible meanings. Those meanings will vary depending on the context, and words in one language will usually not occupy the same semantic range as words in another language. The Committee therefore studies each original word of Scripture in its context to identify its meaning in a particular verse and then chooses an appropriate English word (or phrase) to represent it. It is impossible, then, to translate any given Hebrew, Aramaic or Greek word with the same English word all the time. The Committee does try to translate related occurrences of a word in the original languages with the same English word in order to preserve the connection for the English reader. But the Committee generally privileges clear natural meaning over a concern with consistency in rendering particular words.

Textual Basis

For the Old Testament the standard Hebrew text, the Masoretic Text as published in the latest edition of *Biblia Hebraica*, has been used throughout. The Masoretic Text tradition contains marginal notations that offer variant readings. These have sometimes been followed instead of the text itself. Because such instances involve variants within the Masoretic tradition, they have not been indicated in the textual notes. In a few cases, words in the basic consonantal text have been divided differently than in the Masoretic Text. Such cases are usually indicated in the textual footnotes. The Dead Sea Scrolls contain biblical texts that represent an earlier stage of the transmission of the Hebrew text. They have been consulted, as have been the Samaritan Pentateuch and the ancient scribal traditions concerning deliberate textual changes. The translators also consulted the more important early versions. Readings from these versions, the Dead Sea Scrolls and the scribal traditions were occasionally followed where the Masoretic Text seemed doubtful and where accepted principles of textual criticism showed that one or more of these textual witnesses appeared to provide the correct reading. In rare cases, the translators have emended the Hebrew text where it appears to have become corrupted at an even earlier stage of its transmission. These departures from the Masoretic Text are also indicated in the textual footnotes. Sometimes the vowel indicators (which are later additions to the basic consonantal text) found in the Masoretic Text did not, in the judgment of the translators, represent the correct vowels for the original text. Accordingly, some words have been read with a different set of vowels. These instances are usually not indicated in the footnotes.

The Greek text used in translating the New Testament has been an eclectic one, based on the latest editions of the Nestle-Aland/United Bible Societies' Greek New Testament. The translators have made their choices among the variant readings in accordance with widely accepted principles of New Testament textual criticism. Footnotes call attention to places where uncertainty remains.

The New Testament authors, writing in Greek, often quote the Old Testament from its ancient Greek version, the Septuagint. This is one reason why some of the Old Testament quotations in the NIV New Testament are not identical to the corresponding passages in the NIV Old Testament. Such quotations in the New Testament are indicated with the footnote "(see Septuagint)."

Footnotes and Formatting

Footnotes in this version are of several kinds, most of which need no explanation. Those giving alternative translations begin with "Or" and generally introduce the alternative with the last word preceding it in the text, except when it is a single-word alternative. When poetry is quoted in a footnote a slash mark indicates a line division.

It should be noted that references to diseases, minerals, flora and fauna, architectural details, clothing, jewelry, musical instruments and other articles cannot always be identified with precision. Also, linear measurements and measures of capacity can only be approximated (see the Table of Weights and Measures). Although *Selah*, used mainly in the Psalms, is probably a musical term, its meaning is uncertain. Since it may interrupt reading and distract the reader, this word has not been kept in the English text, but every occurrence has been signaled by a footnote.

As an aid to the reader, sectional headings have been inserted. They are not to be regarded as part of the biblical text and are not intended for oral reading. It is the Committee's hope that these headings may prove more helpful to the reader than the traditional chapter divisions, which were introduced long after the Bible was written.

Sometimes the chapter and/or verse numbering in English translations of the Old Testament differs from that found in published Hebrew texts. This is particularly the case in the Psalms, where the traditional titles are included in the Hebrew verse numbering. Such differences are indicated in the footnotes at the bottom of the page. In the New Testament, verse numbers that marked off portions of the traditional English text not supported by the best Greek manuscripts now appear in brackets, with a footnote indicating the text that has been omitted (see, for example, Matthew 17:[21]).

Mark 16:9−20 and John 7:53−8:11, although long accorded virtually equal status with the rest of the Gospels in which they stand, have a questionable standing in the textual history of the New Testament, as noted in the bracketed annotations with which they are set off. A different typeface has been chosen for these passages to indicate their uncertain status.

Basic formatting of the text, such as lining the poetry, paragraphing (both prose and poetry), setting up of (administrative-like) lists, indenting letters and lengthy prayers within narratives and the insertion of sectional headings, has been the work of the Committee. However, the choice between single-column and double-column formats has been left to the publishers. Also the issuing of "red-letter" editions is a publisher's choice—one that the Committee does not endorse.

The Committee has again been reminded that every human effort is flawed—including this revision of the NIV. We trust, however, that many will find in it an improved representation of the Word of God, through which they hear his call to faith in our Lord Jesus Christ and to service in his kingdom. We offer this version of the Bible to him in whose name and for whose glory it has been made.

The Committee on Bible Translation

Read and Engage with Scripture in a Whole New Way!

The Books of the Bible is a fresh yet ancient presentation of Scripture ideal for personal or small group use. This 4-part Bible removes chapter and verse numbers, headings, and special formatting so the Bible is easier to read. The Bible text featured is the accurate, readable, and clear New International Version.

To get the entire Bible, look for all four books in *The Books of the Bible*:

Covenant History
Discover the Origins of God's People   9780310448037

The Prophets
Listen   God's Messengers Proclaiming Hope and Truth   9780310448044

The Writings
Find Wisdom in Stories, Poetry, and Songs   9780310448051

New Testament
Enter the Story of Jesus' Church and His Return   9780310448020

The Books of the Bible Study Journal   9780310086055

The Books of the Bible Video Study

9780310086109

Join pastor Jeff Manion and teacher John Walton as they look at the context and purpose for each book of the Bible. Included are (32) 10-minute sessions that can be used with large or small groups.

Kids, Read the Bible in a Whole New Way!

The Books of the Bible is a fresh way for kids to experience Scripture! Perfect for reading together as a family or church group, this 4-part Bible series removes chapter and verse numbers, headings, and special formatting. Now the Bible is easier to read, and reveals the story of God's great love for His people, as one narrative. Features the easy-to-read text of the New International Reader's Version (NIrV). Ages 8-12.

Look for all four books in *The Books of the Bible*:

Covenant History
Discover the Beginnings of God's People   9780310761303

The Prophets
Listen to God's Messengers Tell about Hope and Truth   9780310761358

The Writings
Learn from Stories, Poetry, and Songs   9780310761334

New Testament
Read the Story of Jesus, His Church, and His Return   9780310761310

My Bible Story Coloring Book
The Books of the Bible   9780310761068

The Books of the Bible Children's Curriculum
9780310086161

These engaging lessons are formatted around relatable Scripture references, memory verses, and Bible themes. This curriculum has everything you need for 32 complete lessons for preschool, early elementary, and later elementary classes.

Learn how your church can experience the
Bible in community with resources for all ages!

Community Bible Experience

CommunityBibleExperience.com